Official Guide to Using OS/2 Warp

First Edition

Karla Stagray

Linda S. Rogers

An IBM Press Book

Published by IDG Books Worldwide, Inc.

An International Data Group Company

Foster City, CA * Chicago, IL * Indianapolis, IN * Braintree, MA * Dallas, TX

Official Guide to Using OS/2® Warp

Published by
IDG Books Worldwide, Inc.
An International Data Group Company
919 E. Hillsdale Blvd.
Suite 400
Foster City, CA 94404

Library of Congress Catalog Card No.: 95-75384

ISBN: 1-56884-466-2

Printed in the United States of America

10 9 8 7 6 5 4 3 2 1

First Edition

1B/RW/QS/ZV

Distributed in the United States by IDG Books Worldwide, Inc.

Distributed by Macmillan Canada for Canada; by Computer and Technical Books for the Caribbean Basin; by Contemporanea de Ediciones for Venezuela; by Distribuidora Cuspide for Argentina; by CITEC for Brazil; by Ediciones ZETA S.C.R. Ltda. for Peru; by Editorial Limusa SA for Mexico; by Transworld Publishers Limited in the United Kingdom and Europe; by Al-Maiman Publishers & Distributors for Saudi Arabia; by Simron Pty. Ltd. for South Africa; by IDG Communications (HK) Ltd. for Hong Kong; by Toppan Company Ltd. for Japan; by Addison Wesley Publishing Company for Korea; by Longman Singapore Publishers Ltd. for Singapore, Malaysia, Thailand and Indonesia; by Unalis Corporation for Taiwan; by WS Computer Publishing Company, Inc. for the Philippines; by WoodsLane Pty. Ltd. for Australia; by WoodsLane Enterprises Ltd. for New Zealand.

For general information on IDG Books in the U.S., including information on discounts and premiums, contact IDG Books at 800-434-3422 or 415-655-3000.

For information on where to purchase IDG Books outside the U.S., contact IDG Books International at 415-655-3021 or fax 415-655-3295.

For information on translations, contact Marc Jeffrey Mikulich, Director, Foreign & Subsidiary Rights, at IDG Books Worldwide, 415-655-3018 or fax 415-655-3295.

For sales inquiries and special prices for bulk quantities, write to the address above or call IDG Books Worldwide at 415-655-3000.

For information on using IDG Books in the classroom, or ordering examination copies, contact Jim Kelly at 800-434-2086.

is a registered trademark of
International Data Group

Welcome to the world of IDG Books Worldwide.

IDG Books Worldwide, Inc. is a subsidiary of International Data Group, the world's largest publisher of computer-related information and the leading global provider of information services on information technology. IDG was founded more than 25 years ago and now employs more than 7,000 people worldwide. IDG publishes more than 220 computer publications in 65 countries (see listing below). More than fifty million people read one or more IDG publications each month.

Launched in 1990, IDG Books Worldwide is today the #1 publisher of best-selling computer books in the United States. We are proud to have received 3 awards from the Computer Press Association in recognition of editorial excellence, and our best-selling ...*For Dummies*™ series has more than 12 million copies in print with translations in 25 languages. IDG Books, through a recent joint venture with IDG's Hi-Tech Beijing, became the first U.S. publisher to publish a computer book in the People's Republic of China. In record time, IDG Books has become the first choice for millions of readers around the world who want to learn how to better manage their businesses.

Our mission is simple: Every IDG book is designed to bring extra value and skill-building instructions to the reader. Our books are written by experts who understand and care about our readers. The knowledge base of our editorial staff comes from years of experience in publishing, education, and journalism — experience which we use to produce books for the '90s. In short, we care about books, so we attract the best people. We devote special attention to details such as audience, interior design, use of icons, and illustrations. And because we use an efficient process of authoring, editing, and desktop publishing our books electronically, we can spend more time ensuring superior content and spend less time on the technicalities of making books.

You can count on our commitment to deliver high-quality books at competitive prices on topics consumers want to read about. At IDG, we value quality, and we have been delivering quality for more than 25 years. You'll find no better book on a subject than an IDG book.

John J. Kilcullen

John Kilcullen
President and CEO
IDG Books Worldwide, Inc.

IDG Books Worldwide, Inc. is a subsidiary of International Data Group, the world's largest publisher of computer-related information and the leading global provider of information services on information technology. International Data Group publishes over 220 computer publications in 65 countries. More than fifty million people read one or more International Data Group publications each month. The officers are Patrick J. McGovern, Founder and Board Chairman; Kelly Conlin, President; Jim Casella, Chief Operating Officer. International Data Group's publications include: **ARGENTINA'S** Computerworld Argentina, Infoworld Argentina; **AUSTRALIA'S** Computerworld Australia, Computer Living, Australian PC World, Australian Macworld, Network World, Mobile Business Australia, Publish!, Reseller, IDG Sources; **AUSTRIA'S** Computerwelt Oesterreich, PC Test; **BELGIUM'S** Data News (CW); **BOLIVIA'S** Computerworld; **BRAZIL'S** Computerworld, Connections, Game Power, Mundo Unix, PC World, Publish, Super Game; **BULGARIA'S** Computerworld Bulgaria, PC & Mac World Bulgaria, Network World Bulgaria; **CANADA'S** CIO Canada, Computerworld Canada, InfoCanada, Network World Canada, Reseller; **CHILE'S** Computerworld Chile, Informatica; **COLOMBIA'S** Computerworld Colombia, PC World; **COSTA RICA'S** PC World; **CZECH REPUBLIC'S** Computerworld, Elektronika, PC World; **DENMARK'S** Communications World, Computerworld Danmark, Computerworld Focus, Macintosh Produktkatalog, Macworld Danmark, PC World Danmark, PC Produktguide, Tech World, Windows World; **ECUADOR'S** PC World Ecuador; **EGYPT'S** Computerworld (CW) Middle East, PC World Middle East; **FINLAND'S** MikroPC, Tietoviikko, Tietoverkko; **FRANCE'S** Distributique, GOLDEN MAC, InfoPC, Le Guide du Monde Informatique, Le Monde Informatique, Telecoms & Reseaux; **GERMANY'S** Computerwoche, Computerwoche Focus, Computerwoche Extra, Electronic Entertainment, Gamepro, Information Management, Macwelt, Netzwelt, PC Welt, Publish, Publish; **GREECE'S** Publish & Macworld; **HONG KONG'S** Computerworld Hong Kong, PC World Hong Kong; **HUNGARY'S** Computerworld SZT, PC World; **INDIA'S** Computers & Communications; **INDONESIA'S** Info Komputer; **IRELAND'S** ComputerScope; **ISRAEL'S** Beyond Windows, Computerworld Israel, Multimedia, PC World Israel; **ITALY'S** Computerworld Italia, Lotus Magazine, Macworld Italia, Networking Italia, PC Shopping Italy, PC World Italia; **JAPAN'S** Computerworld Today, Information Systems World, Macworld Japan, Nikkei Personal Computing, SunWorld Japan, Windows World; **KENYA'S** East African Computer News; **KOREA'S** Computerworld Korea, Macworld Korea, PC World Korea; **LATIN AMERICA'S** GamePro; **MALAYSIA'S** Computerworld Malaysia, PC World Malaysia; **MEXICO'S** Compu Edicion, Compu Manufactura, Computacion/Punto de Venta, Computerworld Mexico, MacWorld, Mundo Unix, PC World, Windows; **THE NETHERLANDS'** Computer! Totaal, Computable (CW), LAN Magazine, Lotus Magazine, MacWorld; **NEW ZEALAND'S** Computer Buyer, Computerworld New Zealand, Network World, New Zealand PC World; **NIGERIA'S** PC World Africa; **NORWAY'S** Computerworld Norge, Lotusworld Norge, Macworld Norge, Maxi Data, Networld, PC World Ekspress, PC World Nettverk, PC World Norge, PC World's Produktguide, Publish& Multimedia World, Student Data, Unix World, Windowsworld; **PAKISTAN'S** PC World Pakistan; **PANAMA'S** PC World Panama; **PERU'S** Computerworld Peru, PC World; **PEOPLE'S REPUBLIC OF CHINA'S** China Computerworld, China Infoworld, China PC Info Magazine, Computer Fan, PC World China, Electronics International, Electronics Today/Multimedia World, Electronic Product World, China Network World, Software World Magazine, Telecom Product World; **PHILIPPINES'** Computerworld Philippines, PC Digest (PCW); **POLAND'S** Computerworld Poland, Computerworld Special Report, Networld, PC World/Komputer, Sunworld; **PORTUGAL'S** Cerebro/PC World, Correio Informatico/Computerworld, MacIn; **ROMANIA'S** Computerworld, PC World, Telecom Romania; **RUSSIA'S** Computerworld-Moscow, Mir - PK (PCW), Sety (Networks); **SINGAPORE'S** Computerworld Southeast Asia, PC World Singapore; **SLOVENIA'S** Monitor Magazine; **SOUTH AFRICA'S** Computer Mail (CIO),Computing S.A.,Network World S.A., Software World; **SPAIN'S** Advanced Systems, Amiga World, Computerworld Espana, Communications World, Macworld Espana, NeXTWORLD, Super Juegos Magazine (GamePro), PC World Espana, Publish; **SWEDEN'S** Attack, ComputerSweden, Corporate Computing, Macworld, Mikrodatorn, Natverk & Kommunikation, PC World, CAP & Design, Datalngenjoren, Maxi Data,Windows World; **SWITZERLAND'S** Computerworld Schweiz, Macworld Schweiz, PC Tip; **TAIWAN'S** Computerworld Taiwan, PC World Taiwan; **THAILAND'S** Thai Computerworld, MacIn; **TURKEY'S** Computerworld Monitor, Macworld Turkiye, PC World Turkiye; **UKRAINE'S** Computerworld, Computers+Software Magazine; **UNITED KINGDOM'S** Computing / Computerworld, Connexion/Network World, Lotus Magazine, Macworld, Open Computing/Sunworld; **UNITED STATES'** Advanced Systems, AmigaWorld, Cable in the Classroom, CD Review, CIO, Computerworld, Computerworld Client/Server Journal, Digital Video, DOS World, Electronic Entertainment Magazine (E2), Federal Computer Week, Game Hits, GamePro, IDG Books, Infoworld, Laser Event, Macworld, Maximize, Multimedia World, Network World, PC Letter, PC World, Publish, SWATPro, Video Event; **URUGUAY'S** PC World Uruguay; **VENEZUELA'S** Computerworld Venezuela, PC World; **VIETNAM'S** PC World Vietnam.
01/03/95

V

About IBM Press

IBM Press is committed to bringing you high-quality books about IBM products and technologies. You can count on IBM Press to provide books that are of interest to all computer users—home and office users, network and systems administrators, and application developers and programmers.

It is our pleasure to present the first in a series of IBM Press books—*Official Guide to Using OS/2 Warp*. We are especially pleased to introduce this book because it is the first guide to OS/2 Warp that is authorized by IBM.

Inside these pages, readers will learn about the benefits that OS/2 Warp brings to home, office, or mobile computer users. Written in plain English, this user's guide provides complete descriptions of how to use OS/2 Warp. This book also thoroughly describes the BonusPak applications that are included with OS/2 Warp.

The authors of this book use OS/2 Warp every day at IBM to do their work. Within these pages, they share with you their many years of experience using OS/2. Unlike other computing books, this one is written from a user's perspective.

We hope you'll find this user's guide to be the perfect accompaniment to OS/2 Warp. Enjoy this first IBM Press book and your OS/2 Warp experience!

Brenda McLaughlin (IDG Books Worldwide)

Beth Tripi (IBM)

viii

Acknowledgments

The authors wish to thank their family members Bruce, Alex, and Richard Rogers, and Smokey Stagray for all their patience and encouragement which enabled them to see this book to completion.

In addition, they would like to thank Michael Bresnahan for helping them through a few trying situations.

The IBM Press Imprint and Acquisitions Managers wish to thank:

Lois Dimpfel, Jackie Knowles, Nancy Romano, John Schwarz, Tom Smith, and Maria Villar for their support.

Tom Callan, Fred Johnson, Bruce Jobse, and Amy Fliegelman-Olli for their advice and outstanding support.

Brian Black and Jeff Lewis for their excellent graphics and book design.

Liz Jean for her excellent editing and for her infinite patience.

IDG Books Worldwide employees Megg Bonar, Beth Jenkins, Brenda McLaughlin, Eric Stone, Steve Peake, Dwight Ramsey, and Marian Wallace for their support.

A very special thanks to IDG Books Worldwide CEO John Kilcullen, who had the foresight to believe in IBM Press.

x

Credits

xii

Table of Contents

xvii

xix

Introduction

Welcome to the first edition of *Official Guide to Using OS/2 Warp*. This guide is the most comprehensive step-by-step guide to OS/2 Warp available anywhere. The guide shows you how to really use OS/2 Warp and the BonusPak programs that come with OS/2 Warp.

OS/2 Warp is the latest version of IBM's award-winning 32-bit operating system. This version incorporates a number of new operating system features, significant enhancements to the user interface, and includes *nine* BonusPak programs to help you get started quickly.

OS/2 Warp has something for everyone.

If you use your computer at home to play games or electronically shop or communicate with friends, you'll like the games and electronic access that come with OS/2 Warp. If you use your computer at college to write papers or send faxes home to Dad just to say hello (and please send money), you'll like the editor and fax programs that come with OS/2 Warp. If you use your computer at work, you'll like everything OS/2 Warp has to offer. Whether you commute to work, work at home, or work on the road, you'll find OS/2 Warp packs enough power, speed, and versatility to meet all your computing needs.

To Our Readers

We wrote this book for *all* users of OS/2 Warp. We think that our readers will find this book to be the ultimate, no-nonsense, how-to book for everyday users. It is definitely a must-read, must-keep kind of guide!

For our readers who are just learning how to use OS/2 Warp, we've included lots of graphics and step-by-step instructions. If you are already familiar with OS/2 you will find the step-by-step instructions an added benefit over other books written about OS/2. For all readers, we included lots of tips, important information, and previously undocumented, easier ways to do things with OS/2 Warp.

We think all our readers will benefit from reading about the BonusPak programs that come with OS/2 Warp. This guide contains comprehensive information about what the BonusPak programs do, how to install them, and how to use them. Our readers will become productive quickly because most other books about OS/2 Warp don't have any information about the BonusPak programs!

Getting the Most out of This Book

When we wrote this book, we intended that you would use the information in the book interactively along with OS/2 Warp. In most cases, you simply follow the step-by-step procedures and you'll be on your way to using programs, playing games, and surfing the net! We've also provided background information that will help you better understand OS/2 Warp features.

How This Book Is Organized

We tried to organize the book in the order in which we thought you would use OS/2 Warp. After you read the section about how to install OS/2 Warp, you will find plenty of information about the basics to help get you started and information about every possible way to customize OS/2 Warp. Once you've read about the basics and personalized OS/2 Warp, you'll find out how to use printers, programs, multimedia, and all of the BonusPak programs. The following list describes how this book is organized:

Introducing OS/2 Warp

Describes in plain English some of the technical advantages that OS/2 Warp provides. This part also explains what you need to do before you install OS/2 Warp and how to install OS/2 Warp.

Using OS/2 Warp

Provides a tour of OS/2 Warp and describes key features. This part teaches you the basic "moves" and provides information about how to use online help. You'll find out how to perform common tasks, use menus, and how to secure and shut down your system.

Personalizing OS/2 Warp

Shows you how to customize OS/2 Warp to meet your personal needs. This part shows you how to customize every feature! You'll find out how to design a personal desktop, install additional programs, customize menus, create work areas, and more.

Using Productivity, Games, and Multimedia Programs

Describes the productivity, games, and multimedia programs that come with OS/2 Warp. This part explains the purpose of each program and provides information about how to use each one. You'll be editing files, creating your own icons, trying to beat OS/2 Warp in a game of Chess, and playing your favorite CD in no time at all!

Using Printers, Disk Drives, and Utility Programs

Describes printing, using your disk drives, and using utility programs that come with OS/2 Warp. This part shows you how to manage your print jobs and how to view the contents of your disk drives and customize your view. In addition, this part describes utilities that you will find useful if you have a laptop computer, if you need to remove or add operating system features, or if you are running DOS programs.

Enhancing Your Productivity

Describes the *nine* BonusPak programs that come with OS/2 Warp. This part explains the purpose of each program and provides information about how to install and use each one. You'll find out how to record and create movies, how to send and receive faxes, how to edit documents, create spreadsheets, charts, and reports, and how to manage your personal calendar and to-do list. In addition, this part shows you how to communicate person-to-person and how to access and use the Internet!

Conventions

To make it easier for you to learn and use OS/2 Warp, the following conventions are used in this book:

New terms

When a new term is introduced, it is in *italics* and the definition for the term immediately follows. This eliminates the need for a glossary as the definition for the term is right where you need it.

Graphics

When we introduce an OS/2 Warp feature, we've included a graphic of the icon or a picture of the screen you might expect to see on your own computer screen. We've also placed graphics next to the tips, rocket tips, notes, and warnings that appear throughout the book. They are easily recognized as the following graphics appear next to each one:

Tip icon

This icon lets you know about easier ways to do things and indicates practical advice about the task.

Rocket Tip icon

This icon indicates that you can perform the task from the LaunchPad.

Note icon

This icon lets you know about other information related to the task that might be of interest to you.

Warning icon

This icon lets you know about *very important* information.

Part One

Introducing OS/2 Warp

What is OS/2 Warp?

OS/2 Warp is an operating system. An operating system controls and coordinates the activities of the hardware in a computer. In addition, the operating system communicates the needs of the software programs on the computer to the hardware. For example, if a program needs information from the hard disk on the computer, the operating system instructs the hard disk to spin so it can search for the information needed by the program.

In recent years, demands have been placed on operating systems to do more than just coordinate the activities of the computer. Now, operating systems must also be easy to use. In the past, it was sufficient to subject a user to a flashing cursor on a black screen. Today, users want graphics and color to make the screens of the operating system interesting and easy to use.

OS/2 Warp steps up to this challenge by providing a graphical interface that is not only colorful but also easy to learn and use.

Part 1 of this book explains what all the hoopla over OS/2 Warp is about. It also helps you decide whether your computer has what it takes to run OS/2 Warp and which of the installation methods provided with OS/2 Warp is best for you. In addition, you will find simple steps to help you install OS/2 Warp.

The OS/2 *Warp* Advantage

Since its introduction, people have been raving about the speed and power of OS/2 and about its ease of use. In fact, these may have been the very reasons that you bought the newest version, OS/2 Warp. But do you really understand how OS/2 does the things it does?

While it is not necessary to understand a lot of technical details in order to use OS/2 Warp, you might be curious. This chapter explains what all the technical mumbo jumbo really means.

Speed

OS/2 Warp improves the speed of your computer by processing 32 pieces (bits) of information at a time. Compare this to the DOS operating system and Microsoft Windows, which can process only 16 bits of information at a time. OS/2 Warp doubles the amount of information that can be processed by your computer. However, just because OS/2 Warp is a 32-bit operating system doesn't mean that you should throw away your old 16-bit programs. OS/2 Warp can run those too!

TIP: OS/2 Warp protects your software investment because it can run programs written for OS/2, DOS, and Windows (if Windows is installed on your computer). This allows you to continue to use the programs that you've grown to know and love. And from now on, you can purchase the best programs for the jobs you want to do because you are no longer limited by an operating system. For example, you can buy the best DOS spreadsheet program, the best Windows word processor, and the best OS/2 Warp graphics program and run them all on OS/2 Warp!

OS/2 Warp also improves the speed of your computer by effectively managing the reading and writing of information on the hard disk. OS/2 Warp does this in three ways, by:

- Writing information to the hard disk when the hard disk is not being used. This is called "lazy writing." For example, programs typically need to get information from a hard disk, work with the information and then write some of the information back to the hard disk. With lazy writing, OS/2 Warp waits to write information to the hard disk until after the program has finished reading the information from the hard disk. This allows a program to run faster because it doesn't have to wait to use the hard disk. Programs can run without interruptions.

- Placing frequently accessed data in a *high-speed buffer* (temporary storage area). This is called "disk caching." For example, some programs use the same data over and over again. Instead of having to constantly read the information from the hard disk, OS/2 Warp keeps this information in a buffer, where it can be retrieved quickly.

- Detecting sequential read requests and placing the data in a high-speed buffer. This is called "read ahead." When a program needs a piece of information, OS/2 Warp recognizes a pattern and gets more than is requested and places the extra in a buffer. Then when the program needs the next piece of information, OS/2 Warp already has it. This reduces the amount of time needed to retrieve data.

By combining superior hard disk management with 32-bit processing speed, OS/2 Warp leaves the other operating systems light years behind.

Power

OS/2 Warp unleashes the power of your computer by providing the capability to run multiple programs at one time. This is called *multitasking*. As a matter of fact, depending on the amount of memory in your computer, you could run hundreds of programs all at the same time. How does OS/2 Warp do it?

OS/2 Warp uses something called *preemptive multitasking*, which means that tasks (program requests) are assigned a priority. The higher the priority, the more important it is that the task get time in the microprocessor. Those tasks with the highest priority go first. If a task does not need the microprocessor, it is given a very low priority. Now, here is where the preemptive part comes into play. If a task that was a low priority suddenly needs time in the microprocessor, it is reassigned a higher priority so it preempts (goes ahead of) all other tasks waiting for the microprocessor.

DOS and Windows make use of *cooperative multitasking*, which means that all tasks are assigned the same priority. Every task waiting to be processed by the microprocessor is given the same amount of time in the microprocessor.

What makes preemptive so much better than cooperative multitasking? With preemptive multitasking, only those tasks that need the microprocessor time get it, and the microprocessor is never idle. With DOS and Windows cooperative multitasking, all tasks get the same amount of time in the microprocessor whether they need it or not. If they don't need the time, the microprocessor is idle and the time is wasted.

So, while DOS and Windows can multitask, they don't do it as well as OS/2 Warp.

Memory Usage

OS/2 Warp enhances the way *memory* is used by your computer. Memory is a piece of hardware that is used as a temporary storage area for information while it is being processed by the microprocessor. The more programs you want the computer to run at one time, the more space in memory is required.

The minimum amount of memory required to run OS/2 Warp is 4MB (megabytes). This is an unbelievably small amount when you take into account that OS/2 Warp can multitask. OS/2 Warp accomplishes this feat by using a file called SWAPPER.DAT, which is located on the hard disk. This file is used to swap information in and out of memory so the computer will continue to work even when there is not enough memory to store the information. Information that is not currently needed in memory is placed in the SWAPPER.DAT file.

TIP: There is no fixed size for the SWAPPER.DAT file. The actual size of the file is determined by how many programs you run at one time and the amount of memory in your computer. You might expect your SWAPPER.DAT file to be between 10MB and 12MB in size. If the file gets very big or your computer seems to be running slower than usual, it is a result of all the swapping taking place. You can decrease the need to swap information by closing programs that you are not using. When you close programs, OS/2 Warp no longer has to keep the program's information in memory or in the SWAPPER.DAT file.

You can also decrease the size of the SWAPPER.DAT file by installing more memory in your computer. When you install more memory, OS/2 Warp is less likely to have to swap information out to make room for other information. The speed of OS/2 Warp improves because the memory area is larger and less swapping is needed.

Crash Protection

OS/2 Warp provides *crash protection* because it can run so many different programs, some of which might not be bug-free. Typically, when a program encounters a bug, it crashes. Although OS/2 Warp's crash protection won't keep a program from crashing, crash protection ensures that only the program that crashes stops. The rest of the programs running on OS/2 Warp continue to run as though nothing ever happened.

OS/2 Warp was designed so that each program running under OS/2 Warp runs in its own process. Data being used by one program that is running is not available to any other program running under OS/2 Warp.

NOTE: For your protection, OS/2 Warp won't run some Windows programs (those that are labeled VxD) because they try to bypass OS/2 Warp's crash protection and might cause the entire operating system to stop when a problem is encountered.

Multimedia

OS/2 Warp enhances your computer because multimedia is built right in. You can run multimedia programs and presentations that use a combination of voice, high-quality audio, brilliant still images, colorful animation, and full-motion video.

OS/2 Warp comes with its own multimedia programs, so even if you don't own any additional multimedia programs, you can still experience multimedia. (Of course, you will need a CD-ROM drive, audio card, and video capture card to take full advantage of most of these programs.)

However, even without additional hardware, you can enjoy the Ultimotion software motion video technology that is a part of OS/2 Warp. This technology allows you to play movies stored on your hard disk without any special hardware. These movies run smoothly while maintaining excellent picture quality and synchronization of the audio and video. You can even play more than one movie at a time.

Ease of Use

OS/2 Warp maximizes ease-of-use because it has a graphical user interface (GUI, pronounced *goo-ee*). OS/2 Warp uses *icons* (pictures) to make identifying and using the programs, hardware devices, and data files on your computer a snap. All of these icons are placed on something called the *Desktop*. The Desktop and its icons make it easy for you to use OS/2 Warp without having to understand the complexities of the operating system. In fact, once you learn a few basic mouse maneuvers and concepts, you're only a point and click away from getting the most out of your computer. To find out more about the Desktop and its icons, see "Using OS/2 Warp" on page 19 of this book.

Another nice thing about OS/2 Warp's GUI is that you can personalize it to meet your needs. For instance, you can change colors, add audio, create work areas, install programs, move icons—the list could go on and on. If you want to know more about personalizing OS/2 Warp, see "Personalizing OS/2 Warp" on page 63 of this book.

You now know more about the technical advantages of OS/2 Warp. If you need to install OS/2 Warp on your computer, you can go to Chapter 2 now for instructions. If you already have OS/2 Warp installed on your computer, jump ahead to see "Using OS/2 Warp" on page 19.

Happy computing!

Installation

Before you can use OS/2 Warp, it must be installed on your computer. If it has not been installed yet, you can use the information in this chapter to help you decide whether your computer has what it takes to run OS/2 Warp and which of the installation methods provided with OS/2 Warp is best for you. In addition, simple steps are included at the end of the chapter to help you install OS/2 Warp.

Can I Install Over My Current Software?

You can install OS/2 Warp on a brand new computer that has nothing installed on its hard disk, or you can install OS/2 Warp right on top of the following versions of DOS, Windows, and OS/2:

- DOS Version 3.3 or later

- Windows Version 3.1 or 3.1 v2

- Windows for Workgroups 3.1 or 3.1 v2

- OS/2 for Windows or OS/2 Version 1.3

If you install OS/2 Warp over any of the above, you will still be able to use all of the programs that were installed on your computer. OS/2 Warp won't erase or destroy them.

What about any other version of DOS, Windows, or OS/2 you might have on your computer? OS/2 Warp will work only with the versions mentioned above. If you want to continue to use the other versions, you can choose the Advanced Installation method and install OS/2 Warp on a different drive. If you do not want to continue to use the other versions, choose the Advanced Installation method and erase all of the files by formatting the hard disk. To find out more about the Advanced Installation method, see "Advanced Installation Choice" on page 13.

What Hardware Do I Need?

Before you can install OS/2 Warp on your computer, you also need to make sure that your computer has what it takes. If you need help determining whether your computer meets the following criteria, check the documentation that came with it. You will need a computer with:

__ An 80386 SX (or higher) microprocessor

__ A 1.44MB diskette drive

__ A CD-ROM drive (only if you plan to install OS/2 Warp from a CD)

___ A VGA, XGA, 8514, or SVGA display

___ At least 4 megabytes (MB) of memory in the computer (more is better)

___ At least 60MB of unused space on the hard disk where OS/2 Warp will be installed

- If you are installing OS/2 Warp on a new computer, you should be able to check the documentation that came with the computer to find out the size of the hard disk.

- If you have been using the computer, the files on the computer will have taken up some of the space on the hard disk. To determine whether you have enough space on your hard disk to install OS/2 Warp, type DIR at a command prompt and press the Enter key. You will see something like 89014227 bytes free. The number to the left of *bytes free* represents the amount of space left on the hard disk. If the number is greater than 60MB (60000000), you have enough space to install OS/2 Warp.

NOTES:

1. If files exist on the hard disk, make sure that they are not compressed. If they are, decompress them. If you do not know what compressed files are, you are probably not using a compression program and do not need to worry about this item.

2. If you elect not to install all of the software options, you could save up to 16MB of space on the hard disk.

3. If you are going to install OS/2 Warp on a drive that already has OS/2 for Windows or OS/2 Version 1.3, you do not need to be concerned about space. OS/2 Warp will just replace the existing OS/2 files.

What Else Do I Need?

You will also need the following diskettes or CDs to install OS/2 Warp:

___ The OS/2 Warp diskettes or CD

___ The diskettes or CD used to install Windows on your computer.

NOTES:

1. If Windows is not installed on your computer, it is not necessary to have the Windows diskettes or CD.

2. If you want to use Windows or Windows software programs, make sure Windows is installed **before** you install OS/2 Warp.

3. If your computer came with Windows already installed, you will need to create Windows diskettes before you install OS/2 Warp. Refer to the documentation that came with your computer for instructions.

4. If you installed Windows device drivers, fonts, or specific language files on your computer, you will need those diskettes, too. (These files should be reinstalled **after** OS/2 Warp is installed.) If you do not know what these files are, you are probably not using them and do not need to worry about this item.

Choosing an Installation Method

The OS/2 Warp installation program has been greatly improved over programs used to install previous versions of the operating system. It has been revamped to allow both an Easy and an Advanced installation. The hardest decision that you will need to make is which one of these installation methods is right for you.

Use the following information to help you make that decision.

Easy Installation Choice

When you select Easy Installation, the computer makes almost all of the choices about how OS/2 Warp should be installed. This choice is best for most people. To find out if Easy Installation is the best choice for you, look at the tables for both Easy and Advanced Installation before you make your decision. The following table contains details about Easy Installation.

The installation program:	Explanation:
Installs OS/2 Warp on drive C.	OS/2 Warp will coexist on drive C with DOS and Windows if they are installed. If you install OS/2 Warp over OS/2 for Windows or OS/2 Version 1.3, the OS/2 files will be replaced, but the Desktop of the earlier version will be saved.

NOTE: If you want to install OS/2 Warp on a drive with a letter other than C, you cannot use Easy Installation. |

The installation program:	Explanation:
Installs all of the software programs that come with OS/2 Warp.	If there is not enough space on drive C for all of the software programs, a screen is displayed where you can pick which software programs you want installed.
Determines which hardware is installed in your computer.	A screen is displayed where you can change any or all of the hardware choices. **NOTE:** If you have a printer attached to your computer, the installation program might not detect it. Make sure that the printer selection matches the type of printer attached to your computer. If it doesn't, change the selection.

Advanced Installation Choice

When you select Advanced Installation, you must make all of the choices about how OS/2 Warp should be installed. This choice is best left to people who are familiar with their computer and know exactly how they want OS/2 Warp set up. To find out if Advanced Installation is the best choice for you, look at the tables for both Easy and Advanced Installation before you make your decision. The following table contains details about Advanced Installation.

You can:	Explanation:
Add OS/2 Warp to the Boot Manager Menu or set up your computer to use the Boot Manager.	This feature is for computer gurus who want to have multiple operating systems on their computer or who want their operating systems on different partitions or hard disks. It requires knowledge of how to use a program called FDISK.
Select the drive where you want to install OS/2 Warp.	You would use this option only if you wanted to use the Boot Manager. **NOTE:** You must install OS/2 Warp on the drive that contains Windows in order to use Windows from the OS/2 Warp Desktop.

You can:	Explanation:
Format the drive before you install OS/2 Warp	Formatting a drive erases all of the programs and information on the drive. So, unless you plan to back up all the information on a drive before you install OS/2 Warp, you should not choose this option.
Select the HPFS or FAT file system.	This option is available only if you choose to format the drive. If you plan to use DOS and Windows, you must use the FAT file system. **NOTE:** For more information about HPFS and FAT, see "Appendix C, "File Systems: HPFS and FAT" on page 475.
Select which software programs you want installed.	All of the software programs included with OS/2 Warp are selected for installation. These programs take up 16MB of space and are part of the 60MB needed for OS/2 Warp. Unless your hard disk space is severely limited, it will probably be to your advantage to install all of these programs. If, after the installation, you decide that you do not want one of the programs, you can remove it by using Selective Uninstall.
Install the OS/2 Warp multimedia files on a drive other than the one where you are installing OS/2 Warp.	OS/2 Warp multimedia consists of 6.75MB of programs and data files. If you are running out of space on the hard disk partition where you are installing OS/2 Warp, you can install the OS/2 Warp multimedia files on a different drive. To do this, you will have to use the Advanced Installation method to install OS/2 Warp. When you see the Software Configuration screen, press the More button next to Multimedia Software Support and change the Destination drive letter.
Specify the location of the Windows files.	When you installed Windows, you were given the opportunity to change where the Windows files were placed. If you just pressed

Enter and didn't type a different directory name, the Windows files were placed in the \WINDOWS directory. This is exactly where OS/2 Warp thinks they are. If you changed the directory name during the Windows installation, you will have to use the Advanced Installation method of installing OS/2 Warp so you can tell OS/2 Warp where to find the files. When you see the Software Configuration screen, press the More button next to WIN-OS/2 Support and change the path.

Select which hardware is installed in your computer.

The installation program determines which hardware is installed in your computer. You can change any or all of the hardware choices.

NOTE: If you have a printer attached to your computer, the installation program might not detect it. Make sure that the printer selection matches the type of printer attached to your computer. If it doesn't, change the selection.

NOTE: If you perform an Advanced Installation and press the Enter key on every screen (without changing the selections), you will in effect be doing an Easy Installation.

Installing OS/2 Warp

After you make the decision about which installation choice (Easy or Advanced) is right for you, you are ready to begin installing OS/2 Warp. You can use the following instructions for both Easy and Advanced Installation. If at any time during the installation, you get stuck, we recommend you use the online help that comes built into OS/2 Warp. Simply press the F1 key on your keyboard to get help for any screen.

To install OS/2 Warp:
1. Insert the diskette labeled *Installation Diskette* into diskette drive A of your computer.
2. Turn on the computer. If the computer is already on, press the Ctrl+Alt+Del keys to restart the computer.

3. When you see the IBM Logo screen, remove the *Installation Diskette* from drive A and insert *Diskette 1*. If you are installing from a CD, insert the OS/2 Warp CD into the CD-ROM drive at this time.

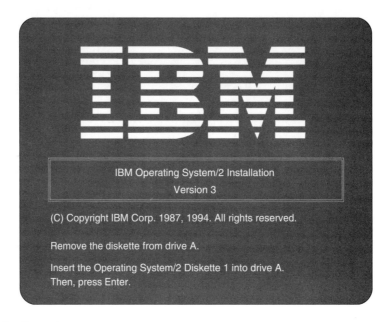

4. Press the Enter key.
5. When you see the *Welcome to OS/2!* screen, use the Up or Down Arrow key to select the installation method that you want to use.

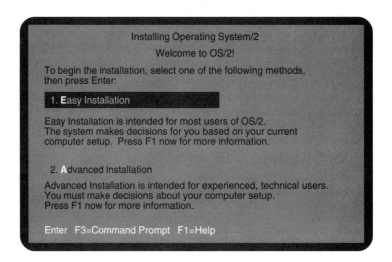

6. Press the Enter key.

7. Follow the instructions on the screens to complete the installation of OS/2 Warp. If you don't know what to select, press the F1 key to display help for the selections on the screen. If, after reading the help, you still don't know what to do, just press the Enter key to select the default choice. In most instances, the default choice is the right choice for you.

8. When the installation of OS/2 Warp is completed, press the Enter key to automatically shut down the computer.

9. When you receive the message Shutdown has completed, press the Ctrl+Alt+Del keys to restart the computer. After you press these keys, OS/2 Warp starts building its graphical user interface to match the installation options that you selected.

   When the hard disk stops whirring and chugging, the building process is completed.

Now that OS/2 Warp is installed, we recommend that you review the tutorial that is displayed on your screen. The tutorial offers an excellent way to become familiar with:

- Using a mouse

- Learning basic moves

- Running programs

- Working with icons (objects)

- Personalizing OS/2 Warp

- Getting help

- Playing games and using multimedia

TIP: Don't try to memorize everything in the tutorial. For your convenience, the tutorial is placed on the Desktop, within easy reach. You can return to it at any time.

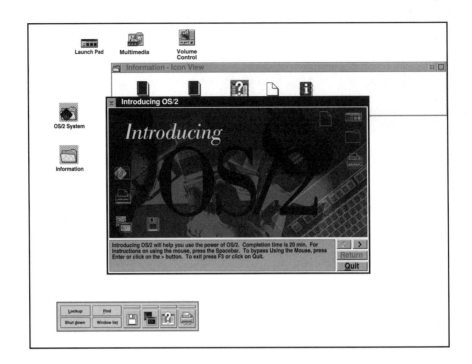

Part Two

Using OS/2 Warp

This part introduces you to the Desktop and provides a quick tour of the Desktop.

After you complete the quick tour, you'll learn about the features of OS/2 Warp that help make it easy to use. You'll find out how OS/2 Warp displays your favorite program and how it is able to display more than one program at a time. This part also shows you how to perform some everyday tasks such as copying and moving icons.

In addition, this part shows you how to use online help, and how to secure and shut down your system.

Chapter 3

Using the Desktop

The OS/2 Warp screen was designed to represent the top of a desk—hence the name Desktop. The Desktop fills the entire screen and is where you will do most of your work with OS/2 Warp. It is much like the place you might already be doing your work except that real things you work with (such as manila folders, a printer, a fax machine, or a shredder) are represented by icons. You can file important documents in folders, print documents, send faxes, and shred documents right from your Desktop using the icons that represent the folder, printer, fax machine, or shredder.

This chapter familiarizes you with the OS/2 Warp Desktop, describes the icons on the Desktop, introduces you to the LaunchPad, and shows you how to use OS/2 Warp to your maximum advantage.

Desktop

The following is an example of what your Desktop might look like:

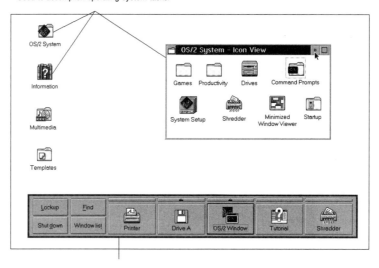

Used to accomplish operating system tasks.

Used to help you organize the Desktop.

Taking a Quick Tour

You are probably wondering where everything is in OS/2 Warp because when you look at the Desktop, all you see are a few icons and the LaunchPad. The sections that follow show you that everything in OS/2 Warp is inside these few icons.

OS/2 System Icon

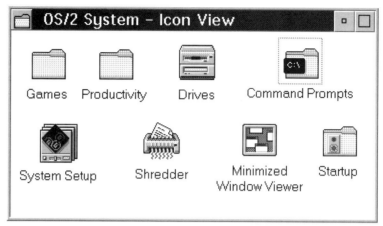

You can use the icons found in the OS/2 System icon to complete a variety of tasks. You can display the contents of your drives (Drives), display command prompts (Command Prompts), or customize and set up your system (System Setup). You can also delete documents (Shredder), access productivity programs (Productivity), or access games programs (Games).

In addition, you can access icons that have been *minimized*—reduced to their smallest possible sizes—(Minimized Window Viewer).

Information Icon

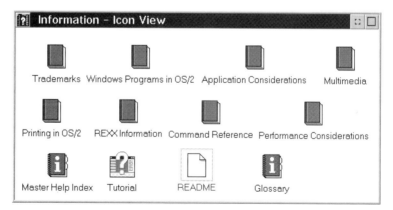

You can consider the Information icon your online library. The online library contains an index, a tutorial, late-breaking OS/2 Warp information, a glossary, a list of trademarks, and online books.

You can use the icons in the Information icon to read short articles about almost any operating system topic (Master Index), read about last-minute updates that were not included in the final OS/2 Warp documentation (README), browse a list of trademarks that are mentioned in the online books and information (Trademarks), or look up an unfamiliar term (Glossary).

In addition, you can choose from *seven* book icons that contain a wide variety of interesting topics and useful information. Each online book has its own table of contents, index, search function, and print function, which allows you to print one or more pages of any book in the library.

The *Command Reference* provides information about the OS/2 and DOS commands that you can use at a command prompt. *Printing in OS/2* provides information for everything you want to know about printing in OS/2 Warp—from installing a printer to solving printer problems. *Windows Programs in OS/2* provides information about using Windows programs with OS/2 Warp. *Application Considerations* provides information about the settings or the tasks you need to perform to make some programs run better with OS/2 Warp. *Performance Considerations* provides information about how to improve the performance of your system and about memory management and COM ports. *Multimedia* provides information about how to use the multimedia programs that come with OS/2 Warp. *REXX Information* provides information about the commands you can use to write powerful REXX programs.

Multimedia Icon

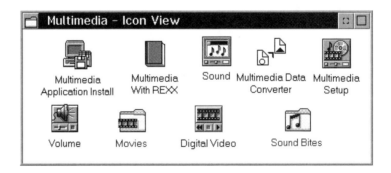

Multimedia is built right into OS/2 Warp, so now you can run multimedia programs and presentations that use voice, high-quality audio, brilliant still images, colorful animation, and full-motion video.

You can use the icons in the Multimedia icon to access data-file icons of sounds that you can attach to computer actions (Sound Bites), play and record digital video movies (Digital

Video), play music CDs (Compact Disc), play movies (Movies), or control the volume of multimedia programs and devices (Volume Control).

The Multimedia icon also contains icons that let you change the settings for all multimedia programs included with OS/2 Warp (Multimedia Setup), let you convert image and sound files to a different format (Multimedia Data Converter), let you connect the sounds found in the Sound Bites icon with computer actions (Sound), and let you install additional multimedia programs (that are included with OS/2 Warp) on your computer (Multimedia Application Install). In addition, the Multimedia icon contains an online book *Multimedia with REXX* that provides information about how to write a REXX program to control multimedia devices.

Templates Icon

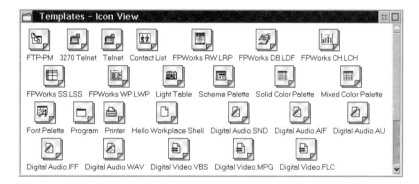

The Templates icon contains icons that you can use to create new icons. There are a number of templates icons that you can use to create additional groups of schemes or colors, to create additional groups of fonts, or to create program, printer, data-file, or folder icons.

Templates icons that you can use with the Picture Viewer and Icon Editor productivity programs that come with OS/2 Warp are also provided. In addition, there are templates icons for the multimedia programs that come with OS/2 Warp. You can use these templates icons with the Digital Video and Digital Audio programs.

LaunchPad

The LaunchPad is an ingenious organizer that you can use to place your favorite or most frequently-used icons in one convenient location. The icons in the LaunchPad are *shadows* of their original icons. (The original icons exist elsewhere on the Desktop. For example, the original icon for the tutorial is in the Information folder.)

The LaunchPad contains the following:

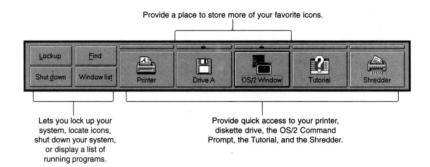

Provide a place to store more of your favorite icons.

Lets you lock up your system, locate icons, shut down your system, or display a list of running programs.

Provide quick access to your printer, diskette drive, the OS/2 Command Prompt, the Tutorial, and the Shredder.

You can add any icons you like to the LaunchPad or to the drawers. To find out how to add icons to the LaunchPad, see "Adding Icons to the LaunchPad" on page 77.

You can also delete icons from the LaunchPad or its drawers when you no longer need them. To find out how to delete icons from the LaunchPad, read "Deleting Icons from the LaunchPad" on page 78.

Throughout the rest of this book, the Rocket Tip symbol is used to indicate that the task that is described can also be performed from your LaunchPad.

Managing Your Windows

When you open an icon, its contents are displayed on the Desktop in a box called a *window*. This window can contain a running software program, other icons, or data. When you finished installing OS/2 Warp, the tutorial was displayed in a window on the Desktop.

This chapter explains the parts of a window and how to use those parts.

Parts of a Window

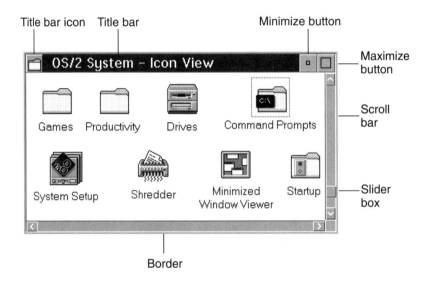

To familiarize yourself with the parts of a window and their purpose, open the OS/2 System icon by pointing to the icon and double-clicking mouse button 1.

A *border* surrounds the window and is used to identify the window that is *active* (it can accept input from you). The border is also used to change the size of the window.

When a window is active, its border is highlighted. An active window always appears in the *foreground* (on top of other windows on the Desktop).

To make a window active, simply click mouse button 1 somewhere within the window.

Sizing a Window

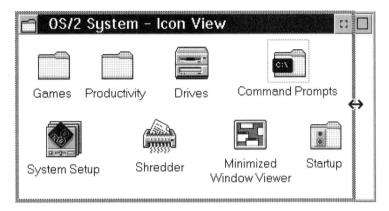

Sometimes a window might appear to be too big or too small for you to work with. You can make a window any size you like.

To size a window:

1. Point to the border of the window.
2. When the mouse pointer looks like this: ↔ press and hold mouse button 1.
3. Drag the border of the window until the window is the size you want.
4. Release mouse button 1.

TIP: You can size two sides of a window at the same time. Point to a corner of the window; then follow steps 2 through 4 above.

In addition to being able to make a temporary change to the size of a window, you also can change its *default size* (the size that comes up each time you open it).

To change the default size of the window:

1. Press and hold the Shift key.
2. Point to the border of the window.
3. When the mouse pointer looks like this: ↔ press and hold mouse button 1.
4. Drag the border of the window until the window is the size you want.
5. Release mouse button 1.
6. Release the Shift key.

TIP: You might want to change the default size of a window if you find that you size the window every time you open it.

Moving a Window

The *title bar* shows you the name of the window. It is also used to move an open window.

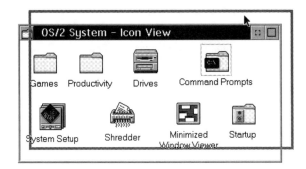

To move a window:

1. Point to the title bar of the window you want to move.
2. Press and hold mouse button 1.
3. Drag the window to a new location.
4. Release mouse button 1.

Scrolling a Window

You can use the *scroll bar* to scroll through the information in a window. A scroll bar is displayed only when more information exists than can be shown in the window. The scroll bar normally appears vertically on the right side of the window; sometimes, one will be displayed horizontally at the bottom of the window, depending on how the window is sized.

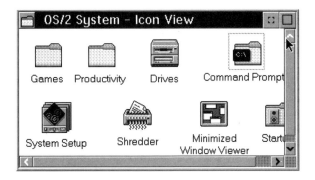

To scroll a window:

1. Point to the Up or Down arrow button on a vertical scroll bar or the Right or Left arrow button on a horizontal scroll bar at either end of the scroll bar.
2. Press and hold mouse button 1 to start scrolling.
3. Release mouse button 1 to stop scrolling.

The *slider box*, located inside the scroll bar, is used to scroll one page of information at a time in the window. It is also used to indicate where you are within the information in the window. For example, if the slider box is in the middle of the scroll bar, you are just about halfway through the information.

To scroll a page vertically, click mouse button 1 on the area above or below the slider box for the vertical scroll bar.

To scroll a page horizontally, click mouse button 1 on the area to the right or left of the slider box for the horizontal scroll bar.

TIP: You can drag the slider box up or down to quickly scroll through the information in the window.

To quickly scroll through the window:

1. Point to the slider box.
2. Press and hold mouse button 1.
3. Drag the slider box until the information you want is displayed in the window.
4. Release mouse button 1.

Minimizing a Window

You can use the *minimize button* to shrink the window to an icon. The minimize button is in the upper-right corner of the window.

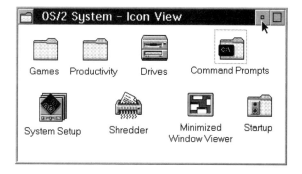

A minimized window is still open and any program that is running in the window continues running. For example, you might open a spreadsheet program icon and prepare a complicated annual report. When you instruct the spreadsheet program to calculate the report, you can minimize the window while the spreadsheet crunches numbers so that you can work with another program until the spreadsheet finishes.

To minimize a window, click mouse button 1 on [□].

Some windows have a *hide button* instead of a minimize button. The kind of program you are running in the window determines whether the button displayed is a minimize or hide button.

To hide a window, click mouse button 1 on [□].

Using the Window List

The titles of minimized and hidden windows are placed in the *Window List*. At any time, you can quickly access a window by displaying the Window List.

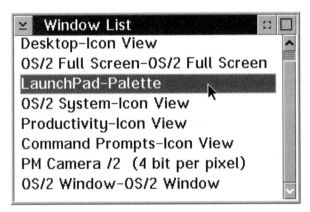

To display the Window List, point to an empty area on the Desktop; then click mouse buttons 1 and 2 at the same time.

To display a minimized or hidden window using the Window List:
1. Point to an empty area on the Desktop.
2. Click mouse buttons 1 and 2 at the same time to display the Window List.
3. Point to the title of the minimized or hidden window; then double-click on the title.

Maximizing a Window

You can use the *maximize button* to make a window its largest possible size. The maximize button is in the upper-right corner of the window. Generally, when a window is maximized, it fills the entire screen. Maximizing a window is useful when you want to see more information than will fit in the window (for example, when you work with a desktop publishing program and want to see more of the content you are creating).

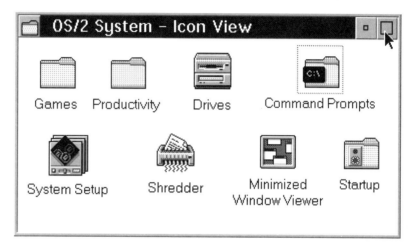

To maximize a window, click mouse button 1 on ▢.

After you have maximized a window, the maximize button changes to a *restore button*. This button is used to return the window to the size it was before it was maximized.

To restore a window, click mouse button 1 on ▣.

Closing a Window

You can use the *title-bar* icon to close the window. The title-bar icon is a little picture that represents the program, data-file, device, or folder you have opened. It is located in the upper-left corner of the window.

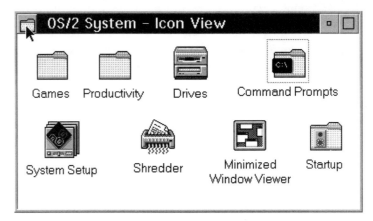

To close a window, point to the title-bar icon; then double-click on the icon.

Chapter 5

Using Menus

The Desktop, icons, and windows have their own menu called a *pop-up menu*. Pop-up menus provide a way to interact with OS/2 Warp because you can use the choices on a pop-up menu to instruct OS/2 Warp to perform a specific action, such as opening or closing an icon. Sometimes, an arrow appears to the right of a menu choice, like this: ➡. This arrow lets you know that there are additional menu choices available. Just click mouse button 1 on the arrow to the right of the menu choice to display the additional choices.

This chapter shows you how to display pop-up menus for the Desktop, icons, and windows.

Displaying the Pop-Up Menu for the Desktop

The pop-up menu for the Desktop contains choices that apply to all the icons on the Desktop and to the operating system. For example, if you select the **Shut down** choice from the Desktop pop-up menu, a housekeeping activity is performed that affects all open icons and the operating system. This housekeeping activity prepares your system before you turn it off.

To display the pop-up menu for the Desktop, point to an empty area on the Desktop; then click mouse button 2.

Displaying the Pop-Up Menu for an Icon

The pop-up menu for an icon contains choices that apply specifically to that icon. For example, if you displayed the pop-up menu for one of the Drives icons, you would find the **Check disk** and **Format** choices. These actions can be applied only to drives, so you won't find these choices on any other pop-up menu.

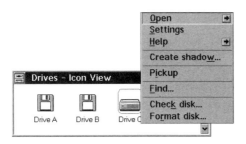

To display the pop-up menu for an icon, point to the icon; then click mouse button 2.

TIP: To be sure the correct pop-up menu is displayed, place the mouse pointer on top of the icon when you click mouse button 2.

There might be times when you want to apply the same pop-up menu choice to more than one icon. For example, you might want to open multiple icons at the same time.

To display a pop-up menu for multiple icons:
1. Press and hold the Ctrl key.
2. Click mouse button 1 on each icon you want to select. (If you click on an icon that you did not really want to select, you can reverse the selection by clicking mouse button 1 on that icon again.)
3. Release the Ctrl key.
4. Point to any one of the icons you selected.
5. Click mouse button 2 to display the pop-up menu.
6. Select a pop-up menu choice.

TIP: If you change your mind before you select the pop-up menu choice, you can reverse your multiple selection very easily. Just point to a blank area of the window or Desktop and click mouse button 1.

Displaying the Pop-Up Menu for a Window

The pop-up menu for a window contain choices that apply specifically to that window. For example, some software programs have a main window (the parent window) and associated windows attached to the main window. If you were working with one of the associated windows and you wanted to quickly return to the main window, you could display the pop-up for the window and select **Open parent.**

To display the pop-up menu for a window, point to an empty area in the window; then click mouse button 2.

TIP: You can choose to display the pop-up menu choices directly from the title-bar icon for the window. The menu that is displayed when you click on the icon is called the *title-bar menu*.

1. Point to the title-bar icon in the upper-left corner of the window.
2. Click mouse button 1 or 2 to display the title-bar menu.

Working with Icons and Windows

You can work with icons and windows in a way that is similar to the way you already work. For example, during your work day, you might write letters or throw things away. With icons, you can do the same kinds of things. You can open a word processor program icon to write a letter or throw an icon away by dragging it to the Shredder.

This chapter shows you how to open an icon or throw one away. It also shows you how to perform other tasks that you might do on a frequent basis such as copying or renaming an icon. You can complete most tasks with or without a pop-up menu. However, for some tasks you must use a pop-up menu.

You will see four kinds of icons as you work with the Desktop:

Program

Represents a software program. Word processors such as WordPerfect, games such as Mahjongg (which comes with OS/2 Warp), productivity programs such as Seek and Scan Files (which comes with OS/2 Warp), and spreadsheet programs such as Lotus 1-2-3 are examples of program icons.

Device

Represents an internal or external piece of hardware attached to your computer. Printers, plotters, displays, modems, fax machines, and a mouse are examples of device icons.

Data-file

Contains information. Text files, memos, letters, and spreadsheets are examples of data-file icons.

Folder

Contains other icons (for example, data-file, program, and other folder icons). You can use folder icons to help you organize your work. For example, all the games that come with OS/2 Warp are organized for you in one place—the Games folder.

TIP: If you try to do something with an icon that OS/2 Warp does not allow, you will see a no-can-do symbol, like this ⬤. The action that you are trying to perform is canceled when you release the mouse button.

Opening an Icon

As mentioned earlier, when you open an icon, you will see its contents displayed in a window on the Desktop.

To open an icon, point to the icon and double-click on it.

Drives

To open an icon using a pop-up menu:
1. Point to the icon.
2. Click mouse button 2 to display the pop-up menu.
3. Click mouse button 1 on the **Open** menu choice.

Copying an Icon

You can make a duplicate of an icon. For example, you might file all memos you write in your Memo icon. However, today you are working on a "Daily Sales" memo to your boss and decide you'd like to keep an extra copy of that memo in your Boss icon. You can copy the memo from one location to the other. When you copy the memo, an exact duplicate of it appears in both the Memo and Boss icons.

If you copy an icon to another location where an icon with the same name is located, the copy will be given a slightly different name. Let's say you copy "Daily Sales" from your Memo icon to your Boss icon. If there is already a memo named "Daily Sales" in the Boss icon, this copy is given a slightly different name, such as "Daily Sales1."

To copy an icon:
1. Point to the icon.
2. Press and hold the Ctrl key.
3. Press and hold mouse button 2.
4. Drag the icon to the place where you want the copy.
5. Release mouse button 2.
6. Release the Ctrl key.

To copy an icon using a pop-up menu:

1. Point to the icon.
2. Click mouse button 2 to display the pop-up menu.
3. Click mouse button 1 on the **Copy** menu choice. The Copy notebook is displayed. Although it is not necessary to change the name of the icon before you copy it, there might be instances where you choose to change the name. If you choose to change the name of the icon before you copy it, type a new name in the **New name** field.
4. Click mouse button 1 on the icon that represents the location where you want the icon to be copied.
5. Click mouse button 1 on the **Copy** push button.

Creating a Shadow Icon

You can create a shadow icon that represents the original icon and its contents. Creating a shadow of an icon is different from copying an icon. An icon that has been copied does not automatically exchange data with the original icon, but a shadow does. In effect, a shadow works with its original, while a copy is independent of its original.

Shadow icons have the following characteristics:

• Changing either the original or the shadow icon causes the change to occur in both icons. For example, if you change the name of an icon that has a shadow icon, the name of the original and shadow icons are changed.

• Deleting the original icon deletes the shadow icon; however, deleting the shadow icon has no effect on the original icon.

• Moving either the original or the shadow icon has no effect on the other icon.

One reason you might want to create a shadow icon is that you want any changes you make to the shadow to occur in the original and vice versa. For example, if you change the text in the original data-file icon, text in the shadow of the data-file icon also changes. This keeps you from having to do work twice.

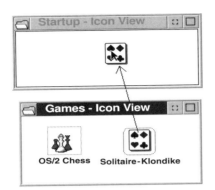

To create a shadow of an icon:

1. Point to the icon.
2. Press and hold the Ctrl+Shift keys.
3. Press and hold mouse button 2.
4. Drag the icon to the location where you want the shadow to appear.
5. Release mouse button 2.
6. Release the Ctrl+Shift keys.

To create a shadow of an icon using a pop-up menu:

1. Point to the icon.
2. Click mouse button 2 to display the pop-up menu.
3. Click mouse button 1 on the **Create shadow** menu choice. The Create Shadow notebook is displayed.
4. Click mouse button 1 on the icon where you want the shadow to be located.
5. Click mouse button 1 on the **Create** push button.

Moving an Icon

You can move an icon to a more convenient location, such as to a different icon or to the Desktop. For example, if you like to play Mahjongg but don't enjoy opening icon after icon to find it, you can move the Mahjongg icon to your Desktop. (If you move an icon to a location that already has an icon with the same name, the icon you move is given a slightly different name.)

To move an icon:

1. Point to the icon.
2. Press and hold mouse button 2.
3. Drag the icon to its new location.
4. Release mouse button 2.

To move an icon using a pop-up menu:
1. Point to the icon.
2. Click mouse button 2 to display the pop-up menu.
3. Click mouse button 1 on the **Move** menu choice. The Move notebook is displayed. Although it is not necessary to change the name of the icon before you move it, there might be instances where you choose to change the name. If you choose to change the name of the icon before you move it, type the new name in the **New name** field.
4. Click on the icon that represents the location where you want the icon to be moved.
5. Click on the **Move** push button.

Deleting an Icon

You can delete an icon when you don't need it anymore. Before you delete an icon, you should realize that you might never see it again.

- If you delete a folder icon, the icon and everything in it is deleted.

- If you delete a shadow of an icon, only the shadow is deleted; the original is not deleted.

- If you delete a program icon, only the program icon is deleted; the actual program files remain intact.

ROCKET TIP: Remember to use the Shredder icon located on the LaunchPad.

To delete an icon:
1. Point to the icon.
2. Press and hold mouse button 2.
3. Drag the icon to the **Shredder** icon.
4. Release mouse button 2.
5. Respond to any messages that are displayed.

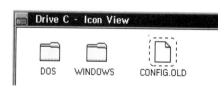

To delete an icon using a pop-up menu:

1. Point to the icon.
2. Click mouse button 2 to display the pop-up menu.
3. Click mouse button 1 on the **Delete** menu choice.
4. Respond to any messages that are displayed.

TIP: On occasion, you might delete an icon that you really need. You can recover your deleted icons. However, you must first set up your computer to do this, as described in "Getting Back a Deleted Icon" on page 172.

Renaming an Icon

You can change the name of an icon as you need to. Sometimes you might find that an icon is named something you just keep forgetting. Or the icon might have an awkward name (or a name that's hard to spell). For example, suppose you buy a software game about dinosaurs and it's named Tyrannosaurus. It's a great game with a great name, but it can be a challenge to spell it. It might be easier to rename the icon for the game to Dinosaur, or Dino Game, or even Dino. Then, if you ever need to find it (which requires that you type the name of the icon you are searching for), you will be able to spell it!

To rename an icon:

1. Point to the text under the icon whose name you want to change.
2. Press and hold the Alt key.
3. Click mouse button 1 to display the input area.
4. Type the new name. Press the Backspace or Del key to erase any unwanted characters or lines. Press the Enter key each time you want to add a line.
5. Point to an empty area on the Desktop or in a window.
6. Click mouse button 1. (The input area disappears and the icon has a new name.)

To rename an icon using a pop-up menu:

1. Point to the icon.
2. Click mouse button 2 to display the pop-up menu.
3. Click mouse button 1 on the **Settings** menu choice. The Settings notebook for the icon is displayed.
4. Click mouse button 1 on the **General** tab located along the right side of the notebook.
5. Type the new name in the **Title** field.
6. Double-click on the title-bar icon of the notebook to close it.

Printing the Contents of an Icon

You can print or plot the contents of a data-file icon on a printer connected to your computer. Data-file icons contain memos, letters, spreadsheets, charts, graphs, and more.

ROCKET TIP: Remember to use the printer icon located on the LaunchPad.

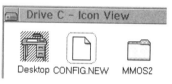

To print a data-file icon:
1. Point to the data-file icon.
2. Press and hold mouse button 2.
3. Drag the data-file icon to a printer icon.
4. Release mouse button 2.
5. Respond to any messages that might be displayed.

To print the contents of a data-file icon on your printer using a pop-up menu:
1. Point to the data-file icon.
2. Click mouse button 2 to display the pop-up menu.
3. Click mouse button 1 on the **Print** menu choice.
4. Respond to any messages that might be displayed.

If your computer is part of a network, you might have access to more than one printer. For example, you might have your own desktop printer in your office to print small jobs. In addition, you might have access to a high-speed printer that is shared by others (such as your co-workers) to print large jobs. If you have access to more than one printer, you can choose which printer you want to use.

To print the contents of a data-file icon and choose the printer name:
1. Point to the data-file icon.
2. Click mouse button 2 to display the pop-up menu.
3. Click mouse button 1 on the arrow to the right of the **Print** menu choice.
4. Click mouse button 1 on the name of the printer you want to use.
5. Respond to any messages that might be displayed.

Picking Up and Dropping Icons

The pickup-and-drop feature provides a handy way to perform a task on a group of icons. When you perform a pickup, your mouse pointer changes to a suitcase.

To pick up a group of icons:
1. Point to the icon.
2. Press and hold the Alt key.
3. Click mouse button 2.
4. Repeat the previous three steps for each icon you want to pick up.
5. Release the Alt key.

To pick up a group of icons using the pop-up menu:
1. Point to the icon.
2. Click mouse button 2 to display the pop-up menu.
3. Click mouse button 1 on the **Pickup** menu choice.
4. Repeat the previous three steps for each icon you want to pick up.

TIP: You can leave the icons picked up for as long as you need to while you do other tasks on the Desktop or go to lunch. When you're done with other tasks (or lunch), then you can complete the task and drop the icons.

After you have picked up the group of icons, you can move, copy, or create shadows of that group. The move task is the default action for a pickup.

To move a group of icons:
1. Pick up the icons (you can pick up as many as you like).
2. Move the mouse pointer to an empty area of the Desktop or a window.
3. Click mouse button 2 to display the pop-up menu.
4. Click mouse button 1 on the **Drop** choice.

In addition to moving a group of icons, you can copy or create shadows of that group.

To copy or create shadows of a group of icons using a pop-up menu:
1. Pick up the icons.
2. Move the mouse pointer to a blank area of the Desktop or a window.
3. Click mouse button 2 to display the pop-up menu.

4. Click mouse button 1 on the arrow to the right of the **Drop** menu choice.
5. Click mouse button 1 on the **Copy** or **Create shadow** menu choice.

If you change your mind, you can cancel a pickup.

To cancel the pickup:
1. Point to one of the icons you picked up.
2. Click mouse button 2 to display the pop-up menu.
3. Click mouse button 1 on the **Cancel drag** menu choice. The mouse pointer returns to an arrow, and the icons are no longer selected.

Sorting Icons

Sometimes it is much easier to find icons if you have them arranged in a certain order on your Desktop or within a window. You can sort icons by name, type, size, creation date, or the last date the file was changed or accessed. For example, you can sort your program icons alphabetically.

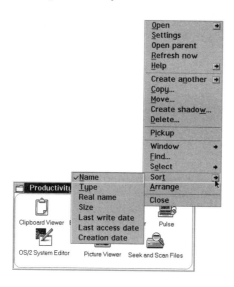

To sort the contents of a window or the Desktop:

1. Point to an icon or to an empty area in the open window or on the Desktop.
2. Click mouse button 2 to display the pop-up menu.
3. Click mouse button 1 on the arrow to the right of the **Sort** menu choice.
4. Click mouse button 1 on the choice that best describes how you want the icons sorted.

Arranging Icons

You can automatically rearrange the icons that are either on the Desktop or displayed in windows. This could make it easier to find everything. When you use the Arrange choice, the icons line up in nice, neat rows across the top of the open window or the Desktop. Any icons that have been minimized to the Desktop will line up across the bottom of the screen.

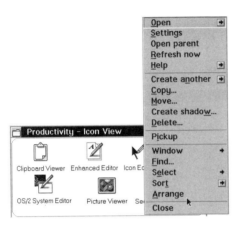

To arrange *all* of the icons in an open window or on the Desktop:

1. Point to an empty area in an open window or on the Desktop.
2. Click mouse button 2 to display the pop-up menu.
3. Click mouse button 1 on the **Arrange** menu choice.

If you arrange the icons on the Desktop or in a window and later decide that you don't like the way the icons are arranged, you can change them back to the way they were previously displayed.

To undo an arrangement:

1. Point to an empty area in an open window or on the Desktop.
2. Click mouse button 2 to display the pop-up menu.
3. Click mouse button 1 on the **Undo arrange** menu choice.

Arranging Windows

When you have many windows open at the same time, the Desktop can start to get cluttered. You can use the Window List to neatly arrange your windows so that you can read their titles.

ROCKET TIP: You can access the Window List quickly using the push button on the LaunchPad. If you click mouse button 1 on the **Window List** push button to display the Window List, you can skip steps 1 and 2 in all of the instructions that appear in this section.

There are two arrangements:

Cascade

Organizes your windows so that they are placed in an overlapped sequence with each title bar visible. In this arrangement, the active window appears on top of all other windows.

Tile

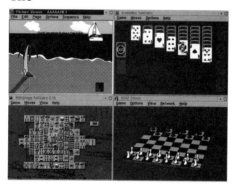

Organizes and sizes your windows so that they are placed side-by-side. In this arrangement, the active window appears in the upper-left corner of the Desktop.

To cascade or tile all of the windows whose titles appear in the Window List:
1. Point to an empty area on the Desktop.
2. Click mouse buttons 1 and 2 at the same time.
3. Point to the title-bar icon.
4. Click mouse button 2 to display the pop-up menu.
5. Click mouse button 1 on the arrow to the right of the **Select** menu choice.
6. Click mouse button 1 on the **Select all** choice.
7. Point to one of the titles in the Window List.
8. Click mouse button 2 to display the pop-up menu.
9. Click mouse button 1 on either the **Cascade** or **Tile** menu choice.

To cascade or tile multiple windows whose titles appear in the Window List:

1. Point to an empty area on the Desktop.
2. Click mouse buttons 1 and 2 at the same time.
3. Press and hold the Ctrl key.
4. Click mouse button 1 on the titles of the windows you want to cascade or tile. (If you change your mind about a title you selected, just click on it again to reverse the selection.)
5. Release the Ctrl key.
6. Point to one of the selected titles.
7. Click mouse button 2 to display the pop-up menu.
8. Click mouse button 1 on either the **Cascade** or **Tile** menu choice.

Switching between Running Programs

OS/2 Warp lets you have multiple programs running at the same time. If you are print-ing charts in one window, writing a memo in another, or sending a fax from still another, you can easily switch between all of these programs.

To switch between running programs, simply click mouse button 1 on the window of your choice.

When you are running multiple programs, one of those programs might be running from a DOS, Windows, or OS/2 full-screen command prompt. If that is the case, you will need to use your keyboard to switch between running programs.

To switch between running programs (when one of the programs is running from a full-screen command prompt), press the Alt+Esc keys.

Closing Windows

You can close windows that you are not using.

TIP: You can improve system performance by:

- Closing programs that are running in a window when you are done using them
- Closing any windows that you do not need to have open
- Moving commonly used functions out of windows and onto the Desktop or the LaunchPad and then closing the windows

You can use the Window List to close each window individually or you can close all windows at the same time.

 ROCKET TIP: You can access the Window List quickly using the push button on the LaunchPad. If you click mouse button 1 on the **Window List** push button to display the Window List, you can skip steps 1 and 2 in all of the instructions that appear in this section.

To close one window using the Window List:
1. Point to an empty area on the Desktop.
2. Click mouse buttons 1 and 2 at the same time.
3. Point to the title of the window in the Window List.
4. Click mouse button 2 to display the pop-up menu.
5. Click mouse button 1 on the **Close** menu choice.

 TIP: Earlier, we showed you how to close one window by double-clicking on the title-bar icon for the window. Although you can use the Window List to close one window, you will find that double-clicking on the title-bar icon is quicker. When you are closing all of the open windows or more than one open window, you will find that the Window List is quicker.

To close *all* of the open windows using the Window List:
1. Point to an empty area on the Desktop.
2. Click mouse buttons 1 and 2 at the same time.
3. Point to the title-bar icon.
4. Click mouse button 2 to display the pop-up menu.
5. Click mouse button 1 on the arrow to the right of the **Select** menu choice.
6. Click mouse button 1 on the **Select all** choice.
7. Point to one of the selected titles in the Window List.
8. Click mouse button 2 to display the pop-up menu.
9. Click mouse button 1 on the **Close** menu choice.

To close multiple windows using the Window List:
1. Point to an empty area on the Desktop.
2. Click mouse buttons 1 and 2 at the same time.
3. Press and hold the Ctrl key.
4. Click mouse button 1 on the titles of the windows you want to close. (If you change your mind abcut any title you selected, click on the title again to reverse the selection.)
5. Release the Ctrl key.

6. Point to one of the selected titles in the Window List.
7. Click mouse button 2 to display the pop-up menu.
8. Click mouse button 1 on the **Close** menu choice.

Locating Icons

You can use the Find program to help you locate icons. For example, if you cannot remember where you put a letter you wrote last week, you can use the Find program to help you locate the data-file icon for the letter.

ROCKET TIP: You can access the Find program quickly using the push button on the LaunchPad. If you click mouse button 1 on the **Find** push button to display the Find program, you can skip steps 1 through 3 in the following instructions.

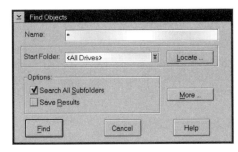

To find an icon:
1. Point to a folder icon or an empty area of the Desktop.
2. Click mouse button 2 to display the pop-up menu.
3. Click mouse button 1 on the **Find** menu choice.
4. Type the name of the icon you want to find in the **Name** field. Type an * if you do not know the name.
5. Click mouse button 1 on the down arrow in the **Start Folder** field. Then click on the drive where you want to search for the icon.
6. Click mouse button 1 on **Search all subfolders** if you want to search every icon.
7. Click mouse button 1 on **Save Results** if you want to create a Find Results window containing shadows of the icons found during the search. When you close this window, a Find Results folder is added to the Desktop.

   If you *do not* select **Save Results**, a *temporary* Find Results window is displayed with icons that represent the original icons. When you close this window a Find Results folder is not added to the Desktop.

WARNING: DO NOT delete icons from the temporary Find Results window because the original icons will be deleted from the computer.

8. Click mouse button 1 on the **Find** push button.

A Find Results windows is displayed, which contains icons found matching your search specification. If no icons are found, a message is displayed.

TIP: The Find Program also has an option that allows you to expand or limit the scope of your search. Use the **Locate** push button as follows, if you want to broaden or narrow your search:

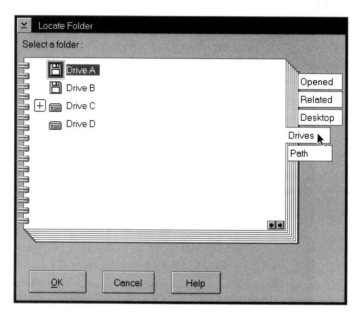

1. Click mouse button 1 on the **Locate** push button to specify where you want to search for the icon. The Locate Folder notebook is displayed. You can choose one of the following tabs to change the way the Find Program searches:

   Opened   Lists all icons that are currently open.

   Related   Lists all the icons on the drive where OS/2 Warp is installed.

   Desktop   Lists all the icons found on the Desktop.

   Drives   Lists all the drives on the computer.

   Path   Allows you to specify a path to search.

2. Click mouse button 1 on a tab on the Locate Folder page. (For example, if you want to search Drive C, you can click on the Drives page and then click on Drive C.)
3. Click mouse button 1 on the **OK** push button.

Chapter 7

Displaying Help

OS/2 Warp comes with an Information icon that contains online books on many topics. In addition to the online information, OS/2 Warp comes with built-in help. You can get help for an icon, a window, a pop-up menu choice, commands, and messages. The best thing about help information is that it is always right at your fingertips.

This chapter describes how to display help for icons, windows, pop-up menu choices, commands, and messages.

Displaying Help Using the F1 Key

Use the F1 key on your keyboard to display general information about the icon, window, or menu choice that is highlighted. Use the F1 key when you are not sure why you might want to use something or when you need help completing a task.

To get help for an icon or window, click mouse button 1 on the icon or window; then press the F1 key.

To get help for a pop-up menu choice:
1. Point to an icon.
2. Click mouse button 2 to display the pop-up menu.
3. Use the Up or Down Arrow key to highlight a menu choice.
4. Press the F1 key.

Displaying Help Using the Pop-Up Menu

You can display help for an icon or a window using the pop-up menu. If you use a pop-up menu to get help, you can select the type of help you want to see.

To display help for an icon or open window:
1. Point to an icon or to an empty area in an open window.
2. Click mouse button 2 to display the pop-up menu.
3. Click mouse button 1 on the **Help** menu choice.

The **Help** choice on the pop-up menu provides you with a list of additional types of help. You can select the following additional types of help:

Help Index
Displays a list of the help topics available in the Master Help Index.

General Help
> Displays general information about an icon or window.   (This choice displays the same help you get when you press F1.)

Using Help
> Displays instructions for the ways you can get help from within OS/2 Warp.

Keys Help
> Displays a list of key combinations you can use with OS/2 Warp.

To display additional help choices, click mouse button 1 on the arrow to the right of the Help choice; then click on the additional help choice.

Displaying Help Using the Help Push Button

You can find Help push buttons at the bottom of notebook pages and some windows. The help that is displayed when you select the push button is specific to the notebook page or window. It details the steps you need to take to complete the task at hand.

To get help for a window that contains a Help push button, click mouse button 1 on the **Help** push button.

Displaying Help for a Command

You can get help for any command by typing HELP from an OS/2 command prompt. When you request help from a command prompt, the OS/2 Command Reference opens to the page that explains the command in question.

To get help for a command from an OS/2 command prompt:
1. Type HELP followed by the command name (for example: HELP COPY).
2. Press the Enter key to display information about the command.
3. After you read the information, press the Alt+F4 keys to return to the command prompt.

Displaying Help for Messages

You can get information that helps you understand and respond to OS/2 Warp messages and correct errors. The way you request help depends upon how and where the message is displayed.

To get help for a message that appears in a window with a Help push button, click mouse button 1 on the **Help** push button.

To get help for a message that appears on a full screen and is enclosed in a box, use the Up or Down Arrow key to highlight **Display Help**; then press the Enter key.

To get help for a message that appears when you are using an OS/2 command prompt, type HELP followed by a space and the message number; then press the Enter key. (It is not necessary to type the letters SYS or the leading zeros.)

For example, if you received this message:

SYS0002: The system cannot find the file specified.

You would type HELP 2 and then press the Enter key. The following help would appear:

SYS0002: The system cannot find the file specified.

EXPLANATION: The file named in the command does not exist in the current directory or search path specified or the file name was entered incorrectly.

ACTION: Retry the command using the correct file name.

Navigating Help

When you display help, a word or phrase is sometimes *highlighted* in a color that is different from the rest of the text in the window. The highlighting means that additional information is available. This information might be a definition of a word, help for an entry field, or additional information related to a topic.

To see the additional information, click mouse button 1 on the highlighted word or phrase.

To return to the previous screen of information, click mouse button 1 on the **Previous** push button or press the Esc key.

Chapter 8

Securing and Shutting Down Your System

When you are not using OS/2 Warp, you should secure your system to prevent other people from using your computer. When you are finished using OS/2 Warp, you should shut down your system so that all data you have been using is properly saved to the hard disk.

This chapter describes how to secure and shut down your system.

Locking Your Computer

You can lock the keyboard and mouse on your computer. The lockup program helps protect important information and also provides a screen saver.

The first time you use the lockup program, you will need to set your password.

To set your password:
1. Point to an empty area on the Desktop.
2. Click mouse button 2 to display the pop-up menu.
3. Click mouse button 1 on the **Lockup now** menu choice.
4. Type a password in the **Password** field.
5. Press the Enter key to move the cursor to the **Password (for verification)** field.
6. Type the same password again. This is to verify that you typed the password correctly.

   NOTE: It is very important that you remember your password.

7. Click mouse button 1 on the **OK** push button.

Your password is set, and your keyboard and mouse are locked. (Remember, you only have to set a password the first time you lock the computer.)

The next time you want to lock your computer, follow the procedure shown below.

To lock your computer:
1. Point to an empty area on the Desktop.
2. Click mouse button 2 to display the pop-up menu.
3. Click mouse button 1 on the **Lockup now** menu choice.

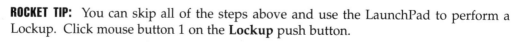

ROCKET TIP: You can skip all of the steps above and use the LaunchPad to perform a Lockup. Click mouse button 1 on the **Lockup** push button.

Each time you lock up your computer, a picture appears on your screen and your keyboard and mouse are locked.

When you want to begin using your computer again, you will need to unlock it.

To unlock your computer, type your password; then press Enter. You will return to the window you were using before you locked up your computer.

No matter how hard you try to remember, sooner or later, you will probably forget the password that you set for lockup.

To recover from a forgotten password:
1. Turn on your computer. If it is already on, press the Ctrl+Alt+Del keys.
2. Watch the upper-left corner of the screen. When you see a small white box, press the Alt+F1 keys.
3. When you see the Recovery Choices screen, press the **c** key.
4. Type **CD\OS2**, and then press the Enter key.
5. Type **MAKEINI OS2.INI LOCK.RC**, and then press the Enter key.
6. When you see the "Successful completion" message, restart your computer by pressing the Ctrl+Alt+Del keys at the same time. Your lockup password is removed. You will now have to go back and set a new lockup password.

TIP: Because it is so easy to remove a lockup password, it should not be your only means of protecting the information on your computer. The lockup password should be used in combination with other security features provided with your computer, such as a power-on password or a keylock.

Shutting Down Your System

Shutdown cleans up information in temporary storage buffers and saves that information to the hard disk. You should avoid turning off the computer without doing a shutdown, because the information in the storage buffers will be lost.

TIP: It might not always be possible to shut down your computer before you turn it off. When it is not possible to perform a shutdown, press the Ctrl+Alt+Del keys at the same time. Then wait until you hear a beep before you turn off the computer.

To shut down your computer:
1. Point to an empty area on the Desktop.
2. Click mouse button 2 to display the pop-up menu.
3. Click mouse button 1 on the **Shut down** menu choice.

ROCKET TIP: You can skip all of the steps above and use the LaunchPad to perform a shutdown. Click mouse button 1 on the **Shutdown** push button.

Before the shutdown is completed, you will see a confirmation message, like this:

> Shutdown has now completed. It is now safe to turn off your computer, or restart the system by pressing Ctrl + Alt + Del.

If you want to continue shutting down your system, click mouse button 1 on the **Yes** push button. If open windows are present, you are asked to verify that you want to close each open window without saving the data.

If you do not want to continue shutting down your system, click mouse button 1 on the **No** push button. The shutdown is canceled.

Part Three

Personalizing OS/2 Warp

When you installed OS/2 Warp on your computer, it was easy to see that a lot of care was taken to provide the best looking and working operating system available today and for many years to come. But did you know that as good as OS/2 Warp is, you can make it better? That's right—you can change the way it works to fit your personality, your way of doing things, your preferences.

The chapters that follow show you how to get the most out of OS/2 Warp by making it your own. You will find out how to customize the LaunchPad, personalize the Desktop with colors, bit maps, and fonts, and change how OS/2 Warp responds in certain situations. You will also find out how to change the location and appearance of the system clock.

This part also provides information about changing your keyboard, mouse, and country settings, and personalizing your printer options. In addition, this part describes how to install new OS/2 Warp, DOS, and Windows programs and provides information about ways to start those programs. You will also find out how to create new icons and how to change the way your icons are displayed.

We'll also share some nifty customizing tricks with you.

Chapter 9

Getting Ready to Personalize OS/2. *Warp*

Many of the personalizing features described in this part are accomplished using a *notebook*. A notebook contains the characteristics of an icon. You might want to spend a few minutes familiarizing yourself with notebooks.

Before you spend time and energy personalizing the OS/2 Warp Desktop, you also might want to make sure that OS/2 Warp saves the changes in the event that something happens to your computer and you might want to set your display so that it provides the best possible resolution.

This chapter explains how to look at a notebook and provides detailed information about the notebooks for folders, devices, programs, printers, and multimedia devices. This chapter explains how to save changes you make to the Desktop so that if your computer should experience a problem, you will be able to recover the latest copy of your Desktop. This chapter also explains how to change your display resolution.

Viewing Icon Notebooks

Every icon has a notebook attached to it. The notebook is where the *settings* for the icon are stored. The settings are used to specify the characteristics of the icon. For example, one of the settings for a program icon is used to tell OS/2 Warp where to find the program and what command is needed to start the program.

When you change a setting in a notebook, the change happens immediately. However, if you change your mind, you can always click on the **Undo** push button located at the bottom of the notebook. The settings will return to what they were before you opened the notebook. Some notebooks also have a **Default** push button. This push button changes the settings in the notebook back to the ones in effect when OS/2 Warp was installed.

When you open the notebook, you will notice tabs along its right side. These tabs represent the different topics in the notebook. If a tab contains more than one page of settings, you will see the words **Page ? of ?** followed by arrows in the lower-right corner of the notebook. By clicking on one of the arrows, you can turn the pages within the tab. For example, if you display the Settings notebook for the Desktop, you will notice **View - Page 1 of 3** in the lower-right corner of the first page of the View tab. Click on the arrow to change to the next page, **View - Page 2 of 3**.

To view the notebook for an icon:
1. Point to the icon whose notebook you want to view.
2. Click mouse button 2 to display the pop-up menu.
3. Click mouse button 1 on the Settings menu choice. The notebook for the icon is displayed.

4. Click mouse button 1 on a tab in the notebook.

5. Repeat step 4 to go to the next tab in the notebook.

6. Double-click on the title-bar icon of the notebook to close it.

Describing Notebook Tabs

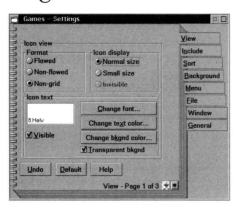

The names that appear on tabs in the notebook depend on the type of icon the notebook is attached to. The following information gives a brief overview of the tabs in notebooks of different types of icons.

Folder and Device Icons

The names on the tabs in a notebook for a folder or device icon include:

View

Use the View tab to change how icons and their text are displayed.

Include

Use the Include tab to include icons that you want in your folder icon and exclude icons you don't want in your folder icon.

Sort

Use the Sort tab to specify which menu items are listed when you click on the arrow to the right of **Sort** in the pop-up menu.

Background

Use the Background tab to choose an image or a color to display in the background of any open icon, including the Desktop. You can choose a different image or color for each icon on the Desktop.

Menu

Use the Menu tab to customize your pop-up menu items. You can add, delete, or change the items on the pop-up menu or the cascaded menu that is displayed when you click on the arrow to the right of a menu item.

File

Use the File tab to view the file name and path of an icon. You can also define the icon as a work-area icon. A work-area icon lets you put together icons that are related to a specific task. For example, you might want to have a work area called MY BRIEF CASE where you can keep programs such as a calculator, a word processor for memos, a printer, or whatever else you need. For more information about work-area icons, see "Creating Work-Area Icons" on page 162.

Window

Use the Window tab to customize the window behavior for each icon on the Desktop. Window behavior includes how and where you want your icon to be minimized, how you want the window to open, and which button (hide or minimize) you want to appear on the window every time you double-click on it.

General

Use the General tab to change the name displayed under an icon or to specify a new icon.

You can get help for settings pages by clicking on the **Help** push button, which is located at the bottom of every page in the notebook.

Program Icons

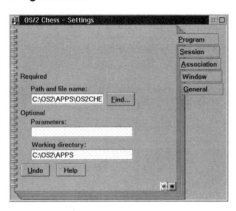

The names on the tabs in a notebook for a program icon include:

Program

Use the Program tab to specify a working directory for the selected icon. When you do this, you control where the program stores the files it creates.

NOTE: Windows programs do not use the **Working Directory** field.

Session

Use the Session tab to select the appropriate session for a program icon. The type of session determines how the program runs. The types are OS/2 Warp, DOS, and WIN-OS/2 full screen and window.

NOTES:

1.   If **WIN-OS/2 window** or **WIN-OS/2 full screen** is selected, then a **WIN-OS/2 settings** push button is displayed instead of a **DOS settings** push button.

Select the settings push button to display the list of DOS or WIN-OS/2 settings for the icon. By fine-tuning these settings, you can improve the way a program runs.

2.   If you change your WIN-OS/2 or DOS settings, you must save the changes with the **Save** push button.

Association

Use the Association tab to create a special link (an association) between the current program icon and one or more data-file icons.

For more information on associating program icons and data-file icons, see "Associating a Program with a Data-File Icon" on page 156 and "Associating Multiple Data-File Icons with a Program" on page 156.

Window

Use the Window tab to change the system default for what happens when you click on the minimize button in the title bar of a program icon. The system default is that an icon is placed in the Minimized Window Viewer icon.

General

Use the General tab to change the name displayed under an icon, specify a new icon, or make the icon a stack of templates.

Data-File Icons

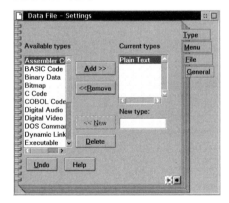

The names on the tabs in a notebook for a data-file icon include:

Type

Use the Type tab to assign one or more file types to the data-file icon.

Menu

Use the Menu tab to customize your pop-up menu items. You can add, delete, or change the items on the pop-up menu or the cascaded menu that is displayed when you click on the arrow to the right of a menu item.

File

Use the File tab to view the file name and path of an icon. You can also define the icon as a work-area icon. A work-area icon lets you put together icons that are related to a specific task. For more information about work-area icons, see "Creating Work-Area Icons" on page 162.

General

Use the General tab to change the name displayed under an icon, specify a new icon, or make the icon a stack of templates.

Printer Icons

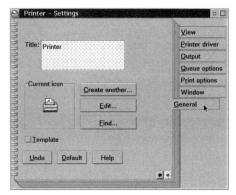

The names on the tabs in a notebook for a printer icon include:

View

Use the View tab to set up how your print jobs are displayed.

Printer driver

Use the Printer driver tab to select printer drivers or change the job properties.

Output

Use the Output tab to select a different port, save your print job as a file, redirect a job to a COM port, and change the communications port setup.

Queue options

Use the Queue options tab to choose a queue driver and store print jobs in a printer-specific file.

Print options

Use the Print options tab to specify start and stop times for printer activity and to add a separator page to your print jobs.

Window

Use the Window tab to change what happens when you click on the hide button in the title-bar of the printer icon window.

General

Use the General tab to change the name displayed under an icon, specify a new icon, or make the icon a stack of templates.

Multimedia Devices

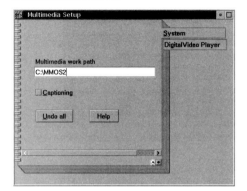

Multimedia devices have two notebooks associated with them. They have a settings notebook for their program icons (see "Program Icons" on page 68) and a settings notebook for the multimedia devices. You can view the settings notebook for the multimedia devices by double-clicking on the **Multimedia** icon and then on the **Multimedia Setup** icon.

The settings in the Multimedia icon are specific to the devices used for OS/2 Warp multimedia. The notebook looks a little different from other notebooks in OS/2 Warp. The tabs for the notebook contain the names of multimedia devices installed on your computer. On the bottom of each device's tab might be other tabs that contain information about the device.

The names on the tabs in the notebook for multimedia device icons can include:

System
Use the System tab to change the path where the data files created with multimedia programs are stored. You can also enable or disable closed captioning.

Compact Disc
Use the Compact Disc tab to change the name that appears below the Compact Disc icon, view a description of the device, and specify whether it is the default Compact Disc player. The **Drive Letter** tab at the bottom allows you to change the drive letter associated with the Compact Disc player.

Digital Audio
Use the Digital Audio tab to change the name that appears below the Digital Audio icon, view a description of the device, and specify whether this is the default Digital Audio player. The **Association** tab at the bottom allows you to change the file extensions associated with the Digital Audio player.

MIDI
Use the MIDI (Musical Instrument Digital Interface) tab to change the name that appears below the MIDI icon, view a description of the device, and specify whether this is the default MIDI player. The **Association** tab at the bottom allows you to change the file extensions associated with the MIDI player. The **Options** tab at the bottom allows you to change the audio card being used by the MIDI player and to specify which channels the audio card should play.

Digital Video

Use the Digital Video tab to change the name that appears below the Digital Video icon, view a description of the device, and specify whether this is the default Digital Video player. The **Association** tab at the bottom allows you to change the file extensions associated with the Digital Video player.

CD-ROM XA

Use the CD-ROM XA tab to change the name that appears below the CD-ROM XA icon, view a description of the device, and specify whether this is the default CD-ROM XA device. The **Association** tab at the bottom allows you to change the file extensions associated with the CD-ROM XA device. The **Drive Letter** allows you to change the drive letter associated with the CD-ROM XA device.

NOTE: Additional tabs might also be provided on your Multimedia Setup notebook if you have other multimedia devices installed.

Saving Changes You Make to Your Desktop

OS/2 Warp provides the capability to save a copy of the Desktop each time you shut down your computer. OS/2 Warp will keep copies of the Desktop from the last three times you shut down.

If you follow the procedure below, you will be able to get back a recent copy of your Desktop in the event that your computer breaks down. Otherwise, your only choice is to get the Desktop as it was originally installed.

Play it safe and do the following steps.

To save a copy of your Desktop every time you shut down the computer:
1. Point to an empty area on the Desktop.
2. Click mouse button 2 to display the pop-up menu.
3. Click mouse button 1 on the **Settings** menu choice.
4. Click mouse button 1 on the **Archive** notebook tab.
5. Click mouse button 1 on **Create archive at each system restart** to place a check mark in the box.
6. Double-click on the title-bar icon of the notebook to close it.

Getting the Best Resolution from Your Display

Before you spend a lot of time personalizing OS/2 Warp, make sure that you are displaying OS/2 Warp at the best resolution that your display is capable of. Resolution is defined by the number of dots that can be displayed on the screen and the number of colors that can be displayed.

To change your screen resolution:

1. Point to an empty area on the Desktop.
2. Click mouse button 2 to display the pop-up menu.
3. Click mouse button 1 on the **System setup** menu choice.
4. Double-click on the **System** icon.
5. Click mouse button 1 on the **Screen** notebook tab.

   NOTE: The **Screen** notebook tab will not appear if you are using the VGA, 8514, or SVGA device driver. If you do not see a **Screen** notebook tab, you cannot change the resolution of your display.

6. Click mouse button 1 on the resolution that you want to use.

   Each resolution is defined by width x height x number of colors. The higher the numbers, the better the resolution.

7. Click mouse button 1 on the **Workplace Shell Palette Aware** choice to improve the appearance of bit maps on your display.
8. Double-click on the title-bar icons of the open windows to close them.

TIP: If you change the screen resolution from a higher resolution to a lower resolution, the display of some windows might be affected. You might have to move the windows so that the windows are visible. If this occurs:

1. Press the Alt and Spacebar keys to display the menu choices for the window.
2. Click mouse button 1 on the **Move** menu choice.
3. Use the mouse or the arrow keys to move the window.
4. Click mouse button 1 or press the Enter key to anchor the window in its new location.

Customizing the LaunchPad

The LaunchPad is one of the best features of OS/2 Warp. It places the OS/2 Window, Shredder, Tutorial, Drive A, and Printer icons in one convenient location. It also puts some of the most commonly used menu choices at your fingertips in the form of push buttons. But did you know that you can make it even more useful by customizing it to your needs?

This chapter shows you how to change the look and location of the LaunchPad, add icons to the LaunchPad, delete icons that you don't want on the LaunchPad, and break off pieces of the LaunchPad so that you can carry them with you to another window.

Changing LaunchPad Settings

You can change the way the LaunchPad is displayed as well as customize the way it displays text.

For example, when OS/2 Warp was installed on your computer, the LaunchPad was set up to be displayed horizontally at the bottom of the Desktop. It did not have a title bar or text beneath the icons. You might decide that you would rather have the LaunchPad displayed vertically with a title bar and text beneath the icons.

TIP: You can move the LaunchPad anywhere on the Desktop by pointing to an empty area on the LaunchPad and dragging it to a new location.

To change the LaunchPad settings:

1. Point to an empty area in the LaunchPad.
2. Click mouse button 2 to display the pop-up menu.
3. Click mouse button 1 on the **Settings** menu choice. You can click mouse button 1 on any of the following choices. The descriptions provided here explain what happens when the choice has a check mark next to it.

   Float on top

   Keeps the LaunchPad on top of all open windows. Open windows will never cover the LaunchPad. This choice might distract you after a while because you will have to physically move the LaunchPad whenever it obstructs your view of a window you are working with.

Hide frame controls

Removes the title bar from the LaunchPad and its drawers so that the LaunchPad occupies less space on the Desktop. The title bar is used to move the LaunchPad and display its pop-up menu. You can still move the LaunchPad and display its pop-up menu without the title bar, but you will need to be particularly adept with the mouse.

Close drawer after icon open

Automatically closes the drawers on the LaunchPad after an icon in the drawer is opened. If this option isn't chosen, you will have to click on the drawer handle in the LaunchPad to close the drawer.

Display vertical

Changes the orientation of the LaunchPad so that it is displayed vertically with the icons on top, the drawers to the right of the icons, and the push buttons at the bottom. This arrangement is nice if you like things up and down rather than left and right.

Display text in drawers

Places text below the icons in the drawers so that they are easier to recognize. This makes the drawers take up more space on the Desktop when they are opened. If you can easily recognize icons, you probably don't need this option.

Display text on LaunchPad

Places text below the icons on the LaunchPad so that they are easier to recognize. This makes the LaunchPad take up more space on the Desktop. However, if you have trouble recognizing icons, it might be worth the trade-off in space.

Small icons

Shrinks the size of the icons displayed on the LaunchPad and in the drawers. This makes the LaunchPad take up less space on the Desktop.

NOTE: However, if you decide that you want to display text on the LaunchPad AND make the icons small, the space needed for the LaunchPad remains the same.

4. Double-click on the title-bar icon of the notebook to close it.

Adding Icons to the LaunchPad

You can add the programs that you use most often to the LaunchPad to eliminate the need to search through icon after icon for the one you want. You can put your icons on the LaunchPad in two different areas: on the front panel and in drawers. Where you put an icon on the LaunchPad depends on how often you will use it. You should put the ones you use most often on the front panel and those you use often, but not quite as frequently, in drawers on the LaunchPad.

To add an icon to the front panel of the LaunchPad:
1. Point to the icon you want to add to the LaunchPad.
2. Press and hold mouse button 2.
3. Drag the icon to the LaunchPad.
4. When you see a bold line between the icons on the LaunchPad, release mouse button 2.

TIP: Try to keep the number of icons on the front panel of the LaunchPad to less than seven if you plan to display text beneath the icons, or less than twelve if you won't be displaying text beneath the icons. Exceeding this number causes some of the icons to be pushed off the screen. When this happens, you will need to move the LaunchPad in order to select some of the icons, which diminishes the usefulness of the LaunchPad.

To add an icon to a drawer on the LaunchPad:
1. Point to the icon you want to add to the drawer.
2. Press and hold mouse button 2.
3. Drag the icon to the drawer.
4. When you see a bold box surrounding the drawer, release mouse button 2.

Deleting Icons from the LaunchPad

Just because an icon was placed on the LaunchPad doesn't mean that you're stuck with it there. You can delete any icons that you don't want from the LaunchPad. Deleting an icon from the front panel or the drawers of the LaunchPad does not remove the icon from your computer. The icons on the LaunchPad are only shadows of the original icons, which reside somewhere else in OS/2 Warp. So, even if you delete the icon from the LaunchPad today, you can put it back on the LaunchPad tomorrow.

To delete an icon from the front panel of the LaunchPad:
1. Point to the icon you want to delete.
2. Press and hold mouse button 2.
3. Drag the icon to the **Shredder** icon.
4. Release mouse button 2.
5. Respond to any confirmation messages that appear on the screen.

To delete an icon from a drawer on the LaunchPad:

1. Click mouse button 1 on the drawer containing the icon you want to delete.
2. Point to the icon you want to delete.
3. Press and hold mouse button 2.
4. Drag the icon to the **Shredder** icon.
5. Release mouse button 2.
6. Respond to any confirmation messages that appear on the screen.

Detaching Drawers

You can set up the LaunchPad in any way that suits your needs. For example, you can put all of the icons you need for a particular project in one of the drawers. After doing this, you can detach the LaunchPad drawer containing all the icons needed for the project and drag it to a more convenient location.

For example, let's say that your job is to write presentations for your boss and you use a graphics program, plotter, and data files for the presentations. You can put the icons that represent your program, plotter, and data files in one of the drawers on the LaunchPad for easy access. Each time you need to do a presentation, you just open the drawer and click on the icon you need. Now let's say that your boss wants you to add multimedia to today's presentation. You can modify your LaunchPad to meet the new requirements in two ways: you can add the multimedia program to your drawer, or you can detach the drawer and drag it to your multimedia window. Because this is a one-time deal, why not just detach the drawer and drag it to the multimedia window.

To detach a drawer from the LaunchPad:

1. Click mouse button 1 on the handle of the drawer that you want to detach from the LaunchPad.
2. Point to the outside edge of the open drawer. Be careful not to point to the icons in the drawer.
3. Press and hold mouse button 2.
4. Drag the drawer to the location on the Desktop where you want the drawer.
5. Release mouse button 2.

 TIP: You can have multiple LaunchPads. Each one can be customized to the particular activities that you perform. For example, if you plan to work with one project for a long time, you might decide that it would be nice to have an entire LaunchPad dedicated to that project. You can copy or create a shadow of an existing LaunchPad and customize it.

When you first open a copy or shadow of the LaunchPad, it will overlay the original LaunchPad. You can move it to another area on the Desktop or to the window where you want to use it. From then on, whenever you open the copy or shadow, it will appear in the new location.

Reattaching Drawers

After you detach a drawer from the LaunchPad, you can move the drawer anywhere you like. This is great, but what do you do with it when you're finished for the day, or when you need the drawer, but it's hidden beneath other open windows? The answer to both situations is the same—just reattach the drawer to the LaunchPad. You don't even have to know where the drawer is physically located.

To reattach a drawer to the LaunchPad, click mouse button 1 on the handle of the drawer that once contained the icons. The drawer is reattached, and ready to be opened or detached again.

Chapter 11

Personalizing Your Desktop with Colors and Bit Maps

OS/2 Warp comes with a predefined set of colors for the Desktop, parts of windows, and text. While they are very nice, you might have a different look for OS/2 Warp in mind.

This chapter shows you how to change the colors of different pieces of the Desktop, add bit maps to the backgrounds of windows and the Desktop, and change the pictures on the icons in OS/2 Warp.

Selecting a Scheme

The people who designed OS/2 Warp had an inkling that not everyone who bought their product would be happy with the colors that they selected. So, in an effort to make changing the colors easier, they put together something called a "scheme." A scheme contains a predefined set of colors for the title bars, scroll bars, Desktop background, window background, and window borders (among other things). OS/2 Warp has 24 of these schemes for you to pick from.

To change the colors of a window or the Desktop using a scheme:

1. Point to an empty area on the Desktop.
2. Click mouse button 2 to display the pop-up menu.
3. Click mouse button 1 on the **System setup** menu choice.
4. Double-click on the **Scheme Palette** icon.
5. Point to a scheme on the palette (for example, **Cool Water**).

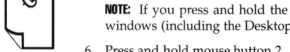

   NOTE: If you press and hold the Alt key while performing the next three steps, all windows (including the Desktop) will be updated to the new color scheme.

6. Press and hold mouse button 2.
7. Drag the color scheme to the window or to a blank area of the Desktop.
8. Release mouse button 2. The colors of the window or the Desktop change to the new scheme.
9. Double-click on the title-bar icons of the open windows to close them.

Creating Your Own Scheme

If you've had a chance to experiment with the different schemes available in OS/2 Warp and couldn't find one to your liking, don't worry. You can create your own scheme. In fact, you can create multiple schemes. When you create a scheme, you get to pick the colors that you want to use for the various parts of the window. This is a great way to individualize the Desktop and make a statement about who you are!

To create your own scheme:

1. Point to an empty area on the Desktop.
2. Click mouse button 2 to display the pop-up menu.
3. Click mouse button 1 on the **System setup** menu choice.
4. Double-click on the **Scheme Palette** icon.
5. Click mouse button 1 on one of the **New scheme** icons.
6. Click mouse button 1 on the **Edit Scheme** push button at the bottom of the window.

   A window appears with a Sample area in the upper-left corner. Use this Sample area to select the items whose colors you want to change. This Sample area changes to reflect the colors that you selected and provides an excellent chance to see whether your color selections look good together. Remember, you do not have to pick a color for each item in the Sample area. You can change as many or as few as you like.

   TIP: The items in the Sample area are also listed in the **Window area** field. You can use this list instead of the Sample area to select the items you want to add color to.

7. Point to an item in the Sample area.
8. Click mouse button 2 to display a pop-up menu containing items that can be changed.
9. Click mouse button 1 on the menu item whose color you want to change. The Edit Colors window is displayed. (You will use the color ball to choose the colors for the item.)

   NOTE: If you are editing either the Desktop Background or the Folder Background, you will see an Edit Background window. Click mouse button 1 on the **Change color** push button to go to the window containing the color ball.

10. Point to anywhere within the color ball.
11. Press and hold mouse button 1.
12. Drag the mouse pointer around the color ball until the color you want is displayed to the right of the color ball.
13. Release mouse button 1.
14. Point to the band in the color bar.
15. Press and hold mouse button 1.
16. Drag the band to the color you want.
17. Release mouse button 1.
18. Repeat steps 7 through 17 until you are satisfied with the colors you have selected for your scheme.
19. Double-click on the title-bar icon of the Edit Colors window to close it. The colors of the window parts on the sample palette change to the colors you selected.
20. Click mouse button 1 on the **Scheme title** field on the Edit Scheme window.

21. Type a name for your new scheme.
22. Double-click on the title-bar icon of the Edit Scheme window to close it.
23. Double-click on the title-bar icons of the open windows to close them.

Your new scheme is ready to use. Follow the instructions under "Selecting a Scheme" on page 82.

Changing Colors Individually or Globally

If the OS/2 Warp schemes aren't quite what you're looking for, and creating your own schemes seems like too much work, you have another option. You can easily select the colors you want to use on the Desktop without all the hassle of a scheme. The following steps show you how to select colors from a palette and use them to change the colors of all the Desktop parts.

To change the colors of the Desktop without using a scheme:
1. Point to an empty area on the Desktop.
2. Click mouse button 2 to display the pop-up menu.
3. Click mouse button 1 on the **System setup** menu choice.
4. Double-click on the **Mixed Color Palette** icon. If your display is not capable of handling high-resolution colors, use the **Solid Color Palette** instead.
5. Make sure that the item you want to change is visible. For example, if you want to change the color of a scroll bar, make sure the scroll bar is visible.
6. Point to a square on the color palette.

NOTE: If you press and hold the Alt key while performing the next three steps, all instances of the item will be changed to the new color. Otherwise, only the item you drag the color to will be changed.

If you press and hold the Ctrl key while performing the next three steps, you will be able to change the color of the titles below the icons in a window or on the Desktop.

7. Press and hold mouse button 2.
8. Drag the color to the item you want to change. The mouse pointer changes to a paint bucket.
9. Release mouse button 2.
10. Repeat steps 5 through 9 until all the items whose color you want to change have been changed.
11. Double-click on the title-bar icons of the open windows to close them.

TIP: If your Desktop ends up looking like an artist's nightmare, you can always recover by following the instructions under "Selecting a Scheme" on page 82 and selecting the **Default** scheme.

Changing the Colors of Icon Titles

When you're designing the overall look of your Desktop and windows, don't forget about the icon titles. You can change the colors so that they stand out or blend in with the background of your Desktop or window. You can even make the icon titles invisible.

To change the colors of the icon titles:

1. Point to an empty area on the Desktop or in a window.
2. Click mouse button 2 to display the pop-up menu.
3. Click mouse button 1 on the **Settings** menu choice.
4. Click mouse button 1 on the **Visible** choice to place a check mark in the box. If no check mark is placed in this box, the icon titles will not be visible.
5. Click mouse button 1 on the **Transparent bkgnd** field if you want the background color of the Desktop or window to show through.
6. Click mouse button 1 on a choice in the **Icon text** field. You can select a color for the icon text or for the background of the icon text.
7. Point to anywhere within the color ball.
8. Press and hold mouse button 1.
9. Drag the mouse pointer around the color ball until the color you want is displayed in the bar to the right of the color ball.
10. Release mouse button 1.
11. Point to the band in the color bar.
12. Press and hold mouse button 1.
13. Drag the band to the color you want.
14. Release mouse button 1.
15. Double-click on the title-bar icon of the Edit Color window to close it.
16. Repeat steps 6 through 15 if you want to change another color associated with the icon text.
17. Double-click on the title-bar icon of the notebook to close it.

Adding a Bit Map to a Background

One of the easiest ways to make working on a computer fun is to add flair to the screens. You can do this by adding a bit map (picture) to your Desktop or window backgrounds. OS/2 Warp comes with a variety of bit maps.

To add a bit map to a background:

1. Point to the icon whose background you want to add a bit map to. If you want to add the bit map to the Desktop, point to an empty area on the Desktop.
2. Click mouse button 2 to display the pop-up menu.
3. Click mouse button 1 on the **Settings** menu choice.
4. Click mouse button 1 on the **Background** notebook tab.
5. Click mouse button 1 on **Color only** to remove the check mark from the box.
6. Click mouse button 1 on the arrow to the right of the File field to display a list of bit maps that you can choose.
7. Click mouse button 1 on the up or down arrow in the scroll bar to the right of the list of bit maps to view the available .BMP (bit map) files.
8. Click mouse button 1 on the bit map of your choice. The bit map is displayed in the **Preview** field. (If you are adding the bit map to the Desktop background, the bit map might also be displayed there, too.)
9. Repeat steps 6 through 8 until you find a bit map that you want to use.
10. Click mouse button 1 on one of the following choices:

    Normal image
    Displays a small image of the bit map in the center of the background area. The bit map usually ends up being too small to enjoy.

    Tiled image
    Displays the same image over and over again until the background area is filled. This is all right for patterns.

    Scaled image
    Sizes the image to fill the background area. The number of images used in the background depends on the setting specified in the field to the right of the choice. For example, if you select 7x7, there will be 49 images covering the background area. If you select 1x1, one image is sized to fill the background area.

    You might need to experiment to find the best choice for your bit map.

11. Double-click on the title-bar icon of the notebook to close it.

TIP: You can use other bit maps as a background. Just copy the bit maps into the \OS2\BITMAP directory, and they will appear in the list of bit maps in the Settings notebook.

Replacing a Bit Map with Color

You can get rid of that bit map background as quickly and easily as you added it. The following steps show you how to remove the bit map and add a splash of color instead. Because this is so easy, you can change your background colors as often as you change your socks.

To add color to a background:
1. Point to the icon whose background you want to change. If you want to change the Desktop, point to an empty area on the Desktop.
2. Click mouse button 2 to display the pop-up menu.
3. Click mouse button 1 on the **Settings** menu choice.
4. Click mouse button 1 on the **Background** notebook tab.
5. Click mouse button 1 on **Color only** to place a check mark in the box.
6. Click mouse button 1 on the **Change color** push button to display the Edit Color window.
7. Point to anywhere within the color ball.
8. Press and hold mouse button 1.
9. Drag the mouse pointer around the color ball until the color you want is displayed in the bar to the right.
10. Release mouse button 1.
11. Point to the band in the color bar.
12. Press and hold mouse button 1.
13. Drag the band to the color you want.
14. Release mouse button 1.
15. Double-click on the title-bar icons of the open windows to close them.

Replacing Icons

Do all the icons on your Desktop look alike? Are you having trouble telling one icon from another? Can anything be done about it? You bet! The little pictures that represent your icons are nothing more than .ICO files, and you can replace them.

NOTE: OS/2 Warp doesn't come with extra .ICO files, but you can buy them or create your own. If you want to create your own, read "Icon Editor" on page 184.

To replace the picture that represents an icon:
1. Point to an icon whose picture you want to change.
2. Click mouse button 2 to display the pop-up menu.
3. Click mouse button 1 on the **Settings** menu choice.
4. Click mouse button 1 on the **General** notebook tab.
5. Display a window containing the icons you want to use to replace the existing icons.
6. Point to the icon that you like and want to use.
7. Press and hold mouse button 2.
8. Drag the icon to the **Current icon** field in the notebook.
9. Release mouse button 2. The icon now has a new picture.
10. Double-click on the title-bar icons of the open windows to close them.

Editing Icons

If you don't have the luxury of having additional icons to choose from, don't worry. You can still change your icons. You can take an existing icon and edit it. While editing an icon, you can make minor changes or go all out and change the entire thing. The choice is yours.

To edit an icon:
1. Point to the icon that you want to edit.
2. Click mouse button 2 to display the pop-up menu.
3. Click mouse button 1 on the **Settings** menu choice.
4. Click mouse button 1 on the **General** notebook tab.
5. Click mouse button 1 on the **Edit** push button. The icon is displayed in the Icon Editor window. The icon is enlarged to make editing easy.
6. Click mouse button 1 on a color on the right side of the window.
7. Point to the area on the icon that you want to change. Your mouse pointer turns into a square. Click mouse button 1. Pointing and clicking changes one square at a time. If you press and hold mouse button 1 while you drag the pointer, you can change multiple squares at the same time.
8. Repeat steps 6 and 7 until you are satisfied with the changes you have made to the icon. To find out how to more effectively edit icons, read "Icon Editor" on page 184.
9. Double-click on the title-bar icon of the Icon Editor window to close it.

10. Click mouse button 1 on the **Yes** push button to save the changes to the icon. (Click mouse button 1 on the **No** push button if you made a mess and don't want to save your masterpiece.)

11. Click mouse button 1 on the button to the left of the **2.0** choice.

12. Click mouse button 1 on the **Save** push button. Your new icon should appear in the **Current icon** field of the notebook.

13. Double-click on the title-bar icon of the notebook to close it.

Official Guide to Using OS/2 Warp

Chapter 12

Personalizing OS/2. *Warp* with Fonts

A font is really nothing more than the look and size of the text that is displayed on the screen. OS/2 Warp comes with a wide variety of fonts: small, large, bold, italic, Times Roman, Helvetica, Courier, and much more. You can use these fonts to personalize the Desktop and make OS/2 Warp more pleasant to work with.

This chapter shows you how to change fonts using the Font Palette or Scheme Palette, install new fonts, add new fonts to the Font Palette, and delete fonts from your computer.

Changing Fonts

You can select the size, line thickness, slant, and style for the text that is displayed on your Desktop, which can actually improve the Desktop's readability and appearance.

You can select one or more fonts and use them for the following areas of the Desktop: icon titles, window titles, pop-up menus, menu bars (which are displayed beneath the title bar of some windows), and, in some instances, the text within a program.

To change the fonts used on the Desktop:

1. Point to an empty area on the Desktop.
2. Click mouse button 2 to display the pop-up menu.
3. Click mouse button 1 on the **System setup** menu choice.
4. Double-click on the **Font Palette** icon.
5. Click mouse button 1 on the sample font that you want to use.

NOTE: If you press and hold the Alt key while performing the next three steps, all instances of the item will be changed to the new font. Otherwise, only the item you drag the font to will be changed.

6. Press and hold mouse button 2. The mouse pointer changes to a pencil.
7. Drag the sample font to the item whose font you want to change. (If you drag a sample font to an icon on the Desktop, the titles of all the icons on the Desktop change to that font. If you drag a sample font to a window, the titles for only the icons within that window will change to that font.)
8. Release mouse button 2.
9. Repeat steps 5 through 8 for each Desktop part whose font you want to change.
10. Double-click on the title-bar icons of the open windows to close them.

TIP: If you switch to a larger font, you might want to arrange the icons on the Desktop or in the window so that the icon titles don't overlap. To do this:

1. Point to an empty area on the Desktop or in a window.

2. Click mouse button 2 to display the pop-up menu.
3. Click mouse button 1 on the **Arrange** menu choice.

Changing Fonts Using a Scheme

You might find it easier to use a scheme to change your fonts. When you use a scheme, you can select the fonts you want for each part of the Desktop. You can view your selections in the Sample area before you drop them on a window or on the Desktop. This could save you a lot of time and aggravation.

To change the fonts used on the Desktop by using a scheme:
1. Point to an empty area on the Desktop.
2. Click mouse button 2 to display the pop-up menu.
3. Click mouse button 1 on the **System setup** menu choice.
4. Double-click on the **Scheme Palette** icon.
5. Click mouse button 1 on the scheme whose font you want to change.

> **NOTE:** If you used a scheme to change the colors of your Desktop, select that same scheme to update the fonts. If you have not changed the colors of the Desktop and do not want to change the colors, select the **Default** scheme. Otherwise, you will overwrite your Desktop colors with different colors.

6. Click mouse button 1 on the **Edit Scheme** push button at the bottom of the window. A window appears with a Sample area in the upper-left corner. Use this Sample area to select the items whose font you want to change. This Sample area changes to reflect the font that you selected and provides an excellent chance to see whether your font selections look good together. Remember, you do not have to pick a font for each item in the Sample area. You can change as many or as few as you like.
7. Point to some text in the Sample area.
8. Click mouse button 2 to display the pop-up menu.
9. Click mouse button 1 on the **Edit Font** menu choice. An Edit Font window appears in which you can make choices about the font you want to use for the Desktop part you selected. Each choice you make is displayed immediately in the Sample area of this window. You can choose from the following fields:

Name
    Determines the name of the font that you want to use.

Style
    Determines the style in which the font should be displayed: bold, italic, bold italic, or normal.

Size
>Determines how big in points the font will be.

Emphasis
>Determines how the font is emphasized: outline character, underscored, or strikeout. You can select more than one item from this field.

10. Click mouse button 1 on the name, style, size, and emphasis that you want to use. The font of the icon title changes.
11. Double-click on the title-bar icon of the Edit Font window to close it.
12. Double-click on the title-bar icon of the Edit Scheme window to close it.
13. Point to the scheme that contains the fonts you want to use.
14. Press and hold mouse button 2.
15. Drag the scheme to a window or to the Desktop. If you drag it to the Desktop, all fonts for the selected Desktop parts will be changed to the new fonts. If you drag the scheme to a window, only the fonts in that window and in its icons will be changed.
16. Double-click on the title-bar icons of the open windows to close them.

Changing the Font of Icon Titles

Another way to change a font is to use the notebook of a particular window or the Desktop. When you change the font using this method, you can preset the fonts that will be used for the different views (icon, tree, or details). Then, when you decide to change the view for the icons on the Desktop or in a window, your icon titles will already be in the font you want.

To change the font of icon titles:
1. Point to an empty area on the Desktop or in a window.
2. Click mouse button 2 to display the pop-up menu.
3. Click mouse button 1 on the **Settings** menu choice.
4. Click mouse button 1 on the **Visible** choice to place a check mark in the box. If no check mark is placed in this box, the icon titles will not be visible.
5. Click mouse button 1 on the **Change font** push button. An **Edit Font** window appears in which you can make choices about the font you want to use for the icon title. Each choice you make is immediately displayed in the Sample area of this window. You can choose from the following fields:

Name
>Determines the name of the font that you want to use.

Style
> Determines the style in which the font should be displayed: bold, italic, bold italic, or normal.

Size
> Determines how big in "points" the font will be.

Emphasis
> Determines how the font is emphasized: outline character, underscored, or strikeout. You can select more than one item from this field.

6. Click mouse button 1 on the name, style, size, and emphasis that you want to use. The font of the icon title changes.
7. Double-click on the title-bar icons of the open windows to close them.

Changing Fonts in a DOS or an OS/2 Window

A DOS Window or an OS/2 Window (command prompt) uses different kinds of fonts from those used by the Desktop. Because of this, you must use a different method to change its fonts. When you change a font in a DOS or an OS/2 Window, you might also affect the font of some of the programs that run in the window.

NOTE: You cannot change the font of a full-screen command prompt.

To change the fonts used in a DOS Window or an OS/2 Window:

1. Double-click on the **OS/2 System** icon.
2. Double-click on the **Command Prompts** icon.
3. Double-click on either the **DOS Window** or **OS/2 Window** icon.
4. Point to the title-bar icon of the open window.
5. Click mouse button 2 to display the pop-up menu.
6. Click mouse button 1 on the **Font size** menu choice.
7. Click mouse button 1 on a font in the **Font size (pels)** field. The font shown is in its actual size in the Font preview window.
8. After you select the perfect font for the window, click mouse button 1 on either the **Change** or **Save** push button.

Change
> Temporarily changes the font to the font you select. The font returns to the previous setting when the window is closed.

Save

Changes the font for all DOS and OS/2 Windows to the font you select. This font stays in effect until you change it again.

9. Double-click on the title-bar icon of the open window to close it.

Selecting Fonts for the Font Palette

OS/2 Warp comes with a wide variety of fonts. The fonts that you see on the Font Palette are only a small sample. If you do not see a font that you want to use, you can add other ones to the palette.

To select other fonts for the Font Palette:

1. Point to an empty area on the Desktop.
2. Click mouse button 2 to display the pop-up menu.
3. Click mouse button 1 on the System setup menu choice.
4. Double-click on the **Font Palette** icon.
5. Click mouse button 1 on the sample font that you want to change.
6. Click mouse button 1 on the **Edit font** push button. An Edit Font window appears in which you can make choices about the font you want to add to the Font Palette. Each choice you make is displayed immediately in the Sample area of this window and in the selected font on the Font Palette. You can choose from the following fields:

Name

Determines the name of the font that you want to use.

Style

Determines the style in which the font should be displayed: bold, italic, bold italic, or normal.

Size

Determines how big in "points" the font will be.

Emphasis

Determines how the font is emphasized: outline character, underscored, or strikeout. You can select more than one item from this field.

7. Click mouse button 1 on the name, style, size, and emphasis that you want to use.
8. Repeat steps 5 through 7 for each font you want to replace on the Font Palette.
9. Double-click on the title-bar icons of the open windows to close them.

Adding Fonts to Your Computer

You can select from a wider variety of fonts if you install additional fonts on your computer. OS/2 Warp uses Adobe Type 1 fonts. There are literally thousands of fonts available in this format. These fonts can be purchased on diskettes and easily installed on your computer.

To add more fonts to your computer:
1. Point to an empty area on the Desktop.
2. Click mouse button 2 to display the pop-up menu.
3. Click mouse button 1 on the **System setup** menu choice.
4. Double-click on the **Font Palette** icon.
5. Click mouse button 1 on the **Edit font** push button. The Edit Font window appears.
6. Click mouse button 1 on the **Add** push button.
7. Follow the instructions on the Add Font window; then click mouse button 1 on the **Add** push button.
8. Click mouse button 1 on the names of the font files that you want to install on your computer.

NOTE: Two files are generally associated with a font. OS/2 Warp requires that both font files be on the same diskette. If you receive an error message during the installation, you might need to copy the fonts you want onto a single diskette.

9. Click on the **Add** push button.
10. Double-click on the title-bar icons of the open windows to close them.

See "Selecting Fonts for the Font Palette" on page 96 if you want to add the new fonts to the Font Palette.

Removing Fonts from Your Computer

If you purchased additional fonts for your computer and installed all of them, they might be taking up a lot of space on your hard disk. If you are cramped for space and have a lot of fonts installed on your computer that you are not using, you might want to consider removing some of them.

NOTE: If you did not install additional fonts after OS/2 Warp was installed, removing a font will not save you that much space and might adversely affect the look of your Desktop.

To remove a font from your computer:

1. Point to an empty area on the Desktop.
2. Click mouse button 2 to display the pop-up menu.
3. Click mouse button 1 on the **System setup** menu choice.
4. Double-click on the **Font Palette** icon.
5. Click mouse button 1 on the **Edit font** push button. The Edit Font window appears.
6. Click on the **Delete** push button.
7. Click on the names of the font files that you want to delete from your computer.
8. Click on the **Delete** push button. The files are deleted.
9. Double-click on the title-bar icons of the open windows to close them.

NOTE: Removing a font deletes the corresponding files from your hard disk unless they are needed by the Windows Adobe Type Manager.

Chapter 13

Changing Message, Window, Logo, Sound, and Closed Captioning Features

OS/2 Warp is installed with default choices for such things as colors and fonts. The OS/2 Warp installation program also presets the way messages appear, how a window acts, how long product logos are displayed, how sound is used, and whether closed-captioning is available.

This chapter shows you how to specify whether messages should appear on the screen when you delete, rename, copy, move, and create shadows of icons. It also shows you how to change the behavior of a window, determine the length of time product logos are displayed, add sounds to the actions that OS/2 Warp performs, and enable closed captioning of some programs.

Selecting Confirmation Messages

Confirmation messages are used by OS/2 Warp to let you know that what you are doing could have repercussions. For example, if you delete an icon, you might not be able to get it back, or if you move an icon to a location where one with the same name exists, you could overwrite one of the icons.

OS/2 Warp's answer to situations like this is to display a message box to warn you. From the message box, you can choose to continue or cancel the action. While these messages are helpful, you might want to change the way the message is displayed.

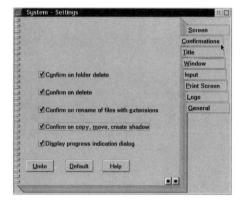

To specify which actions you want confirmation messages for:

1. Point to an empty area on the Desktop.
2. Click mouse button 2 to display the pop-up menu.
3. Click mouse button 1 on the **System setup** menu choice.
4. Double-click on the **System** icon.
5. Click mouse button 1 on the **Confirmations** notebook tab.
6. Click mouse button 1 on each item whose action you want to confirm, so that a check mark appears in the box to the left of the choice. You can confirm the following items:

Confirm on folder delete
Displays a message whenever you try to delete an icon that might contain other icons.

Confirm on delete
> Displays a message whenever you try to delete any icon.

Confirm on rename of files with extensions
> Displays a message whenever you try to rename a file using an extension that is different from the current one.

Confirm on copy, move, create shadow
> Displays a message whenever you try to copy, move, or create a shadow of an icon.

Display progress indication dialog
> Displays a message that allows you to pause during a lengthy copy, move, or create shadow process.

7. Double-click on the title-bar icons of the open windows to close them.

Resolving Title Conflicts

Title conflicts occur when you try to create, copy, or move an icon to a location where an icon with the same name already exists. When title conflicts occur, OS/2 Warp doesn't know whether it should overwrite the icon, rename the icon, or let you know that a problem exists.

You can teach OS/2 Warp what you want it to do so that the next time a title conflict occurs, OS/2 Warp can make the decision on its own.

To indicate how you want title conflicts resolved:

1. Point to an empty area on the Desktop.
2. Click mouse button 2 to display the pop-up menu.
3. Click mouse button 1 on the **System setup** menu choice.
4. Double-click on the **System** icon.
5. Click mouse button 1 on the **Title** notebook tab.
6. Click mouse button 1 on the choice that best describes how you want the computer to respond when a title conflict occurs.

Prompt for appropriate action
> Displays a message box that lets you choose to rename the icon, replace the icon, or append to the existing icon.

Auto-rename object
> Automatically renames the new icon by adding a colon followed by a number to the existing name.

Replace existing object
> Automatically replaces the existing icon with the new icon.

7. Double-click on the title-bar icons of the open windows to close them.

Changing Window Behavior

Windows have a standard way of acting. It is this standard that makes OS/2 Warp so easy to use. However, sometimes the standard is not quite what you want. For example, the standard is that when you double-click on an icon that is already open, the window for that icon is brought to the front of the screen. However, what if you didn't want the window that was already open? What if you wanted a new window for the icon to open? With OS/2 Warp you can change the window behavior so that it will do what you want. For example, you can specify where windows should be minimized to, whether windows should be animated, and what push buttons should appear on the windows.

To change the behavior of a window:

1. Point to an empty area on the Desktop.
2. Click mouse button 2 to display the pop-up menu.
3. Click mouse button 1 on the **System setup** menu choice.
4. Double-click on the **System** icon.
5. Click mouse button 1 on the **Window** notebook tab.
6. Click mouse button 1 on the choices that best describe how you want the windows to behave. You can make changes to the following fields:

Button appearance for windows
> Determines which button appears on the upper-right corner of a window. You can choose either a hide or minimize button.

Animation
> Determines the action that OS/2 Warp takes when you open or close windows. When this choice is selected, windows look like they are zooming in and out.

Minimize button behavior
> Determines what happens when you select the minimize button in a window. You can choose to hide the window, minimize the window to the Minimized Window Viewer, or minimize the window to the Desktop.

Object open behavior
> Determines whether a new window or the already opened window will be displayed when you double-click on the icon.

7. Double-click on the title-bar icons of the open windows to close them.

Specifying Logo Timeouts

Many programs come with logos that are displayed when the programs are started. Some people find them colorful and interesting while other people find them annoying. You can control how long a product logo is displayed before it is removed from the screen.

To specify how long a logo should be displayed:

1. Point to an empty area on the Desktop.
2. Click mouse button 2 to display the pop-up menu.
3. Click mouse button 1 on the **System setup** menu choice.
4. Double-click on the **System** icon.
5. Click mouse button 1 on the **Logo** notebook tab.
6. Click mouse button 1 on the choice that best describes how you want the computer to handle product information and logos. You can choose from the following:

Indefinite
> Displays program logos until you remove them.

None
> Prevents logos from being displayed.

Timed
> Specifies how long logos should be displayed before they are automatically removed. You can indicate a time of 1 to 37 seconds.

7. Double-click on the title-bar icons of the open windows to close them.

Adding or Removing the Warning Beep

OS/2 Warp issues a warning beep when it displays a warning message or when you press an invalid key. If you don't like your computer making noise or announcing to the world that you just did something invalid, you can turn off the beep.

To turn the warning beep off or on:

1. Point to an empty area on the Desktop.
2. Click mouse button 2 to display the pop-up menu.
3. Click mouse button 1 on the **System setup** menu choice.
4. Double-click on the **Sound** icon.
5. Click mouse button 1 on the **Warning beep** notebook tab.
6. Click mouse button 1 on **Warning beep** to place a check mark in the box. This turns on the warning beep. Remove the check mark to disable the beep.
7. Double-click on the title-bar icons of the open windows to close them.

Adding Sound

If you have an audio card installed in your computer, you can add sound to some common actions performed with OS/2 Warp. Sounds can make things like dragging icons, closing and opening windows, and shutting down and starting the computer a little more interesting and sometimes humorous. OS/2 Warp comes with 23 sound (.WAV) files that you can assign to 13 different OS/2 Warp actions. In addition, you can purchase sound files or create your own sounds using the multimedia programs that come with OS/2 Warp. See "Digital Audio" on page 226.

To add sounds to system events:

1. Point to an empty area on the Desktop.
2. Click mouse button 2 to display the pop-up menu.
3. Click mouse button 1 on the **System setup** menu choice.

4. Double-click on the **Sound** icon.
5. Click mouse button 1 on **Enable system sounds** to place a check mark in the box. If no check mark is placed in the box, warning beeps will be played instead of the sounds you pick.
6. If you want to have all of the sounds set to the same volume level, click mouse button 1 on **Apply volume to all sounds** to place a check mark in the box. (The volume level will be controlled by the Volume Control program in the Multimedia icon.) If no check mark is placed in the box, you can individually set the volume level for each system event/sound combination using the volume control to the right of the **Sound file** field.
7. Click mouse button 1 on the arrow keys in the scroll bar of the **System events** field to see the list of events you can connect sounds to.
8. Click mouse button 1 on the system event that you want to connect a sound to.
9. Double-click on as many sounds in the **Sound file** field as you need to, until you find the perfect sound for the system event.

10. If **Apply volume to all sounds** does not have a check mark in the box, click on the + and - buttons next to the volume control to adjust the volume of the sound. (Click on the **Play** push button to test the volume.)
11. Repeat steps 7 through 10 for each system event you want to connect a sound to.
12. Double-click on the title-bar icons of the open windows to close them.

 TIP: The sounds listed in the Sound file field are in the \MMOS2\SOUNDS directory. You can change to a different directory if you have additional sounds on your computer. For example, Windows includes some sound files in its \WINDOWS directory and OS/2 Warp includes some sound files in the \OS2\APPS directory.

To look somewhere else for sounds:
1. Click on the down arrow to the right of the **Sound file** field until {C:} or the drive letter containing the files is displayed.
2. Double-click on the appropriate drive letter.
3. Click on the down arrow to the right of the **Sound file** field to find a directory that contains sounds. (WINDOWS, OS/2, and MMOS2 all have sounds in them. If you installed additional sounds somewhere else, look for that directory instead.)
4. Double-click on **WINDOWS**, or on **OS/2** then **APPS**, or on **MMOS2** and then **SOUNDS** (or another directory of your choice) to get to the sound files.

Adding Closed Captioning

Closed captioning allows you to view the words that are being spoken. On a computer, some programs that emit sounds are closed captioned so that you can read the information. This is a nice feature if you are hearing impaired, or you would prefer that your computer be silent.

If you have multimedia programs that provide closed captioning installed on your computer, you must enable closed captioning in OS/2 Warp before you can use the feature.

To turn on the ability to see closed captioning in OS/2 Warp:
1. Double-click on the **Multimedia** icon.
2. Double-click on the **Multimedia Setup** icon.
3. Click mouse button 1 on the **System** notebook tab.
4. Click mouse button 1 on the **Captioning** choice to place a check mark in the box.
5. Double-click on the title-bar icons of the open windows to close them.

Making Clipboards Public or Private

A clipboard is a temporary storage area on your computer. It is used to hold information that you cut or copy from a document. The information stays in the clipboard until you paste the information somewhere, cut or copy information over it (the clipboard can only hold one chunk of information at a time), or turn off your computer.

One feature of the OS/2 and WIN-OS/2 clipboards is that they can do a dynamic data exchange (DDE). This means that when you copy information from one location to another and then change the information in one of the locations, it is automatically changed in the other, as well.

This chapter shows you how to change the settings for your clipboards.

Setting All Clipboards to Public

OS/2 Warp has a clipboard and so does each WIN-OS/2 icon. When OS/2 Warp is installed, all of the clipboards are set to *private*. OS/2 Warp shares its clipboard only with OS/2 Warp and DOS programs. A WIN-OS/2 icon shares its clipboard only with the programs running within it. For example, programs running in a WIN-OS/2 Full Screen icon can't share the clipboard with programs running in a WIN-OS/2 Window icon.

OS/2 Warp has the ability to unite clipboards so they act as one. This makes a clipboard *public*. When a clipboard is made public, it can share information with other clipboards that are public. For example, let's say that you are running a program from a WIN-OS/2 Window icon that has its clipboard set to public. You have been working diligently all day to create a document. Suddenly, you realize that the program you have been using doesn't allow you to make pie charts, and you need a pie chart! What do you do? Start over? Cry? No, you look for a program that can create pie charts. You find one, but it's an OS/2 Warp program! That's okay! Remember, you have your clipboards set to public and all you have to do is cut or copy the information from one document and paste it into the other.

TIP: For the typical user, setting all the clipboards to public is the best choice.

Clipboard settings do not affect the performance of OS/2 Warp or the programs running on it.

To change all the clipboards to public:
1. Point to an empty area on the Desktop.
2. Click mouse button 2 to display the pop-up menu.
3. Click mouse button 1 on the **System setup** menu choice.
4. Double-click on the **WIN-OS/2 Setup** icon.

108

5. Click mouse button 1 on the **Data Exchange** notebook tab.
6. Click mouse button 1 on the **Public** choice in the **Dynamic data exchange** field.
7. Click mouse button 1 on the **Public** choice in the **Clipboard** field.
8. Double-click on the title-bar icons of the open windows to close them.
9. Double-click on the **OS/2 System** icon.
10. Double-click on the **Command Prompts** icon.
11. Point to a WIN-OS/2 (full-screen or window) program icon.
12. Click mouse button 2 to display the pop-up menu.
13. Click mouse button 1 on each of the following:
    a. The **Settings** menu choice.
    b. The **Session** notebook tab.
    c. The **WIN-OS/2 settings** push button.
    d The **WIN-OS/2 settings** choice.
    e. The **OK** push button.
    f. The **WIN_CLIPBOARD** choice.
    g. The **On** button.
    h. The **WIN_DDE** choice.
    i. The **On** button.
    j. The **Save** push button.
14. Repeat steps 11 through 13 for each WIN-OS/2 icon.
15. Double-click on the title-bar icons of the open windows to close them.

Changing the OS/2 Warp Clipboard to Private

Changing the OS/2 Warp clipboard to private is like creating a new clipboard that no WIN-OS/2 icons can use (even if their clipboards are set to public). Only the programs running within OS/2 Warp and DOS can use it. Having a private OS/2 Warp clipboard might be useful if you frequently cut or copy information to the clipboard, only to have it overwritten by a cut or copy you do from a program running in a WIN-OS/2 icon.

To change the OS/2 Warp clipboard to private:
1. Point to an empty area on the Desktop.
2. Click mouse button 2 to display the pop-up menu.
3. Click mouse button 1 on the **System setup** menu choice.
4. Double-click on the **WIN-OS/2 Setup** icon.
5. Click mouse button 1 on the **Data Exchange** notebook tab.
6. Click mouse button 1 on the **Private** choice in the **Dynamic data exchange** field.

7. Click mouse button 1 on the **Private** choice in the **Clipboard** field.
8. Double-click on the title-bar icons of the open windows to close them.

Changing a WIN-OS/2 Clipboard to Private

Changing a WIN-OS/2 clipboard to private is like creating a new clipboard that no other OS/2 Warp, DOS, or WIN-OS/2 icon can use. Only the programs running within the WIN-OS/2 icon can use it. Having a private clipboard might be useful if you frequently cut or copy information to the clipboard, only to have it overwritten by a cut or copy you do somewhere else in OS/2 Warp.

To change a WIN-OS/2 clipboard to private:
1. Point to the WIN-OS/2 icon whose clipboard you want to change.
2. Click mouse button 2 to display the pop-up menu.
3. Click mouse 1 on each of the following:
    a. The **Settings** menu choice.
    b. The **Session** notebook tab.
    c. The **WIN-OS/2 settings** push button.
    d. The **WIN-OS/2 settings** choice.
    e. The **OK** push button.
    f. The **WIN_DDE** choice.
    g. The **Off** button.
    h. The **WIN_CLIPBOARD** choice.
    i. The **Off** button.
    j. The **Save** push button.
4. Double-click on the title-bar icons of the open windows to close them.

NOTE: If you change the settings for the clipboard or DDE while a program is running in a WIN-OS/2 session, the settings for the program take effect immediately.

Changing a WIN-OS/2 Clipboard to Public

Changing a WIN-OS/2 clipboard to public unites the clipboard with the other clipboards that are set to public. This allows you to cut and copy information from programs running in the WIN-OS/2 icon to programs running in OS/2 Warp, DOS, and other WIN-OS/2 icons with public clipboards.

Official Guide to Using OS/2 Warp

To change a WIN-OS/2 clipboard to public:

1. Point to the WIN-OS/2 icon whose clipboard you want to change.
2. Click mouse button 2 to display the pop-up menu.
3. Click mouse button 1 on each of the following:
    a. The **Settings** menu choice.
    b. The **Session** notebook tab.
    c. The **WIN-OS/2 settings** push button.
    d. The **WIN-OS/2 settings** choice.
    e. The **OK** pushbutton.
    f. The **WIN_DDE** choice.
    g. The **On** button.
    h. The **WIN_CLIPBOARD** choice.
    i. The **On** button.
    j. The **Save** push button.
4. Double-click on the title-bar icons of the open windows to close them.

NOTE: If you change the settings for the clipboard or DDE while a program is running in a WIN-OS/2 session, the settings for the program take effect immediately.

Chapter 15

Personalizing the Clock

The System Clock keeps track of the date and time on your computer. This information is used to time stamp the data-file icons on your computer so you can identify which files are newer or older than others. You can also look at the clock to find out the time or date, and you can set it to act as an alarm clock.

This chapter shows you how to get the clock onto your Desktop, change the date and time, change the look of the clock, and set an alarm so you won't miss important meetings or dinner dates.

Moving the Clock

In order for a clock to be useful, you need to be able to see it. When OS/2 Warp is installed, the clock is buried inside an icon. That's about as useful as being in the bedroom and having to go into the kitchen to find out if it's time to get up for work. Of course, no one would set up a house like that and you might not want to leave OS/2 Warp set up as it is.

To move the clock to your Desktop:

1. Point to an empty area on the Desktop.
2. Click mouse button 2 to display the pop-up menu.
3. Click mouse button 1 on the **System setup** menu choice.
4. Point to the **System Clock** icon.
5. Press and hold mouse button 2.
6. Drag the icon to an empty area on the Desktop.
7. Release mouse button 2.
8. Double-click on the **System Clock** icon.
9. Point to the title bar of the **System Clock** icon.
10. Press and hold mouse button 2.
11. Drag the **System Clock** icon to an empty area on the Desktop.
12. Release mouse button 2.

Changing the Date and Time

A clock can occasionally have the wrong date and time. Perhaps it was never set in the first place, the battery goes bad, or daylight savings time begins or ends. If your System Clock ever has the wrong time and date, no matter what the reason, you can correct it.

To change the date and time:
1. Point to the **System Clock** icon.

   Or, if your System Clock is still in the System Setup icon:
   a. Point to an empty area on the Desktop.
   b. Click mouse button 2 to display the pop-up menu.
   c. Click mouse button 1 on the **System setup** menu choice.
   d. Point to the **System Clock** icon.
2. Click mouse button 2 to display the pop-up menu.
3. Click mouse button 1 on the **Settings** menu choice.
4. Click mouse button 1 on the up and down arrows to change the date and time.
5. Click mouse button 1 on a button to the left of either **AM** or **PM**.
6. Double-click on the title-bar icon of the notebook to close it.

Changing the Date Format

The date can be displayed on your computer in one of three formats: Month-Day-Year, Day-Month-Year, and Year-Month-Day. One is probably more familiar to you than the others. However, if you want to change how the date is displayed on your System Clock and computer, you can use any one that you prefer.

To change the date format:

1. Point to an empty area on the Desktop.
2. Click mouse button 2 to display the pop-up menu.
3. Click mouse button 1 on the **System setup** menu choice.
4. Double-click on the **Country** icon.
5. Click mouse button 1 on the **Date** notebook tab.
6. Click mouse button 1 on one of the choices in the **Date order** field.
7. Click mouse button 1 on the down arrow to the right of the **Separator** field.
8. Click mouse button 1 on the separator that you want to use between the day, month, and year.
9. Double-click on the title-bar icons of the open windows to close them.

NOTE: You must shut down and restart your computer before these changes will be reflected on the System Clock and in other programs.

Changing the Time Format

The time can be displayed in two formats: 12 hours and 24 hours. Twelve-hour clocks use AM and PM to distinguish between 5:00 in the morning and 5:00 at night. 24-hour clocks don't need to distinguish between AM and PM because none of the numbers that represent the hour is repeated on the clock. For example, 5:00 AM is just 5:00 and 5:00 PM is 17:00. You can change the time format so your System Clock and computer use the one that you prefer.

To change the time format:
1. Point to an empty area on the Desktop.
2. Click mouse button 2 to display the pop-up menu.
3. Click mouse button 1 on the **System setup** menu choice.
4. Double-click on the **Country** icon.
5. Click mouse button 1 on the **Time** notebook tab.
6. Click mouse button 1 on the **12 hours** or **24 hours** choice.
7. If you selected 12 hours, click mouse button 1 on the down arrow to the right of the choice. Then, click mouse button 1 on the AM/PM format you want to use.
8. Click mouse button 1 on the down arrow to the right of the **Separator** field.
9. Click mouse button 1 on the separator that you want to use between the hours and minutes.
10. Double-click on the title-bar icons of the open windows to close them.

NOTE: You must shut down and restart your computer before these changes will be reflected on the System Clock and in other programs.

Changing the Clock Face

Some people like clocks with hour and minute hands (analog clocks) while others like clocks with numeric readouts (digital clocks). In addition, some people like clocks that show both the date and the time; others don't. You can change the System Clock face to meet your individual preferences.

To change the look of the clock face:
1. Point to the **System Clock** icon.

   Or, if your System Clock is still in the System Setup icon:
   a. Point to an empty area on the Desktop.
   b. Click mouse button 2 to display the pop-up menu.

c. Click mouse button 1 on the **System setup** menu choice.

d. Point to the **System Clock** icon.

2. Click mouse button 2 to display the pop-up menu.

3. Click mouse button 1 on the **Settings** menu choice.

4. Click mouse button 1 on the **View** notebook tab.

5. Click mouse button 1 on one of the choices in the **Information** field of the notebook.

6. Click mouse button 1 on either **Digital** or **Analog** in the **Mode** field of the notebook.

   Digital
   > Displays the clock with a numeric readout.

   Analog
   > Displays the clock with hour and minute hands. You can also specify whether you want a second hand and whether you want hour and minute marks on the face of the clock.

7. Click mouse button 1 on the **Show title bar** choice to place or remove a check mark in the box. (Removing the check mark means that the title bar will not be shown and you will not be able to move the clock to a different location. If you are happy with where your clock is located, remove the check mark from the box so you save some space on your Desktop.)

8. Double-click on the title-bar icons of the open windows to close them.

Setting an Alarm

Today our lives are governed by time. Who among us doesn't need to be someplace by a certain time? That's where the alarm feature of the System Clock comes in handy. After you install OS/2 Warp on your computer, you will be so wrapped up in its ability, you will need to set an alarm so that you will know when to quit.

To set an alarm or turn an alarm off:

1. Point to the **System Clock** icon.

   Or, if your System Clock is still in the System Setup icon:
   a. Point to an empty area on the Desktop.
   b. Click mouse button 2 to display the pop-up menu.
   c. Click mouse button 1 on the **System setup** menu choice.
   d. Point to the **System Clock** icon.

2. Click mouse button 2 to display the pop-up menu.

3. Click mouse button 1 on the **Settings** menu choice.

4. Click mouse button 1 on the **Alarm** notebook tab.

5. Click mouse button 1 on either **Alarm on** or **Alarm off**. (If you select the **Alarm off** choice, skip to step 8.)

   If you choose **Alarm on**, you can choose one or both of the following:

   Audio alarm
   > Emits a two second beep when the alarm time is reached.

   Message box
   > Displays a message box informing you that the alarm time is reached. This message box stays on the screen until you remove it.

6. Click mouse button 1 on the up and down arrow to set the date and time that you want the alarm to go off.

7. Click mouse button 1 on a button to the left of either **AM** or **PM** in the **Time** field of the notebook.

8. Double-click on the title-bar icon of the notebook to close it.

Changing Keyboard, Mouse, and Country Settings

The keyboard and mouse are the tools you use most often to communicate with your computer. Therefore, it is imperative that they are set for your individual needs. It is also important that the information displayed on your computer be in a format that you are accustomed to.

This chapter shows you how to adjust your keyboard speed, change the keys used for some functions, and make keys on your keyboard "sticky", so you don't need to press more than one key at a time. In addition, it shows you how to adjust the speed of your mouse, set up your mouse for left- or right-hand use, change the mouse buttons used for some functions, pick a different pointer for your mouse, set a trail for the mouse so you can easily track its movement, and display information on your screen in a specific country format.

Adjusting the Keyboard Speed

The speed of the keyboard depends more on the operating system than on the keyboard itself. If the operating system has the keys set too fast for your typing ability, you might find that keys repeat even when you only press them once. When the keys are set too slow for your typing ability, keys don't repeat even when you press them multiple times. You can fix either of these problems by adjusting the keyboard speed.

To adjust the keyboard speed:

1. Point to an empty area on the Desktop.
2. Click mouse button 2 to display the pop-up menu.
3. Click mouse button 1 on the **System setup** menu choice.
4. Double-click on the **Keyboard** icon.
5. Click mouse button 1 on the **Timing** notebook tab.
6. Point to the slider arm above the item you want to adjust. You can make adjustments to the following three items:

   Repeat rate
      Determines how often a key repeats after the repeat delay rate has been met.

   Repeat delay rate
      Determines how long a key must be held down before it starts to repeat.

   Cursor blink rate
      Determines how often the cursor blinks on the screen.

7. Press and hold mouse button 2.
8. Drag the slider arm to a new position. Moving the slider arm to the left decreases the rate. Moving it to the right increases the rate.

9. Release mouse button 2.

10. Click mouse button 1 in the **Test here** field. Then type some characters to test your settings.

11. Repeat steps 6 through 10 until the rates meet your needs.

    (You can return to the default settings at any time by clicking mouse button 1 on the **Default** push button.)

12. Double-click on the title-bar icons of the open windows to close them.

 NOTE: Both OS/2 Warp and WIN-OS/2 allow you to adjust your keyboard settings. You should use only one or the other to make keyboard adjustments. If you make the adjustments in both OS/2 Warp and WIN-OS/2, OS/2 Warp will control the keyboard speed until WIN-OS/2 is started. Then, WIN-OS/2 will take over control until you shut down your computer.

Changing Key Mappings

Key mappings are used to define what action occurs when certain keys are pressed. Sometimes the keys of one program conflict with the keys used by another program. In this situation, you must change the key mappings of one of the programs. If the keys used by a program conflict with those used by OS/2 Warp, you can change the key mappings defined for two of OS/2 Warp's actions.

To change the OS/2 Warp key mappings:

1. Point to an empty area on the Desktop.

2. Click mouse button 2 to display the pop-up menu.

3. Click mouse button 1 on the **System setup** menu choice.

4. Double-click on the **Keyboard** icon.

5. Click mouse button 1 on the **Mappings** notebook tab. You can change which keys you press for the following items:

   Displaying pop-up menus
   Determines the keys you press to see a pop-up menu. By default, this is Shift+F10.

   Editing title text
   Determines the keys you press to edit the title that appears below an icon. By default this is Shift+F9.

6. Click mouse button 1 on the up or down arrow that is to the left of the **Primary key** field to scroll through the list of valid keys.

7. Click mouse button 1 on a choice in the **Additional keys** field.

8. Repeat steps 6 and 7 until you have made the necessary changes.

   (You can return to the default settings at any time by clicking mouse button 1 on the **Default** push button.)

9. Double-click on the title-bar icons of the open windows to close them.

WARNING: If you change these settings, they will not match the key combinations described in the books and online information written for OS/2 Warp.

Setting Sticky Keys

Sticky keys allow you to press and release a series of keys sequentially but have them act as if they were all pressed and released at the same time. This feature was originally developed for people who might have trouble pressing more than one key at a time. However, anyone can use and take advantage of "sticky" keys.

To set sticky keys:

1. Point to an empty area on the Desktop.

2. Click mouse button 2 to display the pop-up menu.

3. Click mouse button 1 on the **System setup** menu choice.

4. Double-click on the **Keyboard** icon.

5. Click mouse button 1 on the **Special Needs** notebook tab.

6. Click mouse button 1 on the **On** button in the **Settings activation** field.

7. Point to the slider arm below the **Settings time-out** field.

8. Press and hold mouse button 2.

9. Drag the slider arm to **Short**. This turns off the time-out function while you are setting your "sticky keys."

NOTE: If you prefer, you can change this setting after the keys are set. When you specify a time by moving the slider from 0, you are telling the computer to wipe out the sticky keys you just set if there has been no keyboard activity within the time limit you specify.

If you went through all the trouble of setting the sticky keys, you will probably want to leave it set to 0.

10. Press the Shift key for five seconds. You will hear two beeps.

11. Point to the slider arm below the item you want to adjust. You can make adjustments to the following three items:

Acceptance delay
> Determines how long a key is pressed before it is recognized.

Delay until repeat
> Determines how long a key is pressed before it starts to repeat.

Repeat rate
> Determines how often a key is repeated after it is pressed.

12. Press and hold mouse button 2.
13. Drag the slider arm to a new position. Moving the slider arm to the left decreases the rate (the minimum is 0 seconds). Moving it to the right increases the rate (the maximum is 10 seconds).
14. Release mouse button 2.
15. Click mouse button 1 in the **Test here** field. Then type some characters to test your settings. Remember that if you set the acceptance delay to 5 seconds, for example, you must hold the key down for 5 seconds for it to be recognized.
16. Repeat steps 11 through 15 until the settings are right for you.
17. Press and hold the Shift key until you hear a beep. Do this 3 times.
18. Press and hold the key you want to "stick" until you hear a beep. For example, normally if you want to display the Window List using the keyboard, you would need to press the Ctrl+Esc keys at the same time. You can make the Ctrl key the sticky key and the Esc key the activating key. Then, whenever you press the Esc key, the computer thinks you are pressing the Ctrl+Esc keys.
19. Press and hold the activating key until you hear a beep.
20. Repeat steps 17 through 19 until all of your sticky keys have been set.
21. Double-click on the title-bar icons of the open windows to close them.

 NOTE: To deactivate the sticky keys from anywhere, just press and release each key in the sticky key combination once.

Enabling Type Ahead

Type ahead lets you communicate with an OS/2 Warp program before it is fully loaded into the computer's memory. For example, if you know which keys you need to press to get to a menu, select a menu item, and start working, you can type them in advance (while the program is loading). This lets you get a head start on the job you need to get done.

To enable or disable type ahead:
1. Point to an empty area on the Desktop.
2. Click mouse button 2 to display the pop-up menu.
3. Click mouse button 1 on the **System setup** menu choice.
4. Double-click on the **System** icon.
5. Click mouse button 1 on the **Input** notebook tab.
6. Click mouse button 1 on the item you want.

> **Enable type ahead**
> Allows a program to accept the keyboard and mouse input while the program is in the process of starting. Selecting this choice might increase the amount of time it takes a program to start.

> **Disable type ahead**
> Prevents a program from accepting keyboard and mouse input while the program is in the process of starting. This is the default choice.

7. Double-click on the title-bar icons of the open windows to close them.

Setting the Lockup Timer

Lockup is used to protect the information on your computer while you are temporarily away from your desk. When you lock up your computer, the keyboard and mouse are locked and a picture covers the screen. No input is accepted by the computer until the correct password is entered.

The lockup timer is used to automatically lock the keyboard and mouse on your computer if there is no keyboard or mouse input after a period of time. The default setting is 3 minutes. You might find that this time is too short. You can change the timer to be any amount of time between 1 and 99 minutes. The automatic lockup timer is great if you momentarily walk away from your computer without locking it and then are detained for a longer period of time than you originally anticipated.

To set the timer setting:
1. Point to an empty area on the Desktop.
2. Click mouse button 2 to display the pop-up menu.
3. Click mouse button 1 on each of the following:
   a. The **Settings** menu choice.
   b. The **Lockup** notebook tab.
   c. The **Automatic lockup** button.

d. The up or down arrow in the **Timeout** field to specify the amount of time that should pass before your computer automatically locks the keyboard and mouse.

4. Double-click on the title-bar icon of the notebook to close it.

 NOTE: An automatic lock up will NOT occur if one of the following icons is opened and displayed on the screen:

- OS/2 Full Screen

- DOS Full Screen

- WIN-OS/2 Full Screen

Changing Your Lockup Password

The lockup password is used to unlock your computer so that you can use the computer again. This password should be kept a secret; otherwise it defeats the purpose of locking the computer in the first place. However, there might be occasions when someone else needs to use your computer and needs to know your password.

If this is a one-time situation, you can prevent that person from using your computer again by changing the lockup password.

To change your lockup password:
1. Point to an empty area on the Desktop.
2. Click mouse button 2 to display the pop-up menu.
3. Click mouse button 1 on the **Settings** menu choice.
4. Click mouse button 1 on the **Lockup** notebook tab.
5. Click mouse button 1 on the right arrow at the bottom of the notebook until you see **Lockup - Page 3 of 3** displayed.
6. Type a password in the **Password** field.
7. Press the Enter key to move the cursor to the **Password (for verification)** field.
8. Type the same password again. This is to verify that you typed the password correctly.

 NOTE: It is very important that you remember your password!

9. Click mouse button 1 on the **OK** push button.
10. Double-click on the title-bar icon of the notebook to close it.

Changing Mouse Settings

Mouse settings are used to tailor the behavior of the mouse to your personal preferences. You can change the speed of the mouse, set it up for left- or right-hand use, select mouse button and key combinations, display a mouse trail, and change what the mouse pointer looks like.

Changing the Mouse Speed

A mouse's speed depends more on the operating system than on the mouse itself. If the operating system has the mouse set too fast for you, the mouse pointer will seem to zip across the screen when you move the mouse. When the mouse is set too slow for you, the mouse pointer will seem to crawl on the screen even if you move the mouse a long way. Another thing that can happen if the mouse speed is not set properly for you is that it takes multiple tries to get the computer to recognize that you are "double-clicking" on the mouse button. You can fix all of these situations by changing your mouse speed.

To change the mouse speed:

1. Point to an empty area on the Desktop.
2. Click mouse button 2 to display the pop-up menu.

3. Click mouse button 1 on the **System setup** menu choice.
4. Double-click on the **Mouse** icon.
5. Click mouse button 1 on the **Timings** notebook tab.
6. Point to the slider arm below the item you want to adjust. You can make adjustments to the following items:

   Double-click
   Specifies the maximum amount of time that can elapse between the clicks of a double-click. If you exceed this time when you double-click, OS/2 Warp treats your input as two single clicks.

   Tracking speed
   Determines how fast the mouse moves across the screen.
7. Press and hold mouse button 2.
8. Drag the slider arm to a new position. Moving the slider arm to the left decreases the rate. Moving it to the right increases the rate.
9. Release mouse button 2.
10. Click mouse button 1 in the **Test here** field. Then double-click and move your mouse around to test your settings.
11. Repeat steps 6 through 10 until the settings are right for you.
12. Double-click on the title-bar icons of the open windows to close them.

Setting Up the Mouse for Left- or Right-Hand Use

Computers are typically designed for right-handed people. If you were left-handed, you just had to learn how to do things right-handed. With OS/2 Warp, left-handed people finally get an even break! You can change the orientation of your mouse so that you can use the mouse on the left side of your computer and have "mouse button 1" under your index finger. If multiple people use the computer, this feature lets left and right-handed people easily tailor the mouse to their personal preferences.

NOTE: Right-handed people might like this feature too!

To set up your mouse for left- or right-hand use:
1. Point to an empty area on the Desktop.
2. Click mouse button 2 to display the pop-up menu.
3. Click mouse button 1 on the **System setup** menu choice.
4. Double-click on the **Mouse** icon.
5. Click mouse button 1 on the **Setup** notebook tab.
6. Click mouse button 1 on one of the following:

   Right-handed
   > Sets mouse button 1 to be on the left side of the mouse. This is the default.

   Left-handed
   > Sets mouse button 1 to be on the right side of the mouse.

7. Double-click on the title-bar icons of the open windows to close them.

Changing Mouse Mappings

Mouse mappings are used to define what actions occur when certain mouse buttons and keys are pressed. If you are accustomed to the mouse buttons and key combinations used by another operating system or program, you might want to change OS/2 Warp so that it uses the same mouse buttons and keys.

WARNING: If you change any of the mouse buttons and key combinations, they will not match the key combinations described in the books and online information written for OS/2 Warp.

To reassign mouse button activities:
1. Point to an empty area on the Desktop.
2. Click mouse button 2 to display the pop-up menu.
3. Click mouse button 1 on the **System setup** menu choice.
4. Double-click on the **Mouse** icon.

5. Click mouse button 1 on the **Mappings** notebook tab.

6. Click mouse button 1 on the mouse buttons, numbers of clicks, and keys you want to assign. You can assign the following activities to mouse buttons:

Dragging objects
> Determines which mouse button you press and hold when you drag an icon.

Displaying Window List
> Determines which mouse buttons you press to display the Window List.

Displaying pop-up menus
> Determines which mouse button, how many clicks, and which keys you press to display a pop-up menu.

Editing title text
> Determines which mouse button, how many clicks, and which keys you press to edit the title that appears below an icon.

7. Double-click on the title-bar icons of the open windows to close them.

Changing the Mouse Pointer

The mouse pointer for OS/2 Warp is used to point to information on the screen, reflect actions that you are taking, let you know when you are doing something illegal, and let you know when the computer is busy.

You can replace the pointers, edit the pointers, change the size (big to small) and color (black to white) of the pointers, or search for other files on the computer with .PTR or .ICO file name extensions.

To change mouse pointers:

1. Point to an empty area on the Desktop.
2. Click mouse button 2 to display the pop-up menu.
3. Click mouse button 1 on the **System setup** menu choice.
4. Double-click on the **Mouse** icon.
5. Click mouse button 1 on the **Pointers** notebook tab. You can select the following choices:

Edit
> Displays the selected pointer in the Icon Editor so that you can make changes to it. For more information about the Icon Editor, see "Icon Editor" on page 184.

Find
> Displays the Find window so that you can search the computer for another icon that you might want to use instead of the selected icon. If you find one, you can display it in a window and drag the icon to the **System Pointers** field to replace the selected pointer.

Load Set
> Allows you to select the size (big or small) and color (black or white) to be used for the pointer.

6. Click mouse button 1 on any of the pointers in the **System Pointers** field.
7. Click mouse button 1 on the **Edit**, **Find**, or **Load Set** push button.
8. Repeat steps 6 and 7 for all the pointers you want to change.
9. Double-click on the title-bar icons of the open windows to close them.

Adding or Changing a Mouse Trail

The mouse trail (also known as a comet cursor) is a group of small circles that follow along behind the mouse. It is used to help people keep track of where the mouse pointer is on their screen. If you have a laptop computer or if you have difficulty finding the mouse pointer on the screen, you might want to add a trail to your mouse pointer.

To add or change a mouse trail:
1. Point to an empty area on the Desktop.
2. Click mouse button 2 to display the pop-up menu.
3. Click mouse button 1 on the **System setup** menu choice.
4. Double-click on the **Mouse** icon.
5. Click mouse button 1 on the **Comet Cursor** notebook tab.
6. Click mouse button 1 on any of the fields you want to set. You can set the following things:

Comet Cursor On
> Turns on the mouse trail; however, you must restart your computer before this choice takes effect.

Disable
> Turns off the mouse trail; however, you must restart your computer before this choice takes effect.

Color
> Determines the color of the circles in the trail. Click mouse button 1 on the down arrow to the right of the field to see a list of colors you can choose.

Border Color

Determines the color of the outline of the circles in the trail. Click mouse button 1 on the down arrow to the right of the field to see a list of colors you can choose.

Trail Length

Determines the length of the trail.

Circle Size

Determines the size of the circles that make up the trail.

Activation Speed

Determines how fast the mouse must be moving before the trail is displayed.

7. Double-click on the title-bar icons of the open windows to close them.

Changing Country Settings

Country settings include things like the date, time, and numeric and monetary formats used by a country. For example, the country format that you select determines how the OS/2 System Clock displays the time. If you were to select a different country's format, the clock might not display the information the same way. For example, some countries use a 24-hour clock and don't use AM and PM.

If you want to change to a different country's format but you are not quite sure of all of the correct choices, you can let OS/2 Warp do most of the work for you.

To change to a specific country format:

1. Point to an empty area on the Desktop.
2. Click mouse button 2 to display the pop-up menu.
3. Click mouse button 1 on the **System setup** menu choice.
4. Double-click on the **Country** icon.
5. Click mouse button 1 on the **Country** notebook tab.
6. Click mouse button 1 on the down arrow to the right of each field, and then click mouse button 1 on a choice in the field. You can change the following fields:

Country

Determines which country's rules will be used for the date, time, and number and monetary format. These items are automatically set when you choose a country. However, the measurement and list separator are not.

Measurement
Determines which measurement system is used (for example, English or metric).

List separator
Determines which punctuation mark will be used to separate items in a list.

7. Double-click on the title-bar icons of the open windows to close them.

NOTE: You must shut down and restart your computer before these changes will be reflected on the System Clock and in other programs.

TIP: If you receive an error message informing you that the code page is not supported, you can solve the problem by using the Selective Install icon to install another code page. For more information, read Chapter 25, "Adding or Removing Features After Installation" on page 255.

Official Guide to Using OS/2 Warp

Chapter 17

Personalizing Print Options

Your printer is used to transfer information that is on your computer to paper. You can get the most out of your printer by changing the settings of the printer and the *spooler*. The spooler is a place where printer jobs are stored until they print.

This chapter shows you how to change your print screen settings, printer properties, and job properties. It also shows you how to add a separator page to your print jobs, set printing hours, and change your printer priority and spooler settings.

Changing Print Screen Settings

You can print the contents of any active window by pressing the Print Screen key on your keyboard. This is great if you want to print a window full of information or just want to impress your friends with a beautiful printout of a window or the entire Desktop.

You can turn off the print screen setting. For example, if you accidentally press the Print Screen key when you meant to press Scroll Lock or F12, you might want to turn off the setting.

To change the print screen setting:
1. Point to an empty area on the Desktop.
2. Click mouse button 2 to display the pop-up menu.
3. Click mouse button 1 on the **System setup** menu choice.
4. Double-click on the **System** icon.

5. Click mouse button 1 on the **Print Screen** notebook tab.
6. Click mouse button 1 on the **Disable** choice if you want to turn off the print screen option. Click on **Enable** if you want to turn on the print screen option.
7. Double-click on the title-bar icons of the open windows to close them.

Setting Printer Properties

Every printer is controlled by a printer driver, which is the file that controls the printer. The printer driver has settings called *printer properties*. These printer properties describe how your printer is physically set up. The number and kind of printer properties available depend upon the type of printer you have.

You can change these properties to customize how you want your jobs to be printed. For example, you might decide that you want your jobs printed in a certain font.

To set the printer properties for your printer:

1. Point to a printer icon.
2. Click mouse button 2 to display the pop-up menu.
3. Click mouse button 1 on the **Settings** menu choice.
4. Click mouse button 1 on the **Printer driver** notebook tab.
5. Point to a printer driver in the **Printer driver** field.
6. Click mouse button 2 to display the pop-up menu.
7. Click mouse button 1 on the **Settings** menu choice.
8. Change the properties to match the way you want your printer to work. Your printer properties window might have some or all of the following choices:

Resolution
Determines the number of dots-per-inch (dpi). The higher the number, the better the resolution of graphical data.

Orientation
Determines the direction (portrait or landscape) that graphical data is printed on the paper.

Printer Fonts
Determines which fonts are available for printing graphical data.

Forms
Allows you to add, change, or delete a form (for example, letter-size or legal-size paper).

Code Page Memory
Determines whether your printer has additional memory installed that can be used for printer fonts for other code pages.

Form Feed Control
Determines whether a blank page is ejected from the printer at the end of each job.

Spool File Type
Determines the format of jobs that are sent to the spooler.

Automatic Mode Switching
Specifies that the printer should take direction from the information being printed. If mode switching is turned off, the Form Feed Control is activated.

Extended NLS Version
Indicates whether your printer supports an extended range of code pages.

Default Font
> Determines the font used for your graphical data and text jobs.

Paper Sources
> Determines what kind of paper feeder your printer is using.

Form Connections
> Determines which forms are in a paper source on the printer.

Code Pages
> Indicates the code pages that can be downloaded to printer memory.

Font Cards
> Indicates which font cards are currently in the printer.

9. Click mouse button 1 on the **OK** push button.
10. Double-click on the title-bar icon of the notebook to close it.

Setting Job Properties

Every job you send to the printer has its own set of properties called *job properties*. These properties allow you to choose specific settings for the jobs that print on your printer.

Some of the setting choices in the job properties window are the same as the setting choices in the printer properties window. Whatever choices you make in the job properties window override those made in the printer properties window.

There are several ways that you can set the properties for a job you are sending to the printer:

- You can set default job properties for all jobs sent to a printer.

- You can specify that you want the computer to prompt you for job properties each time you send a job to the printer.

- You can set the job properties through a program.

Setting Default Job Properties

You can set up your printer so that it uses the same job properties for each job you print. This is the ideal way to set up your jobs if you print the same type of information over and over.

To set default job properties:

1. Point to the printer icon.
2. Click mouse button 2 to display the pop-up menu.
3. Click mouse button 1 on the **Settings** menu choice.
4. Click mouse button 1 on the **Printer driver** notebook tab.
5. Click mouse button 1 on the **Job properties** push button.
6. Change the settings to match the needs of the jobs you print. Your job properties window might have some or all of the following choices:

   Orientation
   Determines the direction (portrait or landscape) that graphical data is printed on the paper.

   Resolution
   Determines the number of dots-per-inch (dpi). The higher the number, the better the resolution of graphical data.

   Select Form
   Determines the form (for example, letter-size or legal-size paper) that should be used for the job.

   Form Configuration
   Indicates how many different forms are used by the job.

   First Page
   Indicates the form that should be used for the first page of the job (when Dual Form is selected).

   Rest of Document
   Indicates the form that should be used for the rest of the pages in the job (when Dual Form is selected).

   Default Font
   Determines the font used for your graphical data and text jobs.

7. Click mouse button 1 on the **OK** push button.
8. Double-click on the title-bar icon of the notebook to close it.

Prompting for Job Properties

You can be prompted for job properties every time you send a job to the printer. When you are prompted, you can view the properties for the job before it is printed and make changes if necessary. This is the ideal way to set up a printer if you print a wide variety of jobs that use different forms, fonts, and orientation.

To set up a printer to prompt for job properties:
1. Point to the printer icon.
2. Click mouse button 2 to display the pop-up menu.
3. Click mouse button 1 on the **Settings** menu choice.
4. Click mouse button 1 on the **Queue options** notebook tab.
5. Click mouse button 1 on the **Job dialog before print** check box to place a check mark in the box.
6. Double-click on the title-bar icon of the notebook to close it.

Now, each time you send a job to the printer, a window will appear in which you can select the job properties.

Setting Job Properties within a Program

Some programs allow you to select the job properties from within the program. Most of these programs have a menu that contains a **Printer Setup** choice. The windows for setting the job properties within a program will differ slightly from the job properties window that you see in OS/2 Warp. However, they will contain similar choices, such as:

- Graphics dpi (dots per inch)
- Paper source
- Orientation
- Number of copies
- Fonts
- Paper size

Adding Separators to Jobs

You can add a piece of paper to the beginning of each job you send to the printer. This piece of paper is called a separator. A separator is used to identify who printed the job, what type of printer was used, the date and time the job was printed, and the spool ID of the job. This information is useful if more than one person prints jobs on the printer, or if you print multiple jobs and need to know what time and date the job was printed.

To add a separator to the beginning of a job:
1. Point to the printer icon.
2. Click mouse button 2 to display the pop-up menu.
3. Click mouse button 1 on the **Settings** menu choice.

4. Click mouse button 1 on the **Print options** notebook tab.
5. Type the drive letter, directory, and name of the separator file in the **Separator file** field. OS/2 Warp comes with two sample separator files:

\OS2\SAMPLE.SEP
A sample separator file that can be used with most printers

\OS2\PSCRIPT.SEP
A sample separator file that can be used with PostScript printers

Both of these files can be changed. For more information, see "Changing the Separator File."

6. Double-click on the title-bar icon of the notebook to close it.

Changing the Separator File

You can improve the usefulness of the information printed on the separator page by changing the information on the separator file.

Following are the valid commands that can be used in a separator file. The most commonly used commands are placed near the top of the list.

Command	Description
@	Used to start every line in the separator page file. This command must appear by itself at the beginning of the file.
@Wnn	Sets the width of the separator page in characters (1-132). For example, @W80.
@n	Skips n number of lines (0-9). Place this in between lines that will print text to make the file easier to read. For example, @2.
.@0	Indicates that a line has ended.
@L	Indicates that text follows. For example, @L Printed by Jim Cook @0.
@D	Prints the date the text was printed. For example, @L Date: @D @0.

Command	Description
@T	Prints the time the text was printed. For example, @L Time: @T @0.
@I	Prints the spool ID number. For example, @L SPL file= @I @0.
@Q	Prints the print queue description followed by the print queue name in parentheses. For example, @L Print Queue @Q @0.
@E	Ejects a page from the printer. Use this to end the separator page.
@N	Prints the machine ID.
@J	Prints the job document name.
@Hnn	Prints a printer-specific control sequence that is understood by the printer. nn is the hexadecimal number sent directly to the printer.
@F"filename"	Prints the file. This could be used to set up printer defaults.
@B	Creates block characters.
@S	Creates single-width block characters. Use this after @B.
@M	Creates double-width block characters. Use this after @B.
@U	Turns off block-character printing.

To create your own separator file:

1. Double-click on the **OS/2 System** icon.
2. Double-click on the **Productivity** icon.
3. Double-click on the **OS/2 System Editor** icon.
4. Type the following information into the file. (Press the Enter key to add a new line, and substitute your name for Jim Cook's name.)

```
@
@L Printed by Jim Cook@0
@2
@W80
```

```
@B@N@0
@2
@L Printed on an @Q@0
@2
@L .SPL file:  @I@U@0
@2
@L Date:  @D@0
@L Time:  @T@0
@E
```

5. Double-click on the title-bar icon of the **OS/2 System Editor** to close it.
6. Click mouse button 1 on the **Save** or **Save as** push button.
7. Type:**\OS2\JOB.SEP** in the **Filename** field.
8. Click mouse button 1 on the **Save** push button.

Setting Printing Hours

You can set up your printer to print only during certain hours of the day or night. This is a nice option if you have a printer that makes so much noise that you can't think straight. By setting the printing hours, you can work in relative quiet and print all of your jobs while you're away.

To set the printing hours:

1. Point to the printer icon.
2. Click mouse button 2 to display the pop-up menu.
3. Click mouse button 1 on the **Settings** menu choice.
4. Click mouse button 1 on the **Print options** notebook tab.
5. Click mouse button 1 on the arrows to the right of the fields in the **Start Time** field to set the time you want the printer to begin printing.
6. Click mouse button 1 on either the **AM** or **PM** choice in the **Start Time** field.
7. Click mouse button 1 on the arrows to the right of the fields in the **Stop Time** field to set the time you want the printer to stop printing.
8. Click mouse button 1 on either the **AM** or **PM** choice in the **Stop Time** field.
9. Double-click on the title-bar icon of the notebook to close it.

Customizing the Spooler Settings

You can send jobs to a printer faster than the printer can actually print them. When this happens, the computer needs to find a place to store the jobs so that they don't get lost or mixed together. This is where the Spooler comes in.

The Spooler manages the jobs that are waiting for an available printer by creating .SPL files for each job. These files are held in the SPOOL directory until the job is printed.

You can view a job in the Spooler while it is waiting to be printed. This comes in handy if you send jobs to the printer and later want to cancel one of them. By double-clicking on the .SPL icons, you can display the text of the file waiting to be printed and determine which one you want to cancel.

Enabling the Spooler

The Spooler keeps the print jobs separate while they are waiting for a printer. If you typically print more than one job at a time, you should enable your Spooler so the jobs don't get mixed together.

To enable the Spooler:
1. Point to an empty area on the Desktop.
2. Click mouse button 2 to display the pop-up menu.
3. Click mouse button 1 on the **System setup** menu choice.
4. Double-click on the **Spooler** icon.
5. Point to the title-bar icon of the open window.
6. Click mouse button 2 to display the pop-up menu.
7. Click mouse button 1 on the **Disable spooler** menu choice. This puts the **Enable spooler** choice on the menu and enables the Spooler.
8. Click mouse button 1 on the **OK** push button for the message that is displayed.
9. Double-click on the title-bar icons of the open windows to close them. (Spooling takes effect immediately. You do not need to restart your system.)

Disabling the Spooler

The spooler keeps the print jobs separate while they are waiting for a printer. When you disable the Spooler, there is nothing to keep track of the print jobs. If you send more than one job to a printer when the Spooler is disabled, the jobs will be mixed together and treated as one job. If you typically print only one job at a time, you can disable the Spooler without having any problems.

To disable the Spooler:

1. Point to an empty area on the Desktop.
2. Click mouse button 2 to display the pop-up menu.
3. Click mouse button 1 on the **System setup** menu choice.
4. Double-click on the **Spooler** icon.
5. Point to the title-bar icon of the open window.
6. Click mouse button 2 to display the pop-up menu.
7. Click mouse button 1 on the **Enable spooler** menu choice. This puts the **Disable spooler** choice on the menu and disables the Spooler.
8. Click mouse button 1 on the **OK** push button for the message that is displayed.
9. Double-click on the title-bar icons of the open windows to close them.
10. Shut down your computer and restart it to disable the spooler.

Printing While a Job Is Spooling

The second you send a job to be printed, the Spooler starts to create an .SPL file for the information (if the Spooler is enabled). The Spooler can do one of the following:

- Start to send the information to the printer immediately. You might want to do this if only one computer is using the printer.

- Wait until it receives all the information from the program before it starts to send the information to the printer. You might want to do this if there are multiple computers using a single printer and you don't want to tie up the printer until all the information is ready to be printed.

You can specify what you want the Spooler to do.

To print a job while it is still spooling:

1. Point to the printer icon.
2. Click mouse button 2 to display the pop-up menu.
3. Click mouse button 1 on the **Settings** menu choice.
4. Click mouse button 1 on the **Queue options** notebook tab.
5. Click mouse button 1 on the **Print while spooling** check box to place a check mark in the box. If you remove the check mark from the check box, your printer will not print the job until it is completely finished spooling.
6. Double-click on the title-bar icon of the notebook to close it.

Changing the Print Priority

The print priority is used to adjust the order in which spooled print jobs are printed. The print priority assigns importance to the jobs in the Spooler. The higher the priority, the more important the computer thinks it is that your job be printed. However, setting the priority too high takes microprocessor time away from other things your computer is trying to do. This means that your computer might run slower. If you set the priority too low, your job might never get printed because everything else the computer is doing is more important than printing your job.

TIP: OS/2 Warp comes with a default setting of 95 for the print priority. You should probably make only minor adjustments to this setting so that you don't give your print jobs too high or low a priority.

To set the print priority:

1. Point to an empty area on the Desktop.
2. Click mouse button 2 to display the pop-up menu.
3. Click mouse button 1 on the **System setup** menu choice.
4. Double-click on the **Spooler** icon.
5. Click mouse button 1 on the **Print priority** notebook tab.
6. Point to the slider arm displayed horizontally across the notebook.
7. Press and hold mouse button 1.
8. Drag the slider arm until the print priority you want is displayed.
9. Double-click on the title-bar icons of the open windows to close them.

Changing the Spool Path

When you send jobs to be printed, they are stored as .SPL files in the SPOOL directory on your computer. You can change the name of the drive and directory where these files are stored. The drive and directory are referred to as the **Spool path**.

If you print very large jobs or lots of small jobs, you might want to change the Spool path to point to a drive that has more space. This frees up space on the drive where OS/2 Warp is installed and gives you more room for programs.

TIP: Before you change the Spool path, make sure that all of the jobs waiting in the Spooler have been printed; otherwise, they never will be printed. After you change the Spooler path to point to another directory, the computer will not know where to find the old .SPL files.

To change the spooler path:

1. Point to an empty area on the Desktop.
2. Click mouse button 2 to display the pop-up menu.
3. Click mouse button 1 on the **System setup** menu choice.
4. Double-click on the **Spooler** icon.
5. Click mouse button 1 on the **Spool path** field.
6. Type a new path in the field.
7. Double-click on the title-bar icons of the open windows to close them.

Adding and Starting Programs

Even though OS/2 Warp comes with many good programs, sooner or later, you will want to add other programs to your computer.

This chapter shows you how to begin installing programs written for OS/2 Warp, DOS, and Windows and how to add program icons to the Desktop. In addition, it shows you how to add an item to a pop-menu, create a cascaded menu, make a menu item the default, choose a menu item that is not the default, associate a program with a data-file icon, and associate multiple data-file icons with a program.

Installing New Programs

OS/2 Warp can run DOS, Windows, and OS/2 Warp programs. Because these programs are written by a multitude of different companies, very few are installed the same way. That is why you need the instructions that come with the program.

The following information is not meant to replace those instructions. Instead, it should be used to get you to the place in OS/2 Warp where you can begin following the instructions that came with the program.

OS/2 Warp Programs

If you are installing a program written specifically for the OS/2 Warp operating system, the instructions that came with the program should take you through the steps on how to get started. If they don't, follow these steps to get to the point where the program instructions start.

To install an OS/2 Warp program:
1. Insert the first diskette for the program into a diskette drive (for example, drive A). If the program is on a CD, insert the CD into the CD-ROM drive.
2. Point to the **Drive A** icon on the LaunchPad and click mouse button 1. If the diskette is in a different drive or if you are installing from a CD:
   a. Double-click on the **OS/2 System** icon.
   b. Double-click on the **Drives** icon.
   c. Double-click on the icon that represents the drive containing the diskette or CD.
3. Double-click on the program-file icon used for installation (for example, INSTALL.EXE).
4. Follow the instructions that came with the program to complete the installation.
5. Remove the diskette or CD from the drive.
6. Double-click on the title-bar icons of the open windows to close them.

Or

1. Place the first diskette for the program into a diskette drive (for example, drive A). If the program is on a CD, insert the CD into the CD-ROM drive.
2. Double-click on the **OS/2 System** icon.
3. Double-click on the **Command Prompts** icon.
4. Double-click on either the **OS/2 Window** icon or the **OS/2 Full Screen** icon.
5. Type the letter of the drive containing the diskette or CD (for example, **A:**); then press the Enter key.
6. Type the command used to install the program (for example: **INSTALL**); then press the Enter key.
7. Follow the instructions that came with the program to complete the installation.
8. Remove the diskette or CD from the drive.
9. Type **EXIT** and then press the Enter key to close the OS/2 Window or Full Screen.
10. Double-click on the title-bar icons of the open windows to close them.

NOTE: After you finish installing the program, check to see if an icon for the program was added to the Desktop. (It might be in another folder on the Desktop.) If no icon was added, you must add one before you can start the program from the Desktop. For instructions on how to do this, read "Adding Programs to the Desktop" on page 151.

DOS Programs

The instructions for installing DOS programs assume that you are installing them from a version of DOS. Because you are running OS/2 Warp, the instructions that come with the program might be missing a few steps that you need to install the program.

If you are installing a program written specifically for the DOS operating system, you can use the following instructions to get you to the point where you can start to use the instructions that came with the program.

To install a DOS program:

1. Insert the first diskette for the program into a diskette drive (for example, drive A). If the program is on a CD, insert the CD into the CD-ROM drive.
2. Double-click on the **OS/2 System** icon.
3. Double-click on the **Command Prompts** icon.
4. Double-click on either the **DOS Window** icon or the **DOS Full Screen** icon.
5. Type the letter of the drive containing the diskette or CD (for example, **A:**); then press the Enter key.
6. Type the command used to install the program (for example: **INSTALL**); then press the Enter key.

7. Follow the instructions that came with the program to complete the installation.
8. Remove the diskette or CD from the drive.
9. Type **EXIT** and then press the Enter key to close the **DOS Window** or **Full-Screen**.
10. Double-click on the title-bar icons of the open windows to close them.

NOTE: Your next step is to add the program to the Desktop. For instructions on how to do this, read "Adding Programs to the Desktop."

Windows Programs

The instructions for Windows programs assume that you are installing either from within Windows or from a DOS prompt. Because you are running OS/2 Warp, the instructions that come with the program might be missing a few steps that you need to install the program.

If you are installing a program written specifically for Windows, you can use the following instructions to get you to the point where you can start to use the instructions that came with the program.

To install a Windows program from the Windows Program Manager:
1. Double-click on the **OS/2 System** icon.
2. Double-click on the **Command Prompts** icon.
3. Double-click on either the **WIN-OS/2 Window** icon or the **WIN-OS/2 Full Screen** icon.
4. Follow the instructions that came with the program to complete the installation.
5. When the installation is completed, double-click on the title-bar icon of the Program Manager window to close it.
6. Respond to the messages on the screen.
7. Double-click on the title-bar icons of the open windows to close them.

To install a Windows program from a DOS command prompt:
1. Click mouse button 1 on the drawer above the **OS/2 Window** icon on the LaunchPad.
2. Click mouse button 1 on the **DOS Window** icon in the LaunchPad drawer.
3. Follow the instructions that came with the program to complete the installation.
4. Type **EXIT** and then press the Enter key to close the **DOS Window**.
5. Double-click on the title-bar icons of the open windows to close them.

NOTE: Your next step is to add the program to the Desktop. For instructions on how to do this, read "Adding Programs to the Desktop."

Adding Programs to the Desktop

Some programs do not place a program icon on the Desktop during their installation. Without the icon, you cannot start the program from the Desktop. There are several ways that you can add a program icon, but this one is by far the easiest. (The other ways require that you know the path, file name, parameters, and settings for the program.)

To add programs (the easy way) to the Desktop:

1. Point to an empty area on the Desktop.
2. Click mouse button 2 to display the pop-up menu.
3. Click mouse button 1 on the **System setup** menu choice.
4. Double-click on the **Add Programs** icon.
5. Click mouse button 1 on the **Add new programs** choice.
6. Click mouse button 1 on the **OK** push button.
7. If a message is displayed stating that no new programs were found, the program you just installed is not in the database of programs that OS/2 Warp knows about. Don't worry—you can still add the program to your Desktop if you:
   a. Click mouse button 1 on the **Yes** push button to search for programs.
   b. Click mouse button 1 on each drive in the **Drives** field that you do not want to search for the program. This removes the highlighting from the drive letter. Only highlighted drive letters will be searched.
   c. Click mouse button 1 on each program type in the **Program Type** field that you do not want to search for. This removes the check mark from the item. Only program types with a check mark will be looked for. (If you are not sure of the program type, look on the outside of the program's package. If you cannot find the package and do not know what kind of program it is, leave all the choices checked.)
   d. Click mouse button 1 on the **OK** push button. The search begins.
   e. When the **Select Programs** window is displayed, click mouse button 1 on each program in the list that you want to add to your Desktop, or click mouse button 1 on the **New**, **All**, or **None** choice.

      New   Adds only the programs that were not added to your Desktop before.

      All   Adds all of the programs in the list to your Desktop.

      None   Does not add any of the programs in the list to your Desktop.
   f. Click mouse button 1 on the **OK** push button.
8. When a message is displayed stating that the process is completed, click mouse button 1 on the **OK** push button.
9. Double-click on the title-bar icons of the open windows to close them.

Icons that represent the programs are added to the following folders on the Desktop:

OS/2 Programs
> Contains icons for the OS/2 Warp programs you added.

DOS Programs
> Contains icons for the DOS programs you added.

Windows Programs
> Contains icons for the Windows programs you added.

WIN-OS/2 Groups
> Contains icons for the Windows Groups programs you added. These are the icons that appear in the Program Manager window of Microsoft Windows.

"Program Name" DOS Programs
> Contains icons of related DOS programs that were installed from a single product (for example, a DOS word processor program that comes with a thesaurus and a spell checker).

"Program Name" Windows Programs
> Contains icons of related Windows programs that were installed from a single product.

TIP: You do not need to leave the program icons in their respective folders. You can move them anywhere you want. If you empty one of the folders, you can then drag it to the Shredder to reduce the clutter on your Desktop.

Other Ways to Start Programs

By now you are used to double-clicking on program icons to start them. But did you know that there are other ways? You can add a program title to a pop-up menu, make it the default choice, associate a program with a data-file icon, and even have programs start automatically every time you turn on your computer.

Adding a Program Choice to the Pop-Up Menu

Sometimes finding the program icon that you want to use can become rather time-consuming. To reduce the amount of time needed to find a program icon, you can add the name of the icon to a pop-up menu. When you add a program to a pop-up menu, you are only one or two clicks away from having the program running.

To add a program to a pop-up menu:

1. Point to an empty area on the Desktop or in a window.
2. Click mouse button 2 to display the pop-up menu that you will add the name of the icon to.
3. Click mouse button 1 on the **Settings** menu choice.
4. Click mouse button 1 on the **Menu** notebook tab.
5. Point to the program icon on the Desktop that you want to add to the menu.
6. Press and hold mouse button 2.
7. Drag the program icon to the **Actions on menu** field.
8. Release mouse button 2.
9. Repeat steps 5 through 8 for each program you want to add to the menu.
10. Double-click on the title-bar icon of the open notebook to close it.

The next time you display the pop-up menu, the programs you added will be shown as menu choices. If you select one of the menu choices, a program will be started.

TIP: When you start a program from a pop-up menu, an error might be displayed. This indicates that an incorrect parameter is being passed to the program. To fix this problem:

1. Point to the program icon you are trying to start.
2. Click mouse button 2 to display the pop-up menu.
3. Click mouse button 1 on the **Settings** menu choice.
4. Click mouse button 1 in the **Parameters** field.
5. Type **%.** This keeps parameters from being passed.
6. Double-click on the title-bar icon of the notebook to close it.

Creating Cascaded Menus

Because starting programs from a pop-up menu is so convenient, you might want to add all of your programs to pop-up menus. This is a great idea, but the pop-up menu could become very long and searching for the item you want could become just as time consuming as double-clicking on icons to find the program icon you want. To lessen the chance of creating long pop-up menus, OS/2 Warp has given you the opportunity to create a mini-menu that connects to the pop-up menu. This is called a cascaded menu. A cascaded menu can be identified by the arrow to the right of the menu choice. An example of a cascaded menu is the **Open** menu choice on a pop-up menu. Cascaded menus allow you to organize your menu items, so that you can find things at a glance. For example, you could create a cascaded menu for Command Prompts, one for Editors, and another one for Games.

To create a cascaded menu:

1. Point to an empty area on the Desktop or in a window.
2. Click mouse button 2 to display the pop-up menu.
3. Click mouse button 1 on the **Settings** menu choice.
4. Click mouse button 1 on the **Menu** notebook tab.
5. Click mouse button 1 on the **Create another** push button in the **Available menus** field.
6. Type a name for the menu in the **Menu name** field. Use a name that describes what you plan to put in the menu (for example, Games, Editors, or Command Prompts).
7. Click mouse button 1 on one of the choices in the **Menu type** field. You can choose one of the following:

   Cascade menu
   > Displays a cascaded menu whenever you click mouse button 1 on the menu choice in the pop-up menu. You must select the program you want to start from the menu.

   Conditional cascade
   > Displays a cascaded menu whenever you click mouse button 1 on the arrow to the right of the menu choice. You can then select one of the programs on the menu to start as the default. If you are undecided about which one you want, choose this one.

8. Click mouse button 1 on the **OK** push button.
9. Click mouse button 1 on the name of the menu in the **Available menus** field that you want to add menu choices to.
10. Point to the program icon that you want to add to the menu.
11. Press and hold mouse button 2.
12. Drag the program icon to the **Actions on menu** field.
13. Release mouse button 2.
14. Repeat steps 10 through 13 for each program that you want to add to the menu.
15. Double-click on the title-bar icon of the notebook to close it.

The next time you display the pop-up menu and then display the cascaded menu, the programs you added will be shown as menu choices. If you select one of the menu choices, a program will be started.

Making an Item on a Cascaded Menu the Default

You can select one of the items on a cascaded menu to be the default. When you make a menu item the default, it means that you want it to start automatically. This is particularly nice if you use one menu item more than the other items on the cascaded menu because it saves you steps. After a menu item is made the default, all you have to do is click mouse button 1 on the menu item in the pop-up menu. You never need to display the cascaded menu again to select that menu choice.

To make an item on a cascaded menu the default:
1. Point to an empty area on the Desktop or in a window.
2. Click mouse button 2 to display the pop-up menu.
3. Click mouse button 1 on the **Settings** menu choice.
4. Click mouse button 1 on the **Menu** notebook tab.
5. Click mouse button 1 on the **Create another** push button in the **Available menus** field.
6. Click mouse button 1 on the name of the menu in the **Available menus** field that you want to select a default item for.
7. Click mouse button 1 on the **Conditional cascade** choice.
8. Click mouse button 1 on the down arrow to the right of the **Default action** field.
9. Click mouse button 1 on the name of the item that you want to start automatically.
10. Click mouse button 1 on the **OK** push button.
11. Double-click on the title-bar icon of the notebook to close it.

Choosing a Non-Default Menu Item

If you have made a menu item on a cascaded menu the default, you will need to know how to select one of the other items on the menu; otherwise, the other menu items will be useless.

For example, let's say that you have a cascaded menu called Editors. You add the OS/2 System Editor, Enhanced Editor, and Icon Editor to the menu. Then you make the Enhanced Editor the default choice. The next time you select Editors from the pop-up menu, the Enhanced Editor is started. But what happens if you want to start the Icon Editor? You will have to manually override the default choice.

To choose a non-default menu item:
1. Point to an empty area on the Desktop or in a window.
2. Click mouse button 2 to display the pop-up menu.
3. Click mouse button 1 on the arrow to the right of the cascaded menu choice.
4. Click mouse button 1 on any choice except the one with the check mark next to it. The program starts.

Associating a Program with a Data-File Icon

Data-file icons are used by programs to store data. You can associate a program with a data-file icon, so that each time you double-click on the data-file icon, it opens up in the program you want to use with it. This makes it much easier to edit a data-file icon because you don't need to locate the program icon for the editor before you edit the data-file icon.

To associate a program with a data-file icon:
1. Point to a data-file icon.
2. Click mouse button 2 to display the pop-up menu.
3. Click mouse button 1 on the **Settings** menu choice.
4. Click mouse button 1 on the **Menu** notebook tab.
5. Click mouse button 1 on the **Open** choice in the **Available menus** field.
6. Point to the program icon on your Desktop that you want to use with this data-file.
7. Press and hold mouse button 2.
8. Drag the program icon to the **Actions on menu** field.
9. Release mouse button 2.
10. Click mouse button 1 on the **Settings** push button to the right of the **Available menus** field. The Menu Settings window appears.
11. Click mouse button 1 on the down arrow to the right of the **Default action** field.
12. Click mouse button 1 on the name of the program you want to use with this data-file.
13. Click mouse button 1 on the **OK** push button.
14. Double-click on the title-bar icon of the notebook to close it.

The next time you double-click on the data-file icon, it is displayed in the program you choose.

Associating Multiple Data-File Icons with a Program

You can associate multiple data-file icons with the same program icon. For example, if you have many existing data files of the same type or extension, you can associate them with one program icon. Then, each time a data-file icon of that type or extension is opened, the program icon is also opened.

To associate multiple data-file icons with a program.
1. Point to the program icon that you want to associate with the data-file icons.
2. Click mouse button 2 to display the pop-up menu.
3. Click mouse button 1 on the **Settings** menu choice.
4. Click mouse button 1 on the **Association** notebook tab.

Choose one of the following ways to associate the data-file icons with a program:

Types
> Allows you to associate types of files with a program. For example, you can associate bit-map files with a program. Then whenever you double-click on a bit-map icon, it is displayed in the program you associated it with.

Names
> Allows you to associate names of data-file icons with a program. For example, if you name your data-file icons *xxxx*.KMS, *oooo*.KMS, and *yyyy*.KMS, you can associate the common part of the name of the data-file icons (.KMS) with a program. Then, whenever you double-click on a data-file icon with the extension .KMS, it is displayed in the program you associated it with.

5. Follow the instructions below that correspond to the way that you want to associate the data-file icon with the program.

   - To associate data-file icons using the type:
      a. In the **Available types** field, click mouse button 1 on the type of file you want to associate with the program.
      b. Click mouse button 1 on the **Add** push button to the right of the **Available types** field. You can add as many types as you want.

      The added types are shown in the **Current types** field.

   - To associate data-file icons using the name:
      a. Click mouse button 1 on the **New name** field.
      b. Type ***.** and then the extension of the file (for example, **DOC, TXT,** or **SCR**).
      c. Click mouse button 1 on the **Add** push button to the right of the **New name** field. You can add as many names as you want.

6. Double-click on the title-bar icon of the notebook to close it.

Opening a Data-File Icon in a Non-Default Program

You can associate data-file icons with multiple programs, and then select one of the programs to be the default. This means that when you double-click on the data-file icon, the data-file icon opens up in the default program.

There might be times when you would like to override the default choice and open a data-file icon in a different program.

To open a data-file icon in a program other than the default one:

1. Point to the data-file icon.
2. Click mouse button 2 to display the pop-up menu.
3. Click mouse button 1 on the arrow to the right of the **Open** menu choice.
4. Click mouse button 1 on a program name that doesn't have a check mark next to it. The data-file icon opens in the program whose name you selected.

Starting Program Icons Automatically

OS/2 Warp has the ability to start program icons automatically every time the computer is turned on. This is a great way to start the programs you use every day. In fact, while the computer is starting the programs, you can be doing something else, such as reading your mail or getting a cup of coffee.

To start a program icon automatically:

1. Double-click on the **OS/2 System** icon.
2. Double-click on the **Startup** icon.
3. Point to the program icon you want to place in the Startup window.
4. Press and hold the Ctrl and Shift keys.
5. Press and hold mouse button 2.
6. Drag the program icon to the Startup window.
7. Release mouse button 2.
8. Release the Ctrl and Shift keys.
9. Repeat steps 3 through 8 for each program you want to automatically start when you turn on the computer.
10. Double-click on the title-bar icons of the open windows to close them.

NOTE: If you decide at a later time that you do not need a program to start automatically every time you turn on the computer, just open the Startup icon and drag the program icon's shadow to the Shredder.

Chapter 19

Creating and Arranging Icons

Icons are used to represent the programs, devices, and data on your computer. A big part of using OS/2 Warp effectively is discovering how to create new icons, modify their settings, and display them where and how you want.

This chapter shows you how to create icons and templates of icons, arrange the icons you use every day into work areas, and change the way icons are arranged in a window or on the Desktop.

Creating a Data-File Icon

A data-file icon contains information in the form of text, pictures, video, sounds, or pointers. Many of the programs that come with OS/2 Warp use these data-file icons to hold the information that is created when you run them. For example, the Digital Audio Player uses data files with the extensions .MID and .WAV to hold the sounds that it plays.

Some programs also come with their own form of data file. When you install these programs, they install templates of their data files in the Templates icon found on the Desktop.

You can easily create a new data-file icon from one of the data files that is already associated with a program.

To create a data-file icon:
1. Double-click on the **Templates** icon.
2. Point to the data-file icon that is used by the specific program.
3. Press and hold mouse button 2.
4. Drag a copy of the data-file icon to the Desktop or to another window.
5. Release mouse button 2. (An empty data-file icon is created.)
6. Point to the title below the icon.
7. Press and hold the Alt key.
8. Click mouse button 1.
9. Type the name that you want to appear below the icon. (Use the Backspace or Del key to erase characters, and use the Enter key to add a new line.)
10. Point to an empty area on the Desktop or in the window, and click mouse button 1.
11. Double-click on the title-bar icon of the Templates window to close it.
12. Double-click on the data-file icon to start the program that it is associated with and begin editing the file.

NOTE: If you double-click on a data-file icon that is not associated with any other program, it automatically opens in the OS/2 System Editor. If you prefer, you can associate the data-file icon with one or more program icons. To find out how, read "Associating Multiple Data-File Icons with a Program" on page 156. To find out more about using the OS/2 System Editor, read "OS/2 System Editor" on page 192.

Creating a Folder Icon

Folder icons are used to "house" other icons. These other icons can be program icons, device icons, data-file icons, or even other folder icons. Without folder icons, the Desktop would be a mess because every icon on your computer would be on the Desktop. You can easily create a folder icon so that you can organize your Desktop the way you want it.

To create a folder icon:
1. Double-click on the **Templates** icon.
2. Point to the **Folder** icon.
3. Press and hold mouse button 2.
4. Drag a copy of the **Folder** icon to the Desktop or to another window.
5. Release mouse button 2. An empty folder icon is created.
6. Point to the title below the icon.
7. Press and hold the Alt key.
8. Click mouse button 1.
9. Type the name that you want to appear below the icon. (Use the Backspace or Del key to erase characters, and use the Enter key to add a new line.)
10. Point to an empty area on the Desktop or in the window and click mouse button 1.
11. Double-click on the title-bar icon of the Templates window to close it.

Now, you can drag any icons you want into the new folder.

Creating a Program Icon

A program icon can be used to start a program after it is set up. Most people do not attempt to create a program icon by using a template because it requires knowledge of the directory path, executable file name, parameters, and working directory. Instead, they use the **Add Programs** program in the **System Setup** icon to create the program icon for them. This program plugs all the necessary information into the program icon.

However, if you want to create the program icon by using a template, you can follow these steps:

To create a program icon:
1. Double-click on the **Templates** icon.
2. Point to the **Program** icon.
3. Press and hold mouse button 2.
4. Drag a copy of the **Program** icon to the Desktop or to another window.
5. Release mouse button 2. A new **Program** icon is created.
6. Type the path and file name of the program in the **Path and file name** field.
7. Press the Tab key twice, and then type the parameters that you want to use in the **Parameters** field.
8. Press the Tab key, and then type the drive and path in the **Working Directory** field. This is where the work you create with this program will be stored.
9. Click mouse button 1 on the **General** notebook tab.
10. Press the Del key to remove **Program** from the **Title** field. Then type the name you want to appear beneath the icon.
11. Double-click on the title-bar icons of the open windows to close them.

Creating Work-Area Icons

Work-area icons are used to organize the icons you use most often. However, they differ from folder icons, because when you close a window for a work-area icon, all of the open icons in the window are closed too. This allows you to close up for the day by double-clicking on one title-bar icon rather than many. In addition, when you open the work-area icon the next time, it remembers which icons were open and puts them in exactly the same place.

The following is an example of how you could use the icons in the list below to set up a work-area window containing:

• A printer (device icon)

• A text editor program (program icon)

• Personnel memos (data-file icons)

• A company newsletter (data-file icon)

1. Create a folder icon.
2. Change the settings for the folder icon. Give it a name like "Dad's Stuff" and specify that you want the folder icon to be a work area.
3. Drag the icons that represent the data-files to the work area.
4. Drag to the work area a shadow of the program (text editor) and device icon (printer) you plan to use.

You might also want to create a work area for each person who will be using the computer. This will make it easier for others to have everything they need to do their work all in one convenient location and lessen the chance that their work will get messed up by someone else using the computer.

To create a work-area icon:
1. Double-click on the **Templates** icon.
2. Point to the **Folder** icon.
3. Press and hold mouse button 2.
4. Drag the **Folder** icon to the Desktop.
5. Release mouse button 2.
6. Point to the **Folder** icon on the Desktop.
7. Click mouse button 2 to display the pop-up menu.
8. Click mouse button 1 on the **Settings** menu choice.
9. Click mouse button 1 on the **File** notebook tab.
10. Click mouse button 1 on the **Work area** check box to place a check mark in the box.
11. Click mouse button 1 on the **General** notebook tab.
12. Press the Del key to remove **Folder** from the **Title** field. Then, type the name you want to appear beneath the icon.
13. Double-click on the title-bar icon of the notebook to close it.

A work-area icon is displayed on the Desktop. You can add program, device, and data-file icons to the work-area icon to create your customized work-area.

To add icons to your work-area icon:
1. Double-click on the work-area icon.
2. Point to a data-file icon (for example, Company Newsletter) that you want to use in the work area.
3. Press and hold mouse button 2.
4. Drag the data-file icon to the work-area window.
5. Release mouse button 2.

6. Point to a program (for example, text editor) or device (for example, a printer) icon that you want to use in the work area.
7. Press and hold the Ctrl+Shift keys and mouse button 2.
8. Drag a shadow of the icon to the work-area window.
9. Release mouse button 2.
10. Release the Ctrl+Shift keys.
11. Repeat these steps until all the icons you want to use are in the work-area window.
12. Double-click on the title-bar icons of the open windows to close them.

Creating a Template from an Icon

We use templates all the time in everyday life. Insurance forms, checks, and job applications are examples of templates. Templates are used to ensure that the information gathered is consistent, no matter how many times they are filled out.

OS/2 Warp comes with its own set of templates. However, you are not limited to them. You can create your own templates. For example, let's say you create the perfect "Thanks for the submission, but sorry" letter and you want to use it over and over again with only a few minor changes. You can easily make the letter into a template and eliminate having to retype the entire letter every time you need another one.

To create a template of an icon:
1. Point to the icon you want to use as a template.
2. Click mouse button 2 to display the pop-up menu.
3. Click mouse button 1 on the **Settings** menu choice.
4. Click mouse button 1 on the **General** notebook tab.
5. Click mouse button 1 on the **Template** check box to place a check mark in the box.
6. Double-click on the title-bar icon of the notebook to close it.

The icon is now displayed as a stack of templates. Each template in the stack has the same settings (such as associations) and contents as the original.

You can peel (drag) a template off the stack whenever you need one and change the name and contents without affecting the text in the stack of templates.

TIP: If you want to move the stack of templates, press the Shift key while dragging the stack.

Creating Another Icon

There is a choice on almost every pop-up menu called Create another. As the name implies, this choice is used to create another icon. The type of icon that is created depends on the icon whose pop-up menu you use. For example, if you use the pop-up menu from the OS/2 System icon, you would create another *folder icon* because the OS/2 System icon is a folder icon. If you use the pop-up menu from the Icon Editor, you would create another *program icon* because the Icon Editor was created from a program icon.

It is important to note that when you use the Create another choice, you are not making a copy of the icon whose pop-up menu you are using. Instead, you are using the template that the icon itself was made from. This means that the icon you create has no predetermined settings. It is blank, just like the ones you pull out of the Templates icon on the Desktop.

Now to add a new wrinkle. If you click on the arrow to the right of the **Create another** menu choice, a cascaded menu appears. The menu could contain two or more items.

- The first item on the menu is the **Default** menu choice. Default creates another icon of the same type as the icon whose pop-up menu you choose. For example, if you chose **Default** from the Create another menu of the OS/2 Chess icon, you would create another program icon, because the OS/2 Chess icon was created from a program icon.

- On the menu below the Default choice is the name of a particular type of icon found in the Templates icon on the Desktop. This choice just identifies what type of icon you will create if you choose **Default**. Exactly the same thing happens whether you choose Default or the menu choice immediately below it.

- Next on some menus is the list of templates you created from this type of icon. For example, if you create a Letterhead template using a Data-File icon, the Create another menu of every icon that was created from a Data-File icon will have the Letterhead menu choice. If you choose Letterhead from the menu, you will get a copy of the Letterhead with all its settings and data intact.

NOTE: If all of this sounds a bit confusing, don't worry. You can use OS/2 Warp just fine without ever understanding this menu item.

To create another icon using a pop-up menu:
1. Point to an icon that was created from the same type of icon you want to create.
2. Click mouse button 2 to display the pop-up menu.
3. Click mouse button 1 on the **Create another** menu choice.

Or

    a. Click mouse button 1 on the arrow to the right of **Create another** menu choice.

    b. Click mouse button 1 on a choice in the menu.

4. Click mouse button 1 in the **New Name** field of the Create Another window.
5. Click mouse button 1 on the location where you want the new icon placed.
6. Click mouse button 1 on the **Create** push button.
7. Click mouse button 1 on the title-bar icon of the open window to close it.

Changing the Way Icons Are Displayed

Icons can be displayed on the Desktop and in windows in three views: icon, tree, or details. Each of these views offers something different for the user. You will need to try out each of the views to discover which one is best for you. After you decide on a view, you can make changes to the format to make the view exactly what you are looking for.

Displaying Icons in an Icon View

Icon view is the default. The Desktop and all the windows are displayed in icon view when you install OS/2 Warp. In this view, the icons are displayed across the top of the Desktop and windows. When the edge of the window or Desktop is reached, the icons wrap to the next line.

To display the icons using Icon view:
1. Point to an empty area on the Desktop or in a window.
2. Click mouse button 2 to display the pop-up menu.
3. Click mouse button 1 on the arrow to the right of the **Open** menu choice.
4. Click mouse button 1 on the **Icon view** menu choice. The Desktop or window is displayed in Icon view.

Changing the Icon View Settings

Your Desktop and windows are set (by default) to display in an icon view. If you decide you like this view, you do not have to change it. You can keep the icon view and make changes to the way it is displayed. Who knows—a few minor changes might make it more appealing.

The settings for the icon view allow you to change the size of the icons or even make the icons invisible (so that only the text beneath the icon is displayed). You can also choose whether you want the icons displayed in columns either vertically or horizontally across the screen.

To change the icon view settings:

1. Point to the Desktop or window whose icon view you want to change.
2. Click mouse button 2 to display the pop-up menu.
3. Click mouse button 1 on the **Settings** menu choice.
4. Click mouse button 1 on the **View** notebook tab.
5. Click mouse button 1 on a choice in the **Format** field. You can choose from the following choices:

   Flowed
   > Vertically lines up the icons within the window starting on the left side. When the icons reach the lower boundary of the open window, they start another vertical column to the right. This pattern is repeated until all icons are lined up.

   Non-flowed
   > Vertically lines up the icons in one column. A scroll bar is added to the window so you can view all the icons.

   Non-grid
   > Horizontally lines up the icons within the window starting on the left side. When the icons reach the right boundary of the open window, they start another horizontal column to the right. This pattern is repeated until all icons are lined up.

6. Click mouse button 1 on a choice in the **Icon display** field. You can choose from the following choices:

   Normal size
   > Specifies the default size for an icon.

   Small size
   > Makes the icons smaller but does not affect the size of the icon title text.

   Invisible
   > Removes the icon so that only the title text remains. (This choice is not available if Non-grid is selected.)

7. Double-click on the title-bar icon of the notebook to close it.

Displaying Icons in a Details View

Even though icons look simple on the surface of your Desktop, hidden within them is a wealth of information. Details such as the icon's creation date, time, and size are available. If you are interested in knowing the details about the icons on the Desktop or in a window, all you need to do is display the icons in the Details view.

To display icons in the Details view:

1. Point to an empty area on the Desktop or in a window.
2. Click mouse button 2 to display the pop-up menu.
3. Click mouse button 1 on the arrow to the right of the **Open** menu choice.
4. Click mouse button 1 on the **Details view** menu choice. The Desktop or window is displayed with details about the icons.

Changing the Details View Settings

When you choose the Details view of the Desktop or a window, information about every field that is available is presented. If you enjoy being able to view the details but want to remove some of the fields, you can change the settings.

To change the Details view settings:

1. Point to the Desktop or window whose details view you want to change.
2. Click mouse button 2 to display the pop-up menu.
3. Click mouse button 1 on the **Settings** menu choice.
4. Click mouse button 1 on the **View** notebook tab.
5. Click mouse button 1 on the arrow in the lower-right corner of the notebook to change to **View - Page 3 of 3**.
6. Click mouse button 1 on any choice in the **Details to display** field that you do not want to display information about. You can choose from the following choices:

Icon
> Picture associated with the icon.

Object Class
> Type of object (for example, folder, program, or data-file.)

Real name
> Actual name of the icon.

Size
> Amount of space in bytes that the icon occupies.

Last write date
> Date that the information in the icon was last changed.

Last write time
> Time of day that the information in the icon was last changed.

Last access date
> Date that the information in the icon was last viewed.

Last access time
Time of day that the information in the icon was last viewed.

Creation date
Date that the icon was created.

Creation time
Time that the icon was created.

Flags
Characteristics of the file that allow it to be used in a certain way.

7. Double-click on the title-bar icon of the notebook to close it.

Displaying Icons in a Tree View

You can display the contents of the Desktop or a window in a structure that is similar to a tree. In a tree view, one icon acts as the trunk and all the other icons branch off it. Its main purpose is to show you how each of the icons is related to the other icons.

To display the icons in a Tree view:
1. Point to an empty area on the Desktop or in a window.
2. Click mouse button 2 to display the pop-up menu.
3. Click mouse button 1 on the arrow to the right of the **Open** menu choice.
4. Click mouse button 1 on the **Tree view** menu choice. The Desktop or window is displayed in a tree-like structure.

Changing the Tree View Settings

With the tree view, you can see the hierarchical structure of the icons on the Desktop or in a window. If you decide you like this setting but want something just a little different, you don't have to "leave" the Tree view behind. You can make changes to the Tree view settings that might improve the look of the Desktop or window.

The tree view settings can be changed to either add or remove the lines that connect the branches in the tree. You can also change the size of the icons or make the icons invisible (so that only the text beside the icon is displayed).

To change the Tree view settings:
1. Point to the Desktop or window whose tree view you want to change.
2. Click mouse button 2 to display the pop-up menu.
3. Click mouse button 1 on the **Settings** menu choice.
4. Click mouse button 1 on the **View** notebook tab.

5. Click mouse button 1 on the arrow in the lower-right corner of the notebook to change to **View - Page 2 of 3**.

6. Click mouse button 1 on a choice in the **Format** field. You can choose from the following choices:

   Lines
   > Shows the connections between the different icons in the tree.

   No Lines
   > Does not show lines drawn between the different icons in the tree.

7. Click mouse button 1 on a choice in the **Icon display** field. You can choose from the following choices:

   Normal size
   > Specifies the default size for an icon.

   Small size
   > Makes the icons smaller but does not affect the size of the icon title text.

   Invisible
   > Removes the icon so only the title text remains. (This choice is not available if Non-grid is selected.)

8. Double-click on the title-bar icon of the notebook to close it.

Chapter 20

Some Nifty Customizing Tricks

While we were writing this book, we discovered some nifty little tricks that you might like to try.

This chapter shows you how to retrieve data files that you accidentally deleted, add the DOS Shell to a DOS Full Screen icon, and write a batch file that brings you back to OS/2 Warp after you use the Dual Boot icon.

Getting Back a Deleted Icon

No matter how careful you are, sooner or later you might delete an icon that you really need. Before this happens to you, you should set up OS/2 Warp so that you can get your deleted icons back. If you wait until after you delete the icon, it will be too late!

Setting up your computer to easily recover a deleted icon involves these three steps:
1. Make a copy of your CONFIG.SYS file
2. Change the CONFIG.SYS file
3. Create the program icon to recover deleted icons.

 TIP: This procedure will recover only data-file icons that have been deleted. OS/2 Warp does not have the capability to recover deleted program or device icons. If you accidentally delete a program icon, you can use Add Programs to add the icon again. If you accidentally delete a device icon, you can use the Selective Install icon to install a new one.

Making a Copy of the CONFIG.SYS File

The CONFIG.SYS icon is one of the most important icons on your computer. It contains information needed to run both the hardware and software on the computer. One wrong move in this icon could prevent OS/2 Warp from starting or could cause errors when it does start.

To ensure that you always have a valid CONFIG.SYS file, make a copy of your good CONFIG.SYS icon before you edit it and start making changes.

To make a copy of your CONFIG.SYS:

1. Double-click on the **OS/2 System** icon.
2. Double-click on the **Drives** icon.
3. Double-click on the icon that represents the drive where OS/2 Warp is installed.
4. Point to an empty area in the window.
5. Click mouse button 2 to display the pop-up menu.

6. Click mouse button 1 on the arrow to the right of the **Open** menu choice.

7. Click mouse button 1 on the **Icon view** menu choice.

8. Point to the **CONFIG.SYS** icon.

9. Press and hold the Ctrl key.

10. Press and hold mouse button 2.

11. Drag the icon to an empty area in the window.

12. Release mouse button 2.

12. Release the Ctrl key.

13. Click mouse button 1 on the field to the right of **Rename object to**.

14. Use the Backspace or Del key to erase the text in the field, and then type CONFIG.OK and press the Enter key.

15. When asked if you want to keep the extension, click mouse button 1 on the **No** push button. The icon is now copied and you can safely set up your computer to recover deleted icons.

Changing the CONFIG.SYS File

The CONFIG.SYS file contains a line that allows OS/2 Warp to keep track of deleted icons for a period of time. Unfortunately, this line is not read by the computer during startup because it has the letters "REM" in front of it. So before you can recover a deleted icon, you need to remove "REM" from the beginning of the line.

To change your CONFIG.SYS file so that you can recover deleted icons:

1. Make sure you make a copy of your CONFIG.SYS before you follow these steps. For instructions on how to do this, read "Making a Copy of the CONFIG.SYS File."

2. Double-click on the **OS/2 System** icon.

3. Double-click on the **Drives** icon.

4. Double-click on the icon that represents the drive where OS/2 Warp is installed.

5. Point to an empty area in the window.

6. Click mouse button 2 to display the pop-up menu.

7. Click mouse button 1 on the arrow to the right of the **Open** menu choice.

8. Click mouse button 1 on the **Icon view** menu choice.

9. Double-click on the **CONFIG.SYS** icon.

10. Click mouse button 1 on the maximize button in the upper-right corner of the window.

11. Click mouse button 1 on the **Edit** menu (found under the title bar of the window).

12. Click mouse button 1 on the **Find** menu choice.

13. Type **DELDIR** in the **Find** field.

14. Click mouse button 1 on the **Find** push button.

15. Click mouse button 1 at the beginning of the line that contains "DELDIR". (Be very careful not to make any other changes!)

16. Press the Del key to erase only **REM** from the beginning of the following line:

    REM SET DELDIR=C:\DELETE,512;

17. Double-click on the title-bar icon of the **OS/2 System Editor** window to close it.

18. Click mouse button 1 on the **Save** push button.

19. Click mouse button 1 on the **Type** push button.

20. Click mouse button 1 on **Plain text**.

21. Click mouse button 1 on the **Set** push button.

22. Double-click on the title-bar icons of the open windows to close them.

23. Click on the **Shut down** push button on the LaunchPad to shut down your computer. Then restart it. (Changes made to the CONFIG.SYS file are not activated until your computer is restarted.)

Creating the Undelete Program Icon

Congratulations! You've made it through the hardest part of preparing OS/2 Warp to recover deleted icons. In fact, if you wanted to, you could use the Undelete command and just forget about creating the program icon, but you would be missing out on the best part.

To create a program icon that makes recovering deleted icons easy:

1. Be sure to make the changes to your CONFIG.SYS file, and then restart your computer. (See "Making a Copy of the CONFIG.SYS File" on page 172 and "Changing the CONFIG.SYS File" on page 173.)

2. Double-click on the **Templates** icon.

3. Point to the **Program** icon.

4. Press and hold mouse button 2.

5. Drag the **Program** icon to an empty area on the Desktop.

6. Release mouse button 2.

7. Type **C:\OS2\UNDELETE.COM** in the **Path** and **file name** field. (If OS/2 Warp is installed on a drive other than C, replace the C with the appropriate drive letter.)

8. Press the Tab key twice. Then type **/S** in the **Parameters** field.

9. Press the Tab key. Then type **C:** in the **Working Directory** field. (If OS/2 Warp is installed on a drive other than C, replace the C with the appropriate drive letter.)

10. Point to the **General** notebook tab and click mouse button 1.

11. Press the Del key to remove **Program** from the **Title** field. Then type **Undelete** (or any name you want).
12. Double-click on the title-bar icons of the open windows to close them.
13. Double-click on the **OS/2 System** icon.
14. Point to the **Undelete** icon on the Desktop.
15. Press and hold mouse button 2.
16. Drag the **Undelete** icon to the drawer above the Shredder in the LaunchPad (for convenient access).
17. When a dark box surrounds the drawer, release mouse button 2. The Undelete icon is now inside the drawer.
18. Double-click on the title-bar icon of the OS/2 System window to close it.

Undeleting an Icon

Now that you've gone through all the trouble of creating the Undelete icon, you probably want to know how to use it to get icons back. The instructions are quite simple.

To undelete an icon:
1. Click mouse button 1 on the drawer above the Shredder icon on the LaunchPad.
2. Click mouse button 1 on the **Undelete** icon. An Undelete window appears.
3. Type a **Y** or an **N** next to each question that appears.
4. After you have recovered the icons that you want, double-click on the title-bar icon of the Undelete window to close it.
5. Click mouse button 1 on the **Yes** push button to respond to the message that is displayed.

Adding the DOS Shell

If you were a DOS user before you bought OS/2 Warp, you might be familiar with an interface called the DOS Shell.

If you had a version of DOS with the DOS Shell on your computer before you installed OS/2 Warp, you can use the DOS Shell whenever you need to use a DOS Command Prompt window.

NOTE: Users of MS DOS 6.2 will not be able to do this, because the DOS Shell is not included with that product.

To add the DOS Shell to a DOS Command Prompt:

1. Double-click on the **OS/2 System** icon.
2. Double-click on the **Command Prompts** icon.
3. Point to the **DOS Full Screen** icon.
4. Press and hold the Ctrl key.
5. Press and hold mouse button 2.
6. Drag the icon to an empty area in the Command Prompts window.
7. Release mouse button 2.
8. Release the Ctrl key.
9. Point to the field to the right of **Rename object to**, and click mouse button 1.
10. Use the Backspace or Del key to erase the text in the field. Then type **DOS Shell** and press the Enter key.
11. Point to the **DOS Shell** icon.
12. Click mouse button 2 to display the pop-up menu.
13. Click mouse button 1 on the **Settings** menu choice.
14. Type **C:\DOS\DOSSHELL** in the **Path and file name** field. (If OS/2 Warp is installed on a drive other than C, replace the C with the appropriate drive letter.)
15. Press the Tab key twice. Then type **%** in the **Parameters** field.
16. Press the Tab key to move to the **Working Directory** field, and press the Del key to delete the text.
17. Double-click on the title-bar icon of the notebook to close it.
18. Point to the **DOS Shell** icon.
19. Press and hold mouse button 2.
20. Drag the **DOS Shell** icon to the drawer above the OS/2 Window icon in the LaunchPad (for convenient access).
21. When a dark box surrounds the drawer, release mouse button 2. The DOS Shell icon is now inside the drawer.
22. Double-click on the title-bar icons of the open windows to close them.

You can now use the DOS Shell whenever you like by clicking mouse button 1 on the **DOS Shell** icon located in the LaunchPad drawer.

Switching from DOS to OS/2 Warp

OS/2 Warp provides a wonderful feature (called Dual Boot) that allows you to switch to the version of DOS that you had on your computer before you installed OS/2 Warp. You can then run DOS programs that do not run under the version of DOS that comes with

OS/2 Warp. One of the downfalls of this feature is that you need to remember a command to get you back from DOS to OS/2 Warp. Forget the command, and you're stuck in DOS!

You can create a file that lets you get back to OS/2 Warp from within the DOS Shell.

To create a file that will restart OS/2 Warp from the DOS Shell:
1. Double-click on the **IBM DOS E Editor** under Main in the DOS Shell.
2. Type **C:\GOBACK.BAT** in the **File to Edit** field. (If OS/2 Warp is installed on a drive other than C, replace the C with the appropriate drive letter.)
3. Click mouse button 1 on the **OK** push button.
4. Type **C:\OS2\BOOT /OS2** and press the F4 key. (If OS/2 Warp is installed on a drive other than C, replace the C with the appropriate drive letter.)
5. Click mouse button 1 on the **File** menu.
6. Click mouse button 1 on the **New** menu choice.
7. Click mouse button 1 on the **Program Item** choice.
8. Click mouse button 1 on the **OK** push button.
9. Type **Return to OS/2** in the **Program Title** field.
10. Type **C:\GOBACK.BAT** in the **Commands** field. (If OS/2 Warp is installed on a drive other than C, replace the C with the appropriate drive letter.)
11. Click mouse button 1 on **Pause after exit** to remove the **X** from the field.
12. Click mouse button 1 on the **OK** push button.
13. Respond to the message that appears.

From now on you can point to **Return to OS/2** under Main in the DOS Shell and double-click on it to return to OS/2 Warp.

Official Guide to Using OS/2 Warp

Part Four

Using Productivity, Games, and Multimedia Programs

If you've read the first three parts of this book, you've installed OS/2 Warp, learned how to use the Desktop, and customized OS/2 Warp to meet your needs. In this part, you will find out how to use the productivity, games, and multimedia programs that come with OS/2 Warp.

The chapters that follow describe how to use the productivity programs to look at information that is stored in your clipboard, help you edit icons and files, and look at information that is waiting to be printed. You will also find out how to view a graph that charts system usage and you'll find out about a productivity program that you can use to find files quickly and easily.

This part describes the games programs that you can play. The rules for each game and the object of the game is also described.

In addition, this part describes the multimedia programs that you can use to play and record sounds, play movies, and listen to CDs. You'll also find out how to install additional multimedia programs.

Official Guide to Using OS/2 Warp

Chapter 21

Using the Productivity Programs

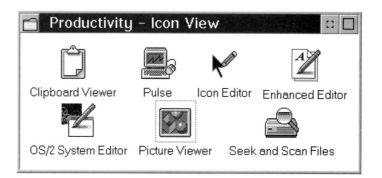

The Productivity icon contains basic programs that are included with OS/2 Warp to help you get started. You can use the programs to look at information that is being held in your clipboard, to create and edit icons, and to create and edit text files. There are also programs that you can use to display files waiting to be printed, to monitor system usage, and to look for files.

This chapter describes the Clipboard Viewer, System and Enhanced Editors, Picture Viewer, Pulse, and Seek and Scan Files programs that come with OS/2 Warp.

Clipboard Viewer

You can use the Clipboard Viewer to look at information in the OS/2 Warp clipboard. The clipboard temporarily holds data that is being passed from one program to another.

To see what's in the OS/2 Warp clipboard:
1. Double-click on the **OS/2 System** icon.
2. Double-click on the **Productivity** icon.
3. Double-click on the **Clipboard Viewer** icon.

TIP: If you want to change the way the information in the Clipboard Viewer is displayed, you can adjust it by clicking on the **Display** menu and then clicking on the **Render** menu choice. The **Render** menu choice lets you decide how you want your information to be displayed in your file. For example, you might have some text that you would rather display as a bit map.

Using the OS/2 Warp Clipboard

The OS/2 Warp clipboard is used to share information between DOS, OS/2, and Windows programs. You can copy or cut information from one program, and the information waits in the clipboard until you are ready to paste it into another program.

You can cut and copy almost anything from text to graphics and, in some cases, even sounds. Sometimes when you try to view some of these items, especially graphics or sounds, you might not see anything or you might get an error message. One reason for this is that you can't see sounds; another reason is that the graphic might not be recognized by the clipboard as a bit map. That's OK—even if it is not displayed in the Clipboard Viewer, you can try to paste it.

TIP: Before you cut or copy information between DOS, Windows, and OS/2 Warp programs, be sure that your clipboard is set to public. Public simply means that the information can be shared by all programs designed to handle cut, copy, and paste options. To find out how to set your clipboard to public, see Chapter 14, "Making Clipboards Public or Private" on page 107.

To copy or cut information:
1. Mark the information you want to copy or cut:
   a. Point to the beginning of the text or graphics you want to copy or cut.
   b. Press and hold mouse button 1.
   c. Drag the mark to the end of the text or graphics you want to copy or cut.
   d. Release mouse button 1. The information is marked.
2. Click mouse button 1 on the **Edit** menu.
3. Click mouse button 1 on either the **Copy** or **Cut** menu choice.

To paste the information from the clipboard:
1. Double-click on the data file where you want to put the information.
2. Point to where you want the information to appear, and click mouse button 1.
3. Click mouse button 1 on the **Edit** menu.
4. Click mouse button 1 on the **Paste** menu choice.

Using the WIN-OS/2 Clipboard

To use the WIN-OS/2 clipboard rather than the OS/2 Warp clipboard, you have to set the WIN-OS/2 clipboard to private so that information is only exchanged between WIN-OS/2 and Windows programs. To find out how to change the WIN-OS/2 clipboard setting to private, see "Changing a WIN-OS/2 Clipboard to Private" on page 110.

To use the cut, copy, and paste features for Windows programs, refer to the information that comes with the program.

Icon Editor

Use the Icon Editor to create, edit, and convert image files into icons, bit maps, or pointers. Icons and pointers are really *bit maps*. A bit map is made up of a series of dots. You can make your own icons and use them on the Desktop. This is great if you become bored with the ones that came with OS/2 Warp or you just want to express yourself with new icons for the files and programs you add to the Desktop.

 To start the Icon Editor, double-click on **OS/2 System**, **Productivity**, and then **Icon Editor**.

Touring the Icon Editor

Before you begin creating and editing your own icons, let's spend a few minutes touring the Icon Editor.

The Icon Editor has a Work area, a Color palette, and a Status area. The Work area provides a place to make your creations and the Color palette provides a selection of colors that you can use to make your creations. The Status area provides information about your creation as follows:

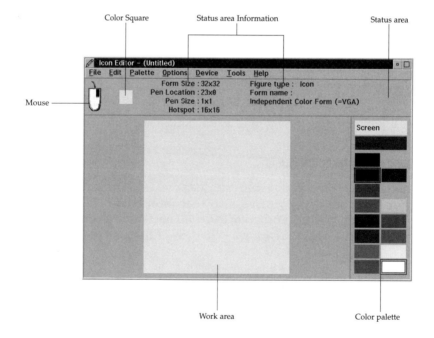

Mouse
> Shows you what colors are assigned to each mouse button.

Color Square
> Shows you what the final creation looks like.

Status area information
> Provides status area information. This information includes the form size (or grid size), the location of the pointer (pen) within the grid, the pen size, the place (hot spot) where the mouse will be active on an icon or pointer, the type of figure you are creating (icon, pointer, or bit map), and the type of resolution that the image is created for.

Creating an Icon

Now that you have a little background, you will learn how to create an icon that you can use in place of the one that exists for the Games folder. The following procedures might appear to be difficult because there are so many steps, but stick with it—it's really very simple. After you follow the steps once, you will be well on your way to being an icon artist.

To create a new icon that looks like a tic-tac-toe game:
1. Double-click on the Icon Editor.
2. Click mouse button 1 on the **File** menu.
3. Click mouse button 1 on the **New** menu choice.
4. When the New figure window is displayed, click mouse button 1 on the **Icon** choice.
5. Click on the **OK** push button.

To make a blue background for your tic-tac-toe icon:
1. Click mouse button 1 on the **Tools** menu.
2. Click mouse button 1 on the **Color fill** menu choice so that when you click on something in the Work area, it will fill the entire area.
3. Move the mouse pointer to the Color palette.
4. Click mouse button 1 on the dark blue square.
5. Move the mouse pointer over the Work area, and click mouse button. Notice that the Mouse (located in the Status area) has assigned dark blue to mouse button 1. Mouse button 1 will remain dark blue until you use mouse button 1 for another color. (You can use either mouse button 1 or mouse button 2 to select colors.)

To create the game board for your tic-tac-toe icon:

1. Click mouse button 1 on each of the following:
   a. The **Tools** menu.
   b. The **Color fill** menu choice. (If you don't do this, the Color fill choice will continue to be in effect and you will just keep switching background colors.)
   c. The **Options** menu.
   d. The **Grid** menu choice. (This places a grid over the work area and makes it a bit easier to see what you are doing.)
   e. The **Options** menu.
   f. The **Draw straight** menu choice.
   g. The **Options** menu.
   h. The **Pen size** menu choice.
   i. The **2x2** menu choice. (This changes the size of the pen.)
2. Move the mouse pointer to the Color palette.
3. Click mouse button 1 on the yellow square.
4. Move the mouse pointer over the Work area. (The mouse pointer changes to a square.) Watch the Pen Location in the Status area change until it reads: **Pen Location: 10x25.**
5. Press and hold mouse button 1. Then, drag the mouse pointer (square) down until the Pen Location in the Status area changes to **Pen Location: 10x5.**
6. Release mouse button 1. You should have a straight yellow line on the left side of the Work area.
7. Move the mouse pointer to **Pen Location: 22x25.**
8. Press and hold mouse button 1. Then, drag the mouse pointer (square) down until the Pen Location in the Status area changes to **Pen Location: 22x5.**
9. Release mouse button 1. You should have a straight yellow line on the right side of the Work area.
10. Move the mouse pointer to **Pen Location: 3x20.**
11. Press and hold mouse button 1. Then, drag the mouse pointer (square) to the right until the Pen Location in the Status area changes to **Pen Location: 29x20.**
12. Release mouse button 1. You should have a straight yellow line that runs horizontally and intersects with both yellow lines you drew on the left and right side of the Work area.
13. Move the mouse pointer to **Pen Location: 3x10.**
14. Press and hold mouse button 1. Then, drag the mouse pointer (square) to the right until the Pen Location in the Status area changes to **Pen Location: 29x10.**
15. Release mouse button 1. You should have a straight yellow line that runs parallel to the first one you drew and a completed tic-tac-toe board.

To create an O for the game board for your tic-tac-toe icon:

1. Click mouse button 1 on each of the following:
   a. The **Options** menu.
   b. The **Draw Straight** menu choice. (This deselects the Draw Straight choice.)
   c. The **Options** menu.
   d. The **Pen size** menu choice.
   e. The **1x1** menu choice. (This changes the size of the pen to a smaller size.)
   f. The **Edit** menu.
   g. The **Select** menu choice.
2. Move the mouse pointer over the Work area. Watch the Pen location in the Status area change until it reads: **Pen location: 4x26.** When you press the mouse button, the Pen location will change to Selection size in the Status area.
3. Press and hold mouse button 1. Then, drag the mouse pointer (square) down and to the right until the Selection size in the Status area changes to **Selection size: 4x4.**
4. Release mouse button 1. You have created a selection box.
5. Move the mouse pointer to the Color palette.
6. Click mouse button 1 on the white square.
7. Click mouse button 1 on each of the following:
   a. The **Edit** menu.
   b. The **Circle** menu choice. (An O is displayed in the upper-left corner of the game board.)

To copy the O to another location:

1. Click mouse button 1 on each of the following:
   a. The **Edit** menu.
   b. The **Select** menu choice. (An O is displayed with a selection box around it, indicating that it is selected.)
   c. The **Edit** menu.
   d. The **Copy** menu choice.
   e. The **Edit** menu.
   f. The **Paste** menu choice.
2. Point to the selection box.
3. Press and hold mouse button 1 to drag the selection box to the center of the game board.
4. Release mouse button 1. (An O is displayed in the center of the game board.)

5. Repeat steps f. through 4. to place an O in the lower-right corner of the game board. You should now have three Os diagonally across the game board.

To create an X for the game board for your tic-tac-toe icon:
1. Move the mouse pointer to the Color palette area.
2. Click mouse button 1 on the light green box. (The Mouse in the Status area should show that mouse button 1 is assigned to light green.)
3. Click mouse button 2 on the dark blue box. (The Mouse in the Status area should show that mouse button 2 is assigned to dark blue.)
4. Move the mouse pointer over the top center area of the game board until the Pen location is at 13x25, and click mouse button 1.

   (The following steps are repetitious but are included to help you locate the coordinates you need to create the X.)

5. Move the mouse pointer over the top center area of the game board until the Pen location is at 14x24, and click mouse button 1.
6. Move the mouse pointer over the top center area of the game board until the Pen location is at 15x23, and click mouse button 1.
7. Move the mouse pointer over the top center area of the game board until the Pen location is at 16x22, and click mouse button 1.
8. Move the mouse pointer over the top center area of the game board until the Pen location is at 17x21, and click mouse button 1.
9. Move the mouse pointer over the top center area of the game board until the Pen location is at 14x22, and click mouse button 1.
10. Move the mouse pointer over the top center area of the game board until the Pen location is at 13x21, and click mouse button 1.
11. Move the mouse pointer over the top center area of the game board until the Pen location is at 16x24, and click mouse button 1.
12. Move the mouse pointer over the top center area of the game board until the Pen location is at 17x25, and click mouse button 1.

You should now have an X in the top center of the game board.

To copy the X to another location:
1. Click mouse button 1 on the **Edit** menu.
2. Click mouse button 1 on the **Select** menu choice. The mouse pointer is displayed as a cross-hair.
3. Move the cross-hair to a corner of the X. Then, press and hold mouse button 1 and drag the cross-hair to the opposite corner of the X.
4. Release the mouse button.

5. Click mouse button 1 on each of the following:
   a. The **Edit** menu.
   b. The **Copy** menu choice.
   c. The **Edit** menu.
   d. The **Paste** menu choice.
6. Point to the selection box.
7. Press and hold mouse button 1 to drag the selection square to the lower-left corner of the game board.
8. Release mouse button 1. (An X is displayed in the lower-left corner of the game board.)
9. Repeat steps d. through 8. to add another X in the lower center area of the game board.

To save your tic-tac-toe icon:
1. Double-click on the title-bar icon of the open window to close it.
2. Click mouse button 1 on the **Yes** push button to save the file.
3. Click mouse button 1 on the **Save as filename** field.
4. Press the Delete or Backspace Key to erase the field.
5. Type **TICTAC.ICO**, and then click mouse button 1 on the **Save** push button. (The Save Options window is displayed.)
6. Click mouse button 1 on the **2.0** choice.
7. Click mouse button 1 on the **Save** push button.

You can use the tic-tac-toe game icon to replace the Games icon that came with your system, as follows:
1. Double-click on the **OS/2 System** icon.
2. Move the mouse pointer to the **Games** icon.
3. Click mouse button 2 to display the pop-up menu.
4. Click mouse button 1 on the **Settings** menu choice.
5. Click mouse button 1 on the **General** notebook tab.
6. Click mouse button 1 on the **Find** push button. (The Find window is displayed.)
7. Type **TICTAC.ICO** in the **Name** field.
8. Click mouse button 1 on the **Find** push button. (A window is displayed with the icon you just created.)
9. Click mouse button 1 on the **OK** push button. (The new icon is displayed in the **Current icon** field.)

10. Double-click on the title-bar icon of the notebook to close it. The Games icon changes to the tic-tac-toe icon you created.

TIP: If you plan to create lots of icons, you might find it useful to create a folder icon to store them in.

Menu Choices

This section describes each menu with its corresponding choices and what they can be used for. Use the following list as a reference to help you when you are using the Icon Editor.

Menu	Choices	
File	New	Lets you create a new icon (.ICO), pointer (.PTR), or bit map (.BMP) file, which is called *untitled* until you save it and give it a name.
	Open	Lets you start working with an .ICO, .PTR, or .BMP file that was already created.
	Save	Lets you save an .ICO, .PTR, or .BMP file and keep it in the window so that you can continue to edit the file. The file must have a name in order for you to save it.
	Save as	Lets you name and save a new .ICO, .PTR or .BMP file, or lets you give an existing file a new name or save the file in a different path or directory or to another disk.
	Next	Lets you open the next .ICO, .PTR, .BMP file in the File list specified from the command line. (This choice can be used only when Icon Editor is started from a command prompt and more than one file is specified.)
Edit	Undo	Removes the last change you made to the figure in the work area.
	Cut	Removes a selected portion of the figure and places it in the clipboard.
	Copy	Copies a selected portion of the figure from the work area and places it in the clipboard.
	Paste	Inserts a selected portion of the figure from the clipboard into the file you are working with at the position of the cursor.

Menu	Choices	
Edit	Clear	Deletes a selected portion of the figure from the file.
	Select	Marks a portion of the figure in the file.
	Select all	Marks all of the figure in the file.
	Stretch paste	Attaches the contents of the clipboard to the current figure, positioned to fit the selected portion of the figure.
	Fill	Colors the selected portion of the figure.
	Flip horizontal	Turns the figure from left to right.
	Flip vertical	Turns the figure from top to bottom.
	Circle	Draws a circle or ellipse within the selected portion of the figure.
Palette	Load Default Palette	Resets palette colors to default.
	Open	Lets you start working with a palette (.PAL) file that was already created.
	Save	Lets you save a .PAL file and keep it in the window so that you can continue to edit the file. The .PAL file must have a name in order for you to save it.
	Save as	Lets you name and save a .PAL file, or lets you give an existing .PAL file a new name or save the .PAL file in a different path, or directory, or to another disk.
	Edit color	Lets you change a color in the Color palette.
	Swap color	Swaps the left mouse button color with the right mouse button color.
	Set default palette	Copies the current palette to the corresponding predefined palette.
Options	Test	Changes the pointer to look like the system pointer or the icon you are designing.
	Grid	Displays vertical and horizontal lines in the work area.

Menu	Choices	
Option	X background	Draws Xs in all areas of the figure that are the screen color or inverse screen color. (This choice is not available for bit maps.)
	Draw straight	Enables the pointer so that it draws only horizontal or vertical lines.
	Pen size	Lets you select the size of the pen you want to draw with.
	Preferences	Lets you specify the settings for the editor.
	Set pen shape	Makes the pen shape equal to the selected area.
	Hotspot	Lets you specify where the mouse is active on an icon or pointer. (This choice is not available for bit maps.)
Device	List	Lets you look at a list of displays that you can create figures for.
	Edit predefined	Lets you set the size of the icon, pointer, bit map, device, or resolution.
Tools	Color fill	Lets you fill a portion of the figure with the color specified on the mouse button.
	Find color	Lets you locate a color in the palette that is used in your figure.

OS/2 System Editor

You can use the OS/2 System Editor to create and edit text files. The System Editor is a basic editor that lets you work on one file at a time in a window. You cannot use it to edit multiple files from within one window. However, you can run several copies of the System Editor and edit a file in each System Editor window you open.

 The System Editor can be useful if you do not have a text editor or word processor and you want to compose a note, letter, or memo. Even though it is a basic editor, you will be able to get by for a while without rushing out to buy some fancy word processor.

Using the OS/2 System Editor

You can follow the instructions that appear below to begin using the OS/2 System Editor.

To open the System Editor, double-click on **OS/2 System**, **Productivity**, and then **System Editor.** The System Editor window is displayed. You can begin composing that note, letter, or memo. When you are finished, you can close the System Editor and save the file at the same time.

To close the System Editor and save the file:
1. Double-click on the title-bar icon of the System Editor window to close it.
2. Click mouse button 1 on the **Save** or **Save as** push button.
3. Type the name you want to use for the file in the **Filename** field. (If you want to save the file in a certain directory on a specific drive, you must include that information when you name the file. For example, to save a file named "Sample.txt" to the OS/2 directory on your C drive, you would type **C:\OS2\SAMPLE.TXT**)
4. Click mouse button 1 on the **Save** push button.

As mentioned, the System Editor is a basic editor and is not able to open several files in one window. However, if you plan to use the System Editor often, you might want to set it up so that each time you click on the System Editor icon, it opens a new window.

To set up the System Editor to open a new window:
1. Double-click on the **OS/2 System** icon.
2. Double-click on the **Productivity** icon.
3. Move the mouse pointer to the **System Editor** icon.
4. Click mouse button 2 to display the pop-up menu.
5. Click mouse button 1 on the **Settings** menu choice.
6. Click mouse button 1 on the **Window** notebook tab.
7. Click mouse button 1 on the **Create new window** choice in the **Object open behavior** area. (This displays another System Editor window on top of the window you originally opened.)
8. Double-click on the title-bar icon of the notebook to close it.

Menu Choices

This section describes each menu with its corresponding choices and what they can be used for. Use the following list as a reference to help you when you are using the System Editor.

Menu	Choices	
File	New	Lets you start creating a new file, which is called untitled until you save it and give it a name.
	Open	Lets you start working with a file that was already created.
	Save	Lets you save a file and keep the text in the window so that you can continue to edit the file. The file must have a name in order for you to save it.
	Save as	Lets you name and save a new file or lets you give an existing file a new name or save the file in a different path or directory or to another disk.
	Autosave	Lets you have your file saved automatically each time you type a specified number of characters. The file must have a name in order for you to use Autosave.
Edit	Undo	Removes the last change you made to the text in the edit window.
	Cut	Removes selected text from the edit window and places it in the clipboard.
	Copy	Copies selected text from the edit window and places it in the clipboard.
	Paste	Inserts text from the clipboard into the file you are working with at the position of the cursor.
	Clear	Deletes selected text from the file.
	Find	Locates specified text within the file.
	Select all	Marks all of the text in the file.

TIP: You can mark selected text easily. Move the mouse pointer to the text you want to mark, and then click mouse button 1. Press and hold down mouse button 1 while dragging the mouse pointer over the area of text you want to mark. Release button 1 when you have finished marking the area of text.

Options	Set font	Lets you change the font of the text displayed in the edit window.

Menu	Choices	
Options	Set colors	Lets you change the colors for the background and text in the edit window.
	Word wrap	Determines the way text is displayed in the edit window. Word wrap is not a tool to help you format text for a final paper. When Word wrap is set to On, the text is displayed wrapped in the window but is not saved that way. When Word wrap is set to Off, the text will continue scrolling to the right until you have reached the 32K characters-per-line limit. You could basically type your whole file on one line.
		If you plan to have formatted text, press the Enter key when you determine where the end of the line should be.

Enhanced Editor

You can use the Enhanced Editor to create and edit text files. It is similar to the System Editor except that it has more features. You can work on multiple files in one window at the same time, calculate equations, check spelling, and more.

The Enhanced Editor also has some very good online help information, which goes to the trouble of explaining how to create REXX macros, along with the basics.

Using the Enhanced Editor

You can follow the instructions that appear below to begin using the Enhanced Editor.

To open the Enhanced Editor, double-click on **OS/2 System**, **Productivity**, and then **Enhanced Editor**. The Enhanced Editor window is displayed. You can begin editing. When you are finished, you can close the Enhanced Editor and save the file at the same time.

To close the Enhanced Editor and save the file:
1. Double-click on the title-bar icon of the Enhanced Editor window to close it.
2. Click mouse button 1 on the **Save** or **Save as** push button.
3. Type the name you want to use for the file in the **Filename** field. (If you want to save the file in a certain directory on a specific drive, you must include that information when you name the file. For example, to save a file named "Sample.txt" to the OS/2 directory on your C drive, you would type **C:\OS2\SAMPLE.TXT**)
4. Click mouse button 1 on the **Save** push button.

As mentioned, the Enhanced Editor is a very functional editor. You can work with multiple files in one window. You only need to change a few settings to do this.

Working with multiple files in the Enhanced Editor:

1. Double-click on the **OS/2 System** icon.
2. Double-click on the **Productivity** icon.
3. Double-click on the **Enhanced Editor** icon.
4. Click mouse button 1 on the **File** menu.
5. Click mouse button 1 on the **Open** menu choice.
6. Open a file to work with by entering its name in the entry field or selecting it from the list.
7. Click mouse button 1 on **OK**
8. When the file is opened, click mouse button 1 on the **Options** menu.
9. Click mouse button 1 on the arrow to the right of the **Preferences** menu choice.
10. Click mouse button 1 on the **Ring enabled** menu choice. Selecting this choice creates a *ring* that allows you to move forward and backward through the files you add to the window.
11. Click mouse button 1 on the **File** menu.
12. Click mouse button 1 on the **Add file** menu choice.

   NOTE: If you do not use the **Add file** menu choice, another Enhanced Editor window will be opened each time you open a new or existing file. (This is done automatically and does not have to be set up).

13. Open another file that you want to work with by entering its name in the entry field or selecting it from the list.
14. Click mouse button 1 on **OK**. The file you selected is added to the window.
15. Repeat steps 5 through 7 to open the remaining files you want to work with.

To move forward and backward through the files, click mouse button 1 on the *rotate button* in the upper-right hand corner of the window next to the title bar.

Menu Choices

The Enhanced Editor has a status area located at the bottom of the window just below the horizontal scroll bar. This status area gives you a brief explanation of the menu choices that are available. It also provides information about where you are in the files or which file in the ring you are working on.

This section describes each menu with its corresponding choices and what they can be used for. Use the following list as a reference to help you when you are using the Enhanced Editor.

Menu	Choices	
File	**New**	Lets you replace the current file with an empty .Untitled file.
	Open.Untitled	Lets you open a new, empty edit window.
	Open	Lets you open a file in a new window.
	Import text file	Lets you copy the contents of an existing text file into the text file in which you are currently working.
	Add file	Lets you add another text file to the active Enhanced Editor window.
	Rename	Lets you change the name of the current file.
	Save	Lets you save a file and keep the text in the window so that you can continue to edit the file. The file must have a name in order for you to save it.
	Save as	Lets you name and save a new file or lets you give an existing file a new name or save the file in a different path or directory or to another disk.
	Save and quit	Lets you save the current file and then quit.
	Quit	Lets you quit the file without saving it.
	Print	Lets you print your document.
Edit	**Undo line**	Removes changes to the current line.
	Undo	Activates the Undo/Redo window, which steps you through the changes you have made to a file.
	Copy	Copies marked text from the edit window and places it in the clipboard.
	Cut	Removes marked text from the edit window and places it in the clipboard.
	Paste	Inserts text from the clipboard into the file you are working with at the position of the cursor.
	Paste lines	Pastes text from the clipboard as new lines.
	Paste block	Pastes text from the clipboard as a rectangular block.

Menu	Choices	
Edit	Style	Changes the font style for marked text within the document.
	Copy mark	Copies marked text to the location of the cursor.
	Move mark	Moves marked text to the location of the cursor.
	Overlay mark	Moves marked text to the location of the cursor and replaces the text that follows the cursor.
	Adjust mark	Fills in the space where marked text was moved from.
	Unmark	Removes the mark from marked text.
	Delete mark	Deletes marked text.
	Print mark	Prints only marked text.

TIP: You can mark selected text easily. Move the mouse pointer to the text you want to mark, and then click mouse button 1. Press and hold down mouse button 1 while dragging the mouse pointer over the area of text you want to mark. Release button 1 when you have finished marking the area of text.

Menu	Choices	
Search	Search	Searches for text within the file in which you are working.
	Find next	Repeats the previous search specification.
	Change next	Repeats the previous change command.
	Bookmarks	Sets, deletes, or goes to a bookmark.
Options	Preferences	Gives you additional choices that let you customize the editor. (It is here that you find the **Ring enabled** choice.)
	Autosave	Lets you view the autosave value and optionally lists the autosave directory.
	Messages	Lets you review previously displayed messages.
	Frame controls	Lets you turn the status line, message line, menu help, scroll bars, and rotate buttons on and off, as well as move the status and message lines to the top or bottom of the window.

Menu	Choices	
Options	Save options	Sets the menu choices you made in the Options menu as the default.
Command	Command dialog	
		Displays a window in which you can type a command for the editor or OS/2 Warp.
	Halt command	Stops a command that is already processing.

Picture Viewer

The Picture Viewer displays metafiles (.MET), picture interchange format (.PIF) files, and spooler (.SPL) files. A .MET file contains a series of attributes that set color, shape, and size, usually of a picture or drawing. Using a program that can interpret these attributes, you can view the assembled image. A .PIF file uses a file format that is compatible with many graphics programs. The file format enables picture files to be exchanged between graphics programs. A .SPL file contains files that you have sent to your printer.

Probably one of the best reasons for using the Picture Viewer is to view spooler files. You can look at the files and decide which print jobs you want to cancel.

Using the Picture Viewer

You can follow the instructions that appear below to begin using the Picture Viewer.

To view print jobs with the Picture Viewer:

1. Double-click on the printer icon where you sent your files. (You will see all the print jobs waiting in the queue to be printed. The files in the print queue are .SPL files.)

2. Point to the title-bar icon in the upper-left corner of the printer window.

3. Click mouse button 2 to display the pop-up menu.

4. Click mouse button 1 on the arrow to the right of the **Change status** menu choice.

5. Click mouse button 1 on the **Hold** menu choice. (This keeps the files in the printer window from printing.)

6. Double-click on any of the files displayed in the printer window. The file you select will be displayed in the Picture Viewer window.

Menu Choices

This section describes each menu with its corresponding choices and what they can be used for. Use the following list as a reference to help you when you are using the Picture Viewer.

Menu	Choices	
File	**Open**	Displays .MET, .PIF, and .SPL files in the Picture Viewer window.
	Save as	Lets you save the files you are working with in the Picture Viewer window.
	Print	Lets you print the contents of the files you are working with.
	Cut	Lets you remove information from the file and place it in the clipboard for future use.
	Copy	Lets you copy information from the file and place it in the clipboard for future use.
	Paste	Lets you paste information that was previously placed in the clipboard into the file you are working with.
Page	**Forward**	Lets you move ahead through the pages of a multipage .SPL file.
	Backward	Lets you move back through the pages of a multipage .SPL file.
	Go to page	Lets you go to a specific page in a multipage .SPL file.
Options	**Fit picture in window**	Displays a picture within the boundaries of the window.
	Fit page in window	Displays the picture within the boundaries set when the picture was created.
	Default Background	Displays the picture on the Picture Viewer background color.
	Black background	Displays the picture on a black background.

Menu	Choices	
Options	Code page	Sets the code page to the country of origin for a .PIF file before you display the file in the window.
Sequence	Next picture	Displays the next picture in a sequence of pictures.
	Quit sequence	Cancels a sequence of pictures.

TIP: You can zoom in or zoom out of a picture after it is displayed. Move the mouse pointer over the part of the picture you want to zoom in on, and then double-click on it.

Pulse

Pulse is a system monitor. It lets you observe a graphic representation of how different activities affect the computer and how much processor power is still available for other programs. In other words, Pulse is like an EKG—you can use it to see the heartbeat of your computer. When the line jumps to the top of the screen, the computer is working very hard. When the line is near the bottom of the screen, the computer is not working too hard.

Use Pulse when you want to see how hard your computer is working.

Using Pulse

You can follow the instructions that appear below to begin using Pulse.

To start Pulse, double-click on **OS/2 System**, **Productivity**, and then **Pulse**.

You might want to change the colors for the Pulse window and graph displayed. This might make it easier for you to see what is going on.

NOTE: If you change the colors or schemes for OS/2 Warp, the changes do not affect Pulse.

To change the background color of the Pulse window:
1. Double-click on the **Pulse** icon.
2. Click mouse button 1 on the **Options** menu.
3. Click mouse button 1 on the arrow to the right of the **Background color** menu choice.
4. Click mouse button 1 on the color you would like to see in the background of the Pulse window.

Now that you have changed the background color, you might not be able to see the graph color very well. You can change the color for the graph line.

To change the graph line color for Pulse:
1. Double-click on the **Pulse** icon.
2. Click mouse button 1 on the **Options** menu.
3. Click mouse button 1 on the **Graph color** menu item.
4. Click mouse button 1 on the color you would like to use for the graph line.

Menu Choices

This section describes additional menu choices with their corresponding choices and what they can be used for. Use the following list as a reference to help you when you are using Pulse.

Smooth
> Creates a smooth, more even graph line without showing drastic spikes in usage.

Centered
> Makes it easier for you to see up-to-the-second activity so that you won't have to wait until the graph line moves away from the edge of the window.

Freeze screen
> Stops the pulse from moving across the window so that you can examine a particularly interesting spike or lull.

Fill
> Colors in the area under the graph line from the bottom up so that it's easier to see the activity.

Seek and Scan Files

 Use the Seek and Scan Files program to quickly search one or more disks for files or text. When a file match is found, it is displayed in a selection list. You can select a file name or a program name from the list, and then open that file or run that program.

Using Seek and Scan Files

You can follow the instructions that appear below to begin using Seek and Scan Files.

To search for files:

1. Double-click on the **OS/2 System** icon.
2. Double-click on the **Productivity** icon.
3. Double-click on the **Seek and Scan Files** icon. (A window is displayed that has search specification input and output fields.)
4. Click mouse button 1 on any of the fields you want to change. You can change the following fields:

   File names to search for
   > Type the name of the file you want to search for. (This field is optional if you intend to use the **Text to search for** field. You can use both fields to narrow down the search specifications.)

   Text to search for (if any)
   > Type the text string you want to search for. (This field is optional if you intend to use the **File names to search for** field. You can use both fields to narrow down the search specifications.)

   Editor filespec
   > Displays the name of the program file for the editor program that will be used to display the file or text you search for. The default editor for OS/2 Warp is the System Editor. (E.EXE is the name of the program file that starts the System Editor. Type a different name if you want to use another editor.)

   Files found
   > Displays the results of the search in a list of directory paths and file names for the file or text. This field does not require any input from you.

   Drives to search
   > Lets you choose which drives you want to search. This Field is not optional; something must be selected so that Seek and Scan can conduct a search.

5. Click mouse button 1 on the **Search** push button to start searching the drives for the specified file or text. When a match is found, the names are listed in the **Files found** field. You can also use the following push buttons:

   Stop
   > Cancels a search in progress.

   Open
   > Opens a file you select in the **Files found** field and displays it in the editor specified in the **Editor filespec** field.

TIP: You can use the * character to broaden the search if you can't remember the exact name you want to search for. The following shows you some examples of how to use this character to search for a file called LSR.TXT:

- **L*.TXT** searches for all text files that begin with L and have .TXT for an extension.

- ***.TXT** searches for all files with the .TXT extension.

- **LSR.*** searches for all files with the name LSR and any extension.

You can use the **?** character in place of any single character within a file name.

Menu Choices

This section describes each menu with its corresponding choices and what they can be used for. Use the following list as a reference to help you when you are using Seek and Scan Files.

Menu	Choices	
File	**Save**	Lets you store the current file name from the **Files found** field with the same name.
	Save as	Lets you store the current file name from the **Files found** field with a different name.
Selected	**Open**	Lets you open a file you select from the **Files found** field and display it in the editor program specified in the **Editor filespec** field.
	Process	Lets you start a program you select from a list of program files in the **Files found** field. Program files have a three-character extension (typically .EXE, .BAT, or .COM).
	Command	Lets you type a command (for example, copy, move, or rename) that you can use on one of the files you select from the **Files found** field.
Edit	**Copy**	Lets you copy files you select from the **Files found** field.
	Clear list	Lets you clear the list of files displayed in the **Files found** field.
Options	**Search subdirectories**	Searches all the subdirectories of the drives you selected in the **Drives to search** field.

Menu	Choices	
File	**Display found text**	
		Displays the text you are looking for with the name of the file and directory path in the **Files found** field.
	Ignore case	Searches for everything regardless of whether the text is in uppercase or lowercase.
	Clear on search	Clears the **Files found** field each time you begin a new search.
	Set default	Saves the choices you made on the Options menu and the editor program you specified in the **Editor filespec** field as the default for the next time you use Seek and Scan Files.

Chapter 22

Using the Games Programs

Games - Icon View

Mahjongg Solitaire   OS/2 Chess   Solitaire - Klondike

The **Games** icon includes three popular games—Solitaire, Chess, and Mahjongg. These games are provided for your enjoyment, but playing them is also a great way to become familiar with using OS/2 Warp.

This chapter describes the object of each game and its rules. You might be familiar with how to play Solitaire, Chess, and Mahjongg, but there might be a thing or two you want to know before you play the computerized versions of these games. These games are very similar to their traditional counterparts. If you are already familiar with how to play them, you might be able to jump right in and start playing. If you are not familiar with them or you just want to know a little more, you have come to the right place.

To open a game, double-click on **OS/2 System**, and on **Games**, and then double-click on the game you want to play.

Klondike Solitaire

The game of Solitaire has been around so long it is practically impossible to pinpoint its exact origin. Documented existence of the game started turning up in the early 1800's. Though there are many variations of the game, Klondike Solitaire is the most popular, yet it is probably one of the hardest to win.

Object of the Game

The object of this game is to find the aces in the deck of cards and build on them to form a stack that includes all cards in a suit. You place cards of the same suit on top of the aces in ascending order. You use the mouse to move the cards from place to place.

Rules of the Game

Before you begin playing a game of Solitaire, it's a good idea to know a few of the rules. The following is a summary of rules for Klondike Solitaire.

- Play cards on the seven columns in descending order (starting with a King and working your way down to a two) using opposite colors to build. For example, if you start with a red King, the next card should be a black Queen, then a red Jack, and so on.

- Build on the aces by suit. For example, if you start with the ace of hearts, you would then build with the two of hearts, then the three of hearts, and so on.

- You can fill empty spaces with a King only.

- You can move a card to the ace stacks by double-clicking on the card you want to move.

Playing the Game

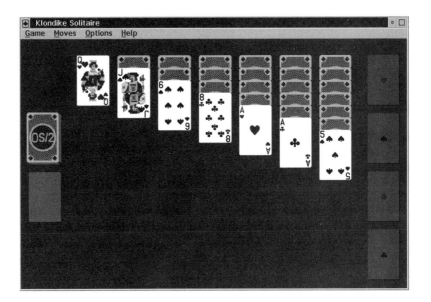

Each time a new game of Klondike Solitaire is dealt, the cards are arranged across the game board in seven columns. Start by looking for cards that can be moved to a column right away and make as many moves as possible before requesting more cards from the deck. Place cards in descending order, using opposite colors to build the column. (For example, you would move a black 9 to a red 10). Use the mouse to drag the cards you want to move. As soon as you see an ace, move it immediately to its corresponding stack on the right side of the game board. This lets you start building the ace stacks, giving you additional move options. Ace stacks are built with cards of the same suit as the ace.

Whenever you remove all the cards from a column, there will be a blank space. Use a King or a King with its attached row of cards to fill in the blank space. Each upturned row can be moved to another column, as long as the bottom card in the upturned row is the opposite color and the next card (in descending order) to the top card in the new column. When an upturned column is moved to another column, a card remains that is face down. Turn the card over by clicking on it, and then continue playing.

When you have made all the moves you can possibly make with the original deal, it's time to move to the remainder of the deck. Click on the top card on the deck to turn over more cards. (The number of cards that are turned over is based on a selection you make with the **Variations** menu choice located under the **Options** menu.) Try to play the top card by moving it to one of the columns. If you can play the top card, then go ahead to the one beneath it and continue play. If you cannot play a card from the deck, click on the deck again to display additional cards. Continue to turn over cards, moving cards from the rows and columns, until you can move no more.

The game is finished when you have been through the deck as many times as allowed and no further plays are possible. If you have managed to build all the ace stacks in ascending order and there are no cards left on the columns, you WIN!

Menu Choices

Klondike Solitaire has menu choices that let you set up the game, cheat at a game, and change the appearance of the game board. Use the following list as a reference to help you when you are playing Klondike Solitaire:

Menu	Choices	
Game	New	Starts a new game.
	Autoplay	Starts an automatic demonstration of how the game is played.
Moves	Take back	Lets you undo your last move.
	Replay	Lets you replay the move you just took back.
	Cheat	Lets you make an illegal move on columns only.
	Auto finish	Lets you have the computer finish the game after all the cards have been turned face up.
Options	Colors	Lets you select from a set of predefined color schemes or create your own.

Menu	Choices	
Options	Sound	Lets you turn warning beeps off and on. A check mark is displayed next to this choice to indicate when it is on.
	Score	Lets you show, hide, or reset the score.
	Time	Shows the time elapsed since the game was started.
	Drag cards	Lets you choose how you want the cards to be displayed while you are dragging them. If a check mark is displayed next to this choice, you will see the actual card being dragged. If the check mark is not displayed next to this choice, the pointer turns to a little card while it is being dragged.
	Variations	Lets you specify the rules for the game based on the draw of the deck.
	Animation	Lets you specify how fast you want the cards to move while you are playing the game.
	Card back	Lets you choose one of nine images for the back of the deck of cards you are playing with.
	Save options	Lets you save any of the options you have changed so that they become the initial settings for the next time you play the game.
	Load options	Restores the last saved options.

OS/2 Chess

Chess is probably one of the most popular board games in the world. It originated in India thousands of years ago. Originally, the idea behind Chess was to simulate two Indian armies at war. Eventually, the Persians came along and made some changes to the game and its rules. These changes spread to the rest of the world, resulting in the game and the rules we know today.

Object of the Game

The object of the game is to place your opponent's king in check (threaten the king with capture). If your opponent can't move his or her king out of check, then the king is in checkmate and you WIN!

With OS/2 Chess, you can play a game of chess against another person on the same computer or on a network workstation. You also can play against the computer.

Rules of the Game

Chess is a challenging game of wit and strategy. Before you begin to play, you should start with some of the basic rules. The following is a summary of rules for the game of Chess.

- There must be two players to lead the two armies—one to claim black and one to claim white.

- Each player starts with a 16-piece army, which is made up of one King, one Queen, two Rooks, two Bishops, two Knights, and eight Pawns.

- The White player always goes first, and then moves alternate between the Black and the White player.

- Only one piece can be moved per turn, except in the case of *castling*. To find out more about castling, read "Castling" on page 213.

- Only the Knight is permitted to jump other pieces when it moves.

- You can capture only pieces of the opposite color.

- It is illegal to move another piece while your King is in check. You must move your King out of check before you can move another piece.

- If your King is placed in check, you must move it out of check on your next move.

- If you can't move your King out of check, then you are in checkmate and the game is over.

- If the game has no winner, it is considered a *draw*. To find out more about the draw, read "The Draw" on page 214.

- The game can be considered to be over if a player does not make a certain number of moves within a predetermined time limit. This rule is generally followed in tournament chess matches.

The following is a summary of rules for moving the game pieces:

Pawn

Each player starts the game with eight pawns worth only 1 point each. The Pawn can move forward only one square at a time, with the exception of the first move, when a Pawn is permitted to advance up to two squares. Your Pawn can capture an opponent's piece only when that piece is located along adjacent diagonal squares from where your Pawn is located (except when using the en passant rule). A Pawn can't move to an occupied square directly in front of it.

Rook

Each player starts the game with two Rooks worth 5 points each. A Rook can be moved in straight rows and columns only. The Rook can become more powerful near the end of the game when there are fewer pieces on the board, because of its mobility. Remember, the Rook is used for the special move of castling.

Knight

Each player starts the game with two Knights worth 3 points each. The Knight moves in an L-shaped pattern, either up two squares and over one square or up one square and over two squares. The Knight is the only piece permitted to jump over another piece to reach its destination, but it doesn't capture jumped pieces. Knights can capture a piece only by landing on an occupied square.

Bishop

Each player starts the game with two Bishops worth 3 points each. The Bishop can be moved only in a diagonal path across the board. One Bishop moves on the white squares and the other on the black squares.

Queen

Each player starts the game with one Queen worth 9 points each. The Queen is the most powerful piece on the board because it can be moved in any direction along rows, columns, or diagonals. The Queen can move almost anywhere on the board as long as another piece does not get in its way.

King

Each player starts the game with one King worth 1 point. The King is considered the most important piece of the game even though its point value is low. The King can be moved only one square at a time, in any direction, provided that you do not place it in check. The only time a King can be moved more than one square is when you intend to try castling.

The following is a summary of some special moves:

Castling

Castling is a special move that you can use to protect your King when you think your opponent's army is closing in. The purpose is to move your King to a safer position on the board. This is the only move in which two pieces—the King and the Rook—can be moved at the same time. You move your King two squares to the left or to the right of its current location, depending on which Rook you intend to use for the move. The Rook is automatically moved to the opposite side of the King. The following restrictions apply when you are castling:

- This move can be used only once per game per player.

- The King and Rook you intend to use must not have been moved prior to castling.

- There must be no other pieces in between the King and Rook you intended to use.

- The King cannot be in check and cannot be moved through or to a space that would place it in check.

En Passant

The en passant rule is the strangest and rarest of the rules of chess. It is used only when a Pawn captures another Pawn. The en passant rule becomes active when your pawn is on its fifth row and your opponent's pawn, on the adjacent column, is moved from its second row to its fourth row. Only on your next move can you capture your opponent's pawn by moving diagonally on the opponent's column, even though there is no Pawn there.

Pawn Promotion

When your Pawn successfully fights its way to the last row on the opposite end of the game board, it can be *promoted*. When a Pawn is promoted, it can be replaced with another, stronger piece that was previously captured by your opponent. You can use a Knight, Bishop, Rook, or Queen to replace the promoted Pawn. There are no restrictions on the number of pieces of one specific type that you can have on the game board for OS/2 Chess. Actually, you can promote all eight Pawns to Queens and end up with nine Queens to finish the game.

The Draw

When you play a game that has no winner or loser, the game is considered a Draw. A Draw is determined by the following conditions of the game:

- A King is not in check, but its final move is to a space that is under attack by an opposing piece. This is considered a "draw by stalemate".

- One player repeatedly places the opponent's King in check. The player placed in check has no other alternative than to make the same moves over and over, which is considered to be a "draw by perpetual check".

- One player makes the same move for three consecutive moves.

- More than fifty moves are made in which no Pawn is moved or no capture is made.

Playing the Game

Before you begin playing OS/2 Chess, you must make some choices about how you want to play the game. You need to decide whether you want to play against a person or the computer. You also need to decide what color you want to be. For example, if you want to play against the computer and you want to play Black, you should select **Computer** on the White side and **Human** on the Black side. Once you select **Computer** from either the White side or the Black side, the **More** push button next to it becomes active.

Click on the **More** push button to display a window that lets you select the level of play. OS/2 Chess is pretty smart when it comes to playing Chess, so it's a good idea to start with a beginner level if you have never played Chess before. You can increase your level as you become a better player.

When the Playing Level window is displayed, you also see a choice called **Select book opening.** This choice lets you select from a number of opening plays that the computer can use to start the game. If you select this choice, you will have the opportunity to recognize specified book openings. This can help you learn strategy and enhance your play capability.

Now that you understand the basic rules, it's time for a few strategic tips. The whole point of Chess is to place your opponent's King in check, so a few tips on how to get there can be worth their weight in gold. Placing an opponent's King in check generally requires a well-planned strategy and is not considered a trivial skill. The strategy described here is very basic, but should provide a good start for a beginner to Chess.

- During the beginning and middle phases of a chess game, it is a good idea to take control of the center squares. This can be done by using the weakest piece, the Pawn, because you can use the Pawn to take control, but it's no big loss if the Pawn is captured.

- Try to castle early in the game to better protect your King.

- Do not stage attacks with your most valuable pieces early in the game. This just provokes attack by your opponent, who will use less valuable pieces to capture you.

- Don't make repeated moves with the same pieces, especially in the beginning of the game, because you will lose momentum.

- Even though a Bishop and a Knight are equally powerful, a Bishop whose diagonals are blocked by other pieces is not as effective as a Knight that is free of obstruction. In such a case, use the Knight if at all possible.

- As the end of the game draws near, it is wise to make use of the more mobile pieces such as the Bishop or the Rook.

- Having a Pawn advantage near the end of the game can result in a winning situation.

- It's a good idea to avoid having two Pawns on the same column because they require more powerful pieces to defend them. Pawns in this situation become difficult to move forward. Stranded Pawns are also at a disadvantage.

Menu Choices

OS/2 Chess has menu choices that let you set up the game, save a game, and display information about the game. Use the following list as a reference to help you when you are playing OS/2 Chess:

Menu	Choices	
Game	**New**	Replaces the current game with a new game.
	Load	Starts a game that you select from a list of games you previously saved.
	Save	Saves a game that you can finish playing at another time.
	Delete	Displays a list of previously saved games that you can individually remove from the list.
	Print	Prints the currently displayed game board along with its game records.
Options	**Set players**	Lets you specify if you want to play against another person or the computer.

Menu	Choices	
Options	**Set position**	Displays all the pieces in the background so that you can drag them to the game board and place them in the location where you want them.
	Set colors	Lets you change the colors of the background, squares, and pieces of the current game.
	Sound	Turns the sound effects on and off. Sound is on when a check mark appears next to this menu choice.
	Warning messages	Turns the warning messages on and off. Warning messages are on when a check mark appears next to this menu choice.
	Label board	Labels the board to help you understand algebraic chess notation. Columns are labeled alphabetically, starting with the far-left column (A). Rows are labeled numerically, starting with the bottom row (1). The white King is usually placed on square **e1**, and the black Queen is usually placed on square **d8**. To find out more about algebraic chess notation, refer to the online help provided with OS/2 Chess.
	Keyboard entry	Lets you type the moves you want to make instead of using the mouse. This method requires an understanding of algebraic chess notation.
	Time	Displays the elapsed playing time for both players.
	Take back move	Lets you undo your last move. If you are playing with another human, it is recommended that you ask permission to take back a move. This is typically not legal during tournament play.
View	**Move status**	Indicates which player moves next, how many moves have been made, and how much time has elapsed in the current move.
	Game record	Shows a list of all the moves that led to the current game positions.
	Valid moves	Shows a list of all the valid moves (in algebraic chess notation) for the current player.

Menu	Choices	
View	**Analysis**	Shows the principal continuation line of play sequences determined as the best possible by the computer.
	Captured pieces	Displays the pieces that have been captured by your opponent.
	Rotate board	Lets you turn the board in any direction you like—clockwise or counterclockwise.
	Flip board	Lets you turn the game board 180 degrees from its current position.
Network	**Send messages**	Lets you send messages to your opponent or another user across the network.
	Disconnect	Detaches you from the network.
	List users	Displays a list of current network users.

Mahjongg Solitaire

Mahjongg Solitaire is a computerized version of the Chinese tile-matching game. Unlike the Chinese version, this game is for only one player.

Mahjongg provides one default tile layout that is displayed the first time you open the game. You can change the layout by selecting one of the following from the **Open** menu.

Castle

The tiles are stacked in the shape of a medieval castle.

Gizeh

The tiles are stacked in the shape of three pyramids, similar to the ones that exist in Gizeh.

Tower Bridge

The tiles are stacked in a shape modeled after the Tower Bridge in London.

Taj Mahal

The tiles are stacked in a shape that outlines the famous Taj Mahal. This layout can be solved more often than the others, making it the easiest of the tile layouts to play.

The layout of the game determines the difficulty of the game. If you select a layout other than Taj Mahal, you will find that the layout produces fewer games that can be solved. This is because the other layouts are more complex, making the tile matching more challenging.

TIP: You can drag a new game layout from the Mahjongg Solitaire window and drop it on the game board to play a game in a different layout.

Object of the Game

Mahjongg is a matching game in which you match symbols on the faces of two tiles to create a pair. You then remove the matched pairs from play. The object of the game is to match and remove as many pairs as you can out of the 144 tiles.

The symbols on the tiles are divided into *suits*. Different tile sets contain different suits. The default tile set is made up of seven suits. Five of the suits contain different pairs of each tile face. The remaining two suits, the Flowers and Seasons suits, each contain only four tiles.

The following describes the suits and the rules for pairing each suit:

- *Character Suit* has Chinese letters with a number in the upper-right corner of the tile face. You must match a character tile to another character tile that has the same number on it.

- *Bamboo Suit* has a different number of stick-like objects on the face of each tile. You must match a bamboo tile to another bamboo tile that has the same number of sticks on it.

- *Dots Suit* has a different number of yin-yang symbols on the face of each tile. You must match a dot tile to another dot tile that has the same number of yin-yang symbols on it.

- *Dragons Suit* has three different colored dragons, one per tile face. You must match a dragon tile to another dragon tile of the same color.

- *Winds Suit* has stars with different color segments representing wind direction. You must match a wind tile to another wind tile that has the same color and wind direction on it.

- *Flowers Suit* has a different flower on the face of each tile. Any flower tile can be matched with any other flower tile.

- *Seasons Suit* has a tree on the face of each tile that represents a different season of the year. Any season tile can be matched with any other season tile.

Rules of the Game

There is really just one rule to this game, and it's that you can remove *free* tiles only. A tile is free only if there is no other tile touching it on the right or left side or there is no other tile stacked on top of it.

Playing the Game

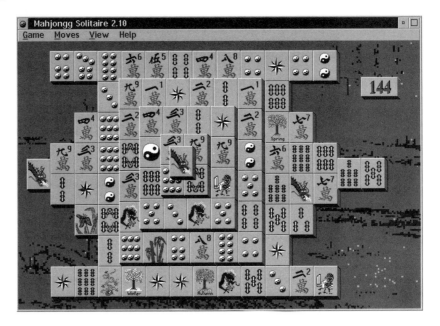

The first time you open Mahjongg, you are given the opportunity to decide how you want to play the game. The following explains the choices:

Hints! It's free!

This choice starts only games that can be solved, uses the pointing-hand cursor to indicate which tiles are free, and automatically displays a match or matches to the free tile you select. If you have never played before, this is a good way to find out which tiles are considered free and which tile faces match.

I like subtle hints.

This choice starts only games that can be solved and uses the pointing-hand cursor to indicate which tiles are free. Tile matches will not be automatically displayed. If you've figured out which tiles match but can't quite grasp which ones are considered free, this is a good choice.

Hints? Me? Never!

This choice leaves you on your own. You will not necessarily be presented with a game that can be solved. The hand-cursor is not displayed, nor are matching tiles. Obviously, this is the most challenging choice.

 TIP: After you make a choice from this window, you won't see it again. But what happens if you finally figure out how to play the game and you are tired of being prompted for every move? No problem! You can easily change the mode of play options by changing the settings available for the game. You can get to the settings by clicking on the **View** menu and then selecting the **Settings** menu choice.

Now that you have made an appropriate choice, you can start to play the game. Move the mouse over the tiles and click on a tile that you think you can match. Click on the matching tile to make a pair, which is then removed from the playing board. When you find a match for every tile and there are no more tiles left on the board, you WIN!

Menu Choices

Mahjongg Solitaire has menu choices that let you set up the game, save a game, show different moves, and edit and customize the game. Use the following list as a reference to help you when you are playing Mahjongg Solitaire:

Menu	Choices	
Game	**New**	Shuffles the tiles in a random manner and displays them in the current game layout. You can specify how the tiles are placed on the game board by clicking on the arrow to the right of the **New** menu choice. The **Random** menu choice is the default choice. The additional menu choices let you use the same game layout and tile order as the game you just finished playing or let you choose a previously played game.
	Default	Starts a new game with the default tile layout.
	Open	Lets you choose the game layout you want to play.
	Save	Saves the current layout into a game file that you can play another time. This does not save a game in its current state to be played at a later time. It only saves the layout of the game you are currently playing. This is a good choice if you have gone to the trouble of creating your own game layout.

Menu	Choices	
Game	**Save as**	Works the same way as the **Save** menu choice, but always requests a new file name.
	Auto play	Shows a demonstration of the game. The computer will continue to play game after game until you select this choice again. If you have never played Mahjongg before, this could be a good way to find out how to get started. The demonstration speed can be adjusted through the Settings notebook.
	Exit	Quits the game.
Moves	**Take back**	Lets you undo quite a few of your most recent moves.
	Replay	Redoes the most recent Take Back actions.
	Show Replay	Highlights the most recently replayed move.
	Cheat	Lets you remove a pair of tiles that don't have matching tile faces. After you use this menu choice, you will inevitably have to use it again to rid the game of the two misfit tiles left behind.
	Show	Highlights in half-a-second intervals all the possible matches that can currently be made.

- Green means that all four tiles can be removed and indicates that this would be a low-risk choice.

- Yellow means that two tiles can be removed and indicates that this would be a medium-risk choice.

- Red means that three tiles match and two can be removed. This indicates a high-risk choice.

TIP: Just because you see a possible tile match does not necessarily mean that it is the right strategic choice.

View	**Play**	Lets you switch from edit mode back to play mode. Play is the Mahjongg Solitaire default mode and needs to be selected only to return you to play mode.
	Edit	Lets you edit the current game board to create your own game boards.

Menu	Choices	
View	Timer	Places a timer in the upper-right corner of the game board window.
	Matches	Places a box in the upper-right corner of the window that displays the number of matches available for the current move.
	Settings	Displays a Settings notebook that lets you change the current settings for Mahjongg Solitaire. The Settings notebook contains the following notebook tabs:

- Options tab, which lets you adjust the animation speed and the 3-D view of the tiles, and lets you change the play options that were originally set the first time you started Mahjongg.

- Sounds tab, which lets you turn the sound effects on or off as well as change the sounds assigned to different actions.

- Color tab, which lets you change the game board background to a solid color and adjust the color that is displayed.

- Bit-map tab, which lets you choose a bit map (instead of a color) for the game board background.

- Tiles tab, which lets you select the different tile sets. The default tile set is called TILEDEF.DLL (in case you're wondering).

- Info tab, which gives you information about the title of the game, the name of the person who created it, and the name of the help file that originally came with the game.

- Icon tab, which displays the current game icon and lets you edit it or create a new one using the Icon Editor.

Menu	Choices	
	Save Settings	Saves the changes you made in the Settings notebook and maintains them as the default for the next time you open a Mahjongg game.

Using Multimedia Programs

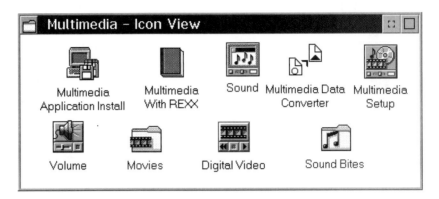

OS/2 Warp comes with multimedia capability built right in, so you can run a variety of multimedia programs you might already own. OS/2 Warp also comes with its very own multimedia programs. If you've never used multimedia on a computer, you will be pleasantly surprised by the way multimedia can make using a computer so much more fun.

This chapter shows you how to play, record, and edit sound files, play movie files, play music CDs, adjust the volume on your computer, view image files, and convert sound and image files to different formats.

Digital Audio

You can use the Digital Audio program to play and record digital sound files. A digital sound file contains sounds that have been converted into digital information. These files usually have an extension of .WAV. OS/2 Warp comes with many sound files, and you can purchase additional sound files or record your own sound files and play them. You can also add special effects to sound files.

The Digital Audio program can be displayed in two views: Player/Recorder or Editor. The Player/Recorder view provides all the functions that you need to play and record sound files. The Editor view provides additional functions (for example, cutting, pasting, deleting, or adding echo) that you can use to edit a sound file.

TIP: You will not have a Digital Audio icon unless you have a sound card installed in your computer.

If you installed a sound card after you installed OS/2 Warp, you can easily add the Digital Audio icon. For instructions about adding this program, see Chapter 25, "Adding or Removing Features After Installation" on page 255.

Playing a Sound File

Sound files contain sound effects and are usually very short, because it takes a lot of space to store digitized sound.

You can use the Digital Audio icon to play sound files in one of these formats: PCM, ADPCM, MU-LAW, and A-LAW. If you purchase additional sound files, make sure they are in one of these formats.

To play a sound file:
1. Double-click on the **Multimedia** icon.
2. Double-click on the **Digital Audio** icon.
3. Click mouse button 1 on the **File** menu.
4. Click mouse button 1 on the **Open** menu choice.
5. Double-click on the sound file that you want to play. You might have to scroll the **File** field to see all of the sound files that are available.
6. Click mouse button 1 on the play button ▶ to begin playing the file.

   a. Click mouse button 1 on the stop button ■ to stop the file from playing.

   b. Click mouse button 1 on the rewind button ◀◀ to rewind the file to the beginning.

7. Double-click on the title-bar icons of the open windows to close them.

TIP: Another way to play a .WAV sound file is to:
1. Double-click on the **Multimedia** icon.
2. Double-click on the **Sound Bites** icon.
3. Double-click on any file that ends with **.WAV**.
4. Click mouse button 1 on the play button ▶.

Recording a New Sound File

You can use the Digital Audio window to record sound files in the PCM format. The typical extension used for these types of files is .WAV. However, you can use any extension you want. The .WAV extension refers to the term "wave" or "waveform", which is a digital representation of a sound wave.

There are two input methods that can be used to record a sound file. You can use a microphone, or you can use a line-in jack on the sound card if it is connected to a device that produces sound output, such as a CD-ROM.

To record into a new sound file:

1. Double-click on the **Multimedia** icon.
2. Double-click on the **Digital Audio** icon.
3. Click mouse button 1 on the **View** menu.
4. Click mouse button 1 on the **Player/Recorder** choice.
5. Click mouse button 1 on the **Options** menu.
6. Click mouse button 1 on the input device that you want to use. A check mark is placed next to the option you choose. You can choose from the following:

   Microphone
   Records from a microphone that is attached to the microphone jack of a sound card.

   Line in
   Records from a device that produces sound and that is attached to the line-in jack of a sound card.

7. Click mouse button 1 on the **Options** menu.
8. Click mouse button 1 on the options that you want to use. A check mark is placed next to the options you select. You can choose from the following:

   Low input level
   Records at a low input level. This choice is good if there is considerable background noise that you do not want to pick up.

   Medium input level
   Records at a medium input level and picks up a moderate amount of background noise.

   High input level
   Records at a high input level and amplifies weak sound levels.

   Monitor input
   Enables the speaker so that you can hear what is being recorded into the file. This is useful if you are recording from the line-in jack of the sound card.

9. Click mouse button 1 on the **File** menu.
10. Click mouse button 1 on the **New** menu choice to create a new file.
11. Click mouse button 1 on the **Type** menu.
12. Click mouse button 1 on the options that you want to use. A check mark is placed next to the options you select. You can choose from the following:

Mono
> Records on one channel and creates a file that is half the size of a file created with the Stereo choice.

Stereo
> Records on both the right and left channels and creates a file that is twice the size of a file created with the Mono choice.

Voice
> Records using a low sampling rate (11.025 kHz), which produces the lowest-quality recording. It should be used only to record speech.

Music
> Records using a moderate sampling rate (22.050 kHz), which produces a higher-quality recording than Voice. It can be used to record speech and music.

High Fidelity
> Records using a high sampling rate (44.100 kHz), which produces the highest-quality recording. It can be used to record all types of sounds.

Low Quality
> Records using an 8-bit (low-quality) sample size.

High Quality
> Records using a 16-bit (high-quality) sample size.

13. Click mouse button 1 on the record button [⬥] to start recording. While recording is in progress, the record button blinks.

14. Click mouse button 1 on the stop button [■] when you want to stop recording.

15. Click mouse button 1 on the rewind button [◀◀] to rewind the file to the beginning.

16. Click mouse button 1 on the play button [▶] to begin playing the file.

17. Double-click on the title-bar icon of the Digital Audio window to close it.

18. Click mouse button 1 on the **Save as** push button.

19. Type a name in the **Save as filename** field, and then press the Enter key. You can use any name that you want. However, if you use the .WAV extension, your file will automatically be associated with the Digital Audio window and you will be able to play the file by just double-clicking on its icon.

20. Double-click on the title-bar icon of the open window to close it.

TIP: If no sound is being recorded into the file, make sure that:

- Your microphone or line-in device is connected to the correct jack on the sound card.

- Your microphone is turned on.

- The volume level in the Digital Audio window is turned up all the way.

- The volume level in the Volume Control window is turned up.

Recording into an Existing Sound File

Suppose you want to add to or change an existing sound file. You can record over all of the information in the sound file, or some of the information, or you can just add information onto the end of the sound file. This gives you the opportunity to fix mistakes in a file without having to re-record the entire file.

To record into an existing sound file:
1. Double-click on the **Multimedia** icon.
2. Double-click on the **Digital Audio** icon.
3. Click mouse button 1 on the **View** menu.
4. Click mouse button 1 on the **Player/Recorder** menu choice.
5. Click mouse button 1 on the **Options** menu.
6. Click mouse button 1 on the input device that you want to use. A check mark is placed next to the option you choose. You can choose from the following:

    Microphone
    Records from a microphone that is attached to the microphone jack of a sound card.

    Line in
    Records from a device that produces sound and that is attached to the line-in jack of a sound card.

7. Click mouse button 1 on the **Options** menu.
8. Click mouse button 1 on the options that you want to use. A check mark is placed next to the options you select. You can choose from the following:

    Low input level
    Records at a low input level. This choice is good if there is considerable background noise that you do not want to pick up.

    Medium input level
    Records at a medium input level and picks up a moderate amount of background noise.

High input level
> Records at a high input level and amplifies weak sound levels.

Monitor input
> Enables the speaker so that you can hear what is being recorded into the file.

9. Click mouse button 1 on the **File** menu.
10. Click mouse button 1 on the **Open** menu choice.
11. Double-click on the name of the file in the **File** field that you want to open. You might have to scroll the list to see all of the files that are available.
12. Click mouse button 1 on an arrow in the **Media Position** field to select the position in the file where you want to start recording. The Media Position field gives you the following information:

Sound Position
> Displays the current position of the file. You can click on the arrow to the right of the field to go forward or backward in the file. Recording will start at the position that is displayed in this field when the record button is selected.

Sound Length
> Displays the total length of the file in the form minutes:seconds.hundredths.

Maximum Recording Time
> Displays the amount of time that sound can be recorded before there is no more hard disk space available. This is displayed in the form seconds.hundredths.

13. Click mouse button 1 on the record button ◆ to start recording. While recording is in progress, the record button blinks.

14. Click mouse button 1 on the stop button ■ when you want to stop recording.

15. Click mouse button 1 on the rewind button ◀◀ to rewind the file to the beginning.

16. Click mouse button 1 on the play button ▶ to begin playing the file.

17. Double-click on the title-bar icon of the Digital Audio window to close it.
18. Click mouse button 1 on the Save push button.
19. Double-click on the title-bar icon of the open window to close it.

TIP: You can use the choices on the Control menu of the Digital Audio window instead of the buttons in the Digital Audio window if you have difficulty remembering which button does what.

Editing an Existing Sound File

When you edit a sound file, you can alter the information in the file. You can remove pauses or mistakes and even add special effects, such as echo or reverb, to the sound file. If you like to create sound files, you will love having the ability to jazz them up.

To edit an existing sound file:

1. Double-click on the **Multimedia** icon.
2. Double-click on the **Digital Audio** icon.
3. Click mouse button 1 on the **View** menu.
4. Click mouse button 1 on the **Editor** menu choice.
5. Click mouse button 1 on the **File** menu.
6. Click mouse button 1 on the **Open** menu choice.
7. Double-click on the name of the file in the **File** field that you want to open. You might have to scroll the list to see all of the files that are available.
8. Click mouse button 1 at the bottom of the **Zoom** field to zoom in on the wave and make it bigger.
9. Click mouse button 1 on the play button [▶]. Watch the cursor as it moves through the wave that is displayed in the Sound field at the bottom of the window.
10. Mark an area of the sound graph for editing.
    a. Point to the beginning of the area that you want to edit.
    b. Press and hold mouse button 1.
    c. Drag the mark to the end of the area that you want to edit.
    d. Release mouse button 1.
11. Click mouse button 1 on the play button [▶] to hear the marked sound.
12. Change the information in the Edit Information field to fine-tune the marked area so that it contains only the information you want to edit. The following fields are displayed:

    View
    > Displays the amount of time used by the file in the form minutes:seconds.hundredths.

    Selected
    > Displays the point in the file where the mark begins and ends. This is displayed in the form minutes:seconds.hundredths. You can change these values by clicking mouse button 1 on the up or down arrow in the fields.

    Modified
    > Informs you that the file has been modified since it was opened.

13. Click mouse button 1 on the **Edit** menu.

14. Click mouse button 1 on the menu choice that you want to use to edit the marked sound. The Edit menu contains the following choices:

Undo
>	Reverses the effect of the last cut, delete, paste, or record operation.

Redo
>	Reverses the effect of the last Undo.

Cut
>	Removes the marked sound area from the file and places it in the clipboard.

Copy
>	Copies the marked sound area into the clipboard.

Paste
>	Copies the sound information from the clipboard into the file at the position of the cursor. If the information in the clipboard was recorded in a different format than the file you are pasting the information into, it will be converted. Possible conversions are mono to stereo and vice versa, 16-bit to 8-bit samples and vice versa, and 11.025kHz to 22.050 or 44.100kHz, 22.050kHz to 11.025 or 44.100kHz, and 44.100kHz to 11.025 or 22.050kHz.

Delete
>	Removes the marked sound from the file.

Select all
>	Marks the entire sound file.

Deselect all
>	Removes the mark from the sound file. It does not affect the sound file.

Mix from file
>	Combines the marked sound area with sound from another sound file.

Mix from clipboard
>	Combines the marked sound area with sound from the clipboard.

Increase volume 25%
>	Increases the volume of the marked sound area by 25%.

Decrease volume 25%
>	Decreases the volume of the marked sound area by 25%.

Maximize Volume

Increases the volume of the marked sound area to its highest level without clipping.

Double-Speed

Increases the speed of the marked sound area so that it plays faster. It also raises the pitch of the sound.

Half-Speed

Decreases the speed of the marked sound area so that it plays slower. It also lowers the pitch of the sound.

Fade in

Increases gradually the volume of the marked sound area until the normal level is reached.

Fade out

Decreases gradually the volume of the marked sound area until no sound is heard.

Reverb

Adds vibration (echo) to the marked sound area so that it sounds as if it was recorded using a reverberating microphone. You can adjust the volume of the reverb information or you can adjust the amount of the delay (in milliseconds) between the reverbs and the original sound.

Reverse

Reverses the marked sound so that it sounds as if it were being played backward.

Echo

Adds echo to the marked sound area so that it sounds as if it were recorded in an echo chamber. You can adjust the volume of the echo information or you can adjust the amount of delay (in milliseconds) between the echo and the original sound.

15. Click mouse button 1 on the rewind button ◄◄ .

16. Click mouse button 1 on the play button ► to begin playing the file.

17. Repeat steps 10 through 16 until you are satisfied with the file.

18. Double-click on the title-bar icon of the Digital Audio window to close it.

19. Click mouse button 1 on the **Save** push button.

20. Double-click on the title-bar icon of the open window to close it.

MIDI

The MIDI icon is used to play sound files that are stored in a MIDI (Musical Instrument Digital Interface) format. This sound format is used by musical equipment such as synthesizers and drum machines. MIDI files can pack a lot of sound information in a small amount of space, because MIDI files do not contain digitized sound (as .WAV files do). Rather, they contain information about which note should be played. This information takes up less space than digitized sounds and makes MIDI files smaller than .WAV files. In addition, because MIDI files contain only information about which notes should be played, the quality of the sound produced is based on the quality of the sound card it is being played on.

Playing a MIDI File

MIDI files can be easily identified because their file names typically end with .MID. OS/2 Warp comes with several MIDI files. If you have MIDI equipment, you can create your own MIDI files and play them on your computer.

To play a MIDI sound file:
1. Double-click on the **Multimedia** icon.
2. Double-click on the **MIDI** icon.
3. Click mouse button 1 on the **File** menu.
4. Click mouse button 1 on the **Open** menu choice.
5. Double-click on the name of the .MID file in the **File** field that you want to open. You might have to scroll the list to see all of the files that are available.
6. Click mouse button 1 on the **play button** to play the file.
7. Double-click on the title-bar icons of the open windows to close them.

TIP: Another way to play a MIDI sound file is to:
1. Double-click on the **Multimedia** icon.
2. Double-click on the **Sound Bites** icon.
3. Double-click on any file that ends with **.MID**.
4. Click mouse button 1 on the play button ▸ .

Digital Video

The Digital Video program allows you to watch high-resolution digital movies on your Desktop without any special hardware. If you have a sound card in your computer, you can listen to the sound that accompanies the video. OS/2 Warp supports the AVI, FLI, FLC, and MPEG formats for movie files.

NOTE: You must have a ReelMagic video playback card in your computer in order to view MPEG (Moving Picture Experts Group) movies.

Playing a Movie

OS/2 Warp comes with one .AVI movie file. If you install the OS/2 Warp BonusPak, you also have another .AVI movie and one .FLC movie. These samples are provided so that you can see what is possible with OS/2 Warp's multimedia.

To play an AVI, MPEG, FLI, or FLC movie:
1. Double-click on the **Multimedia** icon.
2. Double-click on the **Digital Video** icon.
3. Click mouse button 1 on the **File** menu.
4. Click mouse button 1 on the **Open** menu choice.
5. Double-click on the name of the file in the **File** field that you want to open. You might have to scroll the list to see all of the files that are available. If the movie you want to view is not listed in the field, it might be on a different drive or in a different directory. Follow these instructions to find it:
   a. If the files are on a CD, insert the CD into the CD-ROM drive.
   b. Click mouse button 1 on the down arrow to the right of the **Drive** field to see the list of available drives.
   c. Click mouse button 1 on the drive containing the movie files.
   d. Double-click on the names of the directories in the **Directory** field until you open the directory that contains the movie file you want to view.
   e. Double-click on the name of the movie file in the **File** field. You might have to scroll the list to see all of the files that are available. Movie file names ending with .AVI, .MPG, .FLI, or .FLC can be viewed with the Digital Video program.
6. The Digital Video program opens with a smaller window below it. The smaller window is where the movie will be shown. Click mouse button 2 on the title-bar icon of the smaller window.
7. Click mouse button 1 on one of the following choices:

Half Size
>Shrinks the movie window to half of its normal size.

Double Size
>Makes the movie window twice its normal size.

Normal Size
>Returns the movie window to its default size.

Movie Info
>Displays information about the movie file that you selected (if you're interested). This information includes the:

- Name of the file

- Method used to digitize and compress the original video

- Width and height (in pels) in which the movie was created

- Number of frames per second (fps) in which the movie was created

- Average number of kilobytes used by a second of the movie

- Maximum number of kilobytes used by a second of the movie

- Length of the movie in seconds

8. Click mouse button 1 on the play button in the Digital Video window to play the movie.

9. Double-click on the title-bar icons of the open windows to close them. (You cannot use the title-bar icon to close the IBM Ultimotion window. The Digital Video window automatically closes this window.)

TIP: Another way to play a Digital Video movie that is located on your hard disk or a CD is to:

1. Double-click on the **Multimedia** icon.
2. Double-click on the **Movies** icon.
3. Double-click on any file that ends with **.AVI**.
4. Click mouse button 1 on the play button.

NOTE: The additional movies on the CD can be found in the \MOVIES directory.

If you installed the OS/2 Warp BonusPak, you can also record movies on your computer. You can use still images, movie files, a camcorder, videotape recorder (VCR), or video-disc (laserdisc) player that is attached to your computer. To find out more about recording a movie, read Chapter 33, "Video IN Recorder" on page 313.

Compact Disc

If you have a CD-ROM drive and you installed multimedia support, you can use the Compact Disc icon to play music CDs. The Compact Disc icon looks like this when it is open:

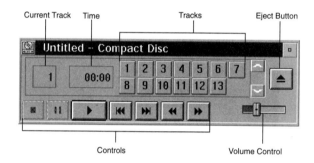

Current track

> Shows the number of the track that is currently being played or the track that is about to be played.

Time

> Displays the amount of time that the current track has been playing.

Tracks

> Displays numbers that represent the tracks on the CD. If the number of tracks exceeds the space provided, the scroll arrows to the right of the tracks become active. You can play a particular track by clicking on the number for the track and then clicking on the play button. If no CD is in the CD-ROM drive, a graphic is displayed that instructs you to insert a CD.

Controls

> Contains buttons that you can use to stop, pause, play a CD, track backward, track forward, scan backward, and scan forward through the CD. (These options are also on the Control menu.)

Volume control

Adjusts the volume of the CD. You can adjust the volume by dragging the box in the slider bar to the left or right.

Eject button

Ejects the CD from the CD-ROM drive.

Playing a Music CD

OS/2 Warp can play a music CD while you continue working. This is a wonderful way to make your computer your all-around entertainment center. Now you can do your work to the beat of your favorite music.

To play a music CD:

1. Insert a CD into the **CD-ROM** drive.
2. Double-click on the **Multimedia** icon.
3. Double-click on the **Compact Disc** icon.
4. Click mouse button 1 on the play button 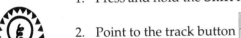.

TIP: You can set the Compact Disc program to play only your favorite tracks on a CD. To do this:

1. Press and hold the **Shift key**.
2. Point to the track button 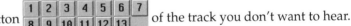 of the track you don't want to hear.
3. Click mouse button 1 to disable the track.
4. Release the **Shift key**.

To enable the track, click mouse button 1 on the disabled track button.

Discovering the Compact Disc Menu Choices

The menus for the Compact Disc window offer a wide variety of choices. To display the menu for the Compact Disc window, click mouse button 2 on the title-bar icon. In addition to standard choices such as move, size, minimize, and close are the following choices:

Menu	Choices	
Options	Automatic play	Starts to play the music CD as soon as it is inserted in the CD-ROM drive.
	Repeat	Starts to play the tracks over again after the last track on the CD is played.
	Shuffle tracks	Rearranges the track buttons in a different order. The tracks then play in the order in which the buttons are displayed.
	Digital transfer	Sends the sound from the CD-ROM drive to a speaker that is connected to a sound card in your computer. This improves the quality of the sound.
Control	Stop	Stops the CD from playing and resets it to the first track.
	Pause	Temporarily stops the CD from playing. The Compact Disc program remembers the exact location of the track that was playing when Pause was selected.
	Play	Starts playing the CD.
	Track backward	Moves to the previous track button.
	Track forward	Moves to the next track button in the list.
	Scan backward	Moves forward through the current track one second at a time.
	Scan forward	Moves backward through the current track one second at a time.
	Eject	Ejects the CD from the CD-ROM drive.
	Mute	Turns off the volume of the CD.
Edit title	Edit title	Displays a window where you can specify a title (up to 32 characters long) for the CD. If you specify a title, it will be displayed in the title bar of the Compact Disc window any time you insert the CD.
Window	Default size	Displays all the controls in the Compact Disc window.
	Compact size	Displays only the Control buttons in the Compact Disc window. This option is used to make the window smaller so that it takes up less space on the Desktop.

Volume Control

The Volume Control program is used to increase or decrease the volume of all the sound-producing programs on your computer. If you have hardware devices with volume controls, the Volume Control program can also adjust the volume of these devices. This does not remove your ability to adjust the volume using the controls on the device or on the individual programs unless the volume in the Volume Control program is set to 0 or Mute.

NOTE: Some hardware devices have only two volume settings, On or Off. The Volume Control program has no effect on these devices.

You might notice that the volume of some programs and devices changes more rapidly than others. This is because the Volume Control program reduces all volumes by the same percentage. For example, if you have one program set at 50% of its maximum volume and another set at 30% and you then decrease the volume (of both) by an additional 30%, the one that was at 30% of the maximum volume will become inaudible before the one that was at 50% of its maximum volume.

Changing the Volume Level

You can use the Volume Control program to adjust the loudness of all the sounds on your computer by using one control. While being able to increase or decrease all of the volumes at one time is nice, the best feature of the Volume Control program is that it can *mute* (silence) all the sound-producing programs and hardware devices on your computer at one time. This allows you to stop the racket whenever you need quiet (for example, when the telephone rings).

To change the volume level:
1. Double-click on the **Multimedia** icon.
2. Double-click on the **Volume Control** icon.
3. Change the volume using one of the following methods:

   - Click mouse button 1 on the plus (+) or minus (-) button. (Hold mouse button 1 down to increase the speed with which you can change the volume level.)

   - Click mouse button 1 on the lines extending out from the volume dial. (Hold mouse button 1 down and drag the pointer over the lines to increase the speed with which you can change the volume level.)

   - Click mouse button 1 inside the lower half of the volume dial. (Hold mouse button 1 down and drag the pointer to the left and right to increase the speed with which you can change the volume level.)

Multimedia Data Converter

 Use the Multimedia Data Converter program to convert sound and image files to different formats. For example, you can convert files from an IBM M-Motion image format to an OS/2 Warp bit-map format so that you can use them as backgrounds for the Desktop and windows.

The following table lists some of the file-name extensions supported by the Multimedia Data Converter.

Extension	Description	Type
_IM and !IM	IBM AVC * still video	Image
VID	IBM M-Motion still video	Image
BMP	OS/2 1.3, 2.0	Bit map (image)
DIB	Microsoft device-independent bit map	Bit map (image)
RDI (image)	RIFF device-independent bit map	Bit map (image)
VOC	Creative Labs voice file	Sound
_AU, _AD	IBM AVC ADPCM digital audio	Sound
WAV	RIFF WAVE digital audio	Sound

 NOTE: Not all image files use these file extensions or have file extensions. The table above summarizes some of the more common extensions used in the industry.

Converting a Sound or an Image File

Sound and image files come in a wide variety of formats. Not all programs accept all formats. By using the Multimedia Data Converter program, you can make an unacceptable file format into a file format that can be used. For example, the Digital Audio program can play only .WAV sound files. If you bought ._AU sound files, you can convert the ._AU file format into a .WAV file format and then use the Digital Audio program to play the files.

To convert a file:
1. Double-click on the **Multimedia** icon.

242

2. Double-click on the **Multimedia Data Converter** icon.

3. Click mouse button 1 on the **Include** push button.

4. Click mouse button 1 on the image formats in the **Image formats** field that you want to convert. If you do not want to convert any image files, do not select anything from this field.

5. Click mouse button 1 on the sound formats in the **Audio formats** field that you want to convert. If you do not want to convert any sound files, do not select anything from this field.

6. Click mouse button 1 on one of the following:

   • **All formats** if you are not sure of the format of the file that you want to convert, or if you want to convert all of the file formats listed.

   • **Selected formats** only if you know the format of the files that you want to convert.

7. Click mouse button 1 on the **OK** push button.

8. Locate the file that you want to convert.

   a. Type the file name and extension of the file you want to convert. If you do not know the file name and extension, you can leave the *.* in the **Filename** field.

   b. Click mouse button 1 on the down arrow to the right of the **Drive** field, and then click mouse button 1 on the drive letter that contains the files you want to convert.

   c. Double-click on directory names in the **Directory** field until the names of the files that you want to convert are displayed in the **File** field.

9. Press and hold the Ctrl key.

10. Click mouse button 1 on the file names in the **File** field that you want to convert.

11. Release the Ctrl key.

12. Click mouse button 1 on the **Convert** push button. The Convert window is displayed.

13. Select the format that you want the files converted to.

   a. Click mouse button 1 on the down arrow to the right of the **Image target format** field, and then click mouse button 1 on the image format that you want the files converted to.

   b. Click mouse button 1 on the **Image extension** field, and then type the extension that you want to use for the newly converted image files.

   c. Click mouse button 1 on the down arrow to the right of the **Audio target format** field, and then click mouse button 1 on the sound format that you want the files converted to.

d. Click mouse button 1 on the **Audio extension** field, and then type the extension that you want to use for the newly converted sound files.

e. Click mouse button 1 on the square to the right of the **Target path**.

f. Double-click on the directory names until the highlighting is on the directory name where you want to place the newly converted files.

g. Click mouse button 1 on the **OK** push button.

14. Click mouse button 1 on the **Convert** push button. The files are converted and placed in the directory that you specified.

15. Double-click on the title-bar icons of the open windows to close them.

Previewing Image Files

Previewing allows you to view the contents of image (picture) files. In addition to finding out what the picture looks like, you can also find out the actual width, height, and color information used in the picture.

To view an image either before or after it has been converted:

1. Double-click on the **Multimedia** icon.

2. Double-click on the **Multimedia Data Converter** icon.

3. Click mouse button 1 on the **Include** push button.

4. Click mouse button 1 on the **All formats** choice.

5. Click mouse button 1 on the **OK** push button.

6. Locate the file you want to view.

a. Click mouse button 1 on the down arrow to the right of the **Drive** field.

b. Click mouse button 1 on the drive letter that contains the files you want to view.

c. Double-click on directory names in the **Directory** field until the names of the files you want to view are displayed in the **File** field.

7. Click mouse button 1 on a file that you want to view.

8. Click mouse button 1 on the **Preview** push button.

9. Click mouse button 1 on the **Cancel** push button to close the Preview window.

10. Repeat steps 6 through 9 for each file you want to view.

 TIP: If you installed the OS/2 Warp BonusPak, you have the ability to record movies from still images. The preview feature lets you see how good a still image really is before you use it in your movie. To find out more about recording movies and capturing still images, see Chapter 33, "Video IN Recorder" on page 313.

Installing Multimedia Programs

You can use the Multimedia Application Install icon to install programs that work with the multimedia programs provided with OS/2 Warp. Examples of such programs are ActionMedia II and M-CONTROL. If you have a multimedia program that does not have its own installation program, try using the Multimedia Application Install icon to install it.

To install additional multimedia programs:

1. Double-click on the **Multimedia** icon.
2. Double-click on the **Multimedia Application Install** icon.
3. Click mouse button 1 on the arrow to the right of the **Source Drive** field.
4. Click mouse button 1 on the letter of the drive that contains the additional multimedia programs.
5. Double-click on the names of directories in the **Directory** field until you find the directory that contains the program files.
6. Click mouse button 1 on any of the features that you **do not** want to install.
7. Click mouse button 1 on the **Install** push button.
8. Click mouse button 1 on the **Yes** push button so that your CONFIG.SYS file is automatically updated with the new information that is needed to run the programs that you are installing. If you click mouse button 1 on the **No** push button, you will have to make the changes to the CONFIG.SYS file yourself.
9. When the installation is completed, click mouse button 1 on the **OK** push button.
10. Shut down and restart OS/2 Warp so that you can use your new multimedia programs.

Part Five

Using Printers, Disk Drives, and Utility Programs

In parts 2 and 3, we showed you how to print a data-file icon and how to customize your printer. This part contains additional information about how to use your printer.

This part also shows you how to use your disk drives, how to display command prompts, and how to use the recovery programs that come with OS/2 Warp.

In addition, this part discusses the utility programs that you can use with a laptop computer, and describes how to add features to the operating system, or install new hardware on your computer. Two utility programs OS/2 Warp provides for DOS users are also discussed.

Using Your Printer

If you installed a printer when you installed OS/2 Warp, a printer icon is on your Desktop. The printer icon is used to print jobs (data files) and check their progress. If you did not add a printer during the installation, you can add one by following the instructions in "Installing a Printer" on page 253.

This chapter shows you how to print the contents of a data-file icon and the contents of your computer screen. You will learn how to look at the contents of a print job and view information about a print job. This chapter also shows you how to stop a job before it prints, release a job that you stopped, change the order in which a job is printed, and delete a job.

Printing Data Files

Printing is the process of transferring information from your computer to paper via a printer.

Rocket Tip: Remember to use the printer icon located on the LaunchPad.

To print the contents of a data-file icon:
1. Point to the data-file icon whose contents you want to print.
2. Press and hold mouse button 2.
3. Drag the data-file icon to the printer icon.
4. Release mouse button 2.

TIP: You can make multiple copies of a printer icon and place a copy inside any icon that contains data-file icons. You will then be able to quickly and easily drag the data-file icon to the printer.

To print the contents of a data-file icon using a menu:
1. Point to the data-file icon whose contents you want to print.
2. Click mouse button 2 to display the pop-up menu.
3. Click mouse button 1 on the **Print** menu choice.

NOTE: If you are using a program (for example, Lotus 1-2-3) and you want to print the data that you are preparing, follow the instructions that came with the program.

Printing Screens

In addition to being able to print the contents of data files, you can print the contents of the Desktop or an active window. This allows you to print only the information displayed in a window rather than all of the information in the data-file icon. You can scroll to the point in the data-file icon that you want, and then print just that screen.

To print the active window or the Desktop, click mouse button 1 on the screen you want to print; then press the Print Screen key.

NOTE: The screen will be printed on your default printer.

Viewing the Contents of a Job

The printer icon contains the jobs that are waiting to be printed. These jobs are in the printer queue. You can view the contents of a job while it is waiting to be printed. This gives you the opportunity to cancel the job if you no longer need it or to change the order in which the job is printed.

To view the contents of a job in the printer queue:
1. Double-click on the printer icon.
2. Double-click on the job whose contents you want to view. (The Picture Viewer window is displayed.)
3. Double-click on the title-bar icon of the Picture Viewer window to close it.

Viewing Information about a Job

The default setting for the printer icon is Icon view. The icon view shows the names of the jobs and the order of the jobs in the printer queue. If you change the setting to **Details view**, the job ID, document name, date, time, status, and owner information is displayed. This can be helpful in identifying which job you want to print next or delete.

To view information about a job:
1. Point to the printer icon.
2. Click mouse button 2 to display the pop-up menu.
3. Click mouse button 1 on the arrow to the right of the **Open** menu choice.
4. Click mouse button 1 on the **Details view** menu choice. Notice the additional details that are displayed about the jobs in the queue.
5. Double-click on the title-bar icon of the open window to close it.

TIP: You can change some of the job information by clicking mouse button 2 on the job icon (Icon view) or on the document name (Details view) and selecting Settings from the pop-up menu.

Holding and Releasing Print Jobs

You can *hold* a job (keep it from printing) or *release* a job (allow it to print). Putting a job on hold is useful if you are not sure whether you really need to print the job or you just want to wait for another time to print it.

To hold or release a print job:
1. Double-click on the printer icon.
2. Point to the job you want to hold or release.
3. Click mouse button 2 to display the pop-up menu.
4. Click mouse button 1 on the **Change status** menu choice.
5. Click mouse button 1 on either the **Hold** or **Release** menu choice.
6. Double-click on the title-bar icon of the open window to close it.

Sometimes it is more convenient to place all of the jobs in a printer queue on hold. For example, if the telephone rings and you want to stop the printer, you can put all the print jobs on hold. Then, when you get off the telephone, you can release the print jobs.

To hold or release all of the print jobs in a printer queue:
1. Point to the printer icon.
2. Click mouse button 2 to display the pop-up menu.
3. Click mouse button 1 on the **Change status** menu choice.
4. Click mouse button 1 on either the **Hold** or **Release** menu choice.
5. Double-click on the title-bar icon of the open window to close it.

TIP: If you put individual jobs on hold before placing all the print jobs in the printer queue on hold, the individual jobs will not be released when you release all jobs. In other words, print jobs placed on hold individually must be released individually.

Changing the Order in Which Jobs Print

The order in which the jobs appear in the printer window is the order in which they will be printed. However, you can change the order. (For example, you can choose which job prints next.) If you send many jobs to the printer, you can send them in any order and then decide which ones you want to print first.

To change the order in which jobs are printed:
1. Double-click on the printer icon.
2. Point to the job you want to print next.

3. Click mouse button 2 to display the pop-up menu.
4. Click mouse button 1 on the **Print next** menu choice.
5. Double-click on the title-bar icon of the open window to close it.

Deleting a Print Job

If you send a job to the printer and then later decide that you do not really need or want the job, you can delete the job before it is printed.

To delete a job before it is printed:
1. Double-click on the printer icon.
2. Point to the job you want to delete.
3. Click mouse button 2 to display the pop-up menu.
4. Click mouse button 1 on the **Delete** menu choice.
5. Double-click on the title-bar icon of the open window to close it.

If you need to, you can delete all of the jobs waiting to be printed.

To delete all of the jobs waiting to be printed:
1. Point to the printer icon.
2. Click mouse button 2 to display the pop-up menu.
3. Click mouse button 1 on the **Delete all jobs** menu choice.
4. Click mouse button 1 on the **Yes** push button.

Installing a Printer

You can easily install a printer for use with OS/2 Warp and WIN-OS/2 after OS/2 Warp is already installed. OS/2 Warp comes with many ways to install a printer, but the one described in the steps that follow is by far the easiest. This procedure takes you through the steps to create a printer icon for OS/2 Warp and also to activate the printer driver for WIN-OS/2 icons.

To install a printer icon:
1. Double-click on the **Templates** icon.
2. Point to the **Printer** template.
3. Press and hold mouse button 2.
4. Drag the template to an icon or to the Desktop.
5. Release mouse button 2.

6. Type a name for the printer in the **Name** field.
7. Click mouse button 1 on the port to which the printer is connected.
8. Click mouse button 1 on the **Install new printer driver** push button.
9. Click mouse button 1 on the name of the printer driver in the **Printer driver** list. If your printer driver is not listed, do the following:
    a. Click mouse button 1 on the **Other OS/2 printer driver** choice.
    b. Insert a diskette containing the printer drivers into drive A, or type the appropriate drive designation and path in the **Directory** field.
    c. Click mouse button 1 on the **Refresh** choice. Wait until the window fills with names of printer drivers.
    d. Click mouse button 1 on one or more drivers. If the driver you need is not listed, insert another diskette or change the information in the **Directory field** and click mouse button 1 on the **Refresh** choice again.
10. Click mouse button 1 on the **Install** push button.
11. Insert the requested media, and then click mouse button 1 on the **OK** push button to begin the installation of the printer driver.
12. Click mouse button 1 on the **OK** push button in the message window.
13. Click mouse button 1 on the **Create** push button in the Create a Printer window.
14. Click mouse button 1 on the **Yes** push button so that you can use this printer while using WIN-OS/2.
15. Insert the requested media, and then click mouse button 1 on the **OK** push button. Repeat this step until all diskette requests have been met.
16. Double-click on the title-bar icon of the Templates window to close it.

A new printer icon is on your Desktop. The printer icon is set up to be used with your WIN-OS/2 icons. If you want to customize the settings for this new printer icon, see "Setting Printer Properties" on page 134.

TIP: Whenever you add a printer icon, the name of that printer is added to the pop-up menu of every other printer icon. This gives you the opportunity to use any printer you want from any printer icon on the Desktop. If you want to choose a printer other than the one represented by the printer icon:

1. Point to a printer icon.
2. Click mouse button 2 to display the pop-up menu.
3. Click mouse button 1 on the **Set default** menu choice.
4. Click mouse button 1 on the name of the printer that you want to use.

Chapter 25

Adding or Removing Features after Installation

255

OS/2 Warp lets you add or remove operating system and hardware features. OS/2 Warp comes with three programs—Selective Install, Device Driver Install, and Selective Uninstall—that help you quickly and easily add or remove features.

This chapter explains how to use the programs that come with OS/2 Warp to help you add or remove features.

NOTE: Keep your OS/2 Warp installation media handy because you will need the media to do the following procedures.

Adding Operating System Features after Installation

If you used the Advanced Installation method to install OS/2 Warp, you might not have installed all of the programs and features available to you. Maybe you made these choices because you didn't have enough space on your computer, or maybe you thought you just didn't need them at the time. You can easily add the programs and features as described in the following procedure.

To add features after installation:

1. Point to an empty area on the Desktop.
2. Click mouse button 2 to display the pop-up menu.
3. Click mouse button 1 on the **System setup** menu choice.
4. Double-click on the **Selective Install** icon.
5. Click mouse button 1 on the **OK** push button.
6. Click mouse button 1 to place a check mark to the left of any item you want to install. If a **More** push button is displayed to the right of an item, click mouse button 1 on it to see additional choices.

You can choose from the following list of options:

Documentation

Lets you install the OS/2 Tutorial, OS/2 Command Reference, or REXX Information.

Fonts

Lets you install Courier, Helvetica, System Mono-Spaced, Times Roman, Courier (outline), Helvetica (outline), or Times Roman (outline) fonts.

Optional System Utilities

Lets you install utilities that back up your hard disk, change file attributes, display a directory tree, manage partitions, label diskettes, link object modules, view pictures, recover files, restore backed up files, and sort filters. Also included are installation utilities and PMREXX support.

Tools and Games

Lets you install the Enhanced Editor, the Search and Scan tool, the Pulse program, and the Solitaire - Klondike, Chess, and Mahjongg Solitaire games.

OS/2 DOS Support

Lets you install the DOS Protect Mode Interface, Virtual Expanded Memory Management, and Virtual Extended Memory Management.

WIN-OS/2 Support

Lets you specify the path where you have Windows installed. You need to change this path only if you installed Windows in a directory other than C:\WINDOWS.

Multimedia Software Support

Lets you install Software Motion Video and other multimedia support and specify the path where you want to have them installed.

High Performance File System

Lets you install HPFS support for OS/2 Warp programs.

Serviceability and Diagnostic Aids

Lets you install utilities that can help an authorized service person in isolating and correcting system problems.

Optional Bitmaps

Lets you install a set of bit maps you can use to change the background of the OS/2 Warp Desktop and its windows.

7. Click mouse button 1 on the **Install** push button.
8. Follow the instructions on the screen.
9. When you see the OS/2 Setup and Installation window, read the instructions on the screen, and then click mouse button 1 on the **OK** push button.

Adding Hardware Features after Installation

If you bought a hardware device (such as a CD-ROM drive) that is OS/2 Warp-compatible, you can install support for it using the Selective Install icon. OS/2 Warp comes equipped with many of the latest hardware *device drivers*, making installation a breeze. Device drivers contains software needed by the computer to recognize and operate the device.

To add hardware after installation:
1. Point to an empty area on the Desktop.
2. Click mouse button 2 to display the pop-up menu.
3. Click mouse button 1 on the **System setup** menu choice.
4. Double-click on the **Selective Install** icon.
5. Click mouse button 1 on the icon next to any of the choices that you want to change.

You can choose from the following list of options:

Country
> Lets you choose which monetary symbol, decimal separator, and date and time format that your computer will use.

Keyboard
> Lets you change the keyboard layout for your computer.

Mouse
> Lets you add or change the type of pointing device you have on your computer.

Serial Device
> Lets you add support for a device such as a modem, serial plotter, or serial printer.

Primary Display
> Lets you change the display adapter used by your primary display.

Secondary Display
> Lets you change the display adapter used by your secondary display.

Advanced Power Management
> Lets you add Advanced Power Management (APM) support, which monitors battery usage in laptop computers.

CD-ROM Device Support
> Lets you install support for CD-ROM devices attached to your computer.

Multimedia Device Support
> Lets you install and change the settings for sound and video cards you select.

PCMCIA Support

Lets you add support for the Personal Computer Memory Card International Association (PCMCIA) standard, which is the industry standard for PC card adapters used in laptop computers.

Printer

Lets you add a printer to your computer that is recognized only by OS/2 Warp.

NOTE: To find out how to add printer support for OS/2 Warp and WIN-OS/2, read "Installing a Printer" on page 253.

SCSI Adapter Support

Lets you add or change support for a SCSI adapter you have in your computer.

6. Click mouse button 1 on the **OK** push button.
7. Click mouse button 1 on the **Install** push button.
8. Follow the instructions on the screen.
9. When you see the OS/2 Setup and Installation window, read the instructions on the screen, and then click mouse button 1 on the **OK** push button.

Installing Device Drivers

Many devices that you attach to your computer, such as a CD-ROM drive, mouse, and display come with a *device driver diskette*. The device driver diskette (sometimes called a device support diskette) contains the software needed by the computer to recognize and operate the device.

NOTE: The Device Driver Install icon can be used to install any device driver except those for printers and plotters. To install a device driver for a printer or plotter, see "Installing a Printer" on page 253.

To install a device driver (other than one for a printer or plotter):
1. Point to an empty area on the Desktop.
2. Click mouse button 2 to display the pop-up menu.
3. Click mouse button 1 on the **System setup** menu choice.
4. Double-click on the **Device Driver Install** icon. When the window is displayed, you will see several push buttons. The **Change** push button, located under the Source directory field, lets you change the path that indicates where the device driver files are located. (This is typically a diskette in drive A.) The **Change** push button located under the Destination directory lets you change the path that indicates where

you want to copy the device driver support. When the directory information is correct, continue on with the following steps.

5. Click mouse button 1 on the **Install** push button.
6. Click mouse button 1 on the device driver that you want to install.
7. Click mouse button 1 on the **OK** push button.
8. Remove the device driver diskette from drive A.
9. Double-click on the title-bar icon of the open window to close it.

To find out more, refer to the documentation that came with the device.

NOTE: Do not use the Device Driver Install icon to install device drivers found on the OS/2 Warp Installation diskettes.

Removing Operating System Features

You can use the Selective Uninstall program to remove operating system files, programs, and device drivers from your hard disk. This program provides a way to change your system as often as your computing needs might change. For example, you might have installed OS/2 Warp and included the documentation feature, but now find that, as a seasoned user, you no longer need to refer to the OS/2 Tutorial. You could elect to selectively uninstall the OS/2 Tutorial and free up the disk space it uses.

The following describes how to selectively uninstall programs you no longer need or are removing so that you can replace them with newer ones.

To remove programs you no longer want:

1. Double-click on the **OS/2 System** icon.
2. Double-click on the **System setup** icon.
3. Double-click on the **Selective Uninstall** icon. You will see the Selective Uninstall window.

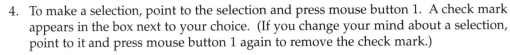

4. To make a selection, point to the selection and press mouse button 1. A check mark appears in the box next to your choice. (If you change your mind about a selection, point to it and press mouse button 1 again to remove the check mark.)

NOTE: When a **More** push button appears next to a choice, it indicates that another window containing additional choices is available. (After you make a selection, the **More** push button becomes available.) Point to the **More** push button and press mouse button 1 to display a list of additional choices that you can remove.

WARNING: When you select **More**, the programs that OS/2 Warp is currently using are listed and a check mark appears next to each one. Make sure you remove the check mark from only those items that you do **NOT** want to selectively uninstall (delete) from your hard disk.

5. Double-click on the title-bar icons of the open windows to close them.

TIP: Your hard disk contains the Adobe Type Manager (ATM) program. Adobe Type Manager uses PostScript outline font technology to produce the sharpest possible character type on the screen and on the printed page.

If you are using the Adobe Type Manager program, you **should not** selectively uninstall the **Fonts** choice. This will cause the ATM program to be deleted.

Official Guide to Using OS/2 Warp

Chapter 26

Using Laptop Computer Utility Programs

The Power icon is used for battery-powered laptop computers. It lets you see how much power is left in the battery of your laptop computer (if your laptop computer supports the Advanced Power Management (APM) standard). The APM standard defines the way the hardware and software work together to reduce the amount of power used by the computer and to help extend the life of the battery.

If your computer has APM support, the Power icon is automatically installed during the installation of OS/2 Warp.

TIP: If APM was not installed, you can install it. Use the Selective Install icon and select **Advanced Power Management**. For information about Selective Install, see Chapter 25, "Adding or Removing Features After Installation" on page 255.

The Power icon gets its power status information from your computer. If you notice incorrect battery life or status information within the Power icon, rely on the LEDs on your computer for accurate power status.

To open the Power icon:
1. Point to an empty area on the Desktop.
2. Click mouse button 2 to display the pop-up menu.
3. Click mouse button 1 on the **System setup** menu choice.
4. Double-click on the **Power** icon.

The Power window displays the following information:

Battery life
Displays the power gauge, which indicates the level of the battery compared to the capacity of the battery. When the power gauge indicator is completely shaded, the battery is at full power. The shaded area of the gauge moves up or down as the battery power level increases or decreases. When the power gauge indicator is dimmed, there is no battery in the computer or the computer cannot provide battery information.

Power source
Indicates whether the computer is being powered by the battery or whether it is plugged into the wall (AC powered). No power source information is displayed if the system cannot determine the power source.

Battery state
Displays the charge state of the battery. Battery state information is displayed as follows:

- **High** indicates that the battery charge is good and you can continue using your computer.

264

- **Low** indicates that you should recharge the battery or switch to another power source such as another battery or AC power.

- **Critical** indicates that the battery charge is depleted. It's time to recharge the battery or switch to another power source immediately to avoid a system failure or data loss.

- **Charging** indicates that the computer is restoring the battery charge.

- **Unknown** indicates that the computer cannot determine the battery state or that there is no battery in your computer.

TIP: If you prefer, you can display only the Power gauge portion of the Power icon window. To do this:
1. Point to the **Power** icon.
2. Click mouse button 2 to display the pop-up menu.
3. Click mouse button 1 on the arrow next to the **Open** menu choice.
4. Click mouse button 1 on the **Battery status** menu choice.

Conserving Power

You can set up your laptop computer to conserve power. When you enable power conservation, you will find that you can use your laptop computer for longer periods of time without having to recharge the battery.

To enable or disable power conservation on your laptop computer:
1. Point to an empty area on the Desktop.
2. Click mouse button 2 to display the pop-up menu.
3. Click mouse button 1 on the **System setup** menu choice.
4. Point to the **Power** icon.
5. Click mouse button 2 to display the pop-up menu.
6. Click mouse button 1 on the **Settings** menu choice.
7. Click mouse button 1 on the **Power** notebook tab.
8. Click mouse button 1 on the **On** choice to reduce the power consumption and track the amount of power left in the battery. (If you click mouse button 1 on the Off choice, you will not be able to track the amount of power left in the battery and you will not be able to use suspend mode.)
9. Click mouse button 1 on the **Confirm on power state changes** to place a check mark in the box. When you place a check mark in this box, you will be notified (a message will be displayed) when your laptop computer is going into suspend mode. If you

do not place a check mark in this box, you will not be notified (no message will be displayed) when your laptop computer is going into suspend mode.

10. Double-click on the title-bar icons of the open windows to close them.

Suspend Mode

Use Suspend mode to help conserve the battery power of your laptop computer. Suspend mode dims the display and turns off devices that you are not using.

To set the suspend mode:

1. Point to the **Power** icon.
2. Click mouse button 2 to display the pop-up menu.
3. Click mouse button 1 on the **Suspend** menu choice.
4. Respond to any messages.

TIP: Because there is such a wide variety of laptop computers available on the market today, each one uses a different method to exit suspend mode and resume operation. Read the documentation that came with your laptop computer for information about its suspend mode features.

After you turn off suspend mode, you will notice a startup delay before you can continue using your laptop computer. This delay, which varies depending on which laptop computer you have, might take a few seconds.

Customizing the Battery Status Window

You might want to customize the window that displays the status of your laptop's battery. You can choose the way the information in the window is displayed. You can choose to show battery power, battery source, and power source in the window or you can choose to show only battery power. You can also choose to automatically update the information in the window.

To customize the battery status window:

1. Point to an empty area on the Desktop.
2. Click mouse button 2 to display the pop-up menu.
3. Click mouse button 1 on the **System setup** menu choice.
4. Point to the **Power** icon.
5. Click mouse button 2 to display the pop-up menu.
6. Click mouse button 1 on the **Settings** menu choice.
7. Click mouse button 1 on the **View** notebook tab.

8. Click mouse button 1 on a choice in the **Default status view** field. You can choose from the following:

Full status

Displays a small window that contains three areas of information:

- A **Battery life** area, which shows a battery with a power gauge in the center of it.

- A **Power source** area, which shows the type of power source (AC/DC).

- A **Battery state** area, which shows the charge state of the battery from high to low.

Battery only

Displays a small window that contains only a **Battery life** area, which shows a battery with a power gauge in the center of it.

9. Click mouse button 1 on one of the choices in the **Refresh** field. You can choose from the following:

On

Enables automatic updates to the battery information. If you select this choice, the battery information is updated at regular intervals. (You specify how often you want the information refreshed.)

Off

Disables automatic updates to the battery information. If you select this choice, the battery information is not updated at regular intervals. (If you set this choice to Off, you will need to display the pop-up menu for the Power or Battery window and then use the **Refresh now** menu choice every time you want to update the battery information.)

10. Double-click on the title-bar icons of the open windows to close them.

TIP: You can also quickly turn the refresh information on or off from the pop-up menu of the Power or Battery window. To do this:

1. Click mouse button 2 on the title-bar icon of the Power or Battery window.
2. Click mouse button 1 on the **Refresh now** menu choice.
3. Click mouse button 1 on either the **On** or **Off** menu choice.

Plug and Play for Laptop Computers

OS/2 Warp provides software support for Personal Computer Memory Card International Association (PCMCIA) hardware. PCMCIA is the standard in *PC card* adapters for laptop computers. A PC card is about the size and shape of a credit card and is plugged into your computer. You can use PC cards with laptops, notebooks, tablets, and other portable computer systems that are equipped with a PCMCIA slot.

If your computer has PCMCIA support, the Plug and Play for PCMCIA icon is automatically installed during the installation of OS/2 Warp.

TIP: If PCMCIA support was not installed, you can install it. Use the Selective Install icon and select PCMCIA. For more information about Selective Install, see Chapter 25, "Adding or Removing Features After Installation" on page 255.

Plug and Play for PCMCIA is an OS/2 Warp program that displays information about a PC card. There are two basic types of PC cards:

- Memory cards, which contain specific types of memory devices

- Input/output (I/O) cards, which contain devices such as modems and disks

Both card types are assigned system resources, which are used to communicate with the card's devices.

Plug and Play for PCMCIA also allows you to start applications automatically when their icons are registered with a PC card type.

To open the Plug and Play for PCMCIA icon:

1. Double-click on the **OS/2 System** icon.
2. Double-click on the **System setup** icon.
3. Double-click on the **Plug and Play for PCMCIA** icon.

Socket and Card Information

The following information is displayed in the Plug and Play for PCMCIA window:

No.
　　Indicates the PCMCIA slot or socket number that is being used.

Card Type
　　Indicates the type of card plugged into the PCMCIA slot. Examples of card types are as follows:

- Boot

- Communication (including 3270, 5250, Ethernet, LAN, SDLC, and Token Ring)

- Hard Disk, AIMS

- I/O (for multi-function, parallel, and SCSI card types)

- Memory

- Modem, Serial

Card Status

Displays an icon that indicates the status of the card. The status for a PCMCIA card can be Empty, Inserted, Ready, Not Ready, or Inserted for Memory.

Additional information about a memory or I/O card is available. To look at this information, double-click on the icon for the memory or I/O card.

For memory cards, the following additional information is available:

Card information

Displays the vendor name and card description.

Write protect

Lets you choose whether you want to write protect the card.

Battery

Displays the state of the computer battery.

Region

Specifies the region of card memory used for memory devices such as SRAM.

For I/O cards, the following additional information is available:

Card information

Displays the vendor name and card description.

Assigned resources

Specifies the type of system resources (such as the interrupt request level and the input/output ports) used by the PC card.

Customizing the Plug and Play for PCMCIA Program

You can customize the Plug and Play for PCMCIA program so that it beeps or automatically opens whenever a PC card is inserted or removed or whenever the PC card is in a ready or not ready state. By setting these cues, you can tell immediately what state the PC card is in.

You can also set the Plug and Play for PCMCIA program to be visible at all times. This prevents other windows from covering it and hiding it from view.

To customize Plug and Play for PCMCIA:
1. Move the mouse pointer to an empty area on the Desktop.
2. Click mouse button 2 to display the pop-up menu.
3. Click mouse button 1 on the **System setup** menu choice.
4. Double-click on the **Plug and Play for PCMCIA** icon.
5. Click mouse button 1 on the **Options** menu.
6. Click mouse button 1 on the **Customize** menu choice.
7. Click mouse button 1 on the choices in the **When card is** field that you want to use. You can have the computer beep or display a window whenever a card is in one of the following states:

   Inserted
   > Beep or display a window whenever a card is inserted.

   Removed
   > Beep or display a window whenever a card is removed.

   Ready
   > Beep or display a window whenever a card is ready to be used.

   Not ready
   > Beep or display a window whenever a card is not configured for use. (Some PC cards are not configured until they are accessed by a user or program.)

8. Click mouse button 1 on a choice in the **Configuration Manager Always Visible** field. You can choose from the following:

   Yes
   > Keeps the Plug and Play for PCMCIA icon or window visible at all times. The icon or window shows through any window placed over it.

   No
   > Lets the Plug and Play for PCMCIA icon or window be covered by other windows.

9. Click mouse button 1 on the **OK** push button.

NOTE: The Plug and Play for PCMCIA program must be running (minimized or in a window) in order for the choices you made in this procedure to work. You can still use your PC cards without having this program running. However, if the Plug and Play for PCMCIA program is not running, you won't hear a beep, the Plug and Play for PCMCIA window won't be displayed automatically, and the Plug and Play for PCMCIA window won't remain visible even though you selected the choices.

Registering Programs with a PC Card

You can use the Plug and Play for PCMCIA icon to register (associate) programs with a PC card so that each time the PC card is inserted, the programs you registered are automatically started. For example, if you use a fax and a communication program every time you insert the Modem PC card, you can set up Plug and Play for PCMCIA to automatically start both programs. This saves you the time and bother of finding the icons for the programs and starting them yourself.

To register programs with PC cards:

1. Point to an empty area on the Desktop.
2. Click mouse button 2 to display the pop-up menu.
3. Click mouse button 1 on the **System setup** menu choice.
4. Double-click on the **Plug and Play for PCMCIA** icon.
5. Click mouse button 1 on the **Options** menu.
6. Click mouse button 1 on the **Register Object** menu choice.
7. Click mouse button 1 on the down arrow to the right of the **Select card type** field.
8. Click mouse button 1 on the card type that you want to register with a program.
9. Point to the program that you want to register with the PC card.
10. Press and hold mouse button 2.
11. Drag the icon to the **Object List** field in the Plug and Play for PCMCIA window.
12. Release mouse button 2.
13. Repeat steps 9 through 12 for each program you want to register with the PC card. If more than one program is registered with a card, a list is presented each time the PC card becomes ready. You can then select the program you want to start from the list.
14. Click mouse button 1 on one of the choices in the **To start or open an object** field. You can choose from the following:

   Automatically
   Starts the registered program automatically when the PC card is in the specified state. (**Automatically** cannot be used when more than one program is registered with a particular PC card.)

Manually
> Displays an Object Launcher window when the PC card is in the specified state so that you can select the program that you want to start. This is the default choice when more than one program is registered with a PC card.

15. Click mouse button 1 on the choices that best describe when you want a program that is registered with a PC card to be launched (started). You can choose from the following:

Inserted
> Launch the program when the card is inserted.

Removed
> Launch the program when the card is removed.

Ready
> Launch the program when the card is ready to be used. (This choice is available only for I/O cards.)

Not ready
> Launch the program when the card is not configured for use. (Some PC cards are not configured until they are accessed by a user or program. This choice is available only for I/O cards.)

16. Click mouse button 1 on the **OK** push button.

Manually Launching Programs with a PC Card

Whenever more than one program is registered with a PC Card, the computer presents a list of programs that are registered with that particular PC card. The list is displayed in the Object Launcher window.

To start a program from the Object Launcher, click mouse 1 on the name of the program in the **Object List**; then click mouse button 1 on the **Launch** push button.

TIP: You can register only one program with a particular PC Card. That way, each time you use a particular PC Card, you will be prompted to start the program. This can be useful for a program that you only occasionally use with a particular PC Card. For example, you might want to register your fax program with your modem PC Card. Then, when you use the modem PC card, you will be prompted to start the fax program. However, if this is an occasion where you are using your modem PC Card for another reason (and you really don't want to use the fax program), you can elect to continue without starting the fax program.

Discontinuing Registration of Programs with a PC Card

When you no longer want to be able to start a program from a PC card, you can choose to discontinue its registration. When you discontinue a registration, you will have to open the program yourself each time you want to use it with the PC card.

To discontinue the registration of a program with a PC card:

1. Point to an empty area on the Desktop.
2. Click mouse button 2 to display the pop-up menu.
3. Click mouse button 1 on the **System setup** menu choice.
4. Double-click on the **Plug and Play for PCMCIA** icon.
5. Click mouse button 1 on the **Options** menu.
6. Click mouse button 1 on the **Register Object** menu choice.
7. Click mouse button 1 on the icon in the **Object List** field.
8. Click mouse button 1 on the **Remove** push button.
9. Click mouse button 1 on the **OK** push button.

27

Using Disk Drives

OS/2 Warp provides a Drives icon that you can use to see the contents of the drives on your computer. Your Drives icon will contain other icons that represent the types of drives that are installed on your computer. For example, if your computer has a diskette drive or a CD-ROM drive, icons that represent them are located in the Drives icon.

This chapter shows you how to look at the contents of your drives and describes how to change the way the contents of your drives are displayed. This chapter also provides information about how to format a disk and check a disk.

Accessing Drives

Most industry-standard computers assign a letter (from A-Z) as an identifier for each drive on the computer. For example, on many computers, the diskette drive is called drive A and the hard disk drive is called drive C. If you have ever used another operating system, you might be familiar with commands that use the drive letter as part of their command syntax. (For example, to look at the contents of your C drive from a command-based operating system, you would type DIR C:.)

With OS/2 Warp, you are less concerned about the physical identifier for your drives (or commands, for that matter), because you simply click on the Drives icon to look at your drives. You can access your hard disk, any diskette drives you might have installed, your CD-ROM drive, a tape backup, or an optical disc. You can review the contents of a drive and you can display files contained on the drive (or on the media supported by the drive).

To look at the contents of a drive:

1. Double-click on the **OS/2 System** icon.
2. Double-click on the **Drives** icon.
3. Double-click on the drive icon you want information about.

Once you have opened a drive, you can look at any file contained on the drive by double-clicking on the file name.

Rocket Tip: You might find it easier to access your drive A or drive C icons from the LaunchPad. (Drive A is located on the front panel and Drive C is located in the drawer.)

Displaying the Contents of Your Drives

The contents of your drives can be displayed in three different views:

Icon view

> Displays the contents of the drive as icons. (This is the default if the drive did not have folders (directories) on it when you installed OS/2 Warp.)

Tree view

> Displays the contents of the drive in a tree-like structure. (This is the default if the drive did have folders on it when you installed OS/2 Warp.) A plus (+) sign to the left of a folder indicates that additional folders exist inside the folder. You can look at the additional folders by clicking on the plus sign. (If you point to a folder and double-click on it, you will display the contents of the folder in an icon view.)

Details view

> Displays the contents of the drive in a table with the following information:
>
> - Icon
> - Title
> - Real name
> - Size
> - Last write date and time
> - Last access date and time
> - Creation date and time
> - Flags

You might find that the default view is not always the most favorable view for you. You can change the way contents of your drives are displayed.

To choose how you want to view the contents of a drive:
1. Double-click on the **OS/2 System** icon.
2. Double-click on the **Drives** icon.
3. Point to the drive icon that you want to display.
4. Click mouse button 2 to display the pop-up menu.
5. Click mouse button 1 on the arrow to the right of the **Open** menu choice.
6. Click mouse button 1 on the menu choice for the view you want to see.
7. Double-click on the title-bar icons of the open windows to close them.

Formatting a Disk

You can *format* a disk. When a disk is formatted, it is checked for defects and prepared to accept data. During this process, all existing data is erased from the disk. Make sure that before you format a disk, it does not contain any information that is important.

TIP: If you are not familiar with formatting disks, look at the OS/2 Tutorial, which provides a nice interactive demonstration of how to format a disk.

To format a disk:
1. Double-click on the **OS/2 System** icon.
2. Double-click on the **Drives** icon.
3. Point to the disk you want to format.
4. Click mouse button 2 to display the pop-up menu.
5. Click mouse button 1 on the **Format disk** menu choice.
6. When the Format Disk window appears, type a Volume Label (a name for the disk).
7. Click mouse button 1 on the type of file system (FAT or HPFS). If you used Easy Installation to install OS/2 Warp, your file system is most likely FAT. If you used Advanced Installation, you might have selected HPFS. (If you are really not sure which file system is installed, use **Check disk** before proceeding. For information about the **Check disk** program, see "Checking a Disk", in the following section.)
8. Click mouse button 1 on the **Format** push button.
9. When the format is completed, click on the **OK** push button.
10. Double-click on the title-bar icons of the open windows to close them.

Checking a Disk

You can check a disk for:

- **Defects**, which are errors in the file allocation table or folders on the disk. If you select Write corrections to disk, any problems found will be fixed.

- **Current usage**, which is the amount of the disk used for folders, files, and any file details. It also indicates the amount of space that is reserved on the disk.

- **File system type**, which is the type of file system on the disk.

- **Total disk space**, which is the capacity of the disk in bytes.

- **Total amount of disk space available**, which is the amount of free space left on the disk.

NOTE: You cannot check a disk that is currently being used or that is locked by another process. (For example, you can't check the disk that OS/2 Warp is running on.)

To check a disk:

1. Double-click on the **OS/2 System** icon.
2. Double-click on the **Drives** icon.
3. Point to the drive that you want to check for errors.
4. Click mouse button 2 to display the pop-up menu.
5. Click mouse button 1 on the **Check disk** menu choice.
6. Click mouse button 1 on the **Write corrections to disk** choice to place a check mark in the box.
7. Click mouse button 1 on the **Check** push button. When the check is done, the Check Disk - Results window is displayed.
8. Click mouse button 1 on the **Cancel** push button to remove the window.
9. Click mouse button 1 on the **Cancel** push button to remove the Check Disk window.
10. Double-click on the title-bar icons of the open windows to close them.

Official Guide to Using OS/2 Warp

Chapter 28

Using Command Prompts

The Command Prompts icon contains icons that start DOS, OS/2, and WIN-OS/2 command prompts. The command prompts for DOS, OS/2, and WIN-OS/2 can be displayed in a window or full screen.

This chapter explains how to start a command prompt and how to start multiple command prompts.

Starting a Command Prompt

After you start a command prompt, you can use it to start programs and enter commands. Each command prompt runs independently of all other command prompts that might be running on your computer.

TIP: In most instances, using command prompts is really a matter of preference because most tasks you perform using OS/2 Warp are performed more efficiently and quickly from the Desktop.

To start a command prompt:
1. Double-click on the **OS/2 System** icon.
2. Double-click on the **Command Prompts** icon.
3. Double-click on the command prompt of your choice.

To close a full-screen command prompt, type **Exit**, and then press the Enter key.

To close a window command prompt, double-click on the title-bar icon of the window.

When you close a command prompt, there might be messages displayed on the screen that you will need to respond to before the command prompt can be closed.

You can temporarily leave a command prompt without closing it. This is considered to be switching from a command prompt to another running program. When you switch from your command prompt to another program, the information in the command prompt window stays the way you left it so that when you switch back, everything is still the same.

To temporarily leave a command prompt and choose to work with another program:
1. Press the Ctrl+Esc keys. (This displays the Window List.)
2. Double-click on a title of the program you want to switch to.

Starting Multiple Command Prompts

You can open more than one command prompt of the same type. (For example, you can have two OS/2 Windows open.) All you need to do is make copies of the icon for the command prompt that you want to run.

To open multiple command prompt icons:
1. Double-click on the **OS/2 System** icon.
2. Double-click on the **Command Prompts** icon.
3. Copy one of the icons (for example, OS/2 Window) by holding down the Ctrl key and mouse button 2 and dragging the icon to another location. Then release the mouse button and the Ctrl key.
4. Double-click on the icon you just made a copy of to start another command prompt.
5. Repeat the steps to make as many copies as you need.

TIP: If you find that you often use multiple copies of a command prompt, you can change the settings of the icon so that it opens another command prompt every time you double-click on it. Do the following:
1. Double-click on the **OS/2 System** icon.
2. Double-click on the **Command Prompt**s icon.
3. Point to the icon that represents the OS/2, DOS, or WIN-OS/2 command prompt you often use.
4. Click mouse button 2 to display the pop-up menu.
5. Click mouse button 1 on the **Settings** menu choice.
6. Click mouse button 1 on the **Window** notebook tab.
7. Click mouse button 1 on the **Create new window** button.
8. Double-click on the title-bar icon of the notebook to close it.

Chapter 29

Some Thoughtful Utilities for DOS Users

285

If you have been using DOS for a long time, you might be using older DOS programs that won't run using the version of DOS that comes with OS/2 Warp. This is generally the exception and not the rule, so try to run your DOS programs using OS/2 Warp because it's faster and more efficient.

If you used Easy Installation to install OS/2 Warp and a version of DOS was installed on your system, then OS/2 Warp created a utility program that you can use to switch back and forth between DOS and OS/2 Warp. OS/2 Warp also provides a utility that you can use to create diskettes that can help you run older DOS programs.

This chapter provides information about both utilities.

Using Dual Boot

When you installed OS/2 Warp, *Dual Boot* was automatically set up for you if there was an existing version of DOS on your computer and you used the Easy Installation method. (If you used the Advanced Installation method, Dual Boot was automatically set up only if you selected drive C as the installation drive.) Dual Boot lets you switch back and forth between OS/2 Warp and DOS so that you can run DOS programs that don't work with the version of DOS that comes with OS/2 Warp.

Dual Boot keeps track of which operating system will be started when you turn on your computer. Each time you shut down and restart your computer, it will start (boot) in the operating system you were using before you shut down your computer. For example, if you shut down your computer while DOS is running, your system will start in DOS the next time you turn it on.

To use Dual Boot to switch to DOS:

1. Double-click on the **OS/2 System** icon.
2. Double-click on the **Command Prompts** icon.
3. Double-click on the **Dual Boot** icon.
4. When a message appears asking if you want your system to be reset, type Y and press the Enter key.

TIP: If you want to run your DOS programs while OS/2 Warp is running, you can use the DOS command prompt icons that are part of OS/2 Warp. You will find that most of your DOS programs can be run from these command prompts. If you use the DOS command prompts, you won't have to use Dual Boot, which shuts down OS/2 Warp. To use a DOS command prompt, open **DOS Window** or **DOS Full Screen** from the Command Prompts icon.

To switch from DOS to OS/2 Warp, at the DOS command prompt, type **C:\OS2\BOOT /OS2**, and then press the Enter key.

TIP: You can create a file that will make it much easier for you to boot from DOS back to OS/2 Warp. To find out how, read "Switching from DOS to OS/2 Warp" on page 176.

Using DOS from Drive A

You can use the DOS from Drive A icon to start a specific version of DOS (3.0 or later) from a diskette. Using a specific version of DOS lets you use programs that run with a version of DOS other than the version of DOS you get with OS/2 Warp.

Before you can start a specific DOS version from a diskette, you must create a DOS Startup diskette (or DOS bootable diskette).

NOTE: If you already have a DOS Startup diskette, skip steps 1 through 5 in the following procedure.

To create a DOS Startup diskette:

1. Start your computer with a version of DOS. You can use a:

   • DOS installation diskette

   • Hard disk that DOS has been installed on

   • Diskette that DOS has been installed on

2. Type **FORMAT A: /S**
3. Insert a blank diskette into drive A.
4. Press the Enter key. This formats the diskette and transfers the DOS system files to the diskette. (When the format and the transfer are completed, remove the diskette.)
5. Start OS/2 Warp by pressing Ctrl+Alt+Del.
6. Double-click on the **OS/2 System** icon.
7. Double-click on the **Drives** icon.
8. Double-click on the **Drive C** icon.
9. Click mouse button 1 on the plus sign (+) to the left of the OS/2 icon.
10. Double-click on the **MDOS** icon.
11. Insert the diskette containing the DOS system files into drive A.
12. Press and hold down the Ctrl key.
13. Point to the **FSACCESS.EXE** icon.

14. Click mouse button 1.

15. Point to the **FSFILTER.SYS** icon.

16. Click mouse button 1.

17. Point to either the **FSACCESS.EXE** or **FSFILTER.SYS** icon.

18. Press and hold down mouse button 2 while dragging the icons to the **Drive A** icon on the LaunchPad.

19. Release mouse button 2.

20. Release the Ctrl key.

21. Double-click on the title-bar icons of the open windows to close them.

22. Double-click on the **Templates** icon.

23. Point to the **Data File** icon.

24. Press and hold mouse button 2.

25. Drag the data-file icon to the Desktop.

26. Release mouse button 2.

27. Double-click on the data-file icon. (The OS/2 System Editor window is displayed.)

28. Type the following information into the data file:

```
DEVICE=FSFILTER.SYS
DEVICE=C:\OS2\MDOS\HIMEM.SYS
DEVICE=C:\OS2\MDOS\EMM386.SYS
DOS=HIGH,UMB
DEVICEHIGH=C:\OS2\MDOS\ANSI.SYS
FILES=20
BUFFERS=20
```

29. Double-click on the title-bar icon of the OS/2 System Editor window to close it.

30. Click mouse button 1 on the **Save as** push button.

31. Type **A:\CONFIG.SYS**. Then press the Enter key.

32. Double-click on the data-file icon again. (The OS/2 System Editor window is displayed again.)

33. Type the following information into the data file:

```
ECHO OFF
PROMPT $P$G
SET COMSPEC=A:\COMMAND.COM
C:\OS2\MDOS\MOUSE.COM
PATH A:\
```

34. Double-click on the title-bar icon of the OS/2 System Editor window to close it.

35. Click mouse button 1 on the **Save as** push button.

36. Type **A:\AUTOEXEC.BAT**. Then press the Enter key.

37. Double-click on the title-icon of the Templates window to close it.

38. Remove the diskette from the drive and label it *DOS Startup*.

Once you have completed making a DOS Startup diskette, you can begin using DOS from drive A.

To start DOS from Drive A:

1. Insert the DOS Startup diskette into drive A.

2. Double-click on the **OS/2 System** icon.

3. Double-click on the **Command Prompts** icon.

4. Double-click on the **DOS from Drive A** icon.

To close DOS from Drive A:

1. Press Ctrl+Esc to display the Window List.

2. Point to the **DOS from Drive A** choice shown in the list.

3. Click mouse button 2 to display the pop-up menu.

4. Click mouse button 1 on the **Close** menu choice.

Chapter 30

Recovering from Problems

OS/2 Warp includes two programs that can help when you are troubleshooting problems. You can use the Recovery Choices and Create Utility Diskette programs to help you when a problem occurs.

This chapter describes the Recovery Choices program, which is available ONLY if you can access your hard disk. This chapter also describes the Create Utility Diskettes program, which you use to create a set of diskettes that can help you troubleshoot problems in case you cannot access your hard disk.

Using the Recovery Choices Program

OS/2 Warp provides you with its own recovery options in case you are unable to start the operating system. If you are not able to start the operating system, the Recovery Choices program might be helpful when you are trying to correct the problem. The program lets you access a command prompt, use the current Desktop files to restart your computer, or reset your primary display to VGA. The Recovery Choices program also allows you to restart your computer using the default Desktop files that came with OS/2 Warp or choose from a set of archived Desktop files.

Getting to a Command Prompt

If you receive error messages that indicate that OS/2 Warp cannot start correctly, you can get to a command prompt so that you can fix the files that are causing you problems.

1. Turn on the computer. If the computer is already on, press Ctrl+Alt+Del to restart it.
2. When a small white box appears in the upper left-hand corner of your screen, press the Alt+F1 keys.
3. When the Recovery Choices screen appears, press C. (A command prompt is displayed where you can access the files you might need to fix.)

Getting Back to VGA Mode

If you selected a resolution mode that is not correct for your display or if you want to add another display adapter to your computer, you can use this procedure to reset the video mode to VGA.

1. Turn on the computer. If the computer is already on, press Ctrl+Alt+Del to restart it.
2. When a small white box appears in the upper left-hand corner of your screen, press the Alt+F1 keys.
3. When the Recovery Choices screen appears, press V.

Getting Back Your Desktop

If you encounter a problem with your Desktop, you can use the Recovery Choices program to recover the original Desktop or one of the last three Desktops you used. OS/2 Warp has an Archive feature that helps you get your Desktop back. The default for the Archive feature is Off. When the Archive feature is set to Off, you can restore the Desktop that was originally installed with OS/2 Warp.

Note: You can change the default setting for the Archive feature to On. If you do this, the Desktop is saved from the last three times you started OS/2 Warp. Then, if you experience a problem getting to your Desktop, you can restore one of the last three archived Desktops. To find out how to turn the Archive feature to On, see "Saving Changes You Make to Your Desktop" on page 72.

1. Turn on the computer. If the computer is already on, press Ctrl+Alt+Del to restart it.
2. When a small white box appears in the upper left-hand corner of your screen, press Alt+F1. The Recovery Choices screen is displayed.

   If the Archive feature was set to Off, you can restore the original Desktop that came with OS/2 Warp. (The original archived installation files are represented by the X.)

   If the Archive feature was set to On, a screen appears listing the three most recent archives and the original archive. Each set of archived files appears on the Recovery Choices screen with the date and time when the files were archived. The files are numbered 1, 2, 3, where 1 is the most recent file and 3 is the oldest file.

3. Type the number of the archive you want to use to restore your system, or type an **X**.

Using the Create Utility Diskettes Program

OS/2 Warp includes a program that creates diskettes called *Utility Diskettes*. You can use these diskettes to help you correct problems if you cannot start your computer from the hard disk. The Utility Diskettes contain programs that provide a way to display a command prompt, start an editor program, check the hard disk for errors or problems, back up and restore your system, format a diskette or hard disk, and define partitions on a hard disk. The idea is to create these diskettes before you run into problems. Keep them in a safe place, so that they are ready when you need them.

Before you begin, you will need three blank, high-density(2MB) diskettes for a 1.44MB drive, or one extended-density (4MB) diskette for a 2.88MB drive.

To create Utility Diskettes:
1. Point to an empty area on the Desktop.

2. Click mouse button 2 to display the pop-up menu.
3. Click mouse button 1 on the **System setup** menu choice.
4. Double-click on the **Create Utility Diskettes** icon. The Create Utility Diskettes window appears.
5. Click mouse button 1 on the arrow to the right of the **Drive Letter** field until the letter of the diskette drive is displayed.
6. Click mouse button 1 on the **Create** push button.
7. Follow the instructions on the screen to create the diskettes.

   Label the diskettes:

   - *Utility Diskette 1*

   - *Utility Diskette 2*

   - *Utility Diskette 3*

NOTE: Store the diskettes in a safe place.

The following sections describe how you might use the Utility Diskettes in the event that you experience a problem. When you are using the Utility Diskettes, you will frequently use commands to help solve the problem; therefore you should plan to become familiar with the commands described in the following sections.

OS/2 Warp comes with an online *Command Reference* that you can use to review information about these commands. But you must remember that if your computer will not start, you will not be able to access the online *Command Reference*. So it is a good idea for you to investigate the commands before you have a crisis on your hands.

Getting to a Command Prompt

The problem you have might include corrective procedures that require you to access a command prompt. A program that lets you get to a command prompt is provided on the Utility Diskettes.

To get to a command prompt:
1. Insert Utility Diskette 1 into drive A, and restart your computer.
2. Follow the directions on the screen until you see a command prompt, (a black screen with A:\> in the upper-left corner of the screen).
3. Remove Utility Diskette 1 from drive A.

Getting to an Editor

The problem you have might include corrective procedures that require you to edit your CONFIG.SYS file or other critical OS/2 Warp files. A very basic editor called the *T-Editor* is provided on the Utility Diskettes.

To access the T-Editor:
1. Start a command prompt.
2. Insert Utility Diskette 3 into drive A.
3. Type **TEDIT** and the name of the file you want to edit. For example, enter:

   TEDIT README

   to view the README for the Utility Diskettes.

   (If you need help using the T-Editor, press the F1 key to see information about how to use the T-Editor. To exit the help, press the F3 key.)

NOTE: Even though you could use the T-Editor from any OS/2 command prompt, we don't recommend that you use it for everyday projects because it is not a very powerful editor. You would be much better off using either the OS/2 System Editor or the Enhanced Editor on the Desktop. To find out how, read "OS/2 System Editor" on page 192 or "Enhanced Editor" on page 195.

Checking a Hard Disk for Errors

The problem you have might include corrective procedures that require you to check the hard disk for errors. A program that checks your hard disk for errors is provided on the Utility Diskettes.

To check your hard disk:
1. Start a command prompt.
2. Insert Utility Diskette 3 into drive A.
3. If you installed OS/2 Warp on your C drive, you would type:

   CHKDSK C: /F:2

   and press the Enter key. (If OS/2 Warp is installed on another drive, for example, your D drive, then substitute D for C in the above example.)

Follow the instructions that appear on your screen to help you correct the problem.

Backing Up and Restoring Files

The problem you have might include corrective procedures that require you to format your hard disk, and then use your backup copy of your system to restore your system. If you do not have a current backup copy of your system, you can use the backup program provided on the Utility Diskettes to make one.

TIP: It makes good computing sense to be prepared. If you back up your system on a regular basis and anything serious happens, you will already have a current backup copy of your system. For information about how to back up your system, refer to the online *Command Reference* that comes with OS/2 Warp.

NOTE: Before you begin, you will need to have a large number of diskettes available to use during this procedure. The number varies from 25 to 45 (or more) depending on how much data is on your system.

To access the backup program:
1. Start a command prompt.
2. Insert Utility Diskette 3 into drive A.
3. If you installed OS/2 Warp on your C drive, you would type:

BACKUP C:*.* A: /S

and press the Enter key. (If OS/2 Warp is installed on another drive, for example, your D drive, then substitute D for C in the above example.)

Most instructions for corrective procedures will require that you use the backup copy of your system to restore it.

To access the restore program:
1. Start a command prompt.
2. Insert Utility Diskette 3 into drive A.
3. If you installed OS/2 Warp on your C drive, you would type:

RESTORE A: C:*.* /S

and press the Enter key. (If OS/2 Warp is installed on another drive, for example, your D drive, then substitute D for C in the above example.)

Formatting a Diskette or a Hard Disk

The problem you have might include corrective procedures that require you to format a diskette or your hard disk. A program that formats a diskette or a hard disk is provided on the Utility Diskettes.

To access the format program:
1. Start a command prompt.
2. Insert Utility Diskette 3 into drive A.
3. If you are formatting a diskette in drive A, remove Utility Diskette 3, insert a blank diskette into drive A, and then type:

   FORMAT A:

   and press the Enter key. (If you are formatting your hard disk, you can leave Utility Diskette 3 in drive A, and substitute the drive identifier you normally use for your hard drive in the above example. For example, if your hard disk is C, then you would type **FORMAT C:**.)

Partitioning a Hard Disk

The problem you have might include corrective procedures that require you to partition your hard disk. A program that partitions your hard disk is provided on the Utility Diskettes. This program can be used to create or delete partitions or logical drives on your hard disk.

 WARNING: This program requires some computer savvy. If you are not familiar with creating or deleting partitions, you might want to get some technical help before you use this procedure. Check the manual that came with OS/2 Warp for some advice, or have a technical support person in your office provide assistance.

To access the partitioning program:
1. Start a command prompt.
2. Insert Utility Diskette 3 into drive A.
3. Type:

   FDISK C:

   and press the Enter key. (If OS/2 Warp is installed on another drive, for example, your D drive, then substitute D for C in the above example.)

Official Guide to Using OS/2 Warp

Part Six

Enhancing Your Productivity

In this part of the book, you will find out how to use the OS/2 Warp BonusPak to enhance your productivity and have some fun!

This part contains information about how to install the BonusPak programs from diskette or CD, how much space the programs require, and what hardware you need to use them. You probably won't have a need to install all the programs, so brief descriptions are provided to help you decide which ones you would like to use.

This part also explains how to use each program. You'll find out how to look at a detailed list of information about your system, how to make movies, how to browse multimedia data-file icons, how to send and receive faxes, and how to organize your life! You'll also find out how to communicate interactively with business associates and friends, and you'll become an Information Superhighway explorer!

Official Guide to Using OS/2 Warp

BonusPak Installation

When you purchase OS/2 Warp, you receive nine *bonus* programs called a BonusPak. These programs are included to make your life more organized and productive in ways you never imagined. You will be able to communicate with people and access information from around the world.

These programs let you organize your work, create and send faxes, create databases, record and edit your own movies, and get you on board the Information Superhighway. Exploring the Superhighway will probably become a daily event. Just think what it would be like to have every library in the world at your fingertips. Truly exciting!

This chapter provides information to help you decide which BonusPak programs you should install. This chapter also discusses the type of hardware you will need to use the programs and the amount of space they will take on your hard disk. The programs included in the BonusPak are as follows:

IBM System Information Tool 2.0

The System Information Tool (SYSINFO) collects information about the hardware in your computer or attached to it and displays that information on the screen. It was designed to identify hardware on IBM computers but might also work with other manufacturers' computers. After you install the IBM System Information Tool, its icon is added to the System Setup folder.

Space Required	Special Hardware Required
1.5MB	None

Video IN for OS/2

Video IN for OS/2 allows you to edit and record movie clips from a variety of sources. These sources include .AVI movie files, still image files, videodiscs (laserdiscs), videotapes (VCR), or camcorders. After you install Video IN for OS/2, the Video IN Recorder, AVI File Utility, and Videodisc icons are added to the Multimedia folder.

NOTE: When you install Video IN for OS/2, you will be asked to select the video devices that you have installed on your computer.

TIP: You can find BMP, FLC, and AVI files in the \MOVIES\SNGLSPIN and \MOVIES\DBLSPIN directories of the BonusPak. You can use these files with the Multimedia Viewer, AVI File Utility, Video IN Recorder, and Digital Video icons. Use the directory that is appropriate for the CD-ROM device you have attached to your computer. (Use SNGLSPIN if you have a single-spin CD-ROM drive. Use DBLSPIN if you have a double-spin CD-ROM drive.)

Space Required	Special Hardware Required	For Full Potential
2.5MB	12MB to 15MB of memory	• Input device (for example, VCR, laserdisc, or camcorder) • Sound Card to record audio and play sounds • Video card to record film clips from an input device

Multimedia Viewer

The Multimedia Viewer lets you play sound, video, animation, image, and text files. It includes programs that can see inside a data-file icon so that you can view or hear its contents. After you install the Multimedia Viewer, its icon is added to the Desktop.

NOTE: When you install the Multimedia Viewer, you will be asked to select the file formats that you intend to use with the Multimedia Viewer.

TIP: You can find PCX, GIF, Targa, and TIF files in the \IMAGES directory of the BonusPak. So even if you don't have files with these formats, you might want to select the ones that are provided with the BonusPak and view them in the Multimedia Viewer and Multimedia Data Converter.

Space Required	Special Software Required	For Full Potential
4.5MB	OS/2 Multimedia installed	Sound card to listen to audio clips

FaxWorks for OS/2

FaxWorks for OS/2 lets you send faxes directly from your computer to another computer, eliminating the need for paper faxes. You can also send faxes to a fax machine and receive faxes from a fax machine. After you install FaxWorks for OS/2, the FaxWorks for OS/2 and FxPrint icons are added to the Desktop.

Space Required	Special Hardware Required
2MB	Fax Modem

IBM Works for OS/2 and Personal Information Manager (PIM)

IBM Works for OS/2 provides you with five tools that let you create documents, spreadsheets, new charts, and charts with data from the spreadsheet, database, and reports programs. It also includes its own Personal Information Manager (PIM), which helps you keep track of daily activities, appointments, and schedules, making your life easier to organize and manage. After you install IBM Works, its icon is added to the Desktop. Inside the IBM Works icon, you will find all of the IBM Works and PIM program icons.

Space Required	For Full Potential
12.5MB	Modem

Person to Person

Person to Person provides a group of programs that let you communicate with other people over a network. After you install Person to Person, its icon is added to the Desktop.

Space Required	Special Hardware Required	For Full Potential
4.5MB	Modem	Camcorder, videodisc, or VCR to send video across the network

CompuServe Information Manager for OS/2 (CIM)

CompuServe Information Manager for OS/2 includes a group of programs that provide menus and windows to make accessing the CompuServe Information service easier for you. Some of the services available on CompuServe are weather reports, electronic mail, stock reports, and forums. You can also communicate with people around the world. After you install CompuServe Information Manager for OS/2, its icon is added to the IBM Information Superhighway icon on the Desktop.

Space Required	Special Hardware Required
2.6MB	Modem

IBM Internet Connection for OS/2

The IBM Internet Connection for OS/2 provides a group of programs that let you register with the Internet, connect to the IBM Global Network, retrieve and install software updates from the Internet, access Gophers, as well as read, subscribe to, and reply to various news forums. You can also find programs that let you create, store, and organize your electronic mail and transfer files and issue commands to remote computers. After you install the IBM Internet Connection for OS/2, its icon is added to the IBM Information Superhighway icon on the Desktop.

Space Required	Special Hardware Required
12MB	Modem

HyperACCESS Lite for OS/2

HyperACCESS Lite for OS/2 provides menus and windows that give you a quick and easy way to access remote computers. By using a modem, telephone, and your computer, you can send and receive information as well as communicate with other people. After you install HyperACCESS Lite for OS/2, its icon is added to the IBM Information Superhighway icon on the Desktop.

Space Required	Special Hardware Required
651KB	Modem

Installing BonusPak Programs

You can install the BonusPak programs from diskette or CD. The instructions below show you how to use the BonusPak Installation Program to install the BonusPak programs. You can install only one program at a time and you must remember to shut down and restart your computer after each installation to make sure the proper statements are added to your CONFIG.SYS file.

To install the BonusPak from diskette:

1. Insert the *BonusPak Installation Diskette* into drive A.
2. Click mouse button 1 on the **Drive A** icon.

   ROCKET TIP: Remember to use the Drive A icon located on the LaunchPad.

3. Double-click on the **INSTALL.CMD** icon to display the BonusPak Installation Program window.
4. Click mouse button 1 on the BonusPak program you want to install.
5. Click mouse button 1 on the **Install** push button.
6. Remove the *BonusPak Installation Diskette* from drive A.
7. Insert the requested diskette.
8. Click mouse button 1 on the **OK** push button, and follow the instructions on the screen.
9. When the installation is completed, shut down and restart your computer.

TIP: You can also install the BonusPak programs individually without using the BonusPak Installation program.

1. Insert Diskette 1 of the program you want to install into drive A.
2. Click mouse button 1 on the **Drive A** icon.
3. Double-click on the icon that represents the installation program for the BonusPak program you want to install.

BonusPak Program	Installation Program
IBM System Information Tool 2.0	SYSI.CMD
Video IN for OS/2	MINSTALL /F:CONTROL.VIN
Multimedia Viewer	MINSTALL /F:CONTROL.MMV
FaxWorks for OS/2	INSTALL.EXE
IBM Works for OS/2	INSTALL.EXE
Person to Person	INSTALL.EXE
CompuServe Information Manager for OS/2	SETUP.EXE
IBM Internet Connection for OS/2	INSTALL.EXE
HyperACCESS Lite for OS/2	HAINST.EXE

4. Follow the instructions on the screen.
5. When the installation is completed, shut down and restart your computer.

To install the BonusPak from CD:

1. Double-click on the **OS/2 System** icon.
2. Double-click on the **Drives** icon.
3. Double-click on the icon that represents the drive containing the BonusPak CD. The icon you want should look like a CD.
4. Double-click on the **US** icon.
5. Double-click on the **INSTALL.CMD** icon to display the BonusPak Installation Program window.
6. Click mouse button 1 on the program you want to install.
7. Click mouse button 1 on the **Install** push button.
8. Follow the instructions on the screen to install the selected program.
9. When the installation is completed, shut down and restart your computer.

32

System Information Tool

The System Information Tool gathers information about the hardware in your computer and displays that information on the screen. It is designed to be used on IBM computers, but it might be able to identify the hardware in other computers too.

This chapter shows you how to view and save the information gathered by the System Information Tool.

Viewing Information about Your Computer

You can use the System Information Tool to determine what hardware is installed on your computer so that you can pinpoint problems with your computer, and, if necessary, supply information about your computer to a service representative. You can also use the System Information Tool (if you are curious) to help you figure out what hardware is installed on your computer.

The System Information Tool provides its information in a series of windows. The amount of information that is displayed in a window depends on the hardware in your computer. You can click on almost any icon in one of the windows and get additional information about your computer. After a window of information is displayed, you can press the F1 key to see additional information.

The following table provides a brief overview of the type of information you might be able to get from the System Information Tool.

Table 1 (page 1 of 3). System Information Tool Contents

Category	Explanation	Contents
Adapter Information	Provides information about the adapters (cards) and slots in the computer.	• Slot numbers • Adapter names • Adapter Addresses
Disk Information	Provides information about the physical and logical drives in the computer.	• Size • Partition • Volume Label • File System • Space Available • Startup Order
Error Log Information	Displays information about the errors that are stored in the system error log.	• Entry number • Error Type • Date and Time

Table 1 (page 2 of 3). System Information Tool Contents

Category	Explanation	Contents
Keyboard Information	Displays information about the keyboard attached to the computer.	• Keyboard Type • Country code • Code Page • Speed
Memory Information	Displays information about the memory in the computer.	• Size and speed • Memory address ranges • Amount of memory • Supported types of memory
Model and Processor Information	Displays a variety of information about the computer.	• Model Name • Expansion Bus Type • Processor • Math Coprocessor • Processor Speed • System Speed • Internal Processor Cache • External Processor Cache • Model Byte • Submodel • BIOS Revision • BIOS ROM Date • System Board POS ID • Reference Disk Type • NVRAM Size
Mouse Information	Displays information about the mouse connected to the computer.	• Mouse Type • Number of Buttons • Mouse Sensitivity • Vertical Scaling Factor • Horizontal Scaling Factor • Mouse Handedness • Double-click Interval
Operating System Information	Provides information about the operating system that is currently running on the computer.	• Operating System Information • Window List • CSD Levels • CONFIG.SYS File Information

Table 1 (page 3 of 3). System Information Tool Contents

Category	Explanation	Contents
Parallel and Serial Port Information	Displays information about the input/output ports on the computer.	• Number of ports • Logical devices • Data transfer rates • Buffer sizes
Printer Information	Provides information about the printers configured for the computer.	• Port assigned • Queue name • Driver • Printer model
Security Information	Provides information about the security features on the computer.	• Power-On Password • Mechanical Case Lock • Privileged Access Password • Unattended Start Mode • Tamper Detection
Video Subsystem Information	Provides information about the video subsystem on the computer.	• Adapter Type • Display Type • Video Memory • Colors Displayed • Screen Resolution • Screen Size • Supported Video Modes

To view information about your computer:

1. Point to an empty area on the Desktop.
2. Click mouse button 2 to display the pop-up menu.
3. Click mouse button 1 on the **System setup** menu choice.
4. Double-click on the **System Information Tool** icon ⬛.
5. Double-click on the icon that represents the category you are interested in (for example, the Memory Information) ⬛.
6. Double-click on the title-bar icon of the System Information Tool window to close it.

Saving the Information

After you finish viewing the information on the screens, you can either print the information so that you can take it with you to purchase new equipment for your computer or save it in a file so that you can view it again later.

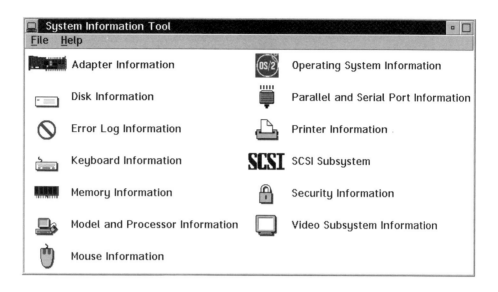

To print all the information about your computer:

1. Point to an empty area on the Desktop.
2. Click mouse button 2 to display the pop-up menu.
3. Click mouse button 1 on the **System setup** menu choice.
4. Double-click on the **System Information Tool** icon.
5. Click mouse button 1 on the **File** menu.
6. Click mouse button 1 on the **Print All System Data To Printer** menu choice.
7. Double-click on the title-bar icon of the System Information Tool window to close it.

To save all the information about your computer to a file:

1. Point to an empty area on the Desktop.
2. Click mouse button 2 to display the pop-up menu.
3. Click mouse button 1 on the **System setup** menu choice.
4. Double-click on the **System Information Tool** icon.
5. Click mouse button 1 on the **File** menu.
6. Click mouse button 1 on the **Print All System Data To File** menu choice.
7. Double-click on the title-bar icon of the System Information Tool window to close it.

Chapter 33

Video IN Recorder

The Video IN Recorder BonusPak program contains three programs — Video IN Recorder, AVI File Utility, and Videodisc. These programs help you record and edit movies and play movies on a videodisc player.

This chapter shows you how to record and edit movies, synchronize the sound in a movie, capture images from a movie, and create your own recording profiles. In addition, it explains how to create a movie from image files, add and remove sound from a movie, fine-tune the sound in a movie, and operate a videodisc player from your computer.

Using the Video IN Recorder Program

The Video IN Recorder program allows you to record and edit movies. These movies can be from software sources, such as existing .AVI movie files, still-image files, or hardware sources, such as videodiscs (laserdisc), videotapes (VCR), or a camcorder. The software sources do not require any extra hardware. The hardware sources require that a video-capture card be installed in your computer so that you can connect the extra hardware to the computer.

NOTE: If you plan to purchase equipment for recording movies, contact your IBM Service Representative to make sure the equipment is compatible with OS/2 Warp.

Recording a Movie

As mentioned, you can record a movie using a videodisc, videotape, camcorder, movie clip on a hard disk or CD, or still images as the source. The source you use will depend on the hardware that you have available.

Creating movies with this program is fun. You will be amazed at how easy it is to create great movies for business presentations and personal entertainment.

NOTE: If you are creating a movie from still images (image files), use "Creating a Movie from Image Files" on page 327 .

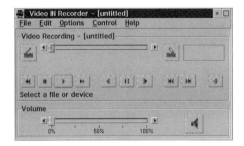

To record a movie:

1. Double-click on the **Multimedia** icon.
2. Double-click on the **Video IN Recorder** icon.
3. Click mouse button 1 on the **Options** menu.

4. Click mouse button 1 on the **Device selections** menu choice. If this option is grayed out, turn the device on and start playing the movie. After waiting a few seconds, check to see if the menu choice is now available.

5. Click mouse button 1 on the device that you will be using to record from. If your device is not listed, click mouse button 1 on the **Line in** choice.

6. Click mouse button 1 on the **OK** push button.

7. Click mouse button 1 on the play button ▶ so that you can set up the **Video IN** window.

8. Click mouse button 1 on the **Options** menu.

9. Click mouse button 1 on the **Monitor video** menu choice. This displays a window so that you can view what you are recording.

10. Click mouse button 1 on the **Options** menu.

11. Click mouse button 1 on the **Adjust video** menu choice to make adjustments to the source that you see in the Monitor window. You can make changes to the following choices:

   Contrast

   The difference in brightness or color between the image and the background.

   Brightness

   The amount of light being emitted by the video signal.

   Color

   The depth of color intensity.

   Tint

   The amount of red or green used in the image.

12. Double-click on the title-bar icon of the Video Adjustments window to close it.

13. Click mouse button 1 on the **Options** menu.

14. Click mouse button 1 on the **Monitor Audio** menu choice to place a check mark next to the choice. This allows you to hear the sound that accompanies the video that you are recording. Don't use this choice if you are recording sound from a microphone because of feedback problems.

15. Click mouse button 1 on the **Options** menu.

16. Click mouse button 1 on the **Record setup** menu choice.

17. Click mouse button 1 on one of the choices to select the recording profile. You can choose from the following:

Real Time

Records information based on the speed in which the information is fed to the computer. This method is usually used to record from a camcorder, videodisc (laserdisc) device, or videotape (VCR) device. If you choose this method, you should use the **Line in** choice from above.

Frame Step

Records information frame by frame from a computer-controlled video source. This method is usually used to record from a previously recorded .AVI file or a source that can be stepped frame by frame, such as a videodisc being controlled by a computer.

18. The Record Setup notebook is displayed with settings that work for most recordings.

19. Double-click on the title-bar icon of the Record Setup notebook to close it. (If in the future you want to use a different Record Setup, you can change the settings in the notebook. See "Changing the Recording Profile" on page 323.)

20. Click mouse button 1 on the **Options** menu.

21. Click mouse button 1 on the **Source time format** menu choice.

22. Click mouse button 1 on one of the choices to select the format used to indicate placement in the source information. You can choose from the following:

HH:MM:SS:FF

This format measures placement in the source by the amount of time it takes to play the movie.

Frames

This format measures placement in the source by the number of video frames in the movie.

23. Click mouse button 1 on the **Options** menu.

24. Click mouse button 1 on the **Recording time format** menu choice.

25. Click mouse button 1 on one of the choices to select the format used to indicate placement in the recording information. You can choose from the following:

HH:MM:SS:FF

This format measures placement in the recording by the amount of time it has been recording.

Frames

This format measures placement in the recording by the number of video frames that have been recorded.

26. Mark the area in the media that you want to record by doing the following:

a. Point to the position in the Video Source slider bar where you want to begin recording.

b. Press and hold mouse button 1.

c. Drag the mark to the position in the Video Source slider bar where you want the recording to end.

d. Release mouse button 1.

To unmark the area so that you can change it, click mouse button 1 anywhere inside the slider bar.

Or

a. Click mouse button 1 on the play ▶, scan forward ▶▶, and scan backward ◀◀ buttons to get close to the desired starting frame.

b. Click mouse button 1 on the step forward ▶ or step backward ◀ button to step to the starting frame.

c. Click mouse button 1 on **Begin Mark** to set the starting frame.

d. Click mouse button 1 on the play ▶, scan forward ▶▶, and scan backward ◀◀ buttons to get close to the desired ending frame.

e. Click mouse button 1 on the step forward ▶ or step backward ◀ button to step to the ending frame.

f. Click mouse button 1 on **End Mark** to set the ending frame.

27. Click mouse button 1 on the seek backward ◀◀ button to go back to the starting frame of the clip.

28. Crop the video image by doing the following:

a. Point to anywhere inside the Monitor Window.

b. Press and hold mouse button 1.

c. Drag the box so that it includes only the information in the window that you want to record.

d. Release mouse button 1. (To remove the box, click mouse button 1 anywhere within the Monitor Window.)

29. Click mouse button 1 on the **Control** menu.

30. Click mouse button 1 on the **Recording** menu choice.

31. Click mouse button 1 on the **Cue for record** menu choice. This cues the recorder so that you can begin to record immediately.

32. Click mouse button 1 on the record ◆ button. (The Monitor Window is removed from the screen while the sound portion of the source is being recorded.)

33. Wait until the end mark is reached, or click mouse button 1 on the stop ■ button in the **Video recording** field if you want to stop recording the sound before the end mark is reached. (The Monitor Window reappears, and the video portion of the source starts to record.)

34. Wait until the end mark is reached, or click mouse button 1 on the stop ■ button in the **Video recording** field if you want to stop recording the video before the end mark is reached. Recording the video portion of the movie is much slower than recording the sound portion of the movie. When recording stops, an IBM Ultimotion Window is displayed on the Desktop. This window will be used to play your movie.

35. Click mouse button 1 on the rewind ◀◀ button in the **Video recording** field to rewind your movie.

36. Click mouse button 1 on the play ▶ button in the **Video recording** field to play your movie.

37. Click mouse button 1 on the **File** menu.

38. Click mouse button 1 on the **Save as** menu choice.

39. Type a name for the movie file. Use .AVI as the extension (for example: SURFING.AVI).

40. Click mouse button 1 on the **OK** push button.

41. Double-click on the title-bar icons of the open windows to close them.

TIP: If you are having difficulty getting the Video IN program to recognize your video-disc player as your source, make sure the baud rate is set to 9800. You can set the baud rate using the Videodisc notebook tab of the Multimedia Setup icon.

Synchronizing the Sound

Sometimes the sound and video of the movies you record are not *synchronized*. This means that the sound of the movie does not match the action. (This makes your film look like a poorly dubbed movie.) You can adjust the synchronization by either delaying or advancing the sound track on the movie.

To synchronize the sound with the video:

1. Double-click on the **Multimedia** icon.
2. Double-click on the **Video IN Recorder** icon.
3. Click mouse button 1 on the **File** menu.
4. Click mouse button 1 on the **Open** menu choice.
5. Double-click on the movie file whose sound you want to synchronize with its video.
6. Click mouse button 1 on the **Options** menu.
7. Click mouse button 1 on the **Adjust Audio Synchronization** menu choice.
8. Point to an arrow at either end of the Sooner or Later bar.
9. Click mouse button 1 to adjust the sound. Each time you click mouse button you adjust the sound by 20 milliseconds.
10. Click mouse button 1 on the rewind [◄◄] button.
11. Click mouse button 1 on the play [►] button.
12. Repeat steps 8 through 11 until you are satisfied with the synchronization of the sound and video.
13. Double-click on the title-bar icon of the Adjust Audio Synchronization window to close it.
14. Click mouse button 1 on the **File** menu.
15. Click mouse button 1 on the **Save as** menu choice.
16. Type a name for the altered movie file. Use .AVI as the extension (for example: BIKING.AVI).
17. Click mouse button 1 on the **OK** push button.
18. Double-click on the title-bar icon of the Video IN Recorder window to close it.

Editing a Movie

After a movie has been completely recorded, many directors like to go back and make changes. You are probably no different. Editing a film can greatly improve its overall quality. You can remove unnecessary frames and you can also repeat movie frames so that they have more impact. For example, if you created a movie about the restoration of your antique auto, you could show a before and after shot at the end of the movie by copying frames from the beginning of the movie and repeating them at the end.

To edit a movie:

1. Double-click on the **Multimedia** icon.

2. Double-click on the **Video IN Recorder** icon.
3. Click mouse button 1 on the **File** menu.
4. Click mouse button 1 on the **Open** menu choice.
5. Double-click on the movie file that you want to edit.
6. Place a mark at the beginning of the clip of movie that you want to edit:

    a. Click mouse button 1 on the play ▶, scan forward ⏩, and scan backward ⏪ buttons in the **Video recording** field to get close to the desired starting frame.

    b. Click mouse button 1 on the step forward ▷ or step backward ◁ button in the **Video recording** field to step to the starting frame.

    c. Click mouse button 1 on the **Begin Mark** 🎬 button in the **Video recording** field to set the starting frame.

7. Place a mark at the end of the clip of movie you want to edit:

    a. Click mouse button 1 on the play ▶, scan forward ⏩, and scan backward ⏪ buttons in the **Video recording** field to get close to the desired ending frame.

    b. Click mouse button 1 on the step forward ▷ or step backward ◁ button in the **Video recording** field to step to the ending frame.

    c. Click mouse button 1 on the **End Mark** 🎬 button in the **Video recording** field to set the ending frame.

8. Click mouse button 1 on the **Edit** menu.
9. Click mouse button 1 on the **Recording** menu choice. Choose an editing option from the menu. You can choose from the following:

    Cut
    Removes the marked clip from the movie and places it in the clipboard.

    Copy
    Places a copy of the marked clip from the movie into the clipboard.

    Paste
    Places the information in the clipboard into the movie at the current location of the slider box. Use the buttons to move the slider box, or click mouse button 1 where you want the clip to be pasted.

Undo
> Reverses the effect of the last cut, copy, paste, or delete operation.

Redo
> Reverses the effect of the last Undo operation.

Delete
> Removes the marked clip from the movie.

10. Click mouse button 1 on the rewind ◀◀ button in the **Video recording** field to rewind your movie.

11. Click mouse button 1 on the play ▶ button in the **Video recording** field to see the results of your edit.

12. Repeat steps 6 through 11 until the movie is edited to your satisfaction.

13. Click mouse button 1 on the **File** menu.

14. Click mouse button 1 on the **Save as** menu choice.

15. Type a name for the edited movie file. Use .AVI as the extension (for example, HIKING.AVI).

16. Click mouse button 1 on the **OK** push button.

17. Double-click on the title-bar icon of the Video IN Recorder window to close it.

Capturing Images from a Movie

You can capture single frames (images) of movies and make them into bit maps. These bit maps can be used to create other movies or as backgrounds for your Desktop, windows, and lockup screen. This means that you can put pictures of your family, favorite movie stars, pets, and prize possessions on your computer screen so that they are never far from your heart.

To capture an image from a movie:

1. Double-click on the **Multimedia** icon.

2. Double-click on the **Video IN Recorder** icon.

3. Click mouse button 1 on the **Options** menu.

4. Click mouse button 1 on the **Device selections** menu choice. If this option is grayed out, make sure that the device is on and that it is playing the movie.

5. Click mouse button 1 on the device that you will be using to capture from. If your device is not listed, click mouse button 1 on the **Line in** choice.

6. Click mouse button 1 on the **OK** push button.

7. Click mouse button 1 on the play button ▶ so that you can set up the Video IN window.

8. Click mouse button 1 on the **Options** menu.

9. Click mouse button 1 on the **Monitor video** menu choice. This displays a window so that you can view the image you are capturing.

10. Click mouse button 1 on the **Options** menu.

11. Click mouse button 1 on the **Bit map capture** menu choice.

12. Click mouse button 1 on the **Auto-increment** choice to place a check mark in front of it. This choice automatically names your image BTMAP000.BMP. The 000 is incremented by 1 every time you capture another image. (You can change the **BTMAP** portion of the name in the next few steps if you want.)

13. Click mouse button 1 on the **Options** menu.

14. Click mouse button 1 on the **Bit map capture** menu choice.

15. Click mouse button 1 on the **Filename selection** choice to choose a directory where you want the bit map stored (and, optionally, to change the BTMAP portion of the file name).

16. Double-click on directory names until the directory where you want to place the image is displayed in the **File** field. If you want to change the name of the file, type a new name for the image in the **Open filename** field (for example, CLOWN000.BMP).

17. Click mouse button 1 on the **OK** push button.

18. Locate the frame in your source movie that you want to capture as an image.

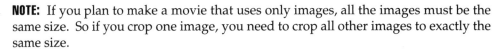

a. Click mouse button 1 on the play ▸ , scan forward ▸▸ , and scan backward ◂◂ buttons to get close to the desired frame.

b. Click mouse button 1 on the step forward ▷ or step backward ◁ button to step to the desired frame.

c. Click mouse button 1 on the pause ‖ button.

19. Crop the image by doing the following:

a. Point to anywhere inside the Monitor Window.

b. Press and hold mouse button 1.

c. Drag the box so that it includes only the information in the window that you want to capture.

d. Release mouse button 1. (To remove the box, click mouse button 1 anywhere within the Monitor Window.)

NOTE: If you plan to make a movie that uses only images, all the images must be the same size. So if you crop one image, you need to crop all other images to exactly the same size.

20. Click mouse button 1 on the **Options** menu.

21. Click mouse button 1 on the **Bit map capture** choice.
22. Click mouse button 1 on the **Capture now** choice.

> **NOTE:** If you plan to capture more images now, you do not need to repeat every step in this procedure. Return to step 11 and follow the procedure from there to capture other images.

23. Double-click on the title-bar icon of the Video IN Recorder window to close it.

Changing the Recording Profile

OS/2 Warp comes with two recording profiles. These profiles provide the most common settings needed to record movies successfully. However, these settings might not meet your needs or match the capabilities of your hardware. Don't fret—you can change the settings to your specifications and save them for future use.

> **NOTE:** You cannot give your recording profile a different name. It will be saved as either the Real Time or Frame Step profile. (Real Time and Frame Step are the names for the two recording profiles that come with OS/2 Warp.)

If the need ever arises to go back to the original settings for either profile, you can easily do so by clicking on the **Default** push button on each page of the notebook.

To change the recording profile settings:
1. Double-click on the **Multimedia** icon.
2. Double-click on the **Video IN Recorder** icon.
3. Click mouse button 1 on the **Options** menu.
4. Click mouse button 1 on the **Record Setup** choice.
5. Click mouse button 1 on the **Real Time** or **Frame Step** menu choice. The Record Setup notebook is displayed.
6. Click mouse button 1 on the **Rate** notebook tab. You can change the following choices:

Recording profile
> Uses the current profile for recording the video when a check mark precedes the choice.

Frame rate - source
> Determines how many frames per second the source movie plays. This option is available only for computer-controlled sources.

Frame rate - output
> Determines how many frames per second the captured movie plays. This value must be less than the source frame rate.

Insert reference frames
> Determines how often a complete frame is saved (instead of a partial frame). The frequency with which reference frames (complete frames) are saved is based on the number supplied in the **Reference frame interval** field. This number should be twice the number specified in the output frame rate to make the editing and synchronizing of the video easier.

7. Click mouse button 1 on the **Size** notebook tab. You can change the following choices:

Capture position
> Determines where the starting point (in pixels) is for the capture box in the Monitor Window. Coordinate 0, 0 is the default and is located in the lower-left corner of the Monitor Window.

Capture size
> Determines the width and height (in pixels) of the capture box in the Monitor Window. The default is the entire Monitor Window.

Output video size
> Determines the output size of the movie. The default size for Real Time recording is 160 x 120. The default size for Frame Step recording is 320 x 240.

8. Click mouse button 1 on the **Quality** notebook tab. You can change the following choices:

Compression type
> Determines which compressor is used to record the movie. (You can view detailed descriptions of the available compressors by clicking mouse button 1 on the **Help** push button.)

Desired video quality
> Determines the quality of the movie. The compressor might have to alter the data rates that you set in order to reach the quality setting you specify.

Maximum data rate
> Determines the maximum number of kilobytes per second that can be used to record the movie. This number is the sum of the **Audio** and **Video** data rates. The actual data rate could be lower than this rate if a low video quality is selected.

9. Click mouse button 1 on the **Audio** notebook tab. You can change the following choices:

Number of channels
> Determines whether the sound will be recorded on one channel (mono) or two channels (stereo).

Sample rate

Determines the rate at which sound waveform sampling will occur based on the type of sound that is being recorded.

Sample size

Determines whether an 8-bit (low quality) or a 16-bit (high quality) sample size is used. This is dependent on the capability of your sound card. Choosing a 16-bit sample size will improve the quality of the sound but will degrade the quality of the video.

10. Click mouse button 1 on the right arrow at the bottom of the notebook. You can change the following choices:

Gain

Determines the level of sound output amplification. You can choose from low, medium, and high.

Audio compression type

Determines the type of sound support for the movie. You can choose no sound, compressed sound (which takes up less space on the hard disk), or uncompressed sound.

Record from

Determines which source you are using for sound. You can choose from microphone and line in.

11. Double-click on the title-bar icon of the notebook to close it. (The changes you made are saved.)

Using the AVI File Utility Program

Use the AVI File Utility to make it easier to work with sound files. For example, you can *merge* a movie's sound and video into one file, *split* a movie's sound and video into two separate files, *interleave* the sound and video data so that they can be accessed efficiently during the playback of the movie, and *skew* the sound so that it plays consistently throughout the movie.

You can also use the AVI File Utility to create a movie from image files and then add sound to that movie.

Merging, Splitting, Interleaving, and Skewing .AVI Files

When you added sound to your movie (either at creation time or after), the video and sound tracks were placed in the same file. This makes it difficult to replace the sound track on a video with another sound track. However, by using the AVI File Utility program, you can replace the sound files and affect how they are meshed with the video file.

To merge, split, interleave, or skew an .AVI file:

1. Double-click on the **Multimedia** icon.
2. Double-click on the **AVI File Utility** icon.
3. Click mouse button 1 on the **File** menu.
4. Click mouse button 1 on the **Open** menu choice.
5. Double-click on the .AVI file that you want to edit.
6. Click mouse button 1 on one of the following push buttons:

Merge

Joins the sound and video into one file. This choice is grayed out until you open a sound file using the **Open Audio File** menu choice in the **File menu**. Use the **Save as** choice to save the newly merged file.

Split

Separates the sound and video into two different files. When you select this option, you must save the sound file using the **Save Audio File** menu choice in the **File menu**. (You must also choose a .WAV extension for the sound file.) Then you must save the video file using the **Save as** menu choice in the **File menu**. (This saves the video portion with an .AVI extension.)

(If you want to play the sound file, you must use the **Digital Audio** icon.)

Interleave

Determines the ratio of video frames to sound frames. The standard ratio is 1 video frame to 1 sound frame. Use the **Save as** choice to save the newly-interleaved file.

Skew

Allows the sound stream to lead the video stream so that the sound buffers stay full while the movie is playing. This does not affect the sound synchronization. However, if the video gets behind the sound, the video might drop video frames during the playback. Adjusting the skew value might fix this problem. Use the **Save as** choice to save the newly-skewed file.

Stop

Stops one of the previous processes before it is completed.

7. Repeat step 6 until the AVI file has been altered to your satisfaction. (To test your changes, you can use the **Digital Video** icon to play the file.)

8. Click mouse button 1 on the **File** menu.

9. Click mouse button 1 on the appropriate choices for saving the files you created or altered.

10. Type a name for the file, and click mouse button 1 on the **OK** push button.

11. Double-click on the title-bar icon of the AVI File Utility window to close it.

Creating a Movie from Image Files

An image file contains a picture of something. OS/2 Warp provides the capability to string individual image files together to create a movie. This process is easy and the end result is very impressive. You can even add sound to the movie after you finish.

You can use image files in any of the following formats to create your movie.

File format	Common file extension
IBM AVC still video	._IM and .!IM
IBM M-Motion still video	.VID
OS/2 1.3 and 2.0 bit map	.BMP
Microsoft device-independent bit map	.DIB
RIFF device-independent bit map	.RDI

To create a movie from image files:

1. Double-click on the **Multimedia** icon.

2. Double-click on the **AVI File Utility** icon.

3. Click mouse button 1 on the **File** menu.

4. Click mouse button 1 on the **New** menu choice.

5. Click mouse button 1 on the **Edit** menu.

6. Click mouse button 1 on the **Generate AVI File from Images** menu choice. The Generate AVI File from Images window is displayed. This window is where you specify which images you want to use to create the movie.

7. Click mouse button 1 on the letter of the drive that contains the image files you want to use in the movie.

8. Double-click on directory names in the **Directory** field until the image files you want to use are displayed in the **Files** field.

9. Click mouse button 1 on an arrow in the **Frames Per Second** field to determine how many frames you want displayed per second. You can stop on any number from 1 to 30.

10. Click mouse button 1 on an image that you want to use in the movie. Select the images in the order that you want them displayed in the movie.

11. Click mouse button 1 on the **Insert** push button. The image file name is added to the **Frame List** field.

12. If you want to add a pause frame in between images, click mouse button 1 on the image file in the **Frame List** field, and then click mouse button 1 on the pause button

    <kbd>||</kbd> . This adds a pause frame after the highlighted image file.

13. Repeat steps 10 through 12 until all of the image files that you want to use in the movie are listed in the **Frame List** field.

14. If you want to remove an image from the **Frame List** field, click mouse button 1 on the image file, and then click mouse button 1 on the **Remove** push button.

15. Click mouse button 1 on the **Generate AVI File** push button.

16. Click mouse button 1 on the **File** menu.

17. Click mouse button 1 on the **Save** menu choice.

18. Type a name for the movie file. Use .AVI as the extension (for example, THERESA.AVI).

19. Click mouse button 1 on the **OK** push button.

20. Double-click on the title-bar icons of the open windows to close them. You can now use the **Digital Video** icon to view your movie.

Adding Sound to a Silent Movie

The AVI File Utility and the Video IN Recorder programs allow you to create movies without a sound track. If you created such a movie, you might want to add narration, sound effects, or music to your video. You can easily do this by merging a .WAV sound file with your movie file.

To add sound to a silent movie:
1. Double-click on the **Multimedia** icon.
2. Double-click on the **AVI File Utility** icon.
3. Click mouse button 1 on the **File** menu.
4. Click mouse button 1 on the **Open** menu choice.
5. Double-click on the name of the file that contains the movie to which you are adding sound.
6. Click mouse button 1 on the **File** menu.
7. Click mouse button 1 on the **Open Audio File** menu choice.
8. Double-click on the .WAV file that you want to use with your movie.
9. Click mouse button 1 on the **Merge** push button.

10. Click mouse button 1 on the **File** menu.

11. Click mouse button 1 on the **Save as** menu choice.

12. Type a name for the movie file. Use .AVI as the extension (for example, KASEY.AVI).

13. Click mouse button 1 on the **OK** push button.

14. Double-click on the title-bar icon of the window to close it. You can now use the **Digital Video** icon to play your movie.

Using the Videodisc Program

Use the Videodisc program to control a videodisc (laserdisc) player that is attached to your computer. You might find this useful if you have a TV monitor attached to the videodisc player and want to be able to play, scan, pause, or stop the videodisc without leaving your computer.

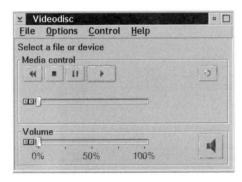

To play a videodisc:

1. Insert the videodisc into the videodisc player.

2. Double-click on the **Multimedia** icon.

3. Double-click on the **Videodisc** icon.

4. Click mouse button 1 on the play button.

5. Click mouse button 1 on the stop button.

6. Double-click on the title-bar icon of the open window to close it.

Chapter 34

Multimedia Viewer

The Multimedia Viewer program provides *browsers* that you can use to play sound, video, animation, image, and text files. Browsers can be useful because you can look inside data-file icons to see their contents. (In the case of sound files, you hear the contents.) The sound, video, animation, image, and text files are shown as "thumbnails," or miniature pictures, as if they were slides on a photographer's light table.

This chapter provides information about how the Multimedia Viewer program uses browsers, how to create other folders that work like the Multimedia Viewer program, and how to place data-file icons in the folders you create.

NOTE: You will need the Multimedia Viewer if you intend to view popular image formats such as GIF, TIFF, TGA, and PCX on CompuServe or the Internet.

Using the Multimedia Viewer Program

When you installed the Multimedia Viewer program, browsers were made available from the Multimedia Viewer window.

The browser programs work with the following data-file types and extensions.

Data-file type	File extension	Browser used	Icon
Sound (Audio)	._AD ._AU .MID .WAV	Continuous Media Browser	Microphone
Image	._IM .!IM .BMP .GIF .ICO .PCX .TGA .TIF .DIB .GIF	Image Browser	Small Picture of Contents
Story	._ST .!ST	Continuous Media Browser	Director's Slate
Text	.TXT .C .DOC .H	Text Browser	Original Icon

Data-file type	File extension	Browser used	Icon
Video	.AVS .DVI .AVI	Continuous Media Browser	Movie Slate

Creating a Light Table Folder

The Multimedia Viewer program also installed a Light Table template in the Templates icon, which you can use to create folders that work in the same way as the Multimedia Viewer program. Then, you can either play a data-file icon when it is located in the Multimedia Viewer icon or you can play a data-file icon when it is located in any other folder you create from the Light Table template in the Templates icon.

TIP: You might find it convenient to create more than one Light Table folder so that you can organize different multimedia project files in those folders.

To create a Light Table folder:
1. Double-click on the **Templates** icon.
2. Point to the **Light Table** icon.
3. Press and hold mouse button 1.
4. Drag the icon to the Desktop or to another folder.
5. Release mouse button 1.

Placing Icons in a Light Table Folder

You can make copies of data-file icons and place them inside a Light Table folder. After a data-file icon is placed inside a Light Table folder, a link is created between the data-file icon and the correct browser program that is needed to play it. The extension of the data-file icon is recognized and associated with the correct browser program.

NOTE: If you place a data-file icon with an unrecognized extension into a Light Table folder, the data-file icon will not have a browser program associated with it; instead, it will open in the default program that is associated with it.

Data-file icons that are placed in a Light Table folder receive a special icon that is larger than a normal icon. If the data-file icon contains an image file, the icon looks like the contents of the file. If it is a sound, video, or animation file, a representative icon is assigned. For example, sound files have a Microphone icon and movies files have a Movie Slate icon.

Around the outside of the larger icon is a border called a frame. When you double-click on this frame, a browser program opens and the contents of the icon can be viewed or heard.

NOTE: Data-file icons that contain text do not receive special icons or frames. In order to use a browser to view their contents, you must double-click on the text below the icon.

Instead of copying the data-file icon, you can place *references* to the icon inside a Light Table folder. A reference to an icon is a special feature that the Multimedia Viewer program uses to point to an icon that exists somewhere else. Using a reference saves space because it eliminates the need to duplicate a data-file icon on your computer.

To place a reference to a data-file icon in a Light Table folder:
1. Double-click on the Light Table folder in which you want to place the data-file icon.
2. Point to the data-file icon that you want to place in the Light Table folder.
3. Click mouse button 2 to display the pop-up menu.
4. Click mouse button 1 on the **Create LT Reference** menu choice.
5. Click mouse button 1 on the Light Table folder where you want to place the data-file icon.
6. Click mouse button 1 on the **OK** push button.

TIP: If the original data-file icon is on removable media, such as a CD or diskette, you cannot browse the contents of the icon if that CD or diskette is not inserted in the drive of the computer. To avoid this problem, you should copy a data-file icon to the computer before you create the reference to it.

Chapter 35

FaxWorks for OS/2 *Warp*

One of the biggest time-savers to come along in recent years is the facsimile (fax) machine. These machines allow you to send information that is printed on paper over the telephone lines. This reduces the amount of time needed to get information from one location to another because transmitting information over the telephone lines is faster than mailing a document.

The FaxWorks for OS/2 program takes the fax machine concept one step further. You can use this program to completely eliminate the use of paper because you can send a fax directly from your computer to another computer. Or, if you prefer, you can send a fax from your computer to a fax machine or even receive a fax from a fax machine on your computer.

This chapter shows you how to view, send, receive, and print faxes. It also shows you how to update the FaxWorks for OS/2 phone book and change the settings for the program.

Viewing a Fax

After you create a fax, you can view its contents to make sure that it looks right before you send it. In addition, you can view faxes that are sent to you.

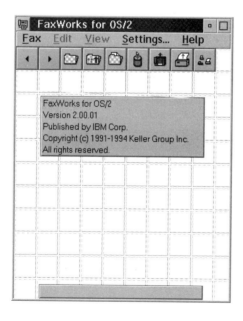

To view a fax:

1. Double-click on the **FAXWorks for OS/2** icon.

2. Click mouse button 1 on the **Fax** menu.

3. Click mouse button 1 on the **Open log** menu choice.

4. Double-click on the fax that you want to view.

5. Click mouse button 1 on the **View** menu.

6. Click mouse button 1 on the choices that best describe how you want the fax displayed. You can choose from the following:

Preview

Displays a full page so that you can see the general layout of the fax. The text will be too small to be read.

Standard

Displays a half page. The text will be small but you might be able to read it. You will have to scroll the window vertically to read the entire page.

Large

Enlarges the information so that you can read it. You will probably have to scroll the window horizontally and vertically to read the entire page.

Bits

Enlarges the information so that you can see all the bits in the fax. You will have to scroll the window horizontally and vertically to read the entire page.

Top up

Displays the fax with the top edge of the fax at the top of the screen. This is normal orientation for viewing a fax.

Left up

Displays the fax with the left edge of the fax at the top of the screen.

Right up

Displays the fax with the right edge of the fax at the top of the screen.

Bottom up

Displays the fax with the bottom edge of the fax at the top of the screen.

Go to page

Allows you to go to a specific page in the fax. This option is grayed out if there is only one page in the fax.

Prev page

Allows you to go to a previous page in the fax. This option is grayed out if there is only one page in the fax. (The PgUp key does the same thing as this choice.)

Next page

Allows you to go to the next page in the fax. This option is grayed out if there is only one page in the fax. (The PgDn key does exactly the same thing as this choice.)

7. Repeat the previous step until the fax is displayed exactly as you want it.

8. Double-click on the title-bar icon of the FaxWorks for OS/2 window to close it.

Sending a Fax

If you have information on your computer that you need to send to someone, you can send it as a fax directly from your computer. This eliminates the need for a fax machine and makes forwarding information fast and easy.

To send a fax:

1. Create the information to be faxed using a DOS, OS/2 Warp, or Windows program.
2. Click mouse button 1 on each of the following:
   a. The **File** menu in the program.
   b. The **Printer Setup** choice in the program. (The actual choice in your program might be different.)
   c. The **FxPrint** choice.
   d. The **Save** push button.
   e. The **File** menu in the program.
   f. The **Print** choice in the program.
3. Click mouse button 1 on the **Enable** choice in the Send Fax window. If this window is not displayed, do the following:
   a. Double-click on the **FaxWorks for OS/2** icon.
   b. Click mouse button 1 on the **Fax** menu.
   c. Click mouse button 1 on the **Send** menu choice.
   d. Click mouse button 1 on the **Enable** choice in the Send Fax window.
4. Fill in the information in the **From** field.
5. Click mouse button 1 on the **Preview** push button to see what your cover page will look like.
6. Click mouse button 1 on one of the following push buttons:

   Manual
   > Allows you to type the recipient's name, company, and fax number.

   Phone book
   > Allows you to search your fax phone book for the recipient's name, company, and fax number. (Double-click on the entry in the phone book to add the information to the Send Fax window.)

7. Type any comments that you have for the recipient.
8. Click mouse button 1 on the **Delay** push button if you want to send the fax at a later date or time.
9. Click mouse button 1 on the **More** push button if you want to add your name and company and the recipient's name and company to the top of each page in the fax.

10. Click mouse button 1 on the **Send** push button at the bottom of the Send Fax window.

TIP: You can eliminate steps 3 through 9 if you change the default settings for your faxes. For information about how to do this, see "Changing the Settings" on page 341.

Receiving a Fax

You can receive a fax directly on your computer. This can eliminate the need for a fax machine. It's also nice to have the information on your computer so that you do not have to retype it if you want to keep it.

To receive a fax:
1. Double-click on the **FaxWorks for OS/2** icon.
2. Click mouse button 1 on the **Fax** menu.
3. Click mouse button 1 on the **Receive** menu choice.
4. Click mouse button 1 on one of the choices in the menu. You can choose from the following:

   Off
   > Specifies that no faxes should be received.

   Current call
   > Specifies that only the fax being sent during the current call should be received.

   One call
   > Specifies that only the next fax that is sent should be received.

   All calls
   > Specifies that all faxes should be received.

5. Double-click on the title-bar icon of the FaxWorks for OS/2 window to close it.

Printing a Fax

One advantage of the FaxWorks for OS/2 program is that it allows you to send and receive faxes without the need for paper. However, sometimes you will want to print the information in a fax so that you can take it with you.

To print a fax:

1. Double-click on the **FaxWorks for OS/2** icon.
2. Click mouse button 1 on the **Fax** menu.
3. Click mouse button 1 on the **Printer Setup** menu choice.
4. Click mouse button 1 on the name of the printer where you want the fax printed.
5. Click mouse button 1 on the **OK** push button.
6. Click mouse button 1 on the **Fax** menu.
7. Click mouse button 1 on the **Open log** menu choice.
8. Point to the fax that you want to print.
9. Click mouse button 2 to display the pop-up menu.
10. Click mouse button 1 on the **Print** menu choice.
11. Double-click on the title-bar icons of the open windows to close them.

Setting Up Your Phone Book

FaxWorks for OS/2 comes with its own phone book that you can personalize with the phone numbers of the people that you usually send faxes to. This eliminates the need to remember a phone number or a company name. After the phone book is set up, all you need to do is double-click on the person's name in the phone book to send a fax to that person.

To set up your phone book:

1. Double-click on the **FaxWorks for OS/2** icon.
2. Click mouse button 1 on the **Fax** menu.
3. Click mouse button 1 on the **Send** menu choice.
4. Click mouse button 1 on the **Phone book** push button.
5. Point to an entry in the phone book.
6. Click mouse button 2 to display the pop-up menu.
7. Click mouse button 1 on one of the choices in the menu. You can choose from the following:

    Edit
    > Allows you to change information about the currently highlighted name in the phone book. (Use this choice to update existing entries.)

    New
    > Allows you to add a new name to the phone book.

Delete
> Allows you to delete the currently highlighted name from the phone book.

Sort by name
> Automatically arranges the entries in the phone book in alphabetic order by last name.

Sort by company
> Automatically arranges the entries in the phone book in alphabetic order by company name.

8. Repeat steps 5 through 7 until you are satisfied with the contents of the phone book.
9. Double-click on the title-bar icons of the open windows to close them.

Changing the Settings

FaxWorks for OS/2 has many settings that specify how it works or what the default information is on the cover sheet. You can change these settings.

To change the settings for FaxWorks for OS/2:
1. Double-click on the **FaxWorks for OS/2** icon.
2. Click mouse button 1 on the **Settings** menu.
3. Change the settings. You can choose from the following:

Cover
> Specifies the default information for the cover sheet that accompanies a fax. You can change this information when you send a fax.

Cover sheet
> Specifies whether you want a cover sheet sent with each fax and whether the cover sheet should be a full page or just long enough to contain the cover sheet information.

Cover bitmap
> Allows you to choose whether you want a bit map displayed at the top of your cover sheet. If you want a specific bit map on your cover sheet, copy that bit map to the \FAXWORKS directory, and then select it.

From
> Allows you to specify your name and phone number on the cover sheet.

Comment
> Specifies the font and additional text you want on the cover sheet.

Cover Sheet Font

Determines which font should be used for the cover sheet. (You should avoid fonts with a "B" after their names because they are harder to read.)

Comment

Allows you to specify additional text that you want on the cover sheet. You can change this information when you send a fax.

Headers

Specifies whether a header line and a To: line should appear at the top of each page of the fax.

Enable

Automatically adds the current date, time, and page count to the top of each page in the fax. You can also specify additional text you want at the top of each page.

Include To: line

Automatically adds the recipient's name and company to the top of each page in the fax. In some instances, this is enough information for the correct person to receive the fax, so the cover sheet becomes unnecessary.

Macros

Allows you to assign long dialing sequences to shorter names. For example, instead of typing your entire telephone number everywhere, you could assign your full phone number to a macro called MINE. Then, whenever you needed to type your phone number, you could just type MINE, which is shorter and easier to remember.

Dial macro

Specifies the macro and the phone number or part of a phone number that you want to assign to the macro. You can assign up to four macros.

Fax

Allows you to set such things as the default note, fax ID, and number of retry attempts that should be made.

Default send notes

Allows you to specify a small reminder about the contents of a fax. This information appears in the Open Fax window. You can change this information when you send a fax.

Dial prefix

Identifies the numbers that must be dialed before you dial the phone number. For example, if you need to reach an outside line, you might need to dial a 9. Add a comma after the number if you want to specify a two-second pause. You can add multiple commas.

Fax local ID

Specifies your fax identifier. This identifier is sent by your fax machine before it sends or receives. It is usually set to your fax telephone number.

Busy

Specifies the number of attempts that should be made to send a fax and the number of minutes between each attempt.

Program

Allows you to set such things as the type of display, audible tones, and the format of the date on the fax.

Monitor type

Specifies the type of display connected to your computer. If you are having difficulty reading information in the FaxWorks for OS/2 windows, select a different monitor type.

Tones

Specifies whether tones should be sounded when the sending or receiving of the fax is completed.

Phone book display

Specifies whether the phone book should be sorted by the last names or the first names of the entries.

Date display

Specifies how the date should be displayed. You can choose text (17-MAR-94) or numeric (03/17/94).

Ports

Lists the ports that are configured for faxes. By double-clicking on a port, you can set a port to Send/Receive, Send only, Receive only, Standby, or Off.

Modem

Specifies the options for your fax hardware.

Baud Rate

Specifies the maximum baud rate in bits per second (BPS) that your fax hardware supports.

Speaker

Specifies the speaker mode for your fax hardware. Dial, which is the default choice, lets you hear the dial tone and dialing sequence. After the call goes through, the speaker is turned off. You can also turn the speaker on or off and select a volume level.

Line Type

Specifies whether your telephone system is tone or pulse and whether the fax hardware should wait for a dial tone.

Answer Rings

Specifies the number of rings before an incoming call is answered.

Modem Type

Specifies the command set that is required by your fax modem. If these settings are incorrect, your faxes might not be correctly sent or received.

Chapter 36

IBM Works

The IBM Works BonusPak program comes with five applications—Word Processor, Spreadsheet, Chart, Data Filer, and Report Writer. These applications let you create documents or documents with pictures, spreadsheets, charts, databases, and reports. These applications were designed to work together so that you can share information between them. This sharing of information can help you to produce high-quality work more efficiently.

The IBM Works BonusPak program also includes a Personal Information Manager (PIM) application. You can use it to organize your life!

This chapter describes the features that are common to the five applications. Then, you'll find out how to create and format documents and spreadsheets and create charts, databases, and reports. This chapter also describes the PIM application and how to use it.

Using Common Features

Because the IBM Works program contains applications that were designed to be used together, there are a number of features that work the same no matter which application you are using. For example, to open any one of the five applications, you always do the following:

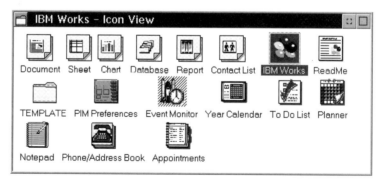

1. Double-click on the **IBM Works** icon (located on the Desktop).
2. Double-click on the **IBM Works** icon (located in the IBM Works window).
3. Double-click on the icon for the application you want to use.

The following list describes other features that work the same no matter which application you are using. (In fact, some of the features are ones you might already be familiar with if you've been using OS/2 Warp.)

Starting one of the applications

You can start each IBM Works application by double-clicking on its icon.

Working with windows

You can arrange (tile or cascade), move, size, close, and switch between open windows in the same way you do with OS/2 Warp.

Formatting text

You can select specific areas of text for formatting purposes.

Opening files

You can open new and existing files by selecting **New** or **Open** from the **File** menu.

Cutting, copying, and pasting

You can cut and copy within the same program or from one program to another by using the **Cut**, **Copy**, and **Paste** menu choices from the **Edit** menu. By using these choices, you will be working with the OS/2 Warp clipboard. To find out more about the OS/2 Warp clipboard, read "Using the OS/2 Warp Clipboard" on page 182.

Using ribbons

Each application has its own *ribbon*, which let you perform different functions. For example, the Spreadsheet ribbon contains choices that you can use to perform calculations and to display charts. Each application's ribbon also contains choices that allow you to open one of the other IBM Works applications or change the font field and point size for that application.

Copying and linking data

You can copy and link data between two or more IBM Works applications, or your can copy and link data between IBM Works applications and non-IBM Works programs. For example, suppose you use the Chart application to create a chart. You then can copy that chart into a document that you create with the Word Processor application. If you change the chart (from within the Chart application), the change is also made to the copy of the chart in the document.

Exiting IBM Works

You can exit from any IBM Works application by selecting the **Exit** menu choice from the **File** menu.

Changing settings

You can establish or change settings for the IBM Works applications in the same way you do using OS/2 Warp.

Display the Settings notebook for the IBM Works icon to set the following for all five applications:

- Page setup, which lets you set up the orientation and size of the pages.

- Preferences, which lets you select such things as units of measure, display characteristics, and the directories you want to search.

- Printers, which lets you check the printer setup. (OS/2 Warp controls the printer setup for IBM Works.)

- Styles, which lets you change the styles of text. You can specify such things as font size and style, emphasis (for example, bold or italic), or position (superscript or subscript).

Word Processor

The Word Processor application is used to create high-quality documents.

The Word Processor application provides a ribbon that contains choices that are common to the other applications. There is also a ruler that you can use to guide you when you are inputting text. The application also provides a spell checker that you can use to check the spelling of a particular word, a selected area of text, or the whole document. You have access to dictionaries, and you can create your own custom dictionaries.

The Word Processor application provides synonym support as well.

In addition, the application has a search-and-replace feature. You can search for words and text strings, and replace existing text with other text in the documents you create.

Working with a Document

You can create a new document or work with an existing document.

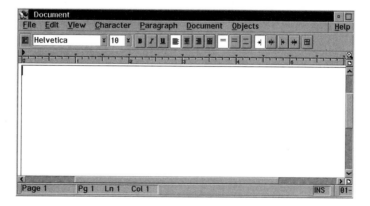

To work with a document:

1. Double-click on the **Word Processor** icon.
2. Click on the **File** menu.
3. Click on **New** (if you are creating a new document). Click on **Open** (if you want to work with an existing document).

To begin working with a document, you simply need to start typing. When you begin working with a document, the default input mode is insert (so that you do not type over existing text). To turn insert mode on or off, press the Insert key.

You can select text (so that you can delete it or cut and paste it to a different location) by moving the mouse pointer to the beginning of the text, and then pressing and holding mouse button 1 while dragging the mouse pointer over the text you want to select. Release mouse button 1 when you are finished.

If you want to delete the selected text, use the Del key or the **Delete** menu choice (located on the **Edit** menu).

 TIP: If you change your mind and really didn't want to delete the text, use the **Undo** menu choice (located on the **Edit** menu). This choice recovers only the most recent deletion, so you need to use it before you delete additional text.

If you want to cut or paste the selected text, use the **Cut** or **Paste** menu choice (located on the **Edit** menu).

When you have finished editing a document, use the **Save** or **Save as** menu choice (located on the **Edit** menu) to save your document.

Drawing Pictures

You can draw pictures right in your document as well as size them and move them around. You can use a Draw Palette or the Tools menu choice from the **Objects** menu. These selections let you create lines, different types of rectangles, circles, ellipses, polygons, and text.

To create a graphic object:

1. Click mouse button 1 on the **View** menu.
2. Click mouse button 1 on the **Draw Palette** menu choice.
3. Click mouse button 1 on the drawing tool you want to use.
4. Start drawing!

To save the graphic object:

1. Click mouse button 1 on the **File** menu.
2. Click mouse button 1 on the **Save** menu choice.
3. Type the name you want to give to the picture.
4. Click mouse button 1 on the **Save** push button.

 TIP: After you have drawn a picture, you can change its appearance with a variety of fills, patterns, colors, and line types. These choices are available on the **Objects** menu.

You can add pictures that you create to any existing document.

To insert a picture into a document:

1. Click mouse button 1 on the **File** menu.
2. Click mouse button 1 on the **Open** menu choice.
3. Click mouse button 1 on the name of the document you want to open.
4. Click mouse button 1 on the **Open** push button.
5. When the document you want to work with is displayed in the Word Processor window, move the mouse pointer to the location where you want to add the picture, and click mouse button 1.
6. Click mouse button 1 on the **File** menu.
7. Click mouse button 1 on the **Import Picture** menu choice.
8. Click mouse button 1 on the Type of **File** field to indicate the type of file that you want to import.
9. Click mouse button 1 on the name of the picture file in the **Files list** field that you want to import.
10. Click on the **OK** push button to add the picture to the document.

Formatting Documents

The Word Processor application provides a wide variety of formatting options. You will need to explore these options on your own to decide which ones are most applicable to the document you are creating. You can do this by reading the online help that describes the option.

To help you get started, the following list describes some of the formatting options:

View menu
Provides a **Layout Mode** menu choice, which you can use to see the way tables and graphs appear on a page and to move them to different locations.

Document menu
> Provides choices that you can use to add hyphens, headers, and footers to your documents.

Paragraph menu
> Provides choices that you can use to set up indentation, page breaks, paragraphs, tables, and tabs for your document.

Spreadsheet

The Spreadsheet application is used to produce spreadsheets.

The Spreadsheet application provides a ribbon that contains choices that are common to the other applications. The ribbon also contains choices that you can use to perform calculations, display charts, and display borders for cells.

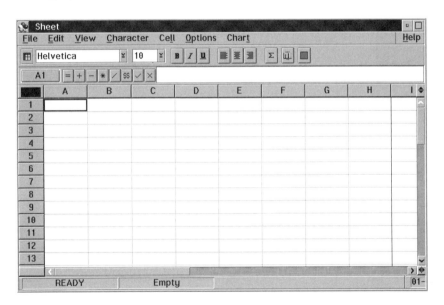

The application also provides support for adding, subtracting, multiplying, and dividing the numbers in the cells.

Working with a Spreadsheet

You can create a new spreadsheet or work with an existing spreadsheet.

To work with a spreadsheet:

1. Double-click on the **Spreadsheet** icon.
2. Click on the **File** menu.
3. Click on **New** (if you are creating a new spreadsheet). Click on **Open** (if you want to work with an existing spreadsheet).

To begin working with a spreadsheet, you will need to enter text, numbers, and formulas. The columns are lettered across the top, and the rows are numbered on the left side. Each area where a column and row connect is considered to be a cell. The cell is the area where you type in text, numbers, or formulas. You can create a spreadsheet that tracks your travel expenses, your business or family expenses, or even your bank account.

To enter text, numbers, or formulas, click mouse button 1 on the cell you want to work with. (Each cell can contain up to 255 characters.)

You can select cells (so that you can delete them or cut and paste them to a different location) by moving the mouse pointer to the beginning of the cell, and then pressing and holding mouse button 1 while dragging the mouse pointer over the cells you want to select. Release mouse button 1 when you are finished.

If you want to delete the selected cells, use the Del key or the **Delete** menu choice (located on the **Edit** menu).

TIP: If you change your mind and really didn't want to delete the cells, you can use the **Undo** menu choice (located on the **Edit** menu). This choice only recovers the most recent deletion, so you need to use it before you delete additional cells.

If you want to cut and paste the selected cells, use the **Cut and Paste** menu choices (located on the **Edit** menu).

The IBM Works Spreadsheet application also provides menu choices that automatically calculate your spreadsheet, allow you to insert new columns and rows, allow you to add special notes in specific cells, and provide a way to protect information in specific cells so that the information cannot be altered.

TIP: You can create a chart and use the data you put together with the Spreadsheet application. Use the Chart icon (located on the ribbon for the Spreadsheet program) to specify the cells of information you want to chart. Then, give the chart a name, and click on the **Show chart** push button to display the information in the default chart view, which is a bar chart. After the chart window is opened, you can choose a different type of chart or further customize the chart to meet your needs.

Formatting Spreadsheets

The Spreadsheet application provides a wide variety of formatting options. You will need to explore these options on your own to decide which ones are most applicable for the spreadsheet you are creating. You can do this by reading the online help that describes the option.

To help you get started, the following list describes some of the formatting options:

Character menu

Provides choices that you can use to format characters and choose fonts.

Options menu

Provides choices that you can use to add headers and footers to your spreadsheets.

Cell menu

Provides choices that you can use to align cells, format numeric cells, and add borders to cells.

Chart

The Chart application is used to create charts.

The Chart application provides a ribbon contains choices that are common to the other applications. The ribbon also contains choices that you can use to select different chart types.

The Chart application provides support for a variety of chart types. You can choose from bar, stacked bar, line, area, bar and line, stacked bar and line, scatter, or pie charts.

You can create a chart that uses the information from the Spreadsheet or Word Processor applications, or you can create a chart from scratch.

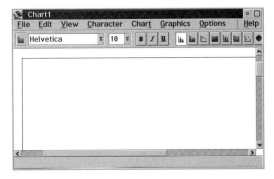

To create a chart from scratch:

1. Double-click on the **Chart** icon.
2. Click mouse button 1 on the **New** push button.
3. Click mouse button 1 on the **Chart** menu.
4. Click mouse button 1 on the **Data input** menu choice.
5. Type labels beside the numbers in the Data series column. These labels identify the graph bar or pie slice of numeric data.
6. Type labels under the numbers at the top of the Data input window. These labels identify the names given to the points appearing on the X-axis of the chart. (These labels are also used to identify parts in the chart legend.)
7. Type numbers in the small boxes under the Legend labels. You can use up to 12 numbers per box.
8. Click mouse button 1 on the **Save** push button. The chart is displayed in a bar graph format. (Although bar graphs are nice, you might want to change the chart to a different type.)
9. Click mouse button 1 on the **Chart** menu.
10. Click mouse button 1 on the **Types** menu choice.
11. Click mouse button 1 on the type of chart you want to create. (The bar chart changes to the type of chart you select.)

NOTE: If you plan to use the Pie chart type, you will be able to display only a single data series. You can display up to eight different data series using the other chart types.

Now that you have created a chart, you can add up to three different types of titles to your chart, as follows:

1. Click mouse button 1 on the **Options** menu.
2. Click mouse button 1 on the arrow that appears to the right of the **Titles** menu choice. (The available title choices are displayed.)
3. Click mouse button 1 on the title choice. The available title choices are:

Main title
> Displays a title in the top center of the chart.

Horizontal title
> Displays a title below the horizontal axis of the chart.

Vertical title
> Displays a title vertically beside the vertical axis.

After a title is displayed in the chart, you can move it anywhere you like by clicking on it and then dragging it to the new location.

Official Guide to Using OS/2 Warp

Data Filer

The Data Filer program is used to create a database. A database is a collection of data with a particular structure used for inputting, storing, and providing information. For example, you could use a database to keep personnel records, product or client listings, or inventory records.

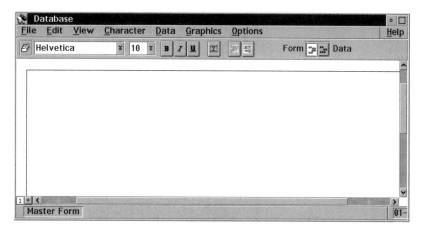

The Data Filer application provides a ribbon that contains choices that are common to the other applications. The ribbon also contains choices that you can use to insert a field on a data form, group or ungroup fields, or activate data entry mode.

Planning Your Database

Before you create a database, some planning is in order. You must decide what type of information your database should provide. For example, it could contain customer names and addresses, particular articles with information about the authors and contents of articles, customer satisfaction results, customer complaints, or possibly project statistics. Next, you need to decide how you want to use the information (for example, to generate mailing lists or monthly reports or to merge data with reports created with the Word Processor application).

When you are through making all these decisions, you can start to think about how you want to design a database form. A database form consists of many different types of fields. Explanations of the types of fields you can chose from follow:

Date Fields

> Are used to store date information about such items as date of hire, transaction date, or possibly the date of a particular customer call.

Logical Fields

Are used to set one of two conditions. For example, you could use **Y** and **N** for Yes or No, **M** and **F** for Male or Female, or **T** and **F** for True or False.

Multi-Line Text Fields

Are used so that you can type long pieces of text or memos. (The text automatically wraps in this field. Press the Enter key each time you want to start a new line.) This field could be useful if you need to type in customer satisfaction or dissatisfaction information or possibly customer wants and needs.

Numeric Fields

Are used to contain numbers. You can specify verification conditions and create calculated fields.

Picture Fields

Are used to store pictures.

Text Fields

Are used to specify the exact size (length) of a text field.

You can set up your database to your specifications by using the fields listed above.

Creating a Database

After you plan your database strategy, you need to set up a database form.

To set up a database form:
1. Double-click on the **Data Filer** icon.
2. Click on the **New** push button. (The Insert Fields window is displayed.)
3. Click mouse button 1 on the type of field in the **Field Type** field that you want to use.
4. Specify the width of the form field in the **Parameters** field.
5. Click on the **Save** push button.
6. When the Database window is displayed, the mouse pointer will look like a rectangle with a + sign inside of it. Move the mouse pointer to the place on the form where you want the field to be located.
7. Repeat steps 3 through 6 until you have created all the database fields you need.

After you set up the fields, use the **Edit field** menu choice (located on the **Data** menu) if you want to edit or delete specific fields. You can select the field you want to edit or delete and then click on the **Save** push button to save any of the changes you made. Click on the **Delete** push button to delete a field.

Report Writer

The Report Writer application is used to create a report (in a columnar format) from a database you created with the Data Filer program. You can create a report directly from the Data Filer program or from the Report Writer program because they were designed to work together.

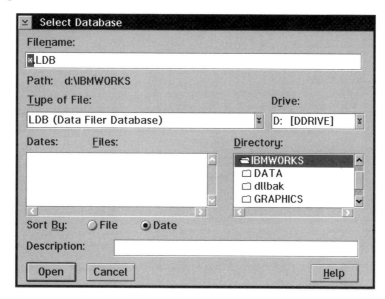

The Report Writer application provides a ribbon that contains choices that are common to the other applications. The ribbon also contains choices that you can use to specify the current sort order or index order and to switch between editing the report or viewing the report.

The application also provides two panels, which are displayed below the ribbon. The Report Format panel lets you select the fields you want your report to contain and select how you want the information grouped. The Sample Report panel displays a condensed version of the report you are creating. (This panel is blank when the Report Writer application is first displayed.)

Planning Your Report

Before you create your report, you should plan it. To do this, you need to open the Report Writer and select the name of the database that contains the data you will use to generate your report. Then, you can review the columns of information you created using the Data Filer application and decide which ones you want to include in your report.

To open the Report Writer program:

1. Double-click on the **Report Writer** icon.
2. Click mouse button 1 on the **New** push button. (The Select Database window is displayed.)
3. Click mouse button 1 on the name of the database that will be used to generate the report.
4. Click mouse button 1 on the **Open** push button to display the Report Writer window.

Review the headings in the Data Fields list located on the Report Format panel. The headings represent the columns of information you created with the Data Filer program. Decide which headings represent the information that you want included in your report.

Creating a Report

After you plan your report strategy, you can create the report.

To create a report:

1. Click mouse button 1 on the headings listed in the **Data Fields** field to establish the columns from which the report will be generated.
2. Click mouse button 1 on the include button. (The include button looks like a right arrow and is located beside the **Data Fields** field.) After you click on the include button, the names you selected are displayed in the **Report Columns** field.

Once the names are included in the **Report Columns** field, you can remove them from the field by clicking mouse button 1 on the remove button located under the include button. As names are included in the **Report Columns** field, you will see the beginning of the report being built in the Sample Report window.

TIP: To rearrange the columns in the report, move the mouse pointer just under the title of the column you want to move. When the pointer turns into a down arrow, press and hold mouse button 2, drag the column to the new location, and then release the mouse button.

Personal Information Manager

The IBM Works BonusPak program provides a Personal Information Manager (PIM). The PIM is a set of applications that can help you manage your business and personal needs.

The collection of applications includes a monthly planner, a calendar, an appointment book, a to-do list, a phone and address book, a notepad, an alarm program, and a notebook that you can use to customize the features of the PIM. The following list describes each PIM application in more detail.

Preferences Notebook

Lets you customize the features in the PIM programs. For example, you can customize holiday types and colors, modem settings, and appointment headings.

Event Monitor

Sets off alarms and launches PIM programs.

Appointments

Provides multiple views of your daily appointments and lets you set alarms, set scheduled program launches, and schedule appointments.

Monthly Planner

Displays monthly appointments in a grid format with either a workday or 24-hour time schedule. Each entry is color-coded by type, and holidays are highlighted. You can reschedule appointments or set up new ones.

Calendar

Displays a full-year calendar with holidays highlighted. You can customize the holiday database, reschedule appointments, and scroll from year to year.

To-Do List

Provides a full month of to-do list activities. You can create a new list item, assign a deadline or priority date to a list item, sort list items by date or priority, attach notes to a list item, or search list items.

Phone/Address Book

Provides details or icon views of business or personal contacts. You can customize icons, create appointments by dragging contact names to the Appointments or Monthly Planner icons, search all fields, place outgoing calls, and log incoming and outgoing calls.

NotePad

Holds text or graphic information. You can add, append, or insert pages into the notepad as well as add chapter headings. Information can be dragged and dropped on the pages in the notepad, and you can rearrange the information by dragging and dropping the headings in the table of contents.

PIM applications were designed to work together. For example, if you add an item to the Appointments icon and link it to the To-Do List, it will show up in both those applications and in the Monthly Planner.

Preferences Notebook

The Preferences Notebook lets you customize certain features of the PIM programs. Use the following list to help you determine what you can change.

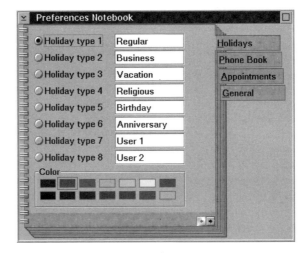

Holidays

This page lets you customize your own set of holidays by assigning colors and types to holiday names. Each type of holiday you set up will have a color assigned to it and will be shown in that color when it is displayed in the To-Do List, Monthly Planner, Appointments, and Calendar applications.

Phonebook

Lets you set up a modem, set up additional labels for different users, and set up additional columns to be displayed within the Phonebook window.

Appointments

Lets you specify settings for the start and end times of your workday, the intervals in which you can schedule events, and other Appointments application options.

General

Lets you specify whether or not you receive a message when you try to delete PIM data or whether or not you receive an event reminder each time a PIM application is opened. You can also specify whether or not the Event Monitor should be opened each time a PIM application is opened.

Event Monitor

The Event Monitor keeps track of all alarms you set when you are using any of the PIM applications. For example, you can set an alarm when you set an appointment (with the Appointments application). You can also set an alarm when you add an item to your to-do list (with the To-Do List application). The Event Monitor is simply the "tracker" for all of the alarms you might possibly set using your PIM applications.

If a PIM application provides the option to set up a program so that it starts at a specified time, then the Event Monitor keeps track of that too.

If you like, you can set up the Event Monitor to open every time you open a PIM application.

Appointments

The Appointments application provides a great way for you to schedule daily events such as an important meeting with a new client or your son's next soccer game. You can attach notes and alarms to appointments to remind yourself of the time of the meeting or event and the subject matter.

When the Appointments application is opened, the current day is displayed in a red box. You use the list box to review scheduled appointments for a specific day. The day is divided into time slots, with the default time slot being 30 minutes. You can change the default time on the Appointments page of the Preferences Notebook.

![Appointment Book window showing January 1995, Week 2, with days 9 Monday through 15 Sunday]

TIP: You can use the arrow buttons at the bottom of the Appointments screen to flip through the pages. The single arrow will flip one week at a time. The double arrow will flip two weeks at a time.

To schedule an appointment:
1. Double-click on the **Appointments** icon.
2. Double-click on the time slot where you want to schedule an appointment.
3. Click mouse button 1 on the up or down arrow beside the **Time** field to set the time for the appointment.
4. Type a description of the appointment in the **Title** field.
5. Click mouse button 1 on the arrow to the right of the **Duration** slider bar to adjust the amount of time needed for the appointment.
6. Click mouse button 1 on the push buttons in the **Options** field to:

   Alarm
   > Set an alarm that goes off to remind you of an appointment.

   Launch
   > Start a program at a specific time.

   Recurring
   > Set recurring meeting times for daily, weekly, monthly, or yearly appointments.

   To-Do List check box
   > Link the appointment to the To-Do List program.

7. Type the subject matter of the appointment or any information you want to remember about the appointment (up to 512 characters) in the **Notes** field.

If an appointment is canceled, you can delete the appointment.

To delete an appointment:
1. Move the mouse pointer to the appointment you want to delete.
2. Click mouse button 2 to display the pop-up menu.
3. Click mouse button 1 on the **Delete** menu choice.
4. Click mouse button 1 on the **Yes** push button.

Planner

The Planner application works with the Appointments application. The Appointments application shows events on a daily or weekly basis only. You can use the Planner to display a month's worth of events at a glance. Use the arrow buttons at the bottom of the Planner window to flip through the months and years. The single-arrow button flips

Official Guide to Using OS/2 Warp

the page forward or backward one month at a time. The double-arrow button flips the page forward or backward one year at a time.

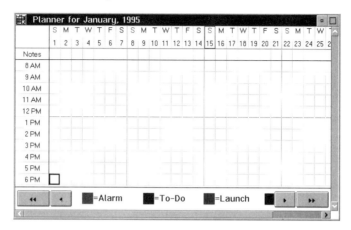

As mentioned, the Planner application works along with the Appointments application. As a result, you can add appointments using either application. The procedure for adding appointments is the same as the procedure for adding appointments with the Appointments application.

To-Do List

The To-Do List application lets you manage and prioritize work items and events from a single list. This can be more useful than creating separate to-do lists for each day or week.

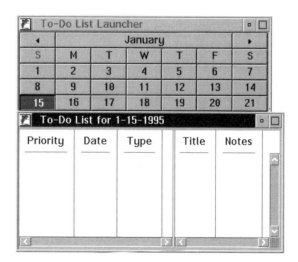

To add an item to your to-do list:

1. Double-click on the **To-Do List** icon. The To-Do List — Launcher calendar and the To-Do List items windows are displayed.
2. Move the mouse pointer to the To-Do List items window.
3. Click mouse button 2 to display the pop-up menu.
4. Click mouse button 1 on the **New** menu choice.
5. Type in the **Title** field the description of the item you want displayed on the to-do list (for example, "Buy Gina's birthday gift"). You can also specify what type of list item you are adding by typing an identifier in the **Type** field. (This field is optional.) For example, *important* or *meeting* will work as to-do types.
6. Assign a priority to the list item. Click mouse button 1 on a number, or type the date in the **Priority** field. (You cannot assign a priority by number and by date. You have to choose one or the other.)

   If you assign a priority to the list item by date, you can use the Recurring push button to set up recurring to-do items. For example, if the list item is "Attend weekly exercise class," you can add it to the to-do list so that it appears every week.

7. If you want to add notes to a list item, you can type up to 512 characters in the note box below the **Options** field.
8. Click mouse button 1 on the **OK** push button.

 TIP: To use the To-Do List — Launcher calendar, you can click on the arrows beside the Month at the top of the calendar to flip through the months of the year. You can click on the arrows beside the Year at the bottom of the calendar to change the calendar year. Double-click on a day to add an item to the to-do list.

After you have completed a to-do list item, you can mark it as completed.

To mark an item as completed:

1. Point to the item you want to mark as completed.
2. Click mouse button 2 to display the pop-up menu.
3. Click on the **Mark complete** menu choice.

If you make an incorrect entry or if an event gets canceled, you can delete it.

To delete an item from the to-do list:

1. Double-click on the **To-Do List** icon. The To-Do List — Launcher calendar and the To-Do List items windows are displayed.
2. Move the mouse pointer to the To-Do List items window.
3. Move the mouse pointer to the list item you want to delete.

4. Click mouse button 2 to display the pop-up menu.
5. Click mouse button 1 on the **Delete** menu choice.
6. Click mouse button 1 on the **Yes** push button.

Calendar

The Calendar application displays a calendar of the current year. The Calendar application works along with other PIM programs and provides several nice options that can save you time. For example, you can easily access any PIM application from the pop-up menu of the Calendar icon.

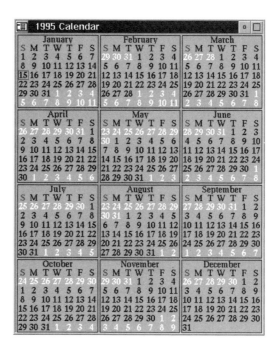

To access any PIM application from the Calendar icon:
1. Point to the **Calendar** icon.
2. Click mouse button 2 to display the pop-up menu.
3. Click mouse button 1 on the **Launch** menu choice. (A list of PIM applications is displayed.)
4. Click mouse button 1 on the name of the PIM application you want to use.

You can also display the pop-up menu for the Calendar icon and use the **Options** menu choice to set an alarm for an event or to schedule holidays. You might find this quicker than opening the Appointments application.

NotePad

The NotePad application lets you store practically any type of information from text to graphics. A table of contents is automatically created for you to keep track of each page you add to the NotePad.

NOTE: The NotePad application stores only bit-map and metafile graphic images.

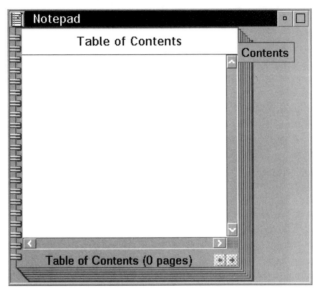

To add pages to the NotePad:

1. Double-click on the **NotePad** icon.
2. Move the mouse pointer to the empty notebook.
3. Click mouse button 2 to display the pop-up menu.
4. Click mouse button 1 on the **Append** menu choice.
5. Type a name in the **Title** field. (This name will be automatically added to the Table of Contents.)
6. Click mouse button 1 on the arrow to the right of the **Insert** field. Click on a number to adjust the number of pages you want to add.
7. Click mouse button 1 on the **Type** field. Click on the type of information you want to add to the NotePad. (If you want the new page to have a notebook tab associated with it, click mouse button 1 on the Chapter check box. Then type in the notebook tab identifier text.)
8. Click mouse button 1 on the **OK** push button.

The NotePad is displayed, and an entry for the new page is displayed in the Table of Contents. To use the new page, double-click on the entry for the new page. (If you chose to create a tab for the new page, you can click mouse button 1 on the tab.) Move the mouse pointer to the location on the page where you want to add the information, and click mouse button 1. Then, start typing.

NOTE: When you close the Notepad, be sure to click mouse button 1 on the **Yes** push button to save any changes or additions to the NotePad.

Phone/Address Book

The Phone/Address Book application is a convenient way for you to record the names, addresses, and phone numbers of friends and relatives or companies you do business with. Everything is recorded in a notebook format and each entry is stored in its own Personal Information notebook. A Personal Information notebook contains five different pages. Each one provides different information about a selected entry.

You can also create contact lists which are subsets of the entries in your phone book. For example, you could set up a mailing list for your holiday greeting cards.

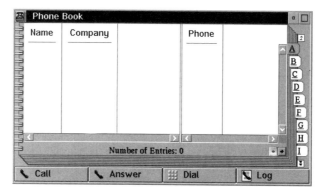

To add an entry to the Phone/Address Book:
1. Double-click on the **Phone/Address Book** icon.
2. Point to the Open Phone Book window.
3. Click mouse button 2 to display the pop-up menu.
4. Click mouse button 1 on the **New** menu choice. (The Personal Information notebook for the new entry is displayed.)
5. Click on the **General** notebook tab. Fill in the information that is requested (for example, the name and address).
6. Click mouse button 1 on the **Add** push button.

7. Click mouse button 1 on the **Phone** notebook tab. Fill in the phone number and associated information.
8. Click mouse button 1 on the **Add** push button.

TIP: To move quickly to an entry, simply press the key on your keyboard that corresponds to the first letter of the entry. You can also click mouse button 1 on the letter tabs along the right side of the notebook.

If a friend moves or you no longer do business with a particular company, you can edit or delete any entry in the Address/Phone Book.

To edit an entry, simply double-click on the entry and make the necessary changes in the notebook. (Don't forget to click on the **OK** push button.)

To delete an entry:
1. Move the mouse pointer to the entry you want to delete.
2. Click mouse button 2 to display the pop-up menu.
3. Click mouse button 1 on the **Delete** menu choice.
4. Click on the **Yes** push button.

You can use the following push buttons at the bottom of the Phone/Address Book to perform additional functions:

Call
> Provides you with a list of phone numbers for an entry so that you can choose the right number when you place a call.

Answer
> Lets you track incoming calls and keep notes about the conversations. You can also schedule follow-up phone calls to be listed in your to-do list.

Dial
> Lets you call someone who is not listed in your phone book and log the conversation.

Log
> Lets you browse through all previously logged phone conversations. It stores the date, time, length, and status of each call. All notes about the call appear in the Notes entry field.

Chapter 37

Person to Person

Person to Person (P2P) is a group of programs that allow you to communicate with other people over a Local Area Network (LAN) or Wide Area Network (WAN). Included in P2P are the following programs:

Call Manager

Manages incoming calls, keeps track of who called, and lets you end calls. The Call Manager must be running in order for you to use any of the other P2P programs during a call.

Address Book

Contains the names of people that you call. You cannot call anyone whose name is not in an address book. You can have multiple address books.

Chalkboard

Displays text or pictures that can be marked up and pointed to by everyone participating in the call.

Talk

Allows you to send text messages to other people participating in the call.

Clip

Allows you to share your clipboard with other people participating in the call.

Video

Allows you to send video to and receive video from other people participating in the call.

Stills Capture

Allows you to capture video images that you send or receive and convert them into bit maps.

This chapter shows you how to start and configure the Call Manager, set up an address book, call people, and use the different P2P programs to communicate with people.

Using Common Features

All of the programs except the Call Manager and the Stills Capture have a P2P menu and a Window menu. These menus work the same way in all of the programs. This section describes the P2P and Window menus.

Using the Window Menu

The Window menu contains a list of the P2P programs that are currently being used (shared) in a call. When a program is no longer being used (unshared), it is removed from the list.

Use the Window menu for quick access to any P2P program that you are using so you don't have to move windows and search the Desktop for them.

Using the P2P Menu

The P2P menu contains choices that you use to start, end, share, and unshare a call. The following list provides a detailed description of the menu choices:

Call

Used to place a call to a person. When you select this choice, a menu is displayed with the names of the last 10 people you called. You can choose a name from this menu or select **People** to display an address book.

If the call goes through, the program that you called from is automatically started on the computer of the person you called. In other words, that person sees the same information that is displayed on your computer.

Add

Adds another person to the call. When you select this choice, a menu is displayed with the names of the last 10 people you called. You can choose a name from this menu or select **People** to display an address book.

If the call goes through, all of the P2P programs that you are currently using are automatically started on the computer of the person you called. In other words, that person sees the same information that is displayed on your computer.

Share

Makes the information in the P2P program when you initiate a call the *share from public* information. This allows everyone who is participating in the call to see the information contained in the program. (If one or more of the participants are not using the P2P program when you initiate the share (perhaps they are away from their computers), the P2P program automatically starts the P2P program that is being used for the call and the information contained in the program is displayed on their computers. If the information that you intend to share is of a confidential nature, you might want to make sure participants plan to be at their computers before you initiate the call.)

Unshare

> Makes the information in the P2P program when you initiate a call the *unshare from private* information. This means only you can see the information contained in the program. (If you are using only one P2P program when you select Unshare, you are disconnected from the call.)

End

> Disconnects you and all the P2P programs you are using from the call. (It does not close the P2P programs.)

Call Manager

The Call Manager must be started before you can make or receive phone calls. It manages incoming calls, keeps track of who called, and end calls. You can also use it to make configuration changes for your P2P programs.

To start the Call Manager:

1. Double-click on the **P2P** icon.
2. Double-click on the **Call Manager** icon.

TIP: If you frequently make or receive calls, you might want to drag a shadow of this icon into the **Startup** folder so that it starts automatically when you start your computer. This eliminates the need to start the Call Manager manually every time you want to use the P2P programs.

During the installation of P2P, you were given the opportunity to provide personal information, give specifics about how you wanted your calls answered, and set up P2P so that it would work with your network. If you made a mistake during the installation or if you just want to change something, you can use the Call Manager to do this.

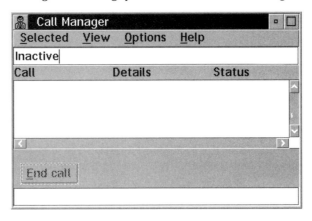

To change your configuration choices:

1. Double-click on the **Call Manager** icon.
2. Click mouse button 1 on the **View** menu.
3. Click mouse button 1 on the **Configuration** menu choice.
4. Click mouse button 1 on the **Personal information** choice.
5. Update any information in the Personal window to meet your needs. You can change the following:

   Name
   > Identifies the person calling or participating in a conference call.

   Telephone number
   > Identifies the telephone number you are calling from.

   Details
   > Specifies your address, department number, job title, and anything else you want to divulge.

   Reject message
   > Identifies the message that you want a caller to receive when you do not respond to a call.

   Bar message
   > Identifies the message that you want a caller to receive when you are barring all incoming calls and not responding.

6. Click mouse button 1 on the **OK** push button.
7. Click mouse button 1 on the **View** menu.
8. Click mouse button 1 on the **Configuration** menu choice.
9. Click mouse button 1 on the **Call timeout** choice.
10. Click mouse button 1 on one of the choices in the window. You can choose from the following:

    No timeout
    > Specifies that you do not want to send a reject message no matter how long a data call remains unanswered.

    Set timeout
    > Specifies the amount of time a data call can go unanswered before a reject message is sent.

11. Click mouse button 1 on the **OK** push button.
12. Click mouse button 1 on the **View** menu.

13. Click mouse button 1 on the **Configuration** menu choice.

14. Click mouse button 1 on the **Async comms port 1** choice.

15. Update any information in the **Async comms port 1** window to meet your needs. You can change the following:

Phone number
Identifies the phone number of your modem. This number is used for data calls only. (Voice calls use the number specified in the **Add person** menu choice of the **Edit** menu.)

Modem
Specifies the name of the modem being used. Select a name from the list.

Initialization
Specifies the string that is used to put the modem in the correct state for making and receiving calls. The string that is displayed is based on the modem you selected.

Baud rate
Specifies the transmission rate for the data.

Dialing
Specifies whether you are using pulse or tone dialing.

Compression
Specifies the compression that is used to send and share data. The default rate is the best choice for most people.

Voice Autodial
Specifies whether you want to use the modem to autodial numbers for voice calls. You should probably choose this option.

16. Click mouse button 1 on the **OK** push button.

17. Click mouse button 1 on the **View** menu.

18. Click mouse button 1 on the **Software video emulation** menu choice.

19. Specify the drive, directory, and file name of the bit map that you want to use when software video emulation is requested. (This bit map will be used if your computer cannot send video images. Even if you cannot send video images, you will still be able to see the video images being sent by other callers.)

20. Click mouse button 1 on the **Enabled** choice to make the software video emulation available to P2P. If it is not enabled, no images will be sent or received.

21. Click mouse button 1 on the **OK** push button.

22. Double-click on the title-bar icon of the Call Manager window to close it. You must then restart the Call Manager so that your changes will be put into effect.

23. Double-click on the **Call Manager** icon to start it.

Address Book

The Address Book is used to hold the names and network addresses of people you call using the P2P programs. You can have as many address books as you want, and there is no limit to their size. However, you might want to make several address books and keep them relatively small so that it is easier to find the name you are looking for.

Setting Up an Address Book

Before you can use an address book, you must provide the names and addresses of the people you plan to call using the P2P programs. You can't place calls to people using the P2P programs unless their names and addresses are specified in an address book. The P2P program provides a sample address book. You can update the sample address book or create a new address book.

To add names, phone numbers, and addresses to an address book:

1. Double-click on the **P2P** icon.
2. Double-click on the **Address Book** icon.
3. If you want to create a new address book:
   a. Click mouse button 1 on the **File** menu.
   b. Click mouse button 1 on the **New** menu choice.

4. Click mouse button 1 on the **Edit** menu.

5. Click mouse button 1 on the **Add person** menu choice.

6. Type in the **Name** field the name of the person you want to add to the address book.

7. Click mouse button 1 in the **Telephone number** field, and type the phone number of the person you want to add to the address book.

8. Click mouse button 1 in the **Details** field, and type in any additional information, such as address or job title.

9. Click mouse button 1 on the communication adapter in the **Communications type** field that you want to use to call this person.

10. Click mouse button 1 on the **Set address** push button, and type the P2P NETBIOS name of the person you are adding. (Only people who share the same type of NETBIOS will be able to communicate using P2P.)

11. Click mouse button 1 on the **OK** push button.

12. Click mouse button 1 on the **Add** push button to add the information to the address book.

13. Repeat steps 4 through 12 for each person you want to add to the address book. (If you make a mistake and press Enter before you complete the information, you can return to the address page for the person by clicking mouse button 1 on **Edit** and then on **Change**.)

14. Click mouse button 1 on the **File** menu.

15. Click mouse button 1 on the **Save as** menu choice.

16. Type a name for the address book. Use a name that will help you identify the names and addresses within it.

17. Click mouse button 1 in the **Save as filename** field, and type a file name for the address book. Use the extension .ABK if possible.

18. Click mouse button 1 on the **Save as** push button.

19. Double-click on the title-bar icons of the open windows to close them.

Accessing an Address Book

After you have a created an address book, you might be surprised to find that it is not in the P2P window. This is because P2P places all of the address books you create inside the Address Book icon. So, if you want to place a call using an address book, you will need to know how to locate the address book.

To access an address book:

1. Double-click on the **P2P** icon.

2. Double-click on the **Address Book** icon.

3. Click mouse button 1 on the **File** menu.

4. Click mouse button 1 on the **Open** menu choice.
5. Double-click on the name of the address book that you want to open.

Calling Someone in Your Address Book

You can use any of the P2P programs to call someone in your address book. The P2P programs you use during the call are entirely up to you. If you are discussing something visual, you might decide on the Chalkboard or Video programs. If you want to send a chunk of information to someone, you might choose the Clip program. But if you just want to chat, Talk might be the best choice.

To call someone in your address book:
1. Select the person that you want to call by doing the following:
   a. Double-click on the **P2P** icon.
   b. Double-click on the **Address Book** icon.
   c. Click mouse button 1 on the **File** menu.
   d. Click mouse button 1 on the **Open** menu choice.
   e. Double-click on the name of the address book that you want to open.
   f. Click mouse button 1 on the up or down arrow to the right of the names in the address book.
   g. Click mouse button 1 on the name of the person you want to call. If you want to call more than one person at the same time, press and hold the Ctrl key while performing this step.
2. Click mouse button 1 on the names of the programs that you want to use to communicate with the person you are calling. You can choose from the following:

   Chalkboard
   > Allows you to use text, simple graphics, and the contents of windows or bitmap files to communicate.

   Clip
   > Allows you to share your clipboard with someone else and vice versa.

   Talk
   > Allows you to use text to communicate.

   Video
   > Allows you to exchange video images.

3. Click mouse button 1 on the **Call** push button.
4. When the call is accepted by the person you are calling, the program you selected to use for communication is displayed.

5. When you are finished with the call, click mouse button 1 on the **P2P** menu of the program you are using to communicate.
6. Click mouse button 1 on the **End** menu choice.

TIP: You can use additional programs after a call has been started.

To add another program:
1. Double-click on the icon for the program you want to use.
2. Click mouse button 1 on the **P2P** menu.
3. Click mouse button 1 on the **Share** menu choice.
4. Click mouse button 1 on the name of the person you want to share the program with.

To stop using a program when more than one program is being used in a call, click mouse button 1 on the **P2P** menu of that program. Then, click mouse button 1 on the **Unshare** menu choice.

Adding Other People to a Call

With P2P you can include as many people as you want in a call. You can even add people to the call at any time during the call. This is especially nice if you are discussing something and realize that you need to include someone else in the discussion.

To add other people to a call:
1. Click mouse button 1 on the **P2P** menu in the window of the program you are using to communicate.
2. Click mouse button 1 on the **Add** menu choice.
3. Click mouse button 1 on the **People** choice.
   a. Look in the list for the name of the person you want to call.
   b. Click mouse button 1 on the name of the person.
   c. Click mouse button 1 on the **Add** push button. The new person is included in the call, and all the P2P programs that you are using are displayed on that person's computer.
4. When you are finished with the call, click mouse button 1 on the **P2P** menu of the program you are using to communicate.
5. Click mouse button 1 on the **End** menu choice.

Autodialing a Voice Call

P2P can automatically dial a number from your computer so that you can talk on the telephone. This gives you the ability to use the information in your Address Book to contact people and also lets you continue to work while the computer places the phone call.

To autodial a voice call:

1. Verify that the Call Manager is set up to autodial a voice call. To find out how to specify this option, see "Call Manager" on page 372.
2. Select the person you want to call by doing the following:
   a. Double-click on the **P2P** icon.
   b. Double-click on the **Address Book** icon.
   c. Click mouse button 1 on the **File** menu.
   d. Click mouse button 1 on the **Open** menu choice.
   e. Double-click on the name of the address book that you want to open.
   f. Click mouse button 1 on the up or down arrow to the right of the names in the address book.
   g. Click mouse button 1 on the name of the person you want to call.
3. Click mouse button 1 on the **Selected** menu.
4. Click mouse button 1 on the **Call** menu choice.
5. Click mouse button 1 on the **Voice** option in the **Call type** field.
6. Click mouse button 1 on the **Call** push button.
7. When a message appears stating that the call has been dialed, lift the handset on your telephone, and click mouse button 1 on the **OK** push button.

Chalkboard

The chalkboard is used to draw and write on. It has two surfaces — a background and a foreground. The background is used to hold a picture of something you want to discuss. This can be text from a file, a bit map, a window, the contents of the clipboard, or nothing at all (blank). The foreground is the surface that you draw and write on.

Using the tools provided with the chalkboard, you can discuss the information on the background of the chalkboard.

Mirroring a Chalkboard

You can use the chalkboard to write notes to the people participating in a call, but you would be missing out on its best feature — its background. The background of the chalkboard can display information from another source (mirror) so that you can make notes about it. You can place text from a file, a bit map, a window, or the contents of the clipboard in the background so that you can discuss it with other people in the call. For example, you can mirror your graduation party list so that other people on the call can make notations, let you know who is missing, and point out incorrect addresses.

NOTE: You cannot mirror full-screen OS/2 and Windows programs or minimized windows. If a window is minimized after it has been mirrored, the mirror image will disappear from the chalkboard.

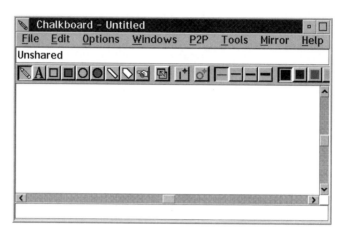

To mirror something onto the background of the chalkboard:

1. Call the person you want to communicate with using the instructions in "Calling Someone in Your Address Book" on page 377. Remember to select **Chalkboard** as the program that you want to use to communicate.
2. Click mouse button 1 on the **Mirror** menu.
3. Click mouse button 1 on the **Start** menu choice. The mouse pointer changes to a crosshair.
4. Move the mouse pointer to the window that you want to mirror in the background of your chalkboard, and then click mouse button 1. The contents of the window are copied to the background of the chalkboard.
5. When you are finished using the mirrored image, click mouse button 1 on the **Mirror** menu.
6. Click mouse button 1 on the **End** menu choice.

TIP: As a shortcut to mirroring a window to your chalkboard background, you can select the name of an open window by clicking mouse button 1 on the **Window list** choice of the **Mirror** menu.

Saving a Mirrored Chalkboard

Many times you will find that the information that ends up on the chalkboard is valuable. Before you refresh the screen or end the mirror, you might want to save the mirrored chalkboard to a file. After a chalkboard is saved, you can look at the information again using any program that can display bit maps.

To save the mirrored chalkboard:

1. Click mouse button 1 on the **File** menu.
2. Click mouse button 1 on the **Save as** menu choice.
3. Click mouse button 1 on the choice in the **Selection** field that best describes what you want to save. You can choose from the following:

   Text
   > Saves the foreground and background text in a single file.

   Bitmap
   > Saves the foreground and background bit maps in a single file.

   Chalkboard
   > Saves the complete chalkboard in a single file exactly as it looked when it was saved.

4. Type a name for the file in the **Save as** filename field.
5. Click mouse button 1 on the **Save as** push button.

Refreshing a Mirrored Chalkboard

After a few minutes of annotating a mirrored chalkboard, it can become very messy, and you might want to refresh it to remove all the notes. There are several ways to erase all the information from the foreground. If you want to save the information in the chalkboard, follow the steps in "Saving a Mirrored Chalkboard" before you refresh the mirrored chalkboard.

To refresh the mirrored chalkboard:

1. Click mouse button 1 on the **Mirror** menu.
2. Click mouse button 1 on the name of the window in the list.

TIP: You can set up a window that appears on the chalkboard to make it more convenient to refresh the mirrored chalkboard.

1. Click mouse button 1 on the **Options** menu.
2. Click mouse button 1 on the **Refresh** button.

After you select the refresh button, a Refresh now window appears on the chalkboard. Just click mouse button 1 on the window at any time to refresh the mirrored chalkboard.

You can also set up a mirrored chalkboard so that refreshes occur automatically at an interval you specify.

1. Click mouse button 1 on the **Options** menu.
2. Click mouse button 1 on the **Periodic mirror** menu choice.
3. Type the number of seconds that you want to elapse between refreshes of the mirrored chalkboard. Choose a number between 1 and 65 seconds.

Writing and Drawing on the Chalkboard

The Chalkboard has tools that you can use to write and draw on it. There are two places from which you can select the tools that you use in the Chalkboard: the tool bar and the **Tools** menu. If you are a beginner, you will probably find it easier to use the **Tools** menu to select tools. After you become familiar with the Chalkboard and its tools, you will probably find the tool bar easier.

To write or draw on the chalkboard:
1. Click mouse button 1 on the Tools menu.
2. Click mouse button 1 on one of the following menu choices:

Pen
> Provides you with a pen so that you can draw freehand on the chalkboard.

Text
> Provides a box that you can type into. After you press the Enter key, the box is removed, and the text is displayed on the line where the box used to be.

Open Box
> Draws a box. Press and hold mouse button 1 while dragging the mouse to change the size of the box.

Filled Box
> Draws a box and then shades the contents of the box. Press and hold mouse button 1 while dragging the mouse to change the size of the box.

Open Circle
> Draws a circle. Press and hold mouse button 1 while dragging the mouse to change the size of the circle.

Filled Circle
> Draws a circle and then shades the contents of the circle. Press and hold mouse button 1 while dragging the mouse to change the size of the circle.

Small Eraser
> Provides a small eraser that can be used to erase information on the foreground of the chalkboard. The size of the eraser is based on the size of the current line width.

Large Eraser
    Provides a large eraser that can be used to erase information on the foreground of the chalkboard. The size of the eraser is based on the size of the current line width.

Remote Pointer
    Provides you with a pointer so that other people participating in the call can see what you are pointing to.

Sync Chalkboards
    Changes the chalkboards of the people participating in the call to look exactly like yours.

Select line width
    Changes the size of the line width used by the pen, box, circle, small eraser, and large eraser.

Select color
    Changes the color used by the pen, text, box, and circle.

NOTE: The tools on the tool bar (at the top of the Chalkboard) are displayed in the same order in which they are listed on the **Tools** menu.

Editing the Chalkboard

Besides being able to write and draw on the chalkboard, you can also cut, copy, paste, and delete information on it. For example, if you are using the chalkboard to discuss landscaping your yard, you might want to delete shrubs from one location or copy trees to another.

To edit the chalkboard:
1. Click mouse button 1 on the **Edit** menu.
2. Click mouse button 1 on the **Mark** menu choice.
3. Point to the area of the chalkboard that you want to edit (cut, copy, or clear information from or paste information to).
4. Press and hold mouse button 1.
5. Drag the crosshairs until a box surrounds the area of the chalkboard that you want to edit.
6. Release mouse button 1.
7. Click mouse button 1 on the **Edit** menu.
8. Click mouse button 1 on one of the following editing menu choices.

Cut
> Removes the marked area from the chalkboard and places it into the clipboard.

Copy
> Copies the marked area into the clipboard.

Paste
> Pastes the information from the clipboard into the marked area. This choice is not available if nothing is in the clipboard.

Clear
> Removes the marked area from the chalkboard.

Clear foreground
> Removes the annotation from the marked area of the chalkboard.

Talk

You can send and receive text messages using several of the P2P programs. However, the Talk program is specially designed for communicating via text. It allows you to communicate as fast as you can type. This gives you the ability to have conversations with people without saying a word (an added plus if you're shy or have trouble talking on the phone).

Sending and Receiving Messages

You can send messages to anyone who is listed in your Address Book using the Talk program. However, unlike other electronic mail programs, this one doesn't require that you write long paragraphs or compose a letter. Instead, the correspondence resembles a phone call more than a letter. This program allows you to write a sentence and then send it. The recipient then reads and responds to your sentence. In fact, because the messages are shorter, spontaneous, and more lively than a letter, you will probably write to people more often.

To send and receive messages:

1. Call the person you want to communicate with using the instructions in "Calling Someone in Your Address Book" on page 377. Remember to select **Talk** as the program that you want to use to communicate.

2. Type a message that you want to send in the field to the left of the **Send** push button. If you want the message to alert the receiver with a beep, place an exclamation point (!) at the beginning of the message.

3. Click mouse button 1 on the **Send** push button. The message is displayed in the Talk window and sent to the other participants in the call.

4. Read the messages received from the other participants in the call. You might have to scroll the window to see all the messages. If a message is sent to you and it is beyond the view of the window, an asterisk is placed next to the name of the person who sent it. The asterisk remains until you scroll the window and display the message.

Modifying the Talk Program

After you have used the Talk program a few times, you will probably want to fine-tune it so that it better serves your needs. For example, if you typically use the Talk program to communicate with an old acquaintance, you might want to increase the number of messages that you can receive before the oldest ones are discarded. That way, you can go back and reread the entire conversation after the call is over to relive the moments.

To modify the Talk program to suit your needs:

1. Double-click on the **P2P** icon.

2. Double-click on the **Talk** icon.

3. Click mouse button 1 on the **Options** menu.

4. Click mouse button 1 on any of the following menu choices that you want to change:

History size

Determines the number of messages that can be displayed before the Talk program discards the oldest messages. If you plan to save the messages to a file for reference, you should select a large number so the messages aren't deleted before you have a chance to save them.

Call log

Enables or disables adding call log events in with the messages you send and receive.

Sound

Enables or disables the beep that is heard when someone prefaces a message with an exclamation point (!).

Bypass save prompt

Allows you the opportunity to turn off the "Do you want to save" message. This message appears whenever you try to exit Talk without saving the messages to a file. If you never save your messages, you will probably want to turn off this prompt.

5. Double-click on the title-bar icon of the Talk window to close it.

Clip

The Clip program is P2P's access to the clipboard. The people participating in the call can use Clip to cut, copy, and paste information between documents. The Clip program also provides dynamic data exchange (DDE). This means that if you paste or copy information into your copy of a document and if the original copy is changed during the call, your copy will be automatically updated.

Sending Clipboard Information

You can send information in your clipboard to another person. This can be useful if you have been working diligently on some information and you find out another person needs the information. All you have to do is copy the information in your document to the clipboard and send it to the other person, who can then paste it into a document. And, if you change something in the information during the call, the information in the other person's document will automatically be changed to reflect your changes.

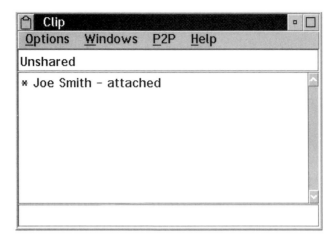

To send information using the P2P clipboard:

1. Call the person you want to communicate with using the instructions in "Calling Some-one in Your Address Book" on page 377. Remember to select **Clip** as the program that you want to use to communicate.
2. Cut or copy the information that you want to share from your document into the clipboard.
3. Click mouse button 1 on the **Options** menu.
4. Click mouse button 1 on the **Attach and send** menu choice.

Receiving Clipboard Information

You can receive information that you need from someone else and paste it into a docu-ment that you are working on. If the person sending the information changes it during the call, your information will automatically be changed to reflect it.

To receive information using the P2P clipboard:

1. Call the person you want to communicate with using the instructions in "Calling Some-one in Your Address Book" on page 377. Remember to select **Clip** as the program that you want to use to communicate.
2. Check the list of participants in the Clip window to see if that person has copied something into the clipboard. If the person has copied information into the clipboard, an asterisk (*) appears next to that person's name.
3. Click mouse button 1 on the **Options** menu.
4. Click mouse button 1 on the **Attach and receive** menu choice. If the **Accept attached** choice in the Options menu has a check mark next to it, these steps will not be neces-sary because the information will automatically be copied into your clipboard.

5. Paste or paste link the information from the clipboard into your program. If you plan to use DDE, you should probably save the file. Many programs do not dynamically exchange data until information from the clipboard has been saved in the file it was copied to.

Preventing Clipboard Overwriting

If you frequently use your clipboard, you might run into a situation in which someone else overwrites the information in your clipboard. This can happen when you are participating in a call and the person sends you something through the Clip program. If you have anything in the clipboard, it is overwritten. Another way in which information in the clipboard can be overwritten is if you are using the clipboard but are not participating in a call with someone, and then you receive a call and information is sent to the clipboard without your knowledge.

To prevent someone with whom you are communicating from overwriting the information in your clipboard:
1. Click mouse button 1 on the **Options** menu.
2. Click mouse button 1 on the **Detach** menu choice.

This protects the information in your clipboard from being overwritten by someone else but does not affect the update of DDE information across the call. In order to receive information into your clipboard, you will have to select **Attach and receive**.

To prevent someone from calling you and sending something to your clipboard while you are using it:
1. Click mouse button 1 on the **Options** menu.
2. Click mouse button 1 on the **Incoming clip** menu choice.
3. Click mouse button 1 on the **Accept detached** choice.
4. Double-click on the title-bar icon of the Clip window to close it.

This protects the information in your clipboard from being overwritten by someone who calls you. In order to receive the information into your clipboard, you will have to select **Attach and receive**.

Video

The Video program allows you to exchange video with other people participating in a call. To send video, you need to have video hardware such as a camera, VCR, or video-disc attached to your computer.

If you don't have one of these, you can send software-only movies. These are movies that are stored on your computer. (You can create these kinds of movies using the Video IN program.) You can use the P2P Video program to display software-only movies as bit maps at up to 4 frames per second. If your video hardware is being used by some other program or you do not have video hardware, you can also use the P2P Video program to send a still image (bit map) to other people participating in a call.

Sending and Receiving Video

You can use P2P to send motion video to other people participating in a call. This might be useful if you want to show someone how to do something or what something looks like, or you simply want to dazzle them with your movie-making abilities.

NOTE: Do not try to send video if you are using asynchronous communications (computer-to-computer via modems) because it will take several seconds to send a single frame of video. This could congest the network and cause other P2P programs to run slower. If you are using asynchronous communications, you can send a still image without causing problems.

To send or receive video within a call:

1. Call the person you want to communicate with using the instructions in "Calling Someone in Your Address Book" on page 377. Remember to select **Video** as one of the programs that you want to use to communicate. When the call goes through, the

video you are transmitting is displayed in the Video Window. (If someone calls you, that person's video is displayed in your Video Window. If Dual view is set, both videos are displayed no matter who calls whom.)

2. Click mouse button 1 on the **Options** menu.
3. Click mouse button 1 on the **Camera controls - Self** menu choice.
4. Adjust the settings in the Camera Control window to improve the quality of the video you are sending.
5. Click mouse button 1 on the **Options** menu.
6. Click mouse button 1 on the **Dual view** menu choice. Dual view is not available if you are sending software-only movies or bit maps.
7. Click mouse button 1 on the **Options** menu.
8. Click mouse button 1 on the **Display control** menu choice.
9. Adjust the settings in the Display Control window to improve the quality of the video you are receiving.
10. Click mouse button 1 on any of the following push buttons:

Off air
Disables your camera so that no video is sent. You will not be able to see the video either. Clicking on this choice again enables the camera so that video can be sent once again.

Freeze
Freezes the frames of a video being received. Clicking on this choice again unfreezes the video that is being received. You cannot freeze your video using this push button.

Self
Switches the video in the Video Window to your video.

Numbers
Displays the video from another person participating in the call when you click mouse button 1 on the number that is assigned to that person.

Arrows
Displays additional numbers if more than four callers are participating in the call.

 TIP: You can release the video hardware so that you can use it with some other program without affecting your call. To do this, click mouse button 1 on the **Hardware available** menu choice in the **Options** menu to remove the check mark.

Stills Capture

The Stills Capture program provides you with the ability to use an ActionMedia II adapter to convert video that is sent during a call into high-quality bit maps. You can then use these bit maps for a variety of purposes. For example, you can use them as backgrounds for windows or the Desktop, or you can use them in a software-only movie created using the AVI File Utility program. You might use one of the bit maps as the lockup screen for your computer or even display one of the bit maps through the P2P Video program. You can also use these bit maps in the P2P Chalkboard and Clip programs.

Capturing Still Images

You can use the P2P Video program to capture images being sent during a call. This might come in handy if you want to discuss a particular image in the video. You can capture the image and place it into the background of the Chalkboard. Then, everyone participating in a call can comment on the contents of the image.

To capture a still image:

1. Call the person you want to communicate with using the instructions in "Calling Someone in Your Address Book" on page 377. Remember to select **Video** or **Chalkboard** as one of the programs that you want to use to communicate.
2. Double-click on the **Stills Capture** icon.
3. Click mouse button 2 on the title-bar icon of the Stills Capture window.
4. Click mouse button 1 on the **Natural Size** menu choice. This changes the window to the best possible size for displaying the video.
5. Click mouse button 1 on the **Options** menu.
6. Click mouse button 1 on the **Video hardware available** menu choice to place a check mark next to it.
7. Click mouse button 1 on the **Options** menu.
8. Click mouse button 1 on the **Control panel** menu choice. This places a small control panel in the Stills Capture window.
9. Click mouse button 1 on one of the following choices in the control panel:

    Live
    > Displays live video in the Stills Capture window. If this choice is grayed out, it means that it is already selected.

    Still
    > Displays a still image in the Stills Capture window. If this choice is grayed out, it means that it is already selected or that no still image that can be displayed has been captured.

Capture still

> Captures the current frame of the incoming video. The Still image choice must be selected in order for you to see the captured frame.

10. Click mouse button 1 on the **Options** menu.
11. Click mouse button 1 on the **Still update** menu choice.
12. Click mouse button 1 on one of the following choices to determine how often the still image should be updated:

Manual

> Updates the image only when requested. This choice is not available if a check mark is next to the **Video hardware available** choice.

Timed

> Updates the image at regular intervals based on the number of seconds you specify.

Continuous

> Updates the image as fast as possible. This places a heavy burden on the computer.

13. Click mouse button 1 on the **Options** menu.
14. Click mouse button 1 on the **Enhanced still** menu choice. This improves the quality of the picture but it takes longer to create.

TIP: If you want to copy the still image to the clipboard automatically, click mouse button 1 on the **Clipboard options** menu choice in the **Options** menu.

Chapter 38

CompuServe Information Manager

The CompuServe Information Manager is a program that allows you to use menus and windows to make accessing information on the CompuServe information service easier.

The CompuServe information service contains information about a variety of topics and allows you to communicate with people all over the world any time of the day or night. Among the services available on CompuServe are weather reports, electronic mail, stock reports, news, and electronic bulletin boards (forums).

This chapter shows you how to sign up to use CompuServe, connect and disconnect from it, access the different CompuServe services, and send, view, and receive mail. It also explains how to set up an address book, send a file, and customize the settings to meet your needs.

Signing Up for CompuServe

Before you can begin using CompuServe, you need to become a CompuServe member. During this process, you will be asked to provide the following information:

- Registration and serial numbers for OS/2 Warp and CompuServe

- The billing method for the services you use

- The membership plan you want to use

- Agreement to CompuServe's rules and regulations

- The settings for your communication port

- The type of modem you are using

If you are already a member of CompuServe, you do not need to complete these steps to use the CompuServe Information Manager for OS/2.

To sign up to use CompuServe:
1. Double-click on the **IBM Information Superhighway** icon.
2. Double-click on the **CompuServe** icon.
3. Double-click on the **Member Signup** icon.
4. Click mouse button 1 on the **Proceed** push button.
5. Click mouse button 1 on the **Signup** menu.
6. Click mouse button 1 on the **Signup** menu choice.
7. Type your registration number for the CompuServe Information Manager in the space provided.
8. Click mouse button 1 on the **Proceed** push button.

9. Fill in the requested Address, Billing, and Membership Options information.

10. Click mouse button 1 on the **Signup** menu.

11. Click mouse button 1 on the **Connect Settings** menu choice.

12. You can change the information to suit your needs. Although this information was prefilled for you when you signed up, you might want to change it. You can change the following:

Primary Network
> Determines the network that you will use to connect to CompuServe.

Baud Rate
> Identifies the baud rate of the modem you plan to use.

Phone
> Identifies the local phone number used to connect to CompuServe.

Connector
> Identifies the communication port to which your modem is attached.

Dial Type
> Identifies how the connection to CompuServe should be dialed.

> **Tone**
>> Use a phone system that uses tones to connect to CompuServe.

> **Pulse**
>> Use a phone system that uses pulses to connect to CompuServe.

> **Direct**
>> Use another computer that is hard-wired to your computer to connect to CompuServe.

13. Click mouse button 1 on the **OK** push button.

14. Click mouse button 1 on the **Signup** menu.

15. Click mouse button 1 on the **Modem Settings** menu choice.

16. Change the information to suit your needs. You can change the following:

Modem
> Determines the modem that you are using for CompuServe. Changing the modem automatically updates most of the other fields in this window.

Speaker Off
> Disables the speaker so that no dial tone, dialing, or connections sounds are made during logon.

Modem Security
    Specifies the user ID and password for those modems that support security access.

17. Click mouse button 1 on the **OK** push button.

18. Double-click on the title-bar icon of the **Signup** window to complete your membership signup.

TIP: If at any time after becoming a member, you are interested in rereading the agreements that you signed during the signup process, do the following:

1. Double-click on the **IBM Information Superhighway** icon.
2. Double-click on the **CompuServe** icon.
3. Double-click on the **Member Signup** icon.
4. Click mouse button 1 on the **Proceed** push button.
5. Click mouse button 1 on the **Signup** menu.
6. Click mouse button 1 on the choice containing the information that you want to read.

Service Agreement Terms
    Provides information about the legal terms that you agree to when you sign up for CompuServe.

Operating Rules
    Provides the rules that you must abide by when you use CompuServe.

Executive Options
    Provides information about the added benefits of becoming an Executive Service member.

Customer Service
    Provides the phone numbers and fax numbers for CompuServe service.

Connecting and Disconnecting

To use CompuServe, you must connect with the network that provides the CompuServe service. After you connect with CompuServe, you can start using the different services. You can choose between *Basic Services* (services provided without additional charge) or other services that charge a fee for their use. The services that are available to you depend on which service agreement you chose during signup.

To connect to a service:

1. Double-click on the **IBM Information Superhighway** icon.

2. Double-click on the **CompuServe** icon.

3. Double-click on the **CIM for OS/2** icon.

4. Click mouse button 1 on the **Connect** push button in the Connect to CompuServe window. If this window is not displayed, click mouse button 1 on the **File** menu and then on the **Connect** menu choice to connect to CompuServe.

Click mouse button 1 on any other service that you want to use. If you connect to a service that is not part of the basic service, you will see a message informing you that you will be charged extra to use the service.

To disconnect from a service:

1. Click mouse button 1 on the **File** menu.

2. Click mouse button 1 on the **Disconnect menu** choice.

TIP: To reduce the cost of using CompuServe, disconnect from a service whenever you are finished using it.

Accessing Services on CompuServe

CompuServe provides a wide variety of services. The services that you use depend on your individual interests. For example, if you are a sports fanatic, you might find the Sports forum more interesting than the Health forum.

To access a service on CompuServe:

1. Double-click on the **IBM Information Superhighway** icon.
2. Double-click on the **CompuServe** icon.
3. Double-click on the **CIM for OS/2** icon.
4. Click mouse button 1 on the icon in the Services window that represents the service you want to use.

Or

1. Click mouse button 1 on the **Services** menu.
2. Click mouse button 1 on one of the following menu choices:

Favorite Places

Displays a list of your favorite services so that you can access them quickly. You can customize this list by adding services, deleting services, or changing the name of a service in the list.

Find

Allows you to search by topic for a service that you want to use.

Browse

Displays the Services window, which contains the icons that represent the available services.

Go

Allows you to go directly to a service by typing the name of the service.

What's New

Provides access to the What's New online service.

Special Events

Provides access to the Special Events online service.

Executive News

Provides access to the Executive News online service, where you can read the latest news stories.

Quotes

Displays the latest stock market quotes. You can customize which stocks are listed in the window.

Portfolio

Allows you to maintain a record of your stock purchases and create a report that shows how well they are doing.

Weather
> Provides a weather report for selected cities in the United States and around the world.

CB Simulator
> Allows you to communicate with people all over the world using your computer keyboard rather than a citizens band radio.

Setting Up the Address Book

Every CompuServe member has a name and address that uniquely identifies the member. If you plan to send letters or files to other people on CompuServe, you need to know their names and addresses. You can try to memorize this information, or you can add the members' names and addresses to your CompuServe Address Book so they can be easily selected from a list.

To set up the address book:
1. Double-click on the **IBM Information Superhighway** icon.
2. Double-click on the **CompuServe** icon.
3. Double-click on the **CIM for OS/2** icon.
4. Click mouse button 1 on the **Mail** menu.
5. Click mouse button 1 on the **Name** and **Addresses** menu choice.
6. Click mouse button 1 on one of the following choices:

Add
> Allows you to add a name and address to the Address Book.

Add Group
> Allows you to add a group of people to the Address Book under one name.

Change
> Allows you to change information about an entry in the Address Book. You must first click on the Address Book entry that you want to change before you select this push button.

Delete
> Allows you to erase an entry in the Address Book. You must first click on the Address Book entry that you want to delete before you select this push button.

OK
> Accepts the changes to the Address Book and removes the Address Book window.

Cancel
> Does not save any of the changes to the Address Book and removes the Address Book window.

7. Repeat step 6 until you are satisfied with the entries in the Address Book.

Sending Mail

You can correspond with other CompuServe members by sending them electronic mail over the network. This is a great way to keep in touch with people who share the same interest. You might even be able to make new friends.

To send mail to a CompuServe member:
1. Double-click on the **IBM Information Superhighway** icon.
2. Double-click on the **CompuServe** icon.
3. Double-click on the **CIM for OS/2** icon.
4. Click mouse button 1 on the **Mail** menu.
5. Click mouse button 1 on the **Create Mail** menu choice.
6. Click mouse button 1 on one of the following choices:

TO
> Sends a letter to the people specified. At least one name must be specified.

CC
> Sends a carbon copy of the letter and lists these names in the distribution list.

BC
> Sends a carbon copy of the letter, but does not list these names in the distribution list.

7. Do one of the following:

- Click mouse button 1 on a name in the **Address Book**, and then click mouse button 1 on the **Copy** push button. The name is added to the **Recipients** field.

- Type the name and address of the recipient in the **Name** and **Address** fields, and then click mouse button 1 on the **Add** push button.

- Click mouse button 1 on the **Search** push button to search the Membership Directory for the address of a CompuServe member.

- Click mouse button 1 on the **Copy Original** push button to send a reply to the originator of the letter. This option is valid only if you are replying to a letter.

8. Repeat step 7 until all the recipients have been specified.
9. Click mouse button 1 on the **Show Recipients** option. A check mark beside the choice means that the names of the recipients will be displayed at the top of the letter.
10. Click mouse button 1 on the **OK** push button.
11. Click mouse button 1 in the **Subject** field, and type a brief summary of the subject of the letter.
12. Click mouse button 1 on one of the following choices:

Reformattable
> Wraps the text in the letter so that it fits within the recipient's screen.

Send as shown
> Does not wrap the text in the letter.

13. Type the text of the letter.
14. Click mouse button 1 on any of the following push buttons:

Out Basket
> Copies the message to your Out Basket. The Out Basket can be used to hold all of your outgoing mail until you are ready to send it.

Send Now
> Sends the letter immediately. If you are not connected to CompuServe at the time you select **Send Now**, it will automatically connect you.

File It
> Saves a copy of the letter to your File Cabinet. If the **Auto-file** choice has a check mark next to it, a copy of your letter will automatically be saved to your File Cabinet.

Cancel
> Discards the letter without saving a copy or sending it to anyone.

Options
> Provides additional attributes that you can attach to the letter.

> **Importance**
>> Determines the importance of the information in your letter. Some systems deliver the most important mail first.

> **Release Date**
>> Determines the date that you want the letter sent. If no date is specified, the mail is sent on the current date.

Sensitivity

Determines how confidential the letter is.

Expiration Date

Determines the date that the letter will automatically be removed from the recipient's mailbox. If no date is specified, the mail can be removed only by the recipient.

Payment Method

Determines who pays for the letter being sent.

Receipt

Determines whether a confirmation message is sent to you when the recipient reads the letter.

Handling Mail

When you receive mail, it is placed in the Get New Mail window. It remains there until you view it and decide what you want to do with it. You can keep it, write a response, use it to update your address book, or delete it. For example, if you receive a letter from your lawyer, you might want to read it and then place a copy of the letter in your File Cabinet for safekeeping.

To handle mail:

1. Double-click on the **IBM Information Superhighway** icon.
2. Double-click on the **CompuServe** icon.
3. Double-click on the **CIM for OS/2** icon.
4. Click mouse button 1 on the **Mail** menu.
5. Click mouse button 1 on the **Get New Mail** menu choice.
6. Click mouse button 1 on the letter that you want to view.
7. Click mouse button 1 on one of the following choices:

Get

Allows you to view the letter. You can also select the following choices after you select Get:

Address

Allows you to add the addresses of the other recipients of this letter to your address book.

From

Allows you to save the sender's address to your address book.

In Basket

Places a copy of the letter in your In Basket.

File It

Places a copy of the letter in your File Cabinet.

Reply

Allows you to respond to a letter.

Forward

Allows you to send the letter to one person or a group of people. You can attach a note to the original letter.

Delete

Erases the letter from your mailbox.

Get All

Moves all letters from your mailbox to your In Basket. You can then view the letters by selecting the **In Basket** choice from the **Mail** menu.

Delete

Erases a letter from your mailbox.

Undelete

Recovers a letter that was accidentally erased.

Sending Files

One of the best things about CompuServe is that you can share information with other people by sending it to them. If the information that you want to send is in a file on your computer, you can easily send it through electronic mail on CompuServe. For example, if you misplaced the instructions for programming your VCR, you could have a friend type up the instructions and send them to you in a file. Then when you receive the file, you can print it, and voila — an instant VCR manual.

To send a file:

1. Double-click on the **IBM Information Superhighway** icon.
2. Double-click on the **CompuServe** icon.
3. Double-click on the **CIM for OS/2** icon.
4. Click mouse button 1 on the **Mail** menu.
5. Click mouse button 1 on the **Send File** menu choice.
6. Click mouse button 1 on one of the following choices:

TO

Sends a file to the people specified. At least one name must be specified.

CC

Sends a carbon copy of the file and lists these names in the distribution list.

BC

Sends a carbon copy of the file, but does not list these names in the distribution list.

7. Do one of the following:

- Click mouse button 1 on a name in the **Address Book**, and then click mouse button 1 on the **Copy** push button. The name is added to the **Recipients** field.

- Type the name and address of the recipient in the **Name and Address** fields, and then click mouse button 1 on the **Add** push button.

- Click mouse button 1 on the **Search** push button to search the Membership Directory for the address of a CompuServe member.

- Click mouse button 1 on the **Copy Original** push button to send a file to the originator of the letter. This option is valid only if you are replying to a letter.

8. Repeat step 7 until all the recipients have been specified.

9. Click mouse button 1 on the **Show Recipients** option. A check mark beside the choice means that the names of the recipients will be displayed at the top of the letter.

10. Click mouse button 1 on the **OK** push button.

11. Click mouse button 1 in the **Subject** field, and type a brief explanation of the contents of the file.

12. Click mouse button 1 on the **Options** push button.

13. Click mouse button 1 on any of the following choices:

Importance

Determines the importance of the information in your file. Some systems deliver the most important files first.

Release Date

Determines the date that you want the file sent. If no date is specified, the file is sent on the current date.

Sensitivity

Determines how confidential the file is.

Official Guide to Using OS/2 Warp

Expiration Date

> Determines the date that the file will automatically be removed from the recipient's mailbox. If no date is specified, the file can be removed only by the recipient.

Payment Method

> Determines who pays for the file being sent.

Receipt

> Determines whether a confirmation message is sent to you when the recipient retrieves the file.

14. Click mouse button 1 on the **OK** push button.

15. Click mouse button 1 on one of the following choices:

Binary

> Specifies that the file being sent is in binary format.

GIF

> Specifies that the file being sent is in a graphical image format.

JPEG

> Specifies that the file being sent is in a Joint Graphical Experts Group format. This format is used in multimedia.

Text

> Specifies that the file being sent contains ASCII text.

16. Type the name and location of the file in the **File** field, or click mouse button 1 on the **File** push button to locate the file.

17. Type into the **Additional information** field any comments that you would like the recipients to see before they retrieve the file.

18. Click mouse button 1 on one of the following push buttons:

Out Basket

> Copies the file to your Out Basket. The Out Basket can be used to hold all of your outgoing mail and files until you are ready to send them.

Send Now

> Sends the file immediately. If you are not connected to CompuServe at the time you select **Send Now**, it will automatically connect you.

Cancel

> Cancels the request to send the file.

Changing Session Settings

Each time you start CompuServe, it uses the session settings to determine your user ID, modem information, CompuServe phone number, and type of telephone system that is being used. Without this information, you would not be able to connect with CompuServe. If you are having difficulty connecting to CompuServe, or you have moved, you will probably need to update your session settings to reflect the changes.

To change session settings:
1. Double-click on the **IBM Information Superhighway** icon.
2. Double-click on the **CompuServe** icon.
3. Double-click on the **CIM for OS/2** icon.
4. Click mouse button 1 on the **Special** menu.
5. Click mouse button 1 on the **Session Settings** menu choice.
6. Change the information in the following fields to update your session settings:

Current
> Determines the group of settings that you want to use for the current session. If none of the listed groups contains the settings you want to use, you can add another group of settings by clicking mouse button 1 on the **Add** push button.

Alternate
> Determines the alternate group of settings to use in case the current group of settings cannot connect you to CompuServe.

Name
> Identifies the person using the session. You should use your legal name, not a nickname.

User ID
> Identifies the user ID for CompuServe. If you have a temporary user ID, you will need to change this information when you receive the permanent user ID.

Password
> Identifies the password that you want to use to prohibit unauthorized use of CompuServe. If no password is specified, you will be prompted to specify a password when you start CompuServe.

Phone
> Identifies the local phone number used to connect to CompuServe.

Connector
> Identifies the communication port used by your modem.

Baud Rate

Identifies the baud rate of your modem.

Network

Identifies the network that you will use to connect to CompuServe.

Dial Type

Identifies how the connection to CompuServe should be dialed.

Tone

Use a phone system that uses tones to connect to CompuServe.

Pulse

Use a phone system that uses pulses to connect to CompuServe.

Direct

Use another computer that is hard-wired to your computer to connect to CompuServe.

Manual

Bypass automatic connection. This gives you the ability to connect to CompuServe if you have an unusual phone system or network, or if you are just having difficulty connecting to CompuServe.

Redial Attempts

Determines the number of times the modem will redial the CompuServe phone number if the first attempt to connect fails.

More Push Button

Specifies additional connection settings for rare situations.

Logon Parameters

Specifies special instructions that are appended to your user ID. This information is provided by a CompuServe Service Representative.

HMI Time Out

Increases the amount of time CompuServe attempts to connect before it fails.

Enable Carrier Detect

Detects when your modem loses carrier. (If you are having difficulty connecting to CompuServe, you might want to disable this feature and try again.)

Modem Push Button
> Specifies the current modem parameters.

Modem
>> Determines the modem that you are using for CompuServe. Changing the modem automatically updates the other fields in this window.

7. Click mouse button 1 on the **OK** push button to accept all of the changes that you made to the session settings.

Changing Preferences

The CompuServe Information Manager is your access to CompuServe. After you've used it for a while, you might want to change some things about it. For example, you might want to change how it handles mail that comes with postage due. Instead of automatically deleting it, you might choose to retrieve it.

To customize CompuServe to match your preferences:

1. Double-click on the **IBM Information Superhighway** icon.
2. Double-click on the **CompuServe** icon.
3. Double-click on the **CIM for OS/2** icon.
4. Click mouse button 1 on the **Special** menu.
5. Click mouse button 1 on the **Preferences** menu choice.
6. Click mouse button 1 on the **General** notebook tab.
7. Change the information to suit your needs. You can change the following:

Address Book Order
> Determines how the entries in the Address Book are alphabetized (by first or last name).

Favorite Places Order
> Determines how the items listed in the **Favorite Places** menu are organized. You can choose to have them in order of the most frequent access, in alphabetic order, or in random order.

Other
> Determines which items should display a confirmation message.

Prompt for Unsent Messages
> Displays a message when you exit a session if there are items in the Out Basket that have not been sent.

Prompt for Unsaved Graphics
> Displays a message if you have viewed a graphic image, but have not saved it to your hard disk.

Always Ask for File Name
> Displays a message asking for new file names whenever you download a file.

8. Click mouse button 1 on the **Display** notebook tab.
9. Change the information to suit your needs. You can change the following:

Initial Desktop
> Allows you to specify which window you want displayed each time you start CompuServe. You can display the Browse or Favorite Places windows or both windows.

Display Parameters
> Allows you to reset the colors and fonts used for CompuServe to their default settings.

10. Click mouse button 1 on the **Directories** notebook tab.
11. Change the information to suit your needs. You can change the following:

Support
> Identifies the directory where CompuServe support files (such as the Address Book) are stored.

Scripts
> Identifies the directory where CompuServe script files (used to automate routine functions) are stored.

Graphics
> Identifies the directory where graphics files that you download from CompuServe are stored.

Filing Cabinet
> Identifies the directory where the files in the File Cabinet are stored.

Download
> Identifies the directory where files other than graphics files that you download from CompuServe are stored.

12. Click mouse button 1 on the **Mail** notebook tab.
13. Change the information to suit your needs. You can change the following:

Postage Due

Identifies what should be done with mail that arrives with postage due. You can retrieve it, not retrieve it, or delete it without retrieving it.

Retrieved Mail Disposition

Identifies what should be done with mail after it has been retrieved. You can keep it, delete it immediately, or delete it after a specified number of days.

Outgoing Messages

Identifies whether you want to have copies of all outgoing mail saved in the File Cabinet. You can also identify which folder in the File Cabinet you want the outgoing mail filed in.

Index File Cabinet

Identifies when the entries are added to the **File** Cabinet. You can choose to add them manually or to have them added after you disconnect or exit from CompuServe.

14. Click mouse button 1 on the **News** notebook tab.

15. Change the information to suit your needs. You can change the following:

Show Folders

Displays the available News folders each time you access the News desktop so that you can select which folder you want to view.

Show Toolbox

Displays a bar across the top of the News window that has icons representing the most commonly used functions.

Delete Retrieved Stories

Deletes news stories from your Personal Folders after you retrieve and read them.

16. Click mouse button 1 on the **Messages** notebook tab.

17. Change the information to suit your needs. You can change the following:

Show News Flash

Displays the news flashes every time you enter a forum.

Show Toolbox

Displays a bar across the top of the forum window that has icons representing the most commonly used functions.

Show Forum Logo

Displays the logo for the forum every time you enter the forum.

Show Numbers

Displays the number of a message in the forum next to the name of the message.

Show List

Displays a list of all the messages in the forum every time you enter the forum.

Automatically File

Saves a copy of all the outgoing forum messages to your File Cabinet. You can also identify which folder in the File Cabinet you want the outgoing messages filed in.

18. Click mouse button 1 on the **Library** notebook tab.

19. Change the information to suit your needs. You can change the following:

Title

Displays CompuServe's name for a file in the Forum Library.

File Name

Displays the actual file name of a file in the Forum Library.

File Size

Displays the actual file size of a file in the Forum Library.

Access Count

Displays how many times a file has been accessed in the Forum Library.

Submission Date

Displays the date that a file was submitted to the Forum Library.

Submitter's ID

Displays the ID of the person who submitted a file to the Forum Library.

Show Numbers

Displays the number of a message in the Forum Library next to the name of the message.

Show List

Displays a list of all the messages in the Forum Library.

Allow Graphics Viewing

Allows you to view .GIF and .JPG files while in the forum.

20. Click mouse button 1 on the **Conference** notebook tab.

21. Change the information to suit your needs. You can change the following:

Nickname

Identifies the name that you will be known by during a forum conference.

People Entering

Displays the nicknames of people entering the forum conference.

People Leaving

Displays the nicknames of people leaving the forum conference.

Switching Locations

Displays the movement of members within a forum.

Changing Nicknames

Informs you when a member of a forum changes his or her nickname.

Accept Group Invitations

Informs you whenever you are invited to join a group conversation on a forum.

Accept Talk Invitations

Informs you whenever you are invited to join a private conversation on a forum.

Room Conversations

Logs all the activity by people in a conference room on CompuServe into a file on your hard disk.

Group Conversations

Logs all activity during a group conversation into a file on your hard disk.

22. Click mouse button 1 on the **CB** notebook tab.
23. Change the information to suit your needs. You can change the following:

Handle

Identifies the Citizens Band (CB) name that you want to be known by.

Show Toolbox

Displays a bar across the top of the CB window that has icons representing the most commonly used functions.

People Entering

Displays the nicknames of people entering CB.

People Leaving

Displays the nicknames of people leaving CB.

Switching Locations

Displays the movement of members within a CB.

Changing Handles

Informs you when a member of a CB changes his or her handle.

Only Friends

Displays only the handles of those members who are listed in your Friends group in the Address Book.

Accept Group Invitations

Informs you whenever you are invited to join a group conversation on a CB.

Accept Talk Invitations

Informs you whenever you are invited to join a private conversation on a CB.

Channel Conversations

Logs all activity on a particular CB channel into a file on your hard disk.

Group Conversations

Logs all activity during a group CB conversation into a file on your hard disk.

24. Click mouse button 1 on the **Terminal** notebook tab.

25. Change the information to suit your needs. You can change the following:

Saved Buffer Lines

Specifies the size of the buffer to be used for capturing data.

Strip High Bit

Allows you to access CompuServe from a communications network other than CompuServe's own network. After you access CompuServe, you should remove the check mark from this option so that all extended characters are displayed correctly.

26. Double-click on the title-bar icon of the open notebook to accept all the changes you made.

Chapter 39

IBM Internet Connection for OS/2

The IBM Internet Connection for OS/2 is a group of programs that make using the Internet easier. Included in the IBM Internet Connection for OS/2 are the following programs:

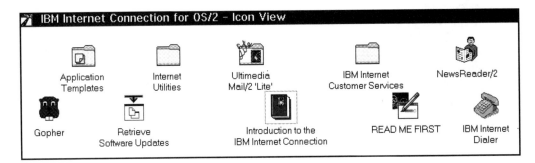

IBM Internet Customer Services

Allows you to register to use the Internet.

IBM Internet Dialer

Establishes the connection to the IBM Global Network. The IBM Global Network links you to the Internet.

Retrieve Software Updates

Allows you to retrieve software packages from the Internet and install them on your computer.

Gopher

Provides a menu-driven interface to help you find, display, and get information from the Internet.

NewsReader/2

Provides an easy way to read, subscribe to, and reply to the various forums (newsgroups) on the Internet.

Ultimedia Mail/2 Lite

Provides an electronic mail facility you can use to create, view, store, and organize the mail you send and receive on the Internet.

Internet Utilities

Provides a way to connect to and issue commands to other computers.

This chapter provides information on how to use all of these programs so that, before long, you'll be an Internet expert.

IBM Internet Customer Services

 The programs located within the IBM Internet Customer Services icon are used to open an account so that you can use the IBM Global Network to access the Internet. If you have an account (are registered) with the IBM Global Network, you can use these programs to change your account information or add or delete a user ID.

Registering to Use the Internet

Before you can access the Internet, you need to set up an account with the IBM Global Network so that it can link you to the Internet. In this account, you will specify how you want to pay for the services you use on the Internet and what type of modem you are using to access the Internet. After you complete the required information, you will be sent a user ID and a password that you can use to connect to the Internet through the IBM Global Network.

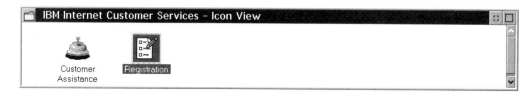

To register to use the Internet:
1. Double-click on the **IBM Information Superhighway** icon.
2. Double-click on the **IBM Internet Connection for OS/2** icon.
3. Double-click on the **IBM Internet Customer Services** icon.
4. Double-click on the **Customer Assistance** icon.
5. Click mouse button 1 on one of the following push buttons:

   Open a new account
   Allows you to open a new account so that you can access the Internet and learn about its services.

   Open a personal account
   Allows you to open a personal account and pay for it using a credit card.

   Open a business account
   Allows you to add Internet access to your existing IBM Global Network business account.

Learn about the Internet
>Provides information about some of the services the Internet has to offer.

Learn about this service
>Provides information about the IBM Global Network, which is used to connect you to the Internet.

Learn about the IBM Network
>Provides the same information as Learn about this service.

Change an existing account
>Allows you to change information in an existing Internet account or close the account.

Create another user ID
>Allows you to add another user to your account. You can have as many as six users per account.

Delete a user ID
>Allows you to remove a user from your account. If you remove the primary user, all users on the account are removed and the account is closed.

Update software
>Allows you to get the latest IBM Internet Connection Service software from the network. You can also use this choice to install or remove the Internet software from your computer and transfer a configuration to or from another computer.

Ask for help
>Provides the telephone numbers for the IBM Global Network help desk. The IBM Global Network is used to access Internet.

6. The following steps are provided only for those users who clicked mouse button 1 on the **Open a personal account** push button.

    a. Read the IBM Internet Service Terms and Conditions information. Use the scroll bar to move forward through the information.

    b. Click mouse button 1 on the **OK** push button.

    c. Fill in the requested information. Do not use spaces in your credit card account number.

    d. Click mouse button 1 on the **OK** push button.

7. Fill in the requested modem configuration information. You will be asked for the following:

Modem name
>Specifies the manufacturer of the modem you use with your computer.

Registration phone number
Specifies the appropriate phone number you should use to access Internet.

Comm port
Specifies which communication port your modem is using.

Dial prefix
Specifies the number that must be dialed in order to reach an outside line. Not everyone will need to specify this.

Dial mode
Specifies whether the telephone system used by your modem uses tones or pulses.

8. Click mouse button 1 on the **OK** push button.
9. Review the choices for IDs in the User ID Preferences window. If you do not like them, change them.
10. Click mouse button 1 on the **OK** push button.
11. Click mouse button 1 on one of the following push buttons:

Send registration to IBM
Sends the registration to IBM and displays the terms and conditions of your subscription. Accepting the terms and conditions activates your subscription; rejecting the terms and conditions cancels the subscription.

Review information
Takes you back through all the windows you just filled in so that you can review the information.

Register some other time
Saves the information you entered so that you can register at another time.

12. Double-click on the title-bar icons of the open windows to close them.

IBM Internet Dialer

 The IBM Internet Dialer is used to provide information such as your account number, user ID, and password to the IBM Global Network so that it can connect you to the Internet. You can also use the dialer to disconnect you from the Internet or change your IBM Global Network password.

Connecting and Disconnecting

When you request to connect to the Internet, the IBM Internet Dialer sends information to the modem. The modem uses this information to dial the phone number of the IBM Global Network. After the connection is made to the IBM Global Network, you are connected to the Internet. Of course, no connection is made to the IBM Global Network if you have not specified your account, user ID, or password during connection.

To connect to the Internet:

1. Double-click on the **IBM Information Superhighway** icon.

2. Double-click on the **IBM Internet Connection for OS/2** icon.

3. Double-click on the **IBM Internet Dialer** icon. If this is the first time that you are accessing the Internet, you might have to click mouse button 1 on the **Already registered** choice before you can complete the next step.

4. If the IBM Internet Dialer **Settings** window appears, follow steps 2 through 9 of "Changing the Settings". Then return here to complete the connection. (The IBM Internet Dialer Settings window only appears the very first time you attempt to connect to the Internet.)

5. Click mouse button 1 on the Dial icon in the Tool bar.

6. Fill in the requested information. You will be asked for the following:

   Account
   Specifies the account name for your subscription to the IBM Global Network and the Internet. (If you are registered to use the IBM Global Network, this field is filled in for you.)

User ID

Specifies your user ID for access to the IBM Global Network and the Internet. (If you are registered to use the IBM Global Network, this field is filled in for you.)

Password

Specifies the password that was given to you when you registered to use the IBM Global Network and the Internet. You must enter this password every time you want to access the Internet. You can change this password by clicking mouse button 1 on the **Change password** push button.

7. Click mouse button 1 on the **OK** push button.

To disconnect from the Internet, click mouse button 1 on the **Hang up** icon in the Tool bar of the IBM Internet Dialer window.

Changing the Settings

The IBM Internet Dialer relies on a combination of settings to connect you to the Internet. Some of these settings were automatically set and others were set by you when you registered to use the IBM Global Network to access the Internet. If you are having difficulty accessing the Internet, the wrong settings might have been specified during registration. For example, the wrong modem, baud rate, or communication port might have been selected.

To change the settings for the dialer:

1. Point to the **IBM Internet Dialer** icon.
2. Click mouse button 2 to display the pop-up menu.
3. Click mouse button 1 on the **Settings** menu choice.
4. Click mouse button 1 on the **Phone** notebook tab.
5. Fill in the requested information. You will be asked for the following:

Primary phone number

Determines the phone number used to connect to Internet. Select the number for the city that is closest to the one from which you are calling.

Backup phone number

Determines the phone number that should be used if the Internet cannot connect using the primary phone number.

Dial prefix

Determines the numbers that need to be dialed to reach an outside line.

Dial mode

Determines whether your telephone system uses pulses or tones.

Dial when loaded

Specifies that the phone number should be dialed when the program starts.

Minimize when loaded

Minimizes the IBM Internet Dialer window when the program starts.

Show detailed information

Displays useful information to help you determine why a connection attempt was unsuccessful.

Update phone list push button

Downloads the latest directory of phone numbers for IBM Internet services.

6. Click mouse button 1 on the **Modem** notebook tab.

7. Fill in the requested information. You will be asked for the following:

Modem name

Determines the modem used to connect to the Internet.

First modem command string

Determines the command string that will be used to configure your modem. This information is automatically updated when you select a modem from the Modem name list.

Second modem command string

Determines the command string that will be used to configure your modem. This information is automatically updated when you select a modem from the Modem name list.

Speed

Determines the baud rate of the modem.

Comm Port

Determines the communication port used by your modem.

Disable modem speaker

Disables the speaker so that no dial tone, dialing, or connection sounds are made during logon.

Update modem list push button

Downloads the latest list of modems.

8. Click mouse button 1 on the **Timeouts** notebook tab.

9. Change any of the following settings:

Enable inactivity timeout
Automatically disconnects the dialer from the Internet when no data is sent or received within the specified time.

Enable call duration timeout
Automatically disconnects the dialer from the Internet after the dialer is connected for the specified time.

Display timeout warning
Displays a warning message before an automatic disconnection. This allows you to postpone or cancel the disconnection.

10. Double-click on the title-bar icon of the notebook window to close it.

Gopher

The Internet contains information about practically anything you can imagine. All of this information makes the Internet very big. Because it is so big, you might have trouble finding what you are looking for. This is where a Gopher comes in. A Gopher uses menus to make it easier for you to find, view, and get information on the Internet.

Navigating the Internet

Not all of the information that you will want to find on the Internet will be located in the same place (on the same remote computer). In order to find the information you are looking for on the Internet, you might need to access different remote computers. A Gopher makes navigating through the Internet easy because it lists topics in a menu and lets you access them regardless of where they are physically located.

To navigate the Internet for information:

1. Double-click on the **IBM Information Superhighway** icon.
2. Double-click on the **IBM Internet Connection for OS/2** icon.
3. Double-click on the **Gopher** icon.
4. Double-click on the icon that represents the information that you are looking for.
5. Repeat step 4 until the information you are looking for is displayed on your screen or you are requested to provide a file name for the file. (The file will be copied to the hard disk drive specified in the Save File As window when you click on the **Save** push button.)

TIP: If you want to save a file to your hard disk drive but are not presented with the Save File As window, you can use the **Get** menu choice on the **Selected** menu to get a copy of the file.

Placing a Bookmark on a Gopher

Because you can go through many Gophers before you find the information you need, you might not remember exactly how you got to a particular Gopher. You can use bookmarks to place a marker on a Gopher so you can easily get back to it. After you place a bookmark, the name of the Gopher is placed in a bookmark window. Selecting a Gopher from the bookmark window takes you directly to that Gopher. This eliminates your having to remember how you got to a particular Gopher. You might want to place a bookmark on a Gopher you frequently access or one you want to refer to at a later time. This provides a fast way to get to those Gophers.

To place a bookmark on a Gopher:

1. Double-click on the **IBM Information Superhighway** icon.
2. Double-click on the **IBM Internet Connection for OS/2** icon.
3. Double-click on the **Gopher** icon.
4. Double-click on the icon that represents the information that you are looking for. Repeat this step until you find the information.

   You can use the **Specify Gopher item** menu choice on the **Gopher** menu to access an information item directly if you know the information for the Gopher server that you want to access.

5. Click mouse button 1 on the **Gopher** menu.
6. Click mouse button 1 on one of the following:

   Menu details
   > Places a bookmark at the currently displayed Gopher window. You can change the name of the bookmark so that you can easily recognize the contents.

   Bookmark this menu
   > Places a bookmark at the currently displayed Gopher window.

   Make this menu the home bookmark
   > Places a bookmark at the currently displayed Gopher window and makes it the default window that appears whenever you open the **Gopher** icon.

TIP: You can also place a bookmark on a particular item in a Gopher window. To do this:

1. Click mouse button 1 on the item.
2. Click mouse button 1 on the **Selected** menu.
3. Click mouse button 1 on the **Bookmark this item** menu choice.

Accessing Bookmarks

After you place a bookmark on a Gopher, it is saved in a bookmark window. This window makes it easy for you to access the Gophers that you have marked because a bookmark takes you directly to the Gopher that you want. If you use a bookmark, you won't need to remember every Gopher that you accessed in order to get to a particular Gopher.

To access bookmarks:

1. Click mouse button 1 on the **Gopher** menu.
2. Click mouse button 1 on the **Open bookmark window** menu choice.
3. Double-click on a Gopher or item you want to access.

NewsReader/2

 NewsReader/2 is a program that lets you share and exchange information with various newsgroups on the Internet. A newsgroup is a collection of articles about a particular topic. There are newsgroups for practically every topic you could imagine. NewsReader/2 lets you read articles, post your own articles, or add information to an existing article in a newsgroup.

Viewing Articles

NewsReader/2 displays a list of the available newsgroups that you can subscribe to. After you subscribe to a newsgroup, you can view the articles it contains. You will find newsgroups that cover every topic under the sun. For example, if you are interested in learning new tricks on roller-blades, you can view the newsgroups that provide information about in-line skating. After you identify the topics you are interested in, you will find that viewing articles can be fun and informative.

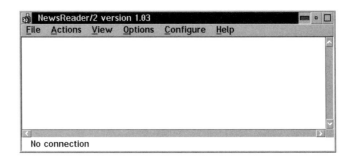

To view articles:

1. Double-click on the **IBM Information Superhighway** icon.
2. Double-click on the **IBM Internet Connection for OS/2** icon.
3. Double-click on the **NewsReader/2** icon.
4. Click mouse button 1 on the **File** menu.
5. Click mouse button 1 on the **List all newsgroups** menu choice.
6. Click mouse button 1 on the entries in the **All groups** window that you want to view.
7. Click mouse button 1 on the **Actions** menu in the **All groups** window.
8. Click mouse button 1 on the **Add Groups** menu choice.
9. Double-click on an entry in the Subscriptions window to display the articles for the entry in the Headers window.
10. Double-click on the article that you want to view.
11. Double-click on the title-bar icon of the Article window to close it so that you can view another article.

TIP: You can customize what NewsReader/2 does with articles that have already been read or that were cancelled by the author, and you can specify whether the news articles are refreshed in your windows. Click mouse button 1 on the **Refreshing** menu choice in the **Options** menu.

Deleting a Subscription

You can view information only in the newsgroups that you subscribe to. You might get tired of looking over the same topics of information or you might have subscribed to a topic that doesn't interest you.

To delete a subscription:

1. Click mouse button 1 on the subscription that you want to delete.
2. Click mouse button 1 on the **Actions** menu.
3. Click mouse button 1 on the **Unsubscribe** menu choice.

Posting an Article

After you have found a newsgroup that interests you, you might want to share some information of your own with other subscribers to the newsgroup. When a subscriber posts an article to a newsgroup, the sharing of information enhances the knowledge of all the subscribers of a particular topic.

To post an article:
1. Double-click on the **IBM Information Superhighway** icon.
2. Double-click on the **IBM Internet Connection for OS/2** icon.
3. Double-click on the **NewsReader/2** icon.
4. Click mouse button 1 on the newsgroup in the Subscription window where you want to post an article.
5. Click mouse button 1 on the **Actions** menu.
6. Click mouse button 1 on the **Post** menu choice.
7. Click mouse button 1 on the **Yes** push button in the Etiquette Reminder window.
8. Verify that the name of the newsgroup that you want to post an article to is displayed in the **Newsgroups** field. (You can specify more than one newsgroup.)
9. Type a title for your article in the **Subject** field.
10. Type the text for the article that you want to post to the newsgroup.
11. Click mouse button 1 on one of the following push buttons:

    Post
    > Sends the article to the selected newsgroup.

    Advanced
    > Displays a window where you can include additional posting information such as distribution lists, keywords, and follow-up information.

    Cancel
    > Removes the posting window without sending or saving the article.

TIP: If you typically post lengthy articles, you might want to use your favorite editor rather than the NewsReader/2 editor to write the article.

To change editors:
1. Click mouse button 1 on the **Configure** menu.
2. Click mouse button 1 on the **Editors** menu choice.
3. Click mouse button 1 on the **Use NewsReader/2 editor** check box to remove the check mark.

4. Fill in the fields with the requested information.
5. Click mouse button 1 on the **OK** push button.

Replying to an Article

After reading an article that was posted by someone else, you might want to respond to the submitter of the article and also add your two cent's worth of information to the article. When you reply to an article, the text of the article is displayed in an editor on your computer. You can add your text anywhere within the existing article.

To reply to an article:
1. Double-click on the **IBM Information Superhighway** icon.
2. Double-click on the **IBM Internet Connection for OS/2** icon.
3. Double-click on the **NewsReader/2** icon.
4. Double-click on the newsgroup in the Subscriptions window to display a list of articles.
5. Double-click on the article in the Headers window that you want to post a reply to.
6. Click mouse button 1 on the **Actions** menu of the Article window.
7. Click mouse button 1 on the **Post reply** menu choice.
8. Click mouse button 1 on the **Yes** push button in the Etiquette Reminder window.
9. Verify that the name of the newsgroup that you want to post a reply to is displayed in the **Newsgroups** field. (You can specify more than one newsgroup.)
10. Verify the title for your reply in the **Subject** field.
11. Type the text for the reply that you want to post to the newsgroup.
12. Click mouse button 1 on one of the following push buttons:

Post
> Sends the reply to the selected newsgroup.

Advanced
> Displays a window where you can include additional posting information such as distribution lists, keywords, and follow-up information.

Cancel
> Removes the posting window without sending or saving the reply.

Creating a Signature File

A signature file contains information about yourself that you can share with other users. The signature file is added to the end of the information that you post in a newsgroup. For example, you might want to list your college degree or area of expertise to lend credence to the information you post in a newsgroup.

To create a signature file:

1. Double-click on the **IBM Information Superhighway** icon.
2. Double-click on the **IBM Internet Connection for OS/2** icon.
3. Double-click on the **NewsReader/2** icon.
4. Click mouse button 1 on the **Options** menu.
5. Click mouse button 1 on the **Signature** menu choice.
6. Choose one of the following:

    Do not use .sig file
    Specifies that you do not want to add a signature file to the end of a post or a reply to a post.

    Use one .sig file
    Specifies that you want to add the selected signature file to the end of a post or a reply to a post.

    Use two .sig files (for post and mail)
    Specifies that you want to add the selected signature file to the end of a post, a reply to a post, and your mail.

7. Click mouse button 1 on the **Create** push button.
8. Type a name for the file that will contain your signature information. Use the .SIG extension.
9. Click mouse button 1 on the **OK** push button to display the editor window.
10. Type the signature that you want to use. For example, you could add your name, address, company name, business title, telephone, fax number, or anything else in this file.
11. Double-click on the title-bar icon of the editor window.
12. Click mouse button 1 on the **Save** push button.
13. Click mouse button 1 on the file name in the Signature Files list to select the signature file that you want to use.
14. Click mouse button 1 on the **Use** push button.
15. Click mouse button 1 on the **OK** push button.

TIP: You can also edit or delete signature files by using push buttons within the Signature window.

Retrieve Software Updates

The IBM Internet Connection for OS/2 posts updates to its software on the Internet. The Retrieve Software Updates program lists any updates found on the Internet and allows you to select which ones you want to download and install on your computer.

To update the software on your computer:
1. Double-click on the **IBM Information Superhighway** icon.
2. Double-click on the **IBM Internet Connection for OS/2** icon.
3. Double-click on the **Retrieve Software Updates** icon.
4. Click mouse button 1 on a software package that you want to install.
5. Click mouse button 1 on the **Install** push button.
6. Follow the instructions displayed on the screen to complete the installation.

Ultimedia Mail/2 Lite

Ultimedia Mail/2 Lite is a set of easy-to-use programs for creating, sending, and receiving electronic mail. It also allows you to add video and audio clips to the mail you send. The recipient can even play these multimedia clips from within the letter.

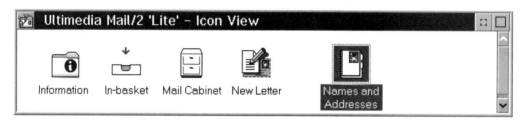

Ultimedia Mail/2 Lite contains the following four programs:

Names and Addresses
Lists the names and addresses of people that you send electronic mail to.

New Letter
Displays a blank letter that you can fill in.

Mail Cabinet
Organizes the mail that you send into folders.

In-basket
Lists the mail that you have received and holds it there until you handle it.

Names and Addresses

 Names and Addresses is a program that lets you add the names and addresses of the people that you plan to correspond with. The addresses you provide in this book are the Internet addresses of people, not their street addresses. If you do not know the Internet address of someone you want to add to your Names and Addresses book, you can use the Directory Service available on Internet to find it.

To add a name and address to the Address Book:

1. Double-click on the **IBM Information Superhighway** icon.
2. Double-click on the **IBM Internet Connection for OS/2** icon.
3. Double-click on the **Ultimedia Mail/2 Lite** icon.
4. Click mouse button 1 on the **Address Book** icon.
5. Click mouse button 1 on the **Person** notebook tab.
6. Fill in the requested information. You will be asked for the following:

    Nickname
    Specifies the nickname of the person you are adding. This field must be filled in.

    Name
    Specifies the actual name of the person you are adding.

    Telephone
    Specifies the telephone number of the person you are adding.

    UserID
    Specifies the Internet user ID of the person you are adding. If this field is left blank, the person's nickname is assumed to be the user ID.

    Domain
    Specifies the Internet address of the person you are adding.

    Folder
    Specifies the name of the folder where you want to store the mail for the person you are adding.

7. Click mouse button 1 on the **Create** push button to add the entry to the address book.
8. Click mouse button 1 on the **Clear** push button to clear the fields so that you can add another name and address.
9. Double-click on the title-bar icon of the notebook window to close it.

TIP: To delete an entry from the address book:

1. Click mouse button 1 on the **Index** notebook tab.
2. Click mouse button 1 on the entry in the **Nicknames** index field.
3. Click mouse button 1 on the **Delete** push button.

Occasionally, you might want to send electronic mail to a group of people instead of an individual. For example, if you needed to let the people in your cooking class know that this Wednesday's class was canceled, you could add the entire cooking class to the Names and Addresses book under one nickname. Then you could send the same letter to all of the people in the group by selecting only one nickname.

To add a group to the address book:

1. Double-click on the **IBM Information Superhighway** icon.
2. Double-click on the **IBM Internet Connection for OS/2** icon.
3. Double-click on the **Ultimedia Mail/2 Lite** icon.
4. Click mouse button 1 on the **Address Book** icon.
5. Click mouse button 1 on the **Group** notebook tab.
6. Fill in the requested information. You will be asked for the following:

   Group Nickname
   Specifies a nickname for the group that you are adding. This field must be filled in.

   Description
   Specifies a description for the group that you are adding. This is used to help you identify the purpose of the group.

   Available Nicknames
   Contains the list of Internet members who can be added to the group. Click mouse button 1 on a name that you want to add to the list.

   Group List
   Specifies the list of Internet members that you selected to be members of the group.

7. Click mouse button 1 on the **Add to Group** push button to add the selected nickname in the Available Nickname List to the Group List.
8. Click mouse button 1 on the **Create** push button to add the group to the address book.
9. Click mouse button 1 on the **Clear** push button to clear the fields so that you can add another name and address.
10. Double-click on the title-bar icon of the notebook window to close it.

432

TIP: To remove a nickname from a group:

1. Click mouse button 1 on a nickname in the Group List.
2. Click mouse button 1 on the **Remove from Group** push button.

New Letter

New Letter displays a form you can use to create an electronic letter. A letter can contain a combination of information formats, such as text, images, and binary data (multimedia clips or programs). The recipient can view the data and run the programs from within the letter.

To send a letter:

1. Double-click on the **IBM Information Superhighway** icon.
2. Double-click on the **IBM Internet Connection for OS/2** icon.
3. Double-click on the **Ultimedia Mail/2 Lite** icon.
4. Double-click on the **New Letter** icon. If a message appears stating that there are no folders available, do the following:
    a. Click mouse button 1 on the **Cancel** push button to remove the message window.
    b. Click mouse button 1 on the **Cabinet** menu.
    c. Click mouse button 1 on the **New Folder** menu choice.
    d. Type a name for the new mail folder.
    e. Click mouse button 1 on the **OK** push button.
    f. Click mouse button 1 on the **Cabinet** menu.
    g. Click mouse button 1 on the **New Letter** menu choice.
5. Click mouse button 1 on the **Names** icon in the Tool bar of the Letter window.
6. Click mouse button 1 on the names of the people you want to receive the letter. If you want the people to receive a carbon copy (cc) of the letter, double-click on their names.
7. Type a topic for the letter in the **Subject** field.
8. Click mouse button 1 on the down arrow to the right of the **Folder** field to select the folder where you want to save a copy of this letter.
9. Click mouse button 1 on one of the following icons in the Tool bar of the Letter window.

    Text
    > Allows you to enter the text that you want to appear in the letter. This is the default choice.

Image

Allows you to drag and drop a bit map into the image part of the letter. You can add text to a bit map after it has been added to the letter.

Binary

Allows you to drag and drop binary data such as an executable program file into the binary part of the letter. The recipient will be able to run the program from the letter.

10. Click mouse button 1 on the **Send** icon in the Tool bar of the Letter window.

In-basket

The In-basket contains all of the electronic mail that you receive. Your mail stays in the In-basket until you discard it or until you place it in a folder in the Mail Cabinet.

To view mail in your In-basket:

1. Double-click on the **IBM Information Superhighway** icon.
2. Double-click on the **IBM Internet Connection for OS/2** icon.
3. Double-click on the **Ultimedia Mail/2 Lite** icon.
4. Double-click on the **In-basket** icon.
5. Double-click on the mail you want to view. (Mail that has not been previously viewed can be identified by a closed envelope icon.)
6. Double-click on an icon in the **Contents** area of the letter window to view the different formats of data in the letter. The formats, which are represented by icons, can be plain text, images, and binary data.
7. Click mouse button 1 on the **Close** icon in the Tool bar of the Letter window to close the letter.
8. Repeat steps 5 through 7 to read the mail in the In-basket.

TIP: To run a program or process binary data from within a letter:

1. Point to an empty area in the Letter window.
2. Click mouse button 2 to display the pop-up menu.
3. Click mouse button 1 on either the **Run or Process data** menu choice.
4. Fill in the requested information.
5. Click on the **OK** push button.

Mail Cabinet

The Mail Cabinet is used to organize the mail that you send and receive. You can create folders within the Mail Cabinet. These folders can be used to store letters about a particular project or from a particular person. Organizing the mail makes it easier to find a letter.

To organize the mail that you receive:
1. Double-click on the **IBM Information Superhighway** icon.
2. Double-click on the **IBM Internet Connection for OS/2** icon.
3. Double-click on the **Ultimedia Mail/2 Lite** icon.
4. Double-click on the **Mail Cabinet** icon.
5. Create a folder for the letters:
    a. Click mouse button 1 on the **Cabinet** menu.
    b. Click mouse button 1 on the **New Folder** menu choice.
    c. Fill in the requested information.
    d. Click mouse button 1 on the **OK** push button.
6. Move the letters from your In-basket or any other mail folder into the new folder you just created.
    a. Press and hold mouse button 1 on the icon representing the letter you want to move.
    b. Drag the letter to the folder where you want the letter stored.
    c. Release mouse button 1 to drop the letter in the folder.

TIP: To access the In-basket, Mail Cabinet, and Address Book windows quickly, just click mouse button 1 on the **Windows** menu and select the window you want to use.

Customizing the Mail Settings

Ultimedia Mail/2 Lite is installed with many default settings. These settings might not be to your liking. For example, you might want to begin all of your letters with an image instead of text. You can change the mail settings so that an image icon is placed in the contents area of the letter instead of a text icon.

To customize your mail settings:
1. Double-click on the **IBM Information Superhighway** icon.
2. Double-click on the **IBM Internet Connection for OS/2** icon.
3. Double-click on the **Ultimedia Mail/2 Lite** icon.
4. Double-click on the **Mail Cabinet** icon.

5. Click mouse button 1 on the **Cabinet** menu.
6. Click mouse button 1 on the **Settings** menu choice.
7. Click mouse button 1 on the **Profile** notebook tab.
8. Change any of the following choices:

Name
> Allows you to change the name that was assigned to you. (The original name was set up by the system administrator.)

ID
> Allows you to change the ID that was assigned to you. (The original ID was set up by the system administrator.)

Password
> Allows you to change your password. (The original password was set up by the system administrator.)

9. Click mouse button 1 on the **Letter 1** tab at the bottom of the notebook.
10. Change any of the following choices:

From
> Allows you to specify an address other than your user ID.

Reply To
> Allows you to specify another address where you want replies to your letters sent.

Address
> Allows you to customize the length of your address in your letters.

Signature
> Allows you to specify the greeting that you want to appear at the beginning of the text of your letters.

Create
> Allows you to select the type of information you want included at the beginning of each letter. For example, you can choose text, video, sound, or an image with which to begin each letter.

11. Click mouse button 1 on the **Letter 2** tab at the bottom of the notebook.
12. Change any of the following choices:

Separator
> Places a line between your text and the forwarded text in a letter.

Annotation

Places a mark in front of each line of forwarded text in a letter.

Signature placement

Places your signature either before or after the forwarded text in a letter.

View all letters

Displays all the letters in one window so that you don't have to open a window for each letter that you want to read.

Beep on new mail

Signals when new mail is received.

13. Click mouse button 1 on the **Session** tab at the bottom of the notebook. The information needed to retrieve your mail is displayed. If you want to log onto a different session to retrieve mail, you can change these settings.

14. Click mouse button 1 on the right arrow at the bottom of the **Session** page to display the **Handler** notebook page.

15. Click mouse button 1 on any of the choices in the **Handler** field to view the settings used by Ultimedia Mail/2 Lite to display the various types of information (text, image, or binary) in a letter. You should not change these settings unless you have a replacement object handler that you want to specify.

16. Click mouse button 1 on the **Time Zone** notebook tab.

17. Change any of the following choices to make sure that your mail is time-stamped with the correct time no matter where in the world you send it.

Time Zone

Determines the time zone you are sending letters from.

Switch to summer time

Determines the week, day of the week, and month that daylight savings time begins.

Switch to standard time

Determines the week, day of the week, and month that daylight savings time ends.

18. Double-click on the title-bar icon of the notebook to close it and save the changes that you made.

Internet Utilities

The IBM Internet Connection for OS/2 provides utility programs to make it easier for you to access remote computers. After you access a remote computer, you can issue commands recognized by the remote computer to make it do what you want it to do. You can even transfer files from the remote computer to your computer or vice versa. For example, your co-worker has files on his computer that you need in order to complete your project. If you have permission to access his computer, you can copy the files you need to your computer.

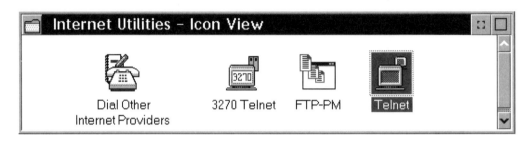

Dial Other Internet Providers

Dial Other Internet Providers allows you to establish and manage Internet connections that you get from an Internet provider other than the Internet Connection Services. Before you can connect to the Internet using a different provider, you will need to get registration and connection information from that Internet provider.

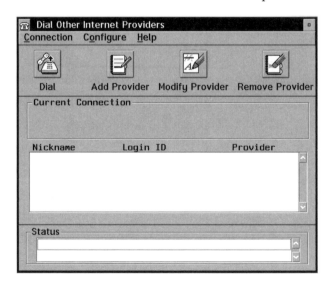

To access a different Internet provider:
1. Double-click on the **IBM Information Superhighway** icon.
2. Double-click on the **IBM Internet Connection for OS/2** icon.
3. Double-click on the **Internet Utilities** icon.
4. Double-click on the **Dial Other Internet Providers** icon.
5. Click mouse button 1 on the service provider that you want to connect to.
6. Click mouse button 1 on the **Dial** push button.

TIP: **To disconnect from an Internet provider:**
1. Click mouse button 1 on the **Connection** menu.
2. Click mouse button 1 on the **Hang-Up** menu choice.

3270 Telnet

3270 Telnet allows you to connect to a remote 3270 computer on the Internet. A 3270 computer is an IBM information display system. Examples of this type of computer are MVS and VM remote computers. Many of the IBM mainframe computers that you can access from the Internet display their information on a 3270.

To connect to a 3270 computer:
1. Double-click on the **IBM Information Superhighway** icon.
2. Double-click on the **IBM Internet Connection for OS/2** icon.
3. Double-click on the **Internet Utilities** icon.
4. Double-click on the **3270 Telnet** icon.
5. Type the name of the remote computer with which you want to connect.
6. Click mouse button 1 on the **Enter** push button.

To disconnect from a 3270 computer:
1. Click mouse button 1 on the **Connection** menu.
2. Click mouse button 1 on the **Exit** menu choice.
3. Click mouse button 1 on the **Yes** push button.
4. Double-click on the title-bar icon of the open window to close it.

Changing the 3270 Telnet Settings

The 3270 Telnet is installed with many default settings. These settings might not be to your liking. For example, you might want to make the screen a full-screen session so that it is easier to see the information. As a by-product of doing this, the session will run faster.

To change the settings for a 3270 Telnet session:

1. Double-click on the **IBM Information Superhighway** icon.
2. Double-click on the **IBM Internet Connection for OS/2** icon.
3. Double-click on the **Internet Utilities** icon.
4. Point to the **3270 Telnet** icon.
5. Click mouse button 2 to display the pop-up menu.
6. Click mouse button 1 on the **Settings** menu choice.
7. Click mouse button 1 on the **3270 Telnet** notebook tab.
8. Fill in the requested information. You can change the following:

   Host
   > Determines the name of the remote computer with which you will connect.

   Port
   > Determines the port number used by the remote computer. If you do not know the port number, you can leave it blank.

   Translation
   > Determines the name of the file that is used to translate between ASCII and EBCDIC characters. (This is an optional field.)

   Enable extended data stream
   > Enables support for extended colors and highlighting and nonstandard screen sizes.

   Disable the bell
   > Determines whether a bell is sounded when a warning message appears on the screen.

   Enable square brackets
   > Displays brackets and backslash characters in a 3270 Telnet session exactly as they appear on your keyboard.

   Maintain screen size
   > Determines whether another program can change the screen size while the 3270 Telnet session is running.

9. Click mouse button 1 on the **Session** notebook tab.
10. Fill in the requested information. You can change the following:

    Session type
    > Determines what type of window the 3270 Telnet session will run in. The OS/2 full-screen session is faster, but the Presentation Manager session is easier to use.

Screen size
> Determines the number of rows and columns of text that will fit in the session window.

11. Double-click on the title-bar icon of the notebook to close it.

TIP: You can also change the definition of the keys and mouse buttons and the colors and fonts used in a 3270 Telnet session. Use the **Options** menu in the 3270 Telnet session to make these changes.

Telnet

Telnet allows you to connect to a remote computer on the Internet. After you have connected to the remote computer, you can access its program and files.

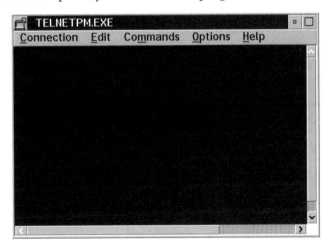

To connect to a remote computer:
1. Double-click on the **IBM Information Superhighway** icon.
2. Double-click on the **IBM Internet Connection for OS/2** icon.
3. Double-click on the **Internet Utilities** icon.
4. Double-click on the **Telnet** icon.
5. Click mouse button 1 on the **Connection** menu.
6. Click mouse button 1 on the **Open session** menu choice.
7. Fill in the requested information. You can specify the following:

Host name
> Determines the name of the remote computer with which you will connect.

Port

Determines the port number used by the remote computer. If you do not know the port number, you can leave it blank.

Emulator

Determines which terminal type you want to emulate. The default is VT220.

Size

Determines the number of rows and columns of text that will fit in the session window.

8. Click mouse button 1 on the **OK** push button.

To disconnect from the remote computer:

1. Click mouse button 1 on the **Connection** menu.
2. Click mouse button 1 on the **Close session** menu choice.
3. Click mouse button 1 on the **Yes** push button.
4. Double-click on the title-bar icon of the open window to close it.

Customizing the Telnet Settings

The Telnet is installed with many default settings. These settings might not be to your liking. For example, you might want to decrease the number of rows and columns of text displayed in the Telnet window. This will change the size of the font in the window.

To change the settings for a Telnet session:

1. Double-click on the **IBM Information Superhighway** icon.
2. Double-click on the **IBM Internet Connection for OS/2** icon.
3. Double-click on the **Internet Utilities** icon.
4. Point to the **Telnet** icon.
5. Click mouse button 2 to display the pop-up menu.
6. Click mouse button 1 on the **Settings** menu choice.
7. Click mouse button 1 on the **Telnet** notebook tab.
8. Fill in the requested information. You can specify any of the following fields; however, all of these fields are optional:

Host

Specifies the name of the remote computer with which you will connect.

Port

Specifies the port number used by the remote computer. If you do not know the port number, you can leave it blank.

Terminal type
> Specifies which terminal type you want to emulate.

Codepage
> Specifies how international keyboard characters are represented.

Country keyboard
> Specifies which country character set your keyboard is emulating.

Configuration file
> Specifies the name of the configuration file that contains the definition of the keys and other configuration options.

Log file
> Specifies the name of the file where the session information will be logged.

Trace file
> Specifies the name of the file where the debug information will be logged.

9. Click mouse button 1 on the **Session** notebook tab.
10. Fill in the requested information. You can specify the following:

Session type
> Determines what type of window the Telnet session will run in. The OS/2 full-screen session is faster, but the Presentation Manager session is easier to use.

Screen size
> Determines the number of rows and columns of text that will fit in the session window.

11. Click mouse button 1 on the **Environment** notebook tab.
12. Type the variables that describe how the session is going to run and the devices it should recognize. Use the *name=value* format.
13. Double-click on the title-bar icon of the notebook to close it.

 TIP: You can change the fonts, the behavior of the Backspace and Enter keys, and the look of the cursor. You can also change the way data is transmitted, and you can create files for traces and logs. Use the **Options** menu in the Telnet session to make these changes.

FTP-PM

 FTP-PM allows you to transfer files from your computer to a remote computer or vice versa. You can transfer both ASCII and binary files using this program. However, you cannot transfer them at the same time because you must specify which file type you are transferring.

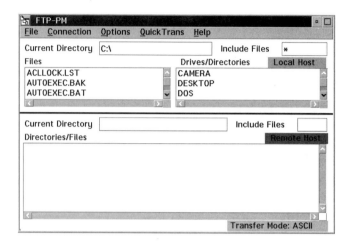

To transfer files from one computer to another computer:

1. Double-click on the **IBM Information Superhighway** icon.
2. Double-click on the **IBM Internet Connection for OS/2** icon.
3. Double-click on the **Internet Utilities** icon.
4. Double-click on the **FTP-PM** icon.
5. Click mouse button 1 on the **Connection** menu.
6. Click mouse button 1 on the **Open remote host** menu choice.
7. Type the appropriate information in the following fields:

   Host
   > Specifies the name of the remote computer with which you will connect.

   User
   > Specifies the ID that the remote computer knows you by. Many remote computers recognize the ID "anonymous".

   Password
   > Specifies your ID on the remote computer. If you are using the anonymous user ID, it is a good idea to use your electronic mail (e-mail) address in this field.

   Account
   > Specifies your account number. It is usually not required.

8. Click mouse button 1 on the **Options** menu.
9. Click mouse button 1 on any of the menu choices that you want to specify. You can choose from the following:

Transfer mode

Specifies whether the contents of the files being transferred are ASCII (text) or binary (packed files, graphics, or executables).

Confirmation

Specifies whether a confirmation message is displayed before a file is transferred or deleted.

Assign unique

Automatically creates a unique file name for a file being transferred (if a file with the same name already exists).

Mark remote file names

Specifies whether you want to be able to mark a file name all at one time (two part) or character by character (free form).

Trace commands/replies

Keep track of communications during the file transfer. This information is used to diagnose problems.

10. Double-click on the name of the directory that contains the files that you want to transfer.
11. Click mouse button 1 on the names of the files that you want to transfer.
12. Double-click on the name of the directory where you want the files transferred. If you want to make a new directory for the files being transferred:
    a. Click mouse button 1 on the **File** menu.
    b. Click mouse button 1 on the **Make directory** menu choice.
    c. Click mouse button 1 on either the **Local or Remote** choice to determine which computer the directory is created on.
    d. Type the drive letter and name for the directory you are creating.
    e. Click mouse button 1 on the **OK** push button.
13. Click mouse button 1 on the **QuickTrans** menu.

NOTE: Instead of using the **QuickTrans** menu to transfer files from one computer to another, you can use the **Get remote files** or **Put local files** menu choice from the **File** menu.

14. Respond to all messages that appear on the screen.
15. Click mouse button 1 on the **Connection** menu.
16. Click mouse button 1 on the **Close all hosts** menu choice.
17. Double-click on the title-bar icons of the open windows to close them.

TIP: To be a considerate user, close all remote computers (hosts) before you exit from the program that connected you to the remote computer.

Application Templates

The Application Templates icon contains templates for creating more 3270 Telnet, Telnet, and FTP-PM icons. You might want to have more than one of these icons if you typically connect to different remote computers for different reasons.

For example, if you connect to Computer A to transfer software programs to your computer and connect to Computer B to transfer your spreadsheet data to your boss's computer, you would probably want to set up an FTP-PM icon for each of these computers. By setting up an FTP-PM icon for each of the computers, you simplify the connection process. You only have to double-click on the appropriate icon instead of changing data each time you want to connect to one of the computers.

TIP: These templates are also located in the Templates icon on your Desktop. They work just like any other template. To eliminate having multiple copies of the templates, you can drag the **Application Templates** icon from the IBM Internet Connection for OS/2 window to the **Shredder** to delete the icon and its contents.

40

HyperACCESS Lite for OS/2

HyperACCESS Lite provides a quick and easy way to use a modem, the telephone system, and your computer to access remote computers. After you connect to a remote computer, you can display information found on the remote computer on your computer screen. You can navigate through this information and even send and receive information.

This chapter shows you how to connect to and disconnect from remote computers, add computers to the HyperACCESS Lite phone book, receive and send files, print text, and customize the settings for the different remote computers.

Connecting and Disconnecting

HyperACCESS Lite provides two ways to connect to a remote computer. The first and easiest way is using the phone book. The phone book provides a visual representation for each system so that you can easily access it. The second way to access a remote computer is by specifying the name and path of the file that contains the settings for the remote computer.

NOTE: You use the telephone line to communicate with remote computers. If the phone number for a system is long distance, you might have large telephone bills. To minimize the cost of connecting to remote computers, disconnect from a remote computer whenever you are not using it.

To disconnect from a remote computer:
1. Click mouse button 1 on the **File** menu.
2. Click mouse button 1 on the **Disconnect** menu choice.

To connect to a remote computer that is listed in the HyperACCESS phone book:
1. Double-click on the **IBM Information Superhighway** icon.
2. Double-click on the **HyperACCESS Lite** icon.

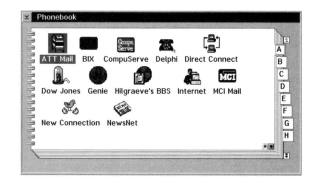

3. Double-click on the icon that represents the remote computer you want to call. If this is the first time that you are trying to access a remote computer, you will be prompted for information about the port, baud rate, and modem you are using.

To connect to a remote computer that is not listed in the HyperACCESS phone book:
1. Double-click on the **IBM Information Superhighway** icon.
2. Double-click on the **HyperACCESS Lite** icon.
3. Double-click on the title-bar icon of the **Phonebook** to close it.
4. Click mouse button 1 on the **File** menu.
5. Click mouse button 1 on the **Open** menu choice.
6. Type the directory and file name of the remote computer with which you want to connect.
7. Click mouse button 1 on the **OK** push button.
8. Click mouse button 1 on the **File** menu.
9. Click mouse button 1 on the **Connect** menu choice.
10. Click mouse button 1 on the **Dial Now** push button.

TIP: If you always connect to the same remote computer every time you start HyperACCESS Lite, you can change a setting so that you are automatically connected to that remote computer when you double-click on the **HyperACCESS Lite** icon. This eliminates one step from the connecting process. To change the setting:
1. Double-click on the **IBM Information Superhighway** icon.
2. Point to the **HyperACCESS Lite** icon.
3. Click mouse button 2 to display the pop-up menu.
4. Click mouse button 1 on the **Settings** menu choice.
5. Type the file name of the remote computer with which you want to automatically connect. The file name ends with the extension .HAL.
6. Double-click on the title-bar icons of the open windows to close them.

Adding Remote Computers to the Phone Book

The HyperACCESS Lite phone book lists the remote computers that you can access. It comes with preset phone numbers for some commonly called remote computers. You can add phone numbers for other remote computers to the phone book so that you can easily access all the remote computers you use from within HyperACCESS Lite.

To add a remote computer to the phone book:
1. Double-click on the **IBM Information Superhighway** icon.
2. Double-click on the **HyperACCESS Lite** icon.

3. Double-click on the **New Connection** icon in the Phonebook window.

4. Type the name of the remote computer that you want to add to the phone book. This name will appear beneath the icon in the phone book.

5. Click mouse button 1 on the icon that you want to represent the new phone book entry. You might have to scroll the window to see all of the icons that are available.

6. Click mouse button 1 on the **OK** push button.

7. Type the phone number for the remote computer that you want to add to the phone book.

8. Click mouse button 1 on the arrow to the right of the **Settings (data-parity-stop)** field.

9. Click mouse button 1 on the setting that best describes the settings you want to use. If none of the settings meets your needs, click mouse button 1 on the **Custom setup** push button and specify your own settings.

10. Click mouse button 1 on the arrow to the right of the **Baud rate** field.

11. Click mouse button 1 on the baud rate used by your modem.

12. Click mouse button 1 on the arrow to the right of the **Port name** field.

13. Click mouse button 1 on the name of the port that your modem is connected to.

14. Click mouse button 1 on the **Port setup** push button. Fill in the requested information. Click mouse button 1 on the **Help** push button for details about each field.

15. Click mouse button 1 on the arrow to the right of the **Modem** field.

16. Click mouse button 1 on the name of the modem that you are using.

17. Click mouse button 1 on the **Modem setup** push button. Fill in the requested information. Click mouse button 1 on the **Help** push button for details about each field.

18. Click mouse button 1 on the **OK** push button in the Communication Settings window.

Receiving Files

Remote computers contain files of information that you might find useful. Files can contain practically anything including graphics, text, sounds, and programs. In order to take full advantage of a remote computer, you will need to be able to receive a file (place a copy on your computer) so that you can use it.

To receive a file from a remote computer:

1. Double-click on the **IBM Information Superhighway** icon.

2. Double-click on the **HyperACCESS Lite** icon.

3. Double-click on the icon that represents the remote computer you want to call.

4. Request that a file be sent from the remote computer. The steps needed to send a file vary depending on the remote computer with which you are connected.

5. Click mouse button 1 on the **Transfer** menu.

6. Click mouse button 1 on the **Receive** menu choice.

7. Specify the directory and file name that you want to use for the information you are receiving.

8. Click mouse button 1 on the down arrow to the right of the **Protocol** field.

9. Click mouse button 1 on the transfer utility that you want to use to receive the file.

10. Click mouse button 1 on the **Receive** push button.

Placing Incoming Text into a File

As you access information on a remote computer, the information is written to the screen of your computer. Occasionally, you might find that you want to keep this information so that you can look at it again at a later time. In order to do this, you need to capture the text and place it into a file.

To place incoming text into a file:

1. Double-click on the **IBM Information Superhighway** icon.

2. Double-click on the **HyperACCESS Lite** icon.

3. Double-click on the icon that represents the remote computer you want to call.

4. Click mouse button 1 on the **File** menu.

5. Click mouse button 1 on the **Capture** menu choice.

6. Specify the directory and file name that you want to use for the information you are capturing.

7. Click mouse button 1 on the **Start** push button. Everything that is displayed from now on will be placed inside the file you specified in the previous step.

   To pause, resume, or stop the capturing of information:

   a. Click mouse button 1 on the **File** menu.

   b. Click mouse button 1 on the **Capture** menu choice.

   c. Click mouse button 1 on the **Pause**, **Resume**, or **Stop** menu choice.

Sending Files

If you have a file that you want to share with other people who are using the remote computer, you can send the file to the remote computer.

To send a file:

1. Double-click on the **IBM Information Superhighway** icon.
2. Double-click on the **HyperACCESS Lite** icon.
3. Double-click on the icon that represents the remote computer you want to call.
4. Request that a file be received by the remote computer. The steps needed to receive a file vary depending on the remote computer with which you are connected.
5. Click mouse button 1 on the **Transfer** menu.
6. Click mouse button 1 on the **Send** menu choice.
7. Specify the directory and file name of the information you are sending.
8. Click mouse button 1 on the down arrow to the right of the **Protocol** field.
9. Click mouse button 1 on the transfer utility that you want to use to send the file.
10. Click mouse button 1 on the **Send** push button.

Printing Text

You might want to print the text that comes across the screen while you are using a remote computer. This allows you to have a permanent copy of the transmission so that you can read it even when you are away from your computer.

To print the text:

1. Double-click on the **IBM Information Superhighway** icon.
2. Double-click on the **HyperACCESS Lite** icon.
3. Double-click on the icon that represents the computer you want to call.
4. Mark the text that you want to print. If you want to print all the text on the screen, go to step 5.
   a. Point to the beginning of the text that you want to print.
   b. Press and hold mouse button 1.
   c. Drag the mouse pointer to the end of the text that you want to print.
   d. Release mouse button 1.
5. Click mouse button 1 on the **File** menu.
6. Click mouse button 1 on the **Print** menu choice.
7. Click mouse button 1 on the **Select Printer** push button, and select the correct printer.
8. Click mouse button 1 on one of the following choices:

   Selected text only
   > Prints only the marked information. If no text is marked, this choice is not available.

Entire terminal screen
    Prints all the information on the screen, whether it's marked or not.

9. Click mouse button 1 on the **Print** push button.

Customizing the Settings

HyperACCESS Lite relies on settings to access and communicate with the different remote computers that are available. These settings include such things as telephone numbers, parity settings, modem baud rates, communication ports, and text formatting. HyperACCESS Lite can automatically detect some things, but not all. If you are having problems accessing a particular remote computer, you might have to change the settings for the computer.

To customize the settings:
1. Double-click on the **IBM Information Superhighway** icon.
2. Double-click on the **HyperACCESS Lite** icon.
3. Double-click on the icon that represents the remote computer whose settings you want to change.
4. Click mouse button 1 on the **Properties** menu.
5. Click mouse button 1 on the **Description** menu choice.
6. Change the settings. You can choose from the following:

    System name
        Determines the name that appears beneath the icon in the phone book.

    Icons
        Determines the icon that appears above the name in the phone book.

7. Click mouse button 1 on the **Communications** notebook tab.
8. Change the settings. You can choose from the following:

    Phone number
        Specifies the phone number that the modem should call to connect to the remote computer.

    Settings (data-parity-stop)
        Determines which transmission settings are required by the remote computer. The default setting is auto-detect. If auto-detect does not work with the remote computer, contact the administrator of the remote computer for the correct settings.

Baud rate
> Determines the maximum transmission speed in bits per second (bps) for your modem.

Port name
> Determines the port that the modem is connected to or is using.

Modem
> Determines the type of modem you are using.

9. Click mouse button 1 on the **ASCII Settings** notebook tab.

10. Change the settings. You can choose from the following:

ASCII Sending
> Specifies formatting options for data you are sending to the remote computer. These options do not affect the format of files you are sending on the remote computer.

Send line end
> Sends a carriage return and line end at the end of each line of text you send. No check mark in this field means that a carriage return only is sent.

Echo type
> Displays on your computer screen the characters you are sending. No check mark in this field means that the characters are not displayed on the screen.

ASCII Receiving
> Specifies formatting options for data you are receiving from the remote computer. These options do not affect the format of files you receive on the remote computer.

Append line feeds
> Adds a carriage return and a line end to the end of each line of text received. Most text is already formatted, so this choice is usually not necessary.

Force incoming data
> Converts 8-bit data to 7-bit with a zero as the 8th bit. This suppresses extraneous characters caused by line noise, incorrect parity, or incorrect bits-per-character settings.

Wrap lines
> Automatically wraps any line of text that exceeds the width of the screen.

11. Click mouse button 1 on the **Terminal Settings** notebook tab.

12. Change the settings. You can choose from the following:

Terminal emulator
Determines which type of remote computer your computer should imitate. The best choice is to let HyperACCESS Lite **auto-detect** the emulator.

Function, Arrow, and Ctrl Keys Act as
Determines whether the keys on your keyboard function like the keys on the terminal being imitated or like your normal computer keys.

13. Click mouse button 1 on the **Fonts** notebook tab.

14. Change the settings. You can choose from the following:

Name
Determines the font to be used when your computer is connected to this remote computer.

Size
Determines the size of the font to be used when your computer is connected to this remote computer.

Style
Determines the style (underline, italic, or bold) of the font to be used when your computer is connected to this remote computer.

15. Click mouse button 1 on the **Properties** menu.

16. Click mouse button 1 on the **Sound** menu choice. Placing a check mark next to this choice indicates that a bell sound should be made whenever a connection to a remote computer is made.

Appendices

This part contains supplemental information about the files that are used to help start up your computer and OS/2 Warp. It also contains information about the file systems that come with OS/2 Warp.

Appendix A
AUTOEXEC.BAT Statements

The AUTOEXEC.BAT file is used to specify parameters to be used by your DOS window and full screen sessions. These parameters can be used, for example, to start your favorite program.

This appendix provides introductory information about the AUTOEXEC.BAT file. It is provided to help give you a basic understanding of the contents of your AUTOEXEC.BAT file.

NOTE: OS/2 Warp comes with an online *Command Reference* which is located in the Information icon on the Desktop. You can refer to the *Command Reference* for more information about the AUTOEXEC.BAT file and the statements.

Understanding Your AUTOEXEC.BAT File

Keep in mind that your AUTOEXEC.BAT file might be different from the one displayed below. The contents of the file depend on what you want to be able to do from your DOS window and full-screen sessions and what you want them to look like.

```
@ECHO OFF
PROMPT $i$p$g
REM SET DELDIR=C:\DELETE,512;D:\DELETE,512;
PATH=C:\OS2;C:\OS2\MDOS;C:\;C:\WINDOWS;
LOADHIGH APPEND C:\OS2;C:\OS2\SYSTEM
SET TMP=C:\
REM LOADHIGH DOSKEY FINDFILE=DIR /A /S /B $*
REM DOSKEY EDIT=QBASIC/EDITOR $*
REM SET DIRCMD=/A
```

@ECHO OFF

Prevents the information in the AUTOEXEC.BAT file from being displayed on the screen when a DOS session is started.

PROMPT ip$g

Changes the command prompt to be equal to the parameters specified after it. (A list of the parameters and what they mean is provided in the online *Command Reference* that comes with OS/2 Warp.)

REM SET DELDIR=C:\DELETE,512;D:\DELETE,512;

Sets the variable DELDIR to be equal to the location and maximum size of the directory used to store deleted files. The REM (remark) command that precedes this statement means that this statement is not read when the computer is started.

PATH=C:\OS2;C:\OS2\MDOS;C:\;C:\WINDOWS;

Sets the search path to be equal to the directories that should be searched for a program or batch file.

LOADHIGH APPEND C:\OS2;C:\OS2\SYSTEM

This statement is a combination of two commands. The LOADHIGH command loads terminate-and-stay resident (TSR) DOS programs into an available upper memory block (UMB) for a particular DOS session. The APPEND command sets the search path to be equal to the directories that should be searched for a data file. When combined, these two commands load the APPEND command into a UMB.

SET TMP=C:

Sets the variable TMP to be equal to the root directory on the drive where OS/2 Warp is installed.

REM LOADHIGH DOSKEY FINDFILE=DIR /A /S /B $*

This statement is a combination of three commands. The LOADHIGH command loads terminate-and-stay resident (TSR) DOS programs into an available upper memory block (UMB) for a particular DOS session. The DOSKEY command creates a macro called FINDFILE that searches for a file in the current directory and all its subdirectories. The REM (remark) command that precedes this statement means that this statement is not read when the computer is started.

REM DOSKEY EDIT=QBASIC/EDITOR $*

The DOSKEY command creates a macro called EDIT that uses the QBASIC editor to edit the command prompt. The REM (remark) command that precedes this statement means that this statement is not read when the computer is started.

REM SET DIRCMD=/A

Sets the variable DIRCMD to display the names of all files including hidden files and system files. The REM (remark) command that precedes this statement means that this statement is not read when the computer is started.

Changing Your AUTOEXEC.BAT File

You can change information in the AUTOEXEC.BAT file or add information to it. For example, if you add a DOS program to the computer and you want to start it from any directory while using a DOS command prompt, you could add the directory where the program resides to the PATH statement, so the computer can find the program.

To change the AUTOEXEC.BAT file:

1. Click mouse button 1 on the drawer button above the **Drive A** icon located on the LaunchPad to open the drawer.
2. Click mouse button 1 on the **Drive C** icon in the drawer of the LaunchPad.
3. Double-click on the **Drive C** icon in the Drive C window.
4. Point to the **AUTOEXEC.BAT** icon.
5. Press and hold the Ctrl key and mouse button 2.
6. Drag the icon to a blank area in the Drive C window.
7. Release the Ctrl key and mouse button 2.
8. Click mouse button 1 on the **OK** push button. This makes a copy of the AUTOEXEC.BAT file as it exists now just in case you make a mistake while changing the original AUTOEXEC.BAT file.
9. Double-click on the **AUTOEXEC.BAT** file in the Drive C window. The file is displayed in the OS/2 System Editor.
10. Make the changes you need and save the file.
11. Open a DOS window or full-screen command prompt to activate the changes.

TIP: A separate AUTOEXEC file is run when you use the Dual Boot feature to switch to DOS. This AUTOEXEC file is located in the C:\OS2\SYSTEM directory. It is named AUTOEXEC.DOS. If you want to make changes to the way your Dual Boot session of DOS is started, change the information in this file, but do not change the name of the file.

Appendix B
CONFIG.SYS Statements

The CONFIG.SYS file is a text file that contains statements. The statements in the file contain information about the different pieces of hardware that your computer uses such as your display, mouse, and printer. When OS/2 Warp is started it uses the CONFIG.SYS file to help set up your computer for a day's work.

This appendix provides introductory information about the CONFIG.SYS file. It is provided to help give you a basic understanding of the contents of your CONFIG.SYS file.

NOTE: OS/2 Warp comes with an online *Command Reference* which is located in the Information icon on the Desktop. You can refer to the *Command Reference* for more information about the CONFIG.SYS file and the statements.

Understanding Your CONFIG.SYS File

The following information is provided to help you understand the contents of your CONFIG.SYS file. Keep in mind that everyone's CONFIG.SYS file is different. The contents of the file depend on the hardware and software installed on your computer and the type of computer you have. You should not replace the information in your CONFIG.SYS file with the information shown in this CONFIG.SYS file. If you do, your computer might not run.

```
IFS=C:\OS2\HPFS.IFS /CACHE:64 /CRECL:4
PROTSHELL=C:\OS2\PMSHELL.EXE
SET USER_INI=C:\OS2\OS2.INI
SET SYSTEM_INI=C:\OS2\OS2SYS.INI
SET OS2_SHELL=C:\OS2\CMD.EXE
SET AUTOSTART=PROGRAMS,TASKLIST,FOLDERS,CONNECTIONS,LAUNCHPAD
SET RUNWORKPLACE=C:\OS2\PMSHELL.EXE
SET COMSPEC=C:\OS2\CMD.EXE
LIBPATH=;C:\OS2\DLL;C:\OS2\MDOS;C:\;C:\OS2\APPS\DLL;C:\MMOS2\DLL;
SET PATH=C:\OS2;C:\OS2\SYSTEM;C:\OS2\INSTALL;C:\;C:\OS2\MDOS;C:\OS2\APPS;C:\WINDOWS;
        C:\MMOS2;
SET DPATH=C:\OS2;C:\OS2\SYSTEM;C:\OS2\INSTALL;C:\;C:\OS2\BITMAP;C:\OS2\MDOS;
        C:\OS2\APPS;C:\WINDOWS;C :\MMOS2;
SET PROMPT=$i[$p]
SET HELP=C:\OS2\HELP;C:\OS2\HELP\TUTORIAL;C:\MMOS2\HELP;
SET GLOSSARY=C:\OS2\HELP\GLOSS;
SET IPF_KEYS=SBCS
PRIORITY_DISK_IO=YES
FILES=20
BASEDEV=IBMKBD.SYS
DEVICE=C:\OS2\BOOT\TESTCFG.SYS
```

```
DEVICE=C:\OS2\BOOT\DOS.SYS
DEVICE=C:\OS2\BOOT\PMDD.SYS
BUFFERS=90
IOPL=YES
DISKCACHE=D,LW,AC:C
MAXWAIT=3
MEMMAN=SWAP,PROTECT
SWAPPATH=C:\OS2\SYSTEM 2048 2048
BREAK=OFF
THREADS=256
PRINTMONBUFSIZE=134,134,134
COUNTRY=001,C:\OS2\SYSTEM\COUNTRY.SYS
SET KEYS=ON
SET BOOKSHELF=C:\OS2\BOOK;C:\MMOS2;
SET SOMIR=C:\OS2\ETC\SOM.IR;C:\OS2\ETC\WPSH.IR;C:\OS2\ETC\WPDSERV.IR
SET SOMDDIR=C:\OS2\ETC\DSOM
REM SET DELDIR=C:\DELETE,512;D:\DELETE,512;
BASEDEV=PRINT02.SYS
BASEDEV=IBM2FLPY.ADD
BASEDEV=IBM1FLPY.ADD
BASEDEV=IBM2SCSI.ADD /LED
BASEDEV=XDFLOPPY.FLT
BASEDEV=OS2DASD.DMD
SET EPMPATH=C:\OS2\APPS;
PROTECTONLY=NO
SHELL=C:\OS2\MDOS\COMMAND.COM C:\OS2\MDOS
FCBS=16,8
RMSIZE=640
DEVICE=C:\OS2\MDOS\VEMM.SYS
DOS=LOW,NOUMB
DEVICE=C:\OS2\MDOS\VXMS.SYS /UMB
DEVICE=C:\OS2\MDOS\VDPMI.SYS
DEVICE=C:\OS2\MDOS\VDPX.SYS
DEVICE=C:\OS2\MDOS\VWIN.SYS
DEVICE=C:\OS2\MDOS\VW32S.SYS
DEVICE=C:\OS2\BOOT\OS2CDROM.DMD /Q
IFS=C:\OS2\BOOT\CDFS.IFS /Q
DEVICE=C:\OS2\MDOS\VCDROM.SYS
BASEDEV=OS2SCSI.DMD
DEVICE=C:\OS2\MDOS\VMOUSE.SYS
DEVICE=C:\OS2\BOOT\POINTDD.SYS
DEVICE=C:\OS2\BOOT\MOUSE.SYS
```

```
DEVICE=C:\OS2\BOOT\COM.SYS
DEVICE=C:\OS2\MDOS\VCOM.SYS
CODEPAGE=437,850
DEVINFO=KBD,US,C:\OS2\KEYBOARD.DCP
BASEDEV=XGA.SYS
DEVICE=C:\OS2\BOOT\XGARING0.SYS
DEVINFO=SCR,VGA,C:\OS2\BOOT\VIOTBL.DCP
SET VIDEO_DEVICES=VIO_XGA
SET VIO_XGA=DEVICE(BVHVGA,BVHXGA)
DEVICE=C:\OS2\MDOS\VVGA.SYS
DEVICE=C:\OS2\MDOS\VXGA.SYS
DEVICE=C:\MMOS2\SBP2D2.SYS 1 1 5 240 4 /N:SBAUD1$
DEVICE=C:\MMOS2\AUDIOVDD.SYS SBAUD1$
SET MMBASE=C:\MMOS2;
SET DSPPATH=C:\MMOS2\DSP;
SET NCDEBUG=4000
DEVICE=C:\MMOS2\SSMDD.SYS
DEVICE=C:\MMOS2\R0STUB.SYS
```

IFS=C:\OS2\HPFS.IFS /CACHE:64 /CRECL:4
> Allows you to use the High Performance File System (HPFS).

PROTSHELL=C:\OS2\PMSHELL.EXE
> Initializes the user interface program and the OS/2 command processor.

SET USER_INI=C:\OS2\OS2.INI
> Sets the variable USER_INI to the INI file that is used by OS/2 Warp for information about such items as program defaults, display options, and file options.

SET SYSTEM_INI=C:\OS2\OS2SYS.INI
> Sets the variable SYSTEM_INI to the INI file that is used by OS/2 Warp for system information about such items as installed fonts and printer drivers.

SET OS2_SHELL=C:\OS2\CMD.EXE
> Sets the variable OS2_SHELL to be equal to the command processor that is used for OS/2 Warp sessions.

SET AUTOSTART=PROGRAMS,TASKLIST,FOLDERS,CONNECTIONS,LAUNCHPAD
> Sets the variable AUTOSTART to be equal to the parts of the Workplace Shell that will be automatically started.

SET RUNWORKPLACE=C:\OS2\PMSHELL.EXE
> Sets the variable RUNWORKPLACE to be equal to the program that starts the Workplace Shell.

SET COMSPEC=C:\OS2\CMD.EXE
Sets the variable COMSPEC to be equal to the command processor.

LIBPATH=.;C:\OS2\DLL;C:\OS2\MDOS;C:\;C:\OS2\APPS\DLL;C:\MMOS2\DLL;
Identifies the directories that should be searched when OS/2 Warp needs to load a dynamic link library (DLL) file.

SET PATH=C:\OS2;C:\OS2\SYSTEM;C:\OS2\INSTALL;C:\; ...
Sets the variable PATH to be equal to the directories that should be searched for a program or batch file.

SET DPATH=C:\OS2;C:\OS2\SYSTEM;C:\OS2\INSTALL;C:\; ...
Sets the variable DPATH to be equal to the directories that should be searched by a program in order to find data files.

SET PROMPT=$i[$p]
Sets the variable PROMPT to be equal to the parameters specified after it. (A list of the parameters and what they mean is provided in the online Command Reference that comes with OS/2 Warp.)

SET HELP=C:\OS2\HELP;C:\OS2\HELP\TUTORIAL;C:\MMOS2\HELP;
Sets the variable HELP to be equal to the directories where help files are located on the computer.

SET GLOSSARY=C:\OS2\HELP\GLOSS;
Sets the variable GLOSSARY to be equal to the directory where the glossary files are located on the computer.

SET IPF_KEYS=SBCS
Sets the variable IPF_KEYS to be equal to the SBCS (Single Byte Character Set).

PRIORITY_DISK_IO=YES
Determines whether the programs running in the foreground receive disk input/output priority over programs running in the background.

FILES=20
Determines the maximum number of files that can be accessed by a program that is running in a DOS session.

BASEDEV=IBMKBD.SYS
Determines the base device driver for the keyboard attached to the computer.

DEVICE=C:\OS2\BOOT\TESTCFG.SYS
Installs the device-driver file that is used to determine the system configuration.

DEVICE=C:\OS2\BOOT\DOS.SYS

Installs the device driver file that is used to communicate between the OS/2 Warp and DOS programs running on the computer.

DEVICE=C:\OS2\BOOT\PMDD.SYS

Installs the device driver file that provides pointer draw support.

BUFFERS=90

Determines the number of disk buffers (1 to 100) that are allocated in memory. Increasing the number of buffers might increase the speed of your computer and decrease the amount of memory available for your programs.

IOPL=YES

Allows input/output privilege to be granted to programs requesting processes.

DISKCACHE=D,LW,AC:C

Determines the number of kilobytes of memory that can be used as a hard disk buffer. The disk cache is used to hold frequently accessed data so that time isn't wasted reading the hard-disk drive. Increasing the size of the disk cache increases the speed of your computer, but decreases the amount of memory available for your programs.

MAXWAIT=3

Determines the amount of time that a thread (an instruction) that is ready to run waits before it is assigned a higher priority.

MEMMAN=SWAP,PROTECT

Permits swapping of data out of memory to a file called SWAPPER.DAT and enables program calls (APIs) to use protected memory.

SWAPPATH=C:\OS2\SYSTEM 2048 2048

Specifies the location and size of the SWAPPER.DAT file. The first (2048) means that a warning message will be displayed if there is less than 2K of free space on the hard disk. The second parameter indicates the initial size of the SWAPPER.DAT file when the operating system was installed.

BREAK=OFF

Determines whether a DOS session should check to see if the Ctrl+Break keys were pressed before it tries to process a request. The Ctrl+Break keys, when pressed, stop a request from processing.

THREADS=256

Determines the maximum number of threads (instructions) that can be performed concurrently.

PRINTMONBUFSIZE=134,134,134

Determines the device-driver buffer size for the parallel port.

COUNTRY=001,C:\OS2\SYSTEM\COUNTRY.SYS

Identifies the three-digit value for the country whose code page you are using. It also specifies the name and location of the file containing the country information.

SET KEYS=ON

Sets the variable KEYS to be equal to the ON state. This allows you to retrieve and edit commands that you issued previously.

SET BOOKSHELF=C:\OS2\BOOK;C:\MMOS2;

Sets the variable BOOKSHELF to be equal to the location of the OS/2 Warp online books.

SET SOMIR=C:\OS2\ETC\SOM.IR;C:\OS2\ETC\WPSH.IR;C:\OS2\ETC\WPDSERV.IR

Sets the variable SOMIR to be equal to the various interface repository (.IR) files. These files are used by the system object model (SOM) to determine what classes are registered and available.

SET SOMDDIR=C:\OS2\ETC\DSOM

Sets the variable SOMDDIR to be equal to the location of the distributed SOM (DSOM) files. The DSOM files provide access to objects located on other computers so that they appear to be on your computer.

REM SET DELDIR=C:\DELETE,512;D:\DELETE,512;

Sets the variable DELDIR to be equal to the location and maximum size of the directory used to store deleted files. The REM (remark) command that precedes this statement means that this statement is not read when the computer is started.

BASEDEV=PRINT02.SYS

Determines the base device driver for the printer attached to the Micro Channel computer.

BASEDEV=IBM2FLPY.ADD

Determines the base device driver for the Micro Channel diskette drives attached to the computer.

BASEDEV=IBM1FLPY.ADD

Determines the base device driver for non-Micro Channel diskette drives. This statement is required for the installation of OS/2 Warp even if there are no non-Micro Channel diskette drives attached to the computer.

BASEDEV=IBM2SCSI.ADD /LED

Determines the base device driver for IBM 32-bit FAST and WIDE Micro Channel cards.

BASEDEV=XDFLOPPY.FLT

Determines the base device driver needed to support extended density format (XDF) diskettes. The OS/2 Warp Installation diskettes use this format.

BASEDEV=OS2DASD.DMD

Determines the base device driver needed to provide communications between adapter device drivers (.ADDs) for hard disk and diskette devices and either the OS/2 Warp kernel or other device drivers.

SET EPMPATH=C:\OS2\APPS;

Sets the variable EPMPATH to be equal to the directory where the Enhanced Presentation Manager files are located on the computer.

PROTECTONLY=NO

Specifies that you want to reserve the lower 640K of memory for running programs in DOS sessions. If this parameter is set to NO, you will not be able to run programs in DOS sessions.

SHELL=C:\OS2\MDOS\COMMAND.COM C:\OS2\MDOS

Loads and starts the DOS command processor.

FCBS=16,8

Determines the number of file control blocks (records that contains all of the information about a file) that can be open and the number of files that can be opened by file control blocks. This statement is used for DOS sessions only.

RMSIZE=640

Specifies the highest address in memory allowed for the DOS operating system.

DEVICE=C:\OS2\MDOS\VEMM.SYS

Specifies the virtual device driver that provides the Expanded Memory Specification (EMS) emulation for DOS sessions. EMS allows DOS programs to allocate and map expanded memory on the Intel 8086 family of computers.

DOS=LOW,NOUMB

Specifies that the DOS kernel will reside in the low memory area and will not control upper memory blocks (UMBs). This means that DOS programs cannot be loaded in UMBs that are between the 640K and 1MB area.

DEVICE=C:\OS2\MDOS\VXMS.SYS /UMB

Specifies the virtual device driver that provides Extended Memory Specification (XMS) emulation for DOS sessions. XMS allows DOS programs to access more than 1MB of memory.

DEVICE=C:\OS2\MDOS\VDPMI.SYS

Specifies the device driver that provides DOS protected-mode interface support.

DEVICE=C:\OS2\MDOS\VDPX.SYS

Specifies the device driver used by DOS protected-mode interface programs.

DEVICE=C:\OS2\MDOS\VWIN.SYS

Specifies the device driver that supports WIN-OS/2 windows on the Desktop.

DEVICE=C:\OS2\MDOS\VW32S.SYS

Specifies the virtual device driver that allows OS/2 Warp to run WIN-32S programs.

DEVICE=C:\OS2\BOOT\OS2CDROM.DMD /Q

Provides support for CD-ROM drives in OS/2 Warp sessions. The /Q parameter suppresses the error message that is displayed if the computer is started when the CD-ROM drive is off.

IFS=C:\OS2\BOOT\CDFS.IFS /Q

Specifies the file that contains the information for loading the CD-ROM file system (CDFS). The /Q parameter suppresses the display of messages during initialization.

DEVICE=C:\OS2\MDOS\VCDROM.SYS

Specifies the device driver that provides CD-ROM support in DOS windows.

BASEDEV=OS2SCSI.DMD

Specifies the device manager that controls the flow and recovery between device drivers written to the OS/2 SCSI Device Driver Specification.

DEVICE=C:\OS2\MDOS\VMOUSE.SYS

Specifies the virtual device driver needed for mouse-pointer draw support in DOS and WIN-OS/2 sessions.

DEVICE=C:\OS2\BOOT\POINTDD.SYS

Specifies the device driver needed for mouse-pointer draw support in OS/2 Warp sessions.

DEVICE=C:\OS2\BOOT\MOUSE.SYS

Specifies the device driver needed for the pointing device attached to the computer.

DEVICE=C:\OS2\BOOT\COM.SYS

Specifies the device driver that enables support for the asynchronous communications interface so that programs can use serial devices. The device drivers for the serial devices attached to the COM ports must appear before this statement in the CONFIG.SYS file.

DEVICE=C:\OS2\MDOS\VCOM.SYS

Specifies the device driver that enables support for the asynchronous communications interfaces so that DOS programs can use serial devices.

CODEPAGE=437,850

Specifies the code pages (defined character sets) to be used by OS/2 Warp for code-page switching.

DEVINFO=KBD,US,C:\OS2\KEYBOARD.DCP

Specifies the file (KEYBOARD.DCP) that contains the keyboard layout table used for translating keystrokes into the characters of each code page specified in the CODEPAGE statement.

BASEDEV=XGA.SYS

Determines the base device driver needed to support the XGA display attached to the computer.

DEVICE=C:\OS2\BOOT\XGARING0.SYS

Specifies the device driver that is used for input/output operations with the XGA (8514) adapter installed in the computer.

DEVINFO=SCR,VGA,C:\OS2\BOOT\VIOTBL.DCP

Specifies the file (VIOTBL.DCP) that contains the video font table used for displaying the characters of each code page specified in the CODEPAGE statement.

SET VIDEO_DEVICES=VIO_XGA

Sets the variable VIDEO_DEVICES to be equal to the video display adapter found in your computer.

SET VIO_XGA=DEVICE(BVHVGA,BVHXGA)

Sets the variable VIO_XGA to be equal to the base video handler DLLs that are specified in the parentheses.

DEVICE=C:\OS2\MDOS\VVGA.SYS

Specifies the virtual device driver that is used to emulate the VGA video adapter when a DOS program is executing in the background or in a window.

DEVICE=C:\OS2\MDOS\VXGA.SYS

Specifies the virtual device driver that is used to emulate the XGA video adapter when a DOS program is executing in the background or in a window.

DEVICE=C:\MMOS2\SBP2D2.SYS 1 1 5 240 4 /N:SBAUD1$

Specifies the device driver that is used by the Creative Labs Sound Blaster card in the computer.

DEVICE=C:\MMOS2\AUDIOVDD.SYS SBAUD1$

Specifies the virtual device driver that is used by the Creative Labs Sound Blaster card for DOS and WIN-OS/2 sessions.

SET MMBASE=C:\MMOS2;

Sets the variable MMBASE to be equal to the directory where the OS/2 Warp multimedia files are located on the computer.

SET DSPPATH=C:\MMOS2\DSP;

Sets the variable DSPPATH to be equal to the directory where the Digital Signal Processors (DSP) modules are located on the computer. These modules are used by the sound card in the computer.

SET NCDEBUG=4000

Sets the variable NCDEBUG to be equal to 4000. It is used by OS/2 Warp multimedia to make multimedia macros work in Lotus 1-2-3.

DEVICE=C:\MMOS2\SSMDD.SYS

Specifies the device driver that is used by OS/2 Warp multimedia for synchronization and stream management. It handles the delivery of multimedia data to the appropriate hardware device and minimizes perceptible delays.

DEVICE=C:\MMOS2\R0STUB.SYS

Specifies the device driver that is used for Ring 0 support with OS/2 Warp multimedia.

If you install the BonusPak programs, additional statements will appear in your CONFIG.SYS file. (For more information about the statements in your CONFIG.SYS, refer to the online Command Reference that comes with OS/2 Warp.)

Changing Your CONFIG.SYS File

Making changes to the CONFIG.SYS file is not for the faint of heart. However, there might come a time when you have no choice, so it's a good idea to at least know how.

Keep in mind that accidentally erasing information in the file, adding incorrect information, or placing a statement in the wrong location within the file, might cause errors during the restart of the computer or could even cause the computer not to start. That is why we recommend that you make a copy of the CONFIG.SYS file before you begin making changes to it. Then, if you make a mistake when you edit the original file, you can use the copy to restart your computer.

The following steps take you through the process of making a copy of the CONFIG.SYS file and changing it.

To change the CONFIG.SYS file:
1. Click mouse button 1 on the drawer button above the **Drive A** icon on the LaunchPad to open the drawer.
2. Click mouse button 1 on the **Drive C** icon in the drawer of the LaunchPad.
3. Double-click on the **Drive C** icon in the Drive C window.
4. Point to the **CONFIG.SYS** icon.
5. Press and hold the Ctrl key and mouse button 2.
6. Drag the icon to a blank area in the Drive C window.
7. Release the Ctrl key and mouse button 2.
8. Click mouse button 1 on the **OK** push button. This makes a copy of the CONFIG.SYS file as it exists now just in case you make a mistake while changing the original CONFIG.SYS file. If your computer won't restart after you change the CONFIG.SYS file, use the instructions in "Getting to a Command Prompt" on page 292. Rename the CONFIG:1.SYS file back to CONFIG.SYS and restart the computer.
9. Double-click on the **CONFIG.SYS** file in the Drive C window. The file is displayed in the OS/2 System Editor.
10. Make the changes you need and save the file.
11. Shut down and restart the computer to activate the changes.

Appendix C
File Systems: HPFS and FAT

A file system is the part of the operating system that provides access to the files and programs on a disk. In other words, it is used to store and retrieve information on a disk. There are many different file systems. OS/2 Warp provides support for two of them - the file allocation table (FAT) and the high performance file system (HPFS).

The file system is selected during the installation of OS/2 Warp. If you use the Easy Installation choice to install OS/2 Warp, the installation program automatically installs the FAT file system. If you use the Advanced Installation choice to install OS/2 Warp, the installation program allows you to decide which file system you want to use.

This appendix provides some facts about each file system and describes naming conventions.

FAT File System

The following table provides information about the FAT file system.

Table 2 (page 1 of 2). FAT File System

Fact	Explanation
The FAT file system was designed to be used with small drives.	The FAT file system places the root directory at either the beginning or the end of the drive. Because of the location of the root directory, the FAT file system has to start searching at either the beginning or end of the drive every time it needs to find or store something. If the information it is looking for is at the opposite end of the drive, the entire drive must be searched. If the drive is large, this can take a long time.
The FAT file system searches the hard drive sequentially.	The FAT file system starts at one end of the drive and searches all the data on the drive until it finds what it needs. If the drive is large or contains a lot of data, the amount of time needed to search the drive increases.
Only the FAT file system works with DOS.	If you have a copy of the DOS operating system on your computer and want to install OS/2 Warp on the same drive as the one containing DOS, you must use the FAT file system. This is because DOS does not understand how to use the HPFS file system.
The FAT file system works with all versions of DOS and OS/2 Warp.	Both the DOS and OS/2 Warp operating system understand how to use the FAT file system.
The FAT file system does not require extra memory to run.	Some file systems, such as HPFS, use some of the memory in the computer to operate. When a file system does this, it takes memory away from the programs that are running on the computer.

Table 2 (page 2 of 2). FAT File System

Fact	Explanation
The FAT file system does not recognize drives that use the HPFS file system.	You can have many drives on your computer. Each drive can use a different file system. If you install OS/2 Warp on a drive that uses the FAT file system, you will not be able to access the drives that use the HPFS file system. For example, you have three drives on your computer that use the following letters and file systems: **Drive C** FAT **Drive D** FAT **Drive E** HPFS If OS/2 Warp is installed on Drive C, you can access the data on both Drives C and D, but not Drive E. This is because the FAT file system does not know how to locate or store information on a drive that uses the HPFS file system. In other words, it can't read it so it doesn't list it as a possible drive.
The FAT file system fragments files.	When the FAT file system saves information to the drive, it locates an empty place on the drive and stores as much of the file as will fit in the location. The part of the file that doesn't fit is split from the file and stored somewhere else on the drive. The larger the file gets, the more pieces the file is broken into. Keep in mind that the FAT file system keeps track of where the different pieces of the file are so you don't really notice the fragmentation.
The FAT file system has a 12-character file-name limitation.	Files on drives that use the FAT file system are limited to a maximum of 12 characters. This limitation means that file names are often cryptic. You must give careful thought when choosing a name so that you can identify the contents of the file by the name. For more information about file naming, see "FAT File Naming Conventions" on page 478.

HPFS File System

The following table provides information about the HPFS file system.

Table 3 (page 1 of 2). HPFS File System

Fact	Explanation
The HPFS file system was designed to be used with large drives.	The HPFS file system places the root directory at the center of the drive. Because of the location of the root directory, a search begins in the center of the drive and moves outward. The amount of time needed to find information is usually decreased because a smaller amount of the drive needs to be searched.

Table 3 (page 2 of 2). HPFS File System

Fact	Explanation
The HPFS file system uses a B-tree (binary tree) to perform file searches.	A B-tree uses binary (yes/no) decision points to search a drive for data. At each decision point, half of the remaining information on the drive is eliminated from the search. Because it takes only a few decision points to find the correct data on a drive, the speed with which a search can be performed is increased. This type of search works very well with large drives and drives that contain a large amount of data.
The HPFS file system works only with OS/2 1.2 and later.	The HPFS file system is a fairly new file system. It wasn't added to the OS/2 product until version OS/2 1.2. Since that time, the HPFS file system has been included in all versions of the OS/2 operating system.
The HPFS file system uses 500K of system memory to run.	Because of the way that the HPFS file system works, it requires the use of memory to locate and store information on the drive. If you have less than 6MB of memory in your computer, the HPFS file system could adversely affect performance.
The HPFS file system recognizes both FAT and HPFS drives.	You can have many drives on your computer. Each drive can use a different file system. If you install OS/2 Warp on a drive that uses the HPFS file system, you will be able to access any drive on your computer that uses either the HPFS or FAT file system. For example, you have three drives on your computer that use the following letters and file systems: **Drive C** HPFS **Drive D** FAT **Drive E** HPFS If OS/2 Warp is installed on Drive C, you can access the data on Drives C, D, and E. This is because the HPFS file system knows how to locate and store information on a drive that uses either the FAT or HPFS file system.
The HPFS file system has a 254-character file-name limitation.	Files and directories on drives that use the HPFS file system can have up to 254 characters in their name. This allows the names of files and directories to be more descriptive. For more information about file naming, see "FAT File Naming Conventions."

FAT File Naming Conventions

Follow these rules when you are naming files and directories intended for a drive formatted using the FAT file system.

- The following symbols cannot be used in the file name or extension:

    \ / : * ? " | , + = [ ] ; .

Although the * and ? symbols cannot be used in file names, they can be used to list files that have similar names. For example, you could enter *.SCR to search for all files that have .SCR as their extension. You could enter ?INE.SCR to list all the files that end with INE.SCR and begin with any other valid character.

- The following device names cannot be used as a file or directory name unless you add an extension to the name.

    KBD$, PRN, NUL, COM1, COM2, COM3, COM$, CLOCK$, LPT1, LPT2, LPT3, CON, SCREEN$, POINTER$, MOUSE$

- The following should not be used as directory names because OS/2 Warp already creates directories with these names.

    OS2, INTRO, INSTALL, SPOOL, DLL, BOOK, NOWHERE, DESKTOP, SYSTEM

- A directory or file name can be up to 12 characters.

    Directory and file names can have up to 12 characters. The file name can have 8 characters. You can add a period, and a maximum of a three character extension (for example: ACCOUNTS.NEW). The period and extension are optional.

- Two files with the same name cannot be saved in the same directory.

    The FAT file system uses the name of the file to determine which file is being requested. If identical file names were permitted, the file system would not know which file should be retrieved or stored.

- A directory or file name can be entered using either upper or lower case; the file system simply converts all names to uppercase.

    The FAT file system saves all file names in upper case no matter how they are entered. This means if you type the file name in lower case letters, it will be saved in upper case letters.

    After a file has been named, you can type the file name in either upper case or lower case and the FAT file system will recognize which file you are referring to.

HPFS File Naming Conventions

Follow these rules when you are naming files and directories intended for a drive formatted using the HPFS file system.

- The following symbols cannot be used in the file name or extension:

\ / : * ? " |

Although the * and ? symbols cannot be used in file names, they can be used to specify files that have similar names. For example, you could enter *.SCR to search for all files that have .SCR as their extension. You could enter ?INE.SCR to list all the files that end with INE.SCR and begin with any other valid character.

- The following device names cannot be used as a file or directory name unless you add an extension to the name.

  KBD$, PRN, NUL, COM1, COM2, COM3, COM$, CLOCK$, LPT1, LPT2, LPT3, CON, SCREEN$, POINTER$, MOUSE$

- The following should not be used as directory names because OS/2 Warp already creates directories with these names.

  OS2, INTRO, INSTALL, SPOOL, DLL, BOOK, NOWHERE, DESKTOP, SYSTEM

- A directory or file name can be up to 254 characters.

  The 254 characters can include blank spaces and punctuation marks. A three-character extension can be placed at the end of the name, but must be included in the 254-character count.

  If you use blank spaces in the file name, you must enclose the file name in quotes (" ") whenever you specify the file name at a command prompt (for example: DEL "BOOKS FOR SALE").

- Two files with the same name cannot be saved in the same directory.

  The HPFS file system uses the name of the file to determine which file is being requested. If identical file names were permitted, the file system would not know which file should be retrieved or stored.

- A directory or file name can be entered using either upper or lower case; the file system does not convert every file name to upper case.

  The HPFS file system saves file names exactly as they are entered. For example, if you type the file name in upper-case letters, it is saved in upper-case. It is important to note, however, that case cannot be used to differentiate between file names. For example, if you have a file named **RADiO** and another file named **RadIo** you cannot place both files in the same directory. Although the case differs, the files have the same name.

  After a file has been named, you can type the file name in either upper case or lower case and the HFPS file system will recognize which file you are referring to.

Index

Index **501**

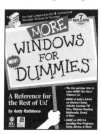

Title	Author	ISBN	Price
			12/20/94
INTERNET / COMMUNICATIONS / NETWORKING			
CompuServe For Dummies™	by Wallace Wang	1-56884-181-7	$19.95 USA/$26.95 Canada
Modems For Dummies™, 2nd Edition	by Tina Rathbone	1-56884-223-6	$19.99 USA/$26.99 Canada
Modems For Dummies™	by Tina Rathbone	1-56884-001-2	$19.95 USA/$26.95 Canada
MORE Internet For Dummies™	by John R. Levine & Margaret Levine Young	1-56884-164-7	$19.95 USA/$26.95 Canada
NetWare For Dummies™	by Ed Tittel & Deni Connor	1-56884-003-9	$19.95 USA/$26.95 Canada
Networking For Dummies™	by Doug Lowe	1-56884-079-9	$19.95 USA/$26.95 Canada
ProComm Plus 2 For Windows For Dummies™	by Wallace Wang	1-56884-219-8	$19.99 USA/$26.99 Canada
The Internet For Dummies™, 2nd Edition	by John R. Levine & Carol Baroudi	1-56884-222-8	$19.99 USA/$26.99 Canada
The Internet For Macs For Dummies™	by Charles Seiter	1-56884-184-1	$19.95 USA/$26.95 Canada
MACINTOSH			
Macs For Dummies®	by David Pogue	1-56884-173-6	$19.95 USA/$26.95 Canada
Macintosh System 7.5 For Dummies™	by Bob LeVitus	1-56884-197-3	$19.95 USA/$26.95 Canada
MORE Macs For Dummies™	by David Pogue	1-56884-087-X	$19.95 USA/$26.95 Canada
PageMaker 5 For Macs For Dummies™	by Galen Gruman	1-56884-178-7	$19.95 USA/$26.95 Canada
QuarkXPress 3.3 For Dummies™	by Galen Gruman & Barbara Assadi	1-56884-217-1	$19.99 USA/$26.99 Canada
Upgrading and Fixing Macs For Dummies™	by Kearney Rietmann & Frank Higgins	1-56884-189-2	$19.95 USA/$26.95 Canada
MULTIMEDIA			
Multimedia & CD-ROMs For Dummies™, Interactive Multimedia Value Pack	by Andy Rathbone	1-56884-225-2	$29.95 USA/$39.95 Canada
Multimedia & CD-ROMs For Dummies™	by Andy Rathbone	1-56884-089-6	$19.95 USA/$26.95 Canada
OPERATING SYSTEMS / DOS			
MORE DOS For Dummies™	by Dan Gookin	1-56884-046-2	$19.95 USA/$26.95 Canada
S.O.S. For DOS™	by Katherine Murray	1-56884-043-8	$12.95 USA/$16.95 Canada
OS/2 For Dummies™	by Andy Rathbone	1-878058-76-2	$19.95 USA/$26.95 Canada
UNIX			
UNIX For Dummies™	by John R. Levine & Margaret Levine Young	1-878058-58-4	$19.95 USA/$26.95 Canada
WINDOWS			
S.O.S. For Windows™	by Katherine Murray	1-56884-045-4	$12.95 USA/$16.95 Canada
MORE Windows 3.1 For Dummies™, 3rd Edition	by Andy Rathbone	1-56884-240-6	$19.99 USA/$26.99 Canada
PCs / HARDWARE			
Illustrated Computer Dictionary For Dummies™	by Dan Gookin, Wally Wang, & Chris Van Buren	1-56884-004-7	$12.95 USA/$16.95 Canada
Upgrading and Fixing PCs For Dummies™	by Andy Rathbone	1-56884-002-0	$19.95 USA/$26.95 Canada
PRESENTATION / AUTOCAD			
AutoCAD For Dummies™	by Bud Smith	1-56884-191-4	$19.95 USA/$26.95 Canada
PowerPoint 4 For Windows For Dummies™	by Doug Lowe	1-56884-161-2	$16.95 USA/$22.95 Canada
PROGRAMMING			
Borland C++ For Dummies™	by Michael Hyman	1 56884-162-0	$19.95 USA/$26.95 Canada
"Borland's New Language Product" For Dummies™	by Neil Rubenking	1-56884-200-7	$19.95 USA/$26.95 Canada
C For Dummies™	by Dan Gookin	1-878058-78-9	$19.95 USA/$26.95 Canada
C++ For Dummies™	by Stephen R. Davis	1-56884-163-9	$19.95 USA/$26.95 Canada
Mac Programming For Dummies™	by Dan Parks Sydow	1-56884-173-6	$19.95 USA/$26.95 Canada
QBasic Programming For Dummies™	by Douglas Hergert	1-56884-093-4	$19.95 USA/$26.95 Canada
Visual Basic "X" For Dummies™, 2nd Edition	by Wallace Wang	1-56884-230-9	$19.99 USA/$26.99 Canada
Visual Basic 3 For Dummies™	by Wallace Wang	1-56884-076-4	$19.95 USA/$26.95 Canada
SPREADSHEET			
1-2-3 For Dummies™	by Greg Harvey	1-878058-60-6	$16.95 USA/$21.95 Canada
1-2-3 For Windows 5 For Dummies™, 2nd Edition	by John Walkenbach	1-56884-216-3	$16.95 USA/$21.95 Canada
1-2-3 For Windows For Dummies™	by John Walkenbach	1-56884-052-7	$16.95 USA/$21.95 Canada
Excel 5 For Macs For Dummies™	by Greg Harvey	1-56884-186-8	$19.95 USA/$26.95 Canada
Excel For Dummies™, 2nd Edition	by Greg Harvey	1-56884-050-0	$16.95 USA/$21.95 Canada
MORE Excel 5 For Windows For Dummies™	by Greg Harvey	1-56884-207-4	$19.95 USA/$26.95 Canada
Quattro Pro 6 For Windows For Dummies™	by John Walkenbach	1-56884-174-4	$19.95 USA/$26.95 Canada
Quattro Pro For DOS For Dummies™	by John Walkenbach	1-56884-023-3	$16.95 USA/$21.95 Canada
UTILITIES / VCRs & CAMCORDERS			
Norton Utilities 8 For Dummies™	by Beth Slick	1-56884-166-3	$19.95 USA/$26.95 Canada
VCRs & Camcorders For Dummies™	by Andy Rathbone & Gordon McComb	1-56884-229-5	$14.99 USA/$20.99 Canada
WORD PROCESSING			
Ami Pro For Dummies™	by Jim Meade	1-56884-049-7	$19.95 USA/$26.95 Canada
MORE Word For Windows 6 For Dummies™	by Doug Lowe	1-56884-165-5	$19.95 USA/$26.95 Canada
MORE WordPerfect 6 For Windows For Dummies™	by Margaret Levine Young & David C. Kay	1-56884-206-6	$19.95 USA/$26.95 Canada
MORE WordPerfect 6 For DOS For Dummies™	by Wallace Wang, edited by Dan Gookin	1-56884-047-0	$19.95 USA/$26.95 Canada
S.O.S. For WordPerfect™	by Katherine Murray	1-56884-053-5	$12.95 USA/$16.95 Canada
Word 6 For Macs For Dummies™	by Dan Gookin	1-56884-190-6	$19.95 USA/$26.95 Canada
Word For Windows 6 For Dummies™	by Dan Gookin	1-56884-075-6	$16.95 USA/$21.95 Canada
Word For Windows For Dummies™	by Dan Gookin	1-878058-86-X	$16.95 USA/$21.95 Canada
WordPerfect 6 For Dummies™	by Dan Gookin	1-878058-77-0	$16.95 USA/$21.95 Canada
WordPerfect For Dummies™	by Dan Gookin	1-878058-52-5	$16.95 USA/$21.95 Canada
WordPerfect For Windows For Dummies™	by Margaret Levine Young & David C. Kay	1-56884-032-2	$16.95 USA/$21.95 Canada

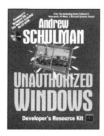

IDG BOOKS

Order Center: **(800) 762-2974** *(8 a.m.–6 p.m., EST, weekdays)*

12/20/94

Quantity	ISBN	Title	Price	Total

Shipping & Handling Charges

	Description	First book	Each additional book	Total
Domestic	Normal	$4.50	$1.50	$
	Two Day Air	$8.50	$2.50	$
	Overnight	$18.00	$3.00	$
International	Surface	$8.00	$8.00	$
	Airmail	$16.00	$16.00	$
	DHL Air	$17.00	$17.00	$

*For large quantities call for shipping & handling charges.
**Prices are subject to change without notice.

Ship to:

Name _____

Company _____

Address _____

City/State/Zip _____

Daytime Phone _____

Payment: ☐ Check to IDG Books (US Funds Only)

☐ VISA   ☐ MasterCard   ☐ American Express

Card # _____ Expires _____

Signature _____

Subtotal _____

CA residents add
applicable sales tax _____

IN, MA, and MD
residents add
5% sales tax _____

IL residents add
6.25% sales tax _____

RI residents add
7% sales tax _____

TX residents add
8.25% sales tax _____

Shipping _____

Total _____

Please send this order form to:

IDG Books Worldwide
7260 Shadeland Station, Suite 100
Indianapolis, IN 46256

Allow up to 3 weeks for delivery.
Thank you!

IDG BOOKS WORLDWIDE REGISTRATION CARD

RETURN THIS REGISTRATION CARD FOR FREE CATALOG

Title of this book: Official Guide to Using OS/2 Warp

My overall rating of this book: ❑ Very good [1] ❑ Good [2] ❑ Satisfactory [3] ❑ Fair [4] ❑ Poor [5]

How I first heard about this book:

❑ Found in bookstore; name: [6]

❑ Advertisement: [8]

❑ Word of mouth; heard about book from friend, co-worker, etc.: [10]

❑ Book review: [7]

❑ Catalog: [9]

❑ Other: [11]

What I liked most about this book:

What I would change, add, delete, etc., in future editions of this book:

Other comments:

Number of computer books I purchase in a year: ❑ 1 [12] ❑ 2-5 [13] ❑ 6-10 [14] ❑ More than 10 [15]

I would characterize my computer skills as: ❑ Beginner [16] ❑ Intermediate [17] ❑ Advanced [18] ❑ Professional [19]

I use ❑ DOS [20] ❑ Windows [21] ❑ OS/2 [22] ❑ Unix [23] ❑ Macintosh [24] ❑ Other: [25]_____
(please specify)

I would be interested in new books on the following subjects:
(please check all that apply, and use the spaces provided to identify specific software)

❑ Word processing: [26]

❑ Data bases: [28]

❑ File Utilities: [30]

❑ Networking: [32]

❑ Other: [34]

❑ Spreadsheets: [27]

❑ Desktop publishing: [29]

❑ Money management: [31]

❑ Programming languages: [33]

I use a PC at (please check all that apply): ❑ home [35] ❑ work [36] ❑ school [37] ❑ other: [38] _____

The disks I prefer to use are ❑ 5.25 [39] ❑ 3.5 [40] ❑ other: [41]_____

I have a CD ROM: ❑ yes [42] ❑ no [43]

I plan to buy or upgrade computer hardware this year: ❑ yes [44] ❑ no [45]

I plan to buy or upgrade computer software this year: ❑ yes [46] ❑ no [47]

Name: _____ Business title: [48] _____ Type of Business: [49] _____

Address (❑ home [50] ❑ work [51]/Company name: _____)

Street/Suite# _____

City [52]/State [53]/Zipcode [54]: _____ Country [55] _____

❑ **I liked this book!** You may quote me by name in future
IDG Books Worldwide promotional materials.

My daytime phone number is _____

IDG BOOKS

THE WORLD OF
COMPUTER
KNOWLEDGE

☐ YES!

Please keep me informed about IDG's World of Computer Knowledge.
Send me the latest IDG Books catalog.

About the Authors

Karla Stagray is an award-winning technical author. Most recently, she was the recipient of a Distinguished Award from the Society for Technical Communication (STC). She has written books for both IBM hardware and software products.

In her spare time, she plays in local golf tournaments (and usually wins).

Linda S. Rogers is an award-winning technical author. Most recently, she was the recipient of an Excellence Award from the STC.

When Linda is not writing, she attends her sons' soccer games and spends time with her family. She enjoys horseback riding and in-line skating.

iv